Moroccan migration in Belgium

CeMIS Migration and Intercultural Studies 1
The Centre for Migration and Intercultural Studies (CeMIS) was founded in 2005 at the University of Antwerp, on the initiative of a group of researchers who were working together within the framework of the Antwerp Centre for Migrant Studies. The centre conducts research as well as providing education and other academic services relating to migration, integration, and intercultural themes in various social fields, including education, the labor market, welfare, family, health, and law. Collaborating with civil society, policymakers, and other academic partners, the research centre addresses the challenges arising from migration and intercultural life in today's society. CeMIS seeks to provide an open and pluralistic research platform that fosters collaboration between society and academia.

Series editors
Christiane Timmerman (University of Antwerp), Noel Clycq (University of Antwerp), An Daems (University of Antwerp)

Series board
Dirk Vanheule (University of Antwerp), Lore Van Praag (University of Antwerp), Sunčica Vujić (University of Antwerp), Paul Van Royen (University of Antwerp), Godfried Engbersen (Erasmus University Rotterdam), Kevin Smets (University of Antwerp /Vrije Universiteit Brussel), Hilde Greefs (University of Antwerp), François Levrau (Centre Pieter Gillis/ University of Antwerp)

Moroccan migration in Belgium

More than 50 years of settlement

Edited by
Christiane Timmerman, Nadia Fadil, Idesbald Goddeeris,
Noel Clycq and Karim Ettourki

LEUVEN UNIVERSITY PRESS

© 2017 by Leuven University Press / Presses Universitaires de Louvain / Universitaire Pers Leuven.
Minderbroedersstraat 4, B-3000 Leuven (Belgium).

ISBN 978 94 6270 116 8
D / 2017/ 1869 / 38
NUR: 763

Lay-out: Coco Bookmedia
Cover: Johan Van Looveren

Contents

Part 5: Religion and devotion   **305**

Introduction

Christiane Timmerman, Nadia Fadil,
Idesbald Goddeeris, Noel Clycq & Karim Ettourki

In 2014 Belgium celebrated 50 years of Moroccan and Turkish migration. The year commemorated the signature of bilateral agreements with Morocco and Turkey in 1964, which resulted into the migration of tens of thousands of workers to Belgium. The celebrations of 2014 were also, at once, the occasion to acknowledge the presence and the history of these migrants which have become an incumbent part of society. Yet, despite more than fifty years having passed now, Belgium's growing cultural and religious diversity is occasionally at the grips of social anxieties or moral panics. These various societal tensions are part and parcel of the increasing awareness of the changing demographic composition of the native population, and the fact that its multicultural composition is an irreversible fact. Scholars and scientists have played a key role in disseminating this idea, and in acknowledging the ways in which migration flows deeply impact upon the receiving countries.

This book is an attempt to offer an overview of the various studies that have appeared in this regard, and which have played a central role in offering insights, vocabularies and imaginaries in order to account for, and acknowledge, this multicultural society. It focusses on Moroccan migration in Belgium, with an explicit attention to the scientific knowledge its history produced. It deals with Belgium as a whole, although it once in a while will draw comparison with other countries (e.g. the Netherlands) and even with other migration groups (e.g. people of Turkish descent). Most of its authors are based at Flemish universities, which epitomizes the greater deal of attention that these universities pay to migration.

We deliberately opt for a focus on Moroccan migration, because of the important role this group played in triggering various societal debates on multiculturalism and migration. The Moroccan immigration was, together with the Turkish one, the first large wave of non-European immigration in the 20th century in Belgium. By now, the number of Belgians with Moroccan roots is estimated at 300,000, thus making this group one of the largest non-EU minorities. Furthermore, various members of this minority group have played a central role in the recent years in modeling and shaping the debate on multiculturalism. Many of the major societal debates on immigration and multiculturalism from the eighties onwards have often taken the Belgian-Moroccan community as main target in these discussions, to the extent that some right wing analysts even speak of the existence of a 'Moroccan problem'.[1]

Furthermore, in the recent attacks in Paris and Brussels in 2015 and 2016, several perpetrators were of Moroccan origin and came from Belgium, thus feeding into the already existing stigmatization of the community.

The large societal attention (positive and negative) accorded to this group has coincided with the creation of public policies geared towards a better inclusion of immigrants (and more specifically of Moroccan background). A major boost came with the establishment of the Royal Commission for Migrant Policy (*Koninklijk Commissariaat voor het Migrantenbeleid*) in 1989 that strengthened the policies in place aiming for the integration of the immigrant communities (*categoriaal beleid*). In Flanders, a specific policy for newcomers was developed (*inburgeringsbeleid*) focusing mainly on Dutch language acquisition and introduction into the labor market. By the beginning of the 21st century in the context of major terrorist attacks associated with Islam in the West, public opinion became more skeptical, if not hostile, towards Muslim immigrants, including the Moroccan community. From then on, the specific integration policies were abandoned and instead a policy of general social inclusion was installed, aiming to improve the situation and participation of all vulnerable groups in society, including Moroccan immigrants. Transnational contacts on an institutional as well as individual level remained important over the years. In general, Moroccans living in Belgium stayed well connected to their regions of origin and started, during the last decades, to develop a diaspora policy from below. From the side of Morocco a lot of energy was invested in an institutional diaspora policy to make their citizens abroad staying well connected to their country of origin. During the last years a turn in the Moroccan diaspora policy can be witnessed, focusing much more on the relevance for the Moroccans living abroad to become integrated in the countries of destination, including Belgium.

The growing visibility of this minority group has, consequently, generated a large amount of scientific studies. The Belgian Moroccans – as the group will regularly be called in this book for practical reasons (it reads more fluently than the correct name 'people of Moroccan descent') – represent one of the most studied groups in the Belgian context, and several aspects of their presence have been subjected to a scholarly scrutiny. Yet this book is not only a comprehensive overview of the scholarly *status quaestionis* on Moroccan migration. By taking this minority group as a reference point, it also seeks to offer an overview of the most representative trends in the rapidly developing scholarly field of migration studies in Flanders.

Despite the presence of some pioneering researches already in the seventies, migration studies remain a rather young and minor sub-disciplinary field in Belgium, restricted to sociology and anthropology. In the recent years, however, one can witness a growing interest from various disciplines (history, religious and cultural studies, economy, political sciences, demography, media and urban studies), thus turning it into one of the fastest growing research domains. By attending to the particularity of the scientific production on Moroccan minorities in Belgium, this volume is simultaneously an attempt to identify some current trends in this newly emerging field and to bring more established and new scholars in conversation. The book is divided into five parts.

The first part of this volume needs to be read as three general thematic introductions into the rich and diverse body of scholarship that was generated by 50 years of Moroccan migration in Belgium. Rather than providing a general and comprehensive introduction, which covers the various topics within one text, we have chosen to develop these themes into separate chapters: a first one which goes more deeply into migration as a phenomenon and sketches its diachronic resonance in different academic disciplines; a second one that turns to the attention that has been given to Islam in the study of Moroccan migration in Belgian scholarship; and a last contribution that looks at how history has related to the phenomenon of (Moroccan) migration. These three texts must be read as interdependent and are illustrative of the richness and vastness of the academic knowledge produced so far.

Christiane Timmerman's contribution outlines migration history in Belgium and describes this dynamic process by using a theoretic model of Hein de Haas.

She shows how the different stages in this migration process have influenced the scientific research over time. While at first these studies were descriptive in nature, research nowadays is no longer simply descriptive but is built upon analysis and theory.

Nadia Fadil's contribution offers an account of how Islam was considered by Belgian scholars interested in (Moroccan) migration. She notes that while the focus on Islam will emerge quite late compared to the other themes raised in this volume, recent years have witnessed an exponential increase in researches focused on this theme – often as a result of the growing public anxieties around the visibility of Islam in the public sphere. Whereas the early studies were marked by an interest in the institutional aspects of the presence of Islam in Belgium, recent works have paid more attention to the individual and collective dimensions of their religious experiences. An important element, Fadil notes in her review, is the relative neglect of the component of ethnicity as well as the role that the "home countries" and other, non-European, transnational agents continue to play in the organization of the religious lives of Belgian Moroccans.

Karim Ettourki, Sam De Schutter and Idesbald Goddeeris, finally, offer an overview of historical research into Moroccan immigration in Belgium. They argue that the research is still in its infancy. There are some valuable studies, both written in academia and by some people within the Moroccan community, on a variety of topics, from local cases to Berber activism. Yet, an abundance of primary sources remain untouched so far. The three scholars discuss some of them, such as institution archives (e.g. the alien policy), media (both Belgian and migrant periodicals), private papers (e.g. the ones of Johan Leman), and interviews.

The second part offers an account of some historical facets and contemporary developments of this migration that was initiated as a program of temporary labor migrants (*gastarbeiders*). Albert Martens – the emeritus Leuven social scientist who has been pioneering Belgian migration studies since the seventies – discusses Moroccan migration to Belgium from a labor perspective and by means of statistical data, most importantly labor cards (i.e. work permits). He paints a different picture than the classical one that highlights the watersheds of the bilateral agreement of 1964 and the migration halt of 1974. Martens elaborates, for instance, on the so-called touristic migration between 1963 and 1967, which he calls 'a fitting euphemism for the pure and simple acceptation of immigrants non-conforming to the law and accordingly illegal'. A foreign worker could come to Belgium with a tourist passport and could easily regularize his situation if he was able to find employment. In the second part of his chapter,

Martens denounces the continuing ethno-stratification of the labor market. In spite of the fact that it is difficult to conduct quantitative research on the occurrence of discrimination in the social field because many second generation immigrants have become Belgians, the work situation (selection, remuneration, unemployment, etc.) of 'Belgians of allochthonous origin' is clearly less favorable than that of 'autochthonous' Belgians.

The Ghent scholars Emilien Dupont, Bart Van de Putte, John Lievens and Frank Caestecker examine the evolutions in intra-ethnic partner choices in Belgium among residents of Moroccan origin. This topic has recently been considered particularly relevant for migration policies and dominates public debates because marrying a spouse from the country of origin could potentially hinder or even fully inhibit the integration process (although there are different views, suggesting that choosing a partner from the country of origin could also be seen as a way of emancipating oneself). The team compared the choice of partner migration to the choice of a Moroccan partner in Belgium by means of 24,723 first partner choices among residents of Moroccan origin between 2001 and 2008. In general, they compute that partner migration still prevails (54,5% for women and 51,3% for men), but they simultaneously observe a shift towards a more local partner choice. They also find differentiation between age, generation, and gender. While Moroccan women from the second generation increasingly opt for a local partner, Moroccan men who were born in Belgium, are keen on marrying a wife migrated from Morocco. Men from the first generation, in contrast, are more likely to choose a local partner compared to the second generation.

Drawing on the 2001 Belgian census data as well as on birth registrations from 2002 to 2005, the Antwerp social scientists Jonas Wood, Layla Van den Berg and Karel Neels study the household organization among 176,048 co-residential couples of Belgian, Moroccan, or mixed Belgian-Moroccan origin. Since the seventies, women are increasingly active on the labor market, inter alia due to higher female educational attainment, rising earning potential, and the expansion of subsidized childcare. However, this evolution is not entirely visible among Moroccan migrants in Belgium. First, couples in which one or both partners are of Moroccan origin exhibit much lower shares of dual earner households, and much higher shares of male breadwinner models, female breadwinner models, or households without an earner. This may be related to less favorable labor market prospects for Moroccan men. Second, there is a difference in entering into parenthood. Whereas among Belgian couples the dual earner model yields the highest first birth odds, the male breadwinner model plays this part for Moroccan couples. The outsourcing of childrearing and household tasks may be too costly for these groups due to lower wage potentials, although this may also be caused by less favorable attitudes toward female labor force participation.

The third part of this book looks into the policy dimensions of this history. It investigates the various facets of the policies of integration, and also attends to the ways in which this minority group is not simply a recipient or passive actor in this process but in many cases actively negotiated, contested or engaged with the various demands from stakeholders and society at large. A particular attention is thus paid to the role of minority networks, and the ways in which these fulfill a central role in the integration and participation process of this minority group.

In the early years of immigration policy makers were not focused on designing and implementing a comprehensive reception and integration policy aimed at the settlement of migrant workers. These laborers were seen as temporary guests who sooner or later would return to their country of origin. It is only when reality refuted this assumption that in the eighties the first seeds of a more elaborate integration policy became implemented. Noel Clycq and François Levrau tackle the transformations that occurred in the development of integration policies from the eighties until present day. They focus on the shift from a Belgian migration and asylum policy to a Flemish (civic) integration policy, and simultaneously from a shift from a more group oriented to an individual oriented definition of integration. In many of these policies Moroccans were often – together with Turks – the 'ultimate other' or individuals that needed to be integrated, even though policies seldom explicitly targeted 'Moroccan' migrants as such. In a final section they discuss these processes in light of a more general discussion of the rationale underlying integration policies.

It has been common practice to conceive of people from Moroccan descent as an ethnic community that finds its origins in a common national heritage. Concomitantly, immigrant associations have in general been considered as the most fundamental expressions of this collective national identity. Nicolas Van Puymbroeck asks whether Belgian Moroccans indeed organize unlike other immigrant groups, thus giving a different form to their cultural heritage and shared origins. He draws on a historical study of immigrant organizations of two most similar groups (Moroccan and Turkish) in two most similar cities (Ghent and Antwerp) and points to the importance of the city context, as assumed by political opportunity structure explanations, but also highlights idiosyncratic national traditions, as highlighted in resource models.

A few decades ago, integration of the expatriate Moroccans in the receiving countries was totally rejected by the Moroccan state as it was deemed to undermine their homeland affiliation. Remarkably, in the current Moroccan diaspora policies, we find that policy discourses are increasingly focusing on the improvement of their expatriate citizens' integration in the receiving societies. This shift is remarkable, as it implies a total rupture with previous Moroccan diaspora policy discourses. Rilke Mahieu, Nadia Fadil and Christiane Timmerman put focus on diaspora policies of the Moroccan state regarding the *Marocains Résident à l'étranger* (Moroccans Living Abroad), the increasingly diverse group of Moroccan emigrants and their descendants currently estimated at 5 million. They analyze how integration and its relationship with transnationalism are conceptualized in these current diaspora policy narratives.

The sociological reality of the Moroccan community in Belgium is, however, not only one of history, or policy, but elements of culture and identity have also been central in this. Whereas early research has tended to pay attention to the impact of the socio-economic dimensions on settlement and incorporation processes, it is mostly from the nineties onwards that researchers increasingly pay attention to the role of cultural markers such as language or food in ethnic identity construction processes. Building upon this academic legacy the papers selected in this **fourth part** focus on the ways in which Moroccan ethnicity emerges as an important (or sometimes rather the opposite is the case) variable in and across various social domains.

Norah Karrouche starts with a broader scope on a topic that is almost absent in the research on the Moroccan identity in Belgium. Up until the late nineties, Berber culture and languages in the Maghreb countries were neglected and at times even severely and violently oppressed. Since the late eighties, Berber cultural associations in France, Germany and the Netherlands have been advocating the rights of Berbers in the Maghreb and its diaspora. These associations continue to strive for the recognition and dissemination of knowledge on Berber languages, history and culture both in the Maghreb and among Moroccan and Algerian migrants and their descendants in the diaspora. Karrouche describes and analyzes the history of Berber associations and their members in Belgium, and in Antwerp and Brussels in particular. She explains why and how these associations in Flanders/Belgium developed late in comparison to other Western European countries and addresses their public lives and roles as secular actors in Flemish society. In so doing, she takes into account both local Belgian politics and transnational ties.

In the second chapter Anna Berbers, Leen d'Haenens and Joyce Koeman study how identity processes are intertwined with individual's social networks, in particular Belgian and Dutch Moroccans. It examines how personal networks and interactions of minorities with society at large shape their daily identity negotiations and constructions. The authors analyze the 'lived' experience of social networks, with an emphasis on related identification processes, as well as the structure and composition of networks. The findings show how minority individuals with a more dense and homogeneous network (in terms of ethnicity) and a smaller number of subgroups are more likely to self-identify ethnic-exclusively (e.g. Moroccan), whereas other types of networks may lead to ethnic-inclusive (e.g. Moroccan-Belgian) and generic identifications (e.g. as a woman).

A third chapter focuses on the use of language(s) and relates this to a continuing concern among policy makers and educators on the position of minority language usage at school and in the home environment. Over the recent years, this concern has become the object of growing scientific interest. Jürgen Jaspers' detailed ethnographic description of the language usage at school seeks to gain insight into the way in which students and teachers try to reconcile the effects of migration within an institution that is often not geared to them. On the basis of ethnographic research in two schools where youth with a Moroccan background play a significant role, Jaspers describes how teachers and pupils cope with the contradictions between top down language policy and on the ground linguistic diversity.

In a final chapter of this section Wim Peumans studies the issue of same-sex sexuality in Moroccan communities and doing so he provides a unique insight into contemporary ethnic, racial, sexual and gender dynamics in Belgian society. His research assesses the attitudes of Belgian Moroccans towards same-sex sexuality and situates these attitudes in broader moral frameworks. Through an ethnographic content analysis of online and print media, the author discusses a series of events that took place during his fieldwork. All events were heavily mediatized and caused public and political scrutiny as they revolved around same-sex sexuality, Islam and migration.

Finally, **the fifth and last part** of this book will focus on the religious dimension of this migration history. In difference to the previous sections, the attention is given to the centrality of Islam or other forms of divination. In his chapter Philip Hermans sketches the nature of divination practices by traditional Moroccan healers. Many Moroccans assume that misfortune as well as many illnesses can be caused by demons (*jinn*) and other supernatural powers. Because of this, they often find themselves misunderstood by western therapists and seek help from traditional healers who use popular Islamic elements in their treatments. This article depicts healing practices and rituals as they are still performed in Morocco and tries to explain the healers' relative success as well as their patients' dependencies on them in terms of psychological and social processes as well as the power of symbols in the placebo effect.

In just a few decades Islam has become the second largest religion in most European countries, including Belgium. This impacts on how our contemporary multicultural and multi-religious society deals with birth, marriage, and with death and dying and the philosophical and religious outlook on the attitudes toward bio-ethical issues. This evolution constitutes an important challenge to European health care (including palliative care), as this is still deeply influenced by secular-Western and/or Christian approaches. Bert Broeckaert, Chaïma Ahaddour, Goedele Baeke and Stef Van den Branden analyze real world end of life views and attitudes of elderly Muslims in Flanders, Belgium. Drawing on semi-structured interviews with elderly Moroccan men and women, their paper shows that among the respondents euthanasia and assisted suicide are strongly rejected; non-treatment decisions and the refusal of treatment are only allowed in exceptional circumstances; pain control does not pose an ethical problem. God, for their respondents, controls illness and health, life and death and many consider it unacceptable to interfere in this divine plan. Patience is considered a central virtue. Another important observation were the striking similarities between the guidelines in the international normative sources and the actual attitudes of the respondents. The attitudes of the generation of Belgian Muslims studied here are deeply influenced by a shared religious framework. Nevertheless, even in these very homogeneous groups a few dissident voices were found. Indeed, in palliative care it remains essential to start from the ethical and religious views of the unique individual in front of you; not from the views that are typically associated with the community he/she belongs to.

In the multicultural context of Brussels, Mieke Groeninck notes that there is a growing demand from the Muslim community for initiatives for the Islamic education of women. The main *leitmotiv* through the lessons is the subjective reform toward a more pious version of the self. In this process, a growing attention is paid to the instruction and transference of correct Islamic knowledge, *'ilm al-Islam*. In her paper, she describes how the question of correct knowledge (transference) is similarly the object of continuous debate. Drawing on two years (2013-2015) of participant observation in women-only and gender separated courses on Islam in three mosques and three Islamic institutes in the region of Brussel she looks into the curriculum offered courses in Qur'anic exegesis (*tafseer*), Qur'anic recitation (*tajweed*), Islamic jurisprudence (*fiqh*), the biography of the prophet (*al-sirah*), Islamic dogma (*'aqidah*), and Islamic ethics. The most important theme of the courses, she notes, is the idea of personal and communal reform. Therefore attention is paid to the perfection of one's *'ibadat* (five pillars of Islam), as well as to one's ethical behavior towards others (*almu'amalat*), and one's spiritual relation with the ultimate Other. In her paper, she describes how, in the process of reforming and 'becoming pious', these three elements relate to each other during, but ideally also outside of the courses. Knowledge acquaintance, then, is not only aimed at disciplining the *self*, but also of the self's *being* in the world next to and in a mutual relation with similar and dissimilar, visible and invisible o/Others. Her paper thus describes how *politics of 'ilm* relate to the private, public and universal sphere of existence.

Iman Lechkar's chapter finally concludes this section through her study of Moroccan Belgians who were born as Sunni but converted into Shiism during their life. Her work thus offers a unique insight into an underexplored theme, and also shows the complexity and diversity of Islam within the Belgian-Moroccan community. Lechkar's contribution furthermore proposes a novel understanding of conversion by highlighting the affective and visceral dimensions that are often entailed in such life course changes. Through a detailed ethnographic description of the life story of one of her informants, she shows how this turn from Sunnism into Shi'ism was as much a matter of intellectual and existential interrogations as it was a consequence of being moved and touched by carriers and proponents of Shi'ism.

The different sections proposed in this book offer a multifaceted introspection into the dynamic nature of migration studies in Flanders in general, and Moroccan studies in particular. Of course, they are not comprehensive, and certain other aspects, such as psychological research on acculturation or social research on the religiosity of Moroccan migrants, certainly deserve to be further analyzed in the future. Still, because of the large degree of comprehensiveness of the individual contributions, this book can not only appeal to scientific peers working on this domain, but also to teachers, social workers, policy advisors and other interested people who work from close or afar with this minority group.

Note

1. Expressions such as 'het marokkanenprobleem', 'kutmarokkanen' and others are routinely used by (mostly conservative) commentators in Flanders and the Netherlands to suggest a high rate of criminality and social fraud among Belgian-Moroccans and to link this with their cultural background. This formulation even figured as the official designation of a parliamentary debate in 2012 in the Netherlands

Part 1
Research and context

1. Social sciences and Moroccan migration in Belgium

Christiane Timmerman

Belgian migration in a nutshell

In the past, certainly between 1850 and 1950, Belgium has been a country of emigration. Initiatives such as the recent creation of the Red Star Line Museum in Antwerp make sure that this important fact is not forgotten. Migration dynamics in Belgium began to change in the second half of the 20th century, and immigration began to prevail. Labor migration gained force in the Mediterranean region. First, guest workers from Spain and Italy were recruited; however, especially following the major mining disaster in Marcinelle (1956), it became difficult to convince Southern Europeans to work in Belgium under dangerous conditions for relatively low wages. Belgium was forced to look elsewhere for its heavy industry workers. In the early '60s, Belgium entered into agreements with Morocco and Turkey, upon which the guest worker migration began in earnest. Unlike other European countries, Belgium has remarkably few immigrants from its former colonies, and as a result of the Cold War, the number of refugees from the communist world remains limited. In the early '70s, the Western world was facing the Oil Crisis. The oil producing countries refused to continue to sell their oil at cheap prices, and as a result, the economic tide in Western Europe resulted in many workers losing their jobs. The rapid increase in the number of unemployed and the bleak economic outlook also had an impact on migration. In 1974 Belgium, like many other European countries, put a stop to migration. This did not, however, prevent migration from happening after 1974. Migrants no longer entered the country to be guest workers, but mainly with the goal of 'family reunification'. The regions of origin of immigrants became more diverse at that point; from the '80s onward, Belgium welcomed immigrants from around the world, and no longer exclusively low-skilled workers but also highly skilled workers, refugees, asylum seekers, students, and undocumented migrants. The immigrant profile became unprecedentedly diverse. Migration also no longer implied a permanent establishment; mobility began to characterize migration – both in terms of successive visits to the homeland as well as between different countries.

The research follows...

It is evident that this important social phenomenon, namely migration, also attracted the attention of the scientific community in Belgium. In the beginning, in the sixties and seventies, the focus remained rather reluctant and migration was approached as an 'exotic' phenomenon, but by now, migration has become a factor that all areas of social science research take into account.

Migration is a dynamic process, not a static phenomenon; it evolves over time. At a certain moment, the migration of a particular group begins. Sometimes this migration is a great success and catalyzes a significant migration chain, developing into a real migration *system*; but after a certain period this migration system will also probably die out. A number of researchers have tried to understand these processes via theories. Hein de Haas offers an interesting exercise in this respect (see Figure 1).

De Haas distinguishes five phases – from beginning to end – in a migration system. This model is relevant first of all for its clarification that no migration system can continue to exist indefinitely. Several factors on macro, meso and micro levels ensure that migration will increase under certain conditions, and will thereafter decrease. It is interesting to apply this model to the Belgian situation and also to consider how the existing research has responded to these different phases. We note that there is a clear link between migration phenomena, in this case in Belgium, and the genre of research that it generates. To get a more thorough view on the historical research on Moroccan migration in Belgium we refer to the contribution of Karim Ettourki, Sam De Schutter and Idesbald Goddeeris to this volume.

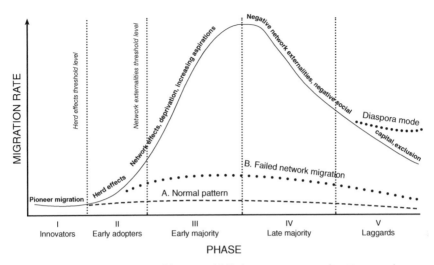

Figure 1: An ideal-typical trajectory of the rise and fall of a migration system (De Haas, 2010).

The first phase, namely that of the **'pioneer migration'**, ended in Belgium in the early '60s with the signing of bilateral agreements that included Morocco and Turkey. Until then, migration was mainly a matter of individual adventurers and/or entrepreneurial individuals who dared to take risks. For example, in 1960 only 461 Moroccan nationals were registered in Belgium (DG Statistic Belgium).

The period 1964-1974 can be described as the second stage, that of the **'novice chain migration'**, in which the migration was effectively set in motion. At the end of this period, in 1974, already 40 000 persons with Moroccan nationality were living in Belgium (DG Statistic Belgium).

However, only a minority of immigrants used official immigration procedures; spontaneous migration was still the most common. The phenomenon called "herd effect" was apparent during this phase. Many migrants follow in full trust those who have preceded them, anchoring their confidence on migrants who have already made the crossing – despite lacking information about the migrant situation in the destination country. It is also at this stage that we find the first Belgian studies dealing specifically with migration, more specifically with the so-called 'guest workers'. The studies are primarily descriptive in nature since it is a completely new phenomenon: One first had to get an overview migration in Belgium. Another remarkable finding is that these studies were often carried out in close consultation with key figures from the immigrant community. The subjects of these initial studies are closely linked to the status of these migrants: namely, "labor" (Martens, 1969; Hanotiau, 1973). The first doctorate on this subject was realized by Albert Martens in 1973: "25 years of disposable workers". We also see some studies on health and welfare (Van Mol, 1974; 1976a) and even already on integration (Van Mol, 1976).

The third phase, namely that of **'the flourishing chain migration'** (1974-1989), is the heyday of Moroccan immigration: The number of Moroccans in Belgium in 1974 was, as mentioned before, 40,000, which increased to 140,000 by 1989. The labor migration indeed stopped due to the oil crisis, but the immigration continued largely on the basis of family reunification. This allowed a feminization of the migrant population and the emergence of the so-called 'second generation' migrants, children born in Belgium of immigrant parents. Along with this chain migration, intense transnational networks developed, particularly between regions of origin and destination. Such networks involve a substantial exchange of information which can facilitate the migration process of prospective migrants. These transnational networks thus increase the potential for migration and reduce the costs thereof. The migration process itself thus creates an internal dynamic that perpetuates migration. We note that the migration aspirations in emigration regions of Morocco are increasing.

It was also in 1974 that Islam was officially recognized as one of Belgium's religions. In response to the new migration phenomenon, the extreme right gained more wind in the sails, and alarming election results showing that a significant proportion of the population was struggling with the new reality of a more culturally diverse society resulted in the establishment of the Royal Commission for Migrant Policy, led by Paula D'Hondt. We note that in this period the policy regarding the reception of migrants became more professionalized. More specific, they began building policy specifically aimed at migrants as a group.

This new situation was also reflected in academic research. As the number of immigrants increased, so did the amount of research on this theme. Migrants are increasingly becoming part of society and are no longer perceived as the exotic outsiders that they once were. In the meantime, a substantial amount of knowledge about the migrant groups has been gathered, research that is no longer simply descriptive but is built upon analysis and theory. In this phase, research was often done in close consultation with the categorical integration policy (Martens & Moulaer, 1985; Royal Commission for Migrant Policy, 1989). The period where a handful of key individuals were able to oversee the entire migrant situation is over.

The research themes were closely linked to the new migration landscape. Research was conducted on the changing profile of migrants (Bastenier & Dassetto, 1981;

Paula D'Hondt, the Royal Commissioner for Migrant Policy, visiting a school in Gent (source: KADOC)

Dassetto & Bastenier, 1984; Dumon, 1982; Pauwels & Deschamps, 1989; Poulain & Eggerickh, 1990); as well as on the 'second generation migrants', wherein education occupies an important place (Gailly & Leman, 1982; Van Loock, 1988). Scholars also kept an eye on what was changing in the health domain (Schillemans, 1989). In anthropological research, the regions of origin became an interesting research topic (Leman, Gailly, Hermans, 1980; Cammaert, 1985; Hermans, 1985). Inspired by research in countries with a longer tradition of immigration, namely the United States and the United Kingdom, Belgian scholarship also began to focus on processes of ethnic identification (Roosen, 1989).

1989 was a significant year worldwide because of the fall of the Iron Curtain. In the following years, there were a number of events which thoroughly reshaped the international context and which also had a strong impact on Belgian migration dynamics. Therefore, we propose that we entered the fourth phase in 1989, namely that of the **'late chain migration'**. First there was the fall of the Iron Curtain and the collapse of the Soviet Union, whereby the East-West relation had to be redefined. In Belgium the so-called 'Fast Belgian Law' came into force, through which foreigners could acquire Belgian nationality in a very short time.

Many foreigners also became Belgian through regularization, as was the case among the Moroccans living in Belgium[1]. On September 11, 2001, there were the terrorist attacks of Al Qaeda on the Twin Towers in New York. This helped to reinforce the image of the Muslim as the ultimate 'Other' in the Western world, thus further increasing polarization.

In the Belgian context, we see that the profile of immigrants is becoming more diverse. The majority of immigrants in Belgium are still coming in on the basis of family reunification, usually through marriage migration, but the proportion of students, migrant workers and so-called "illegals" is increasing. Compared with the previous phases, more highly skilled individuals, more women, and citizens of a wider variety of countries belong to this group of newcomers. The second and subsequent generations of immigrants are also increasing, and most of them acquire Belgian nationality. The feminization of the migrant population is continuing, and the ageing of the migrant population must also be considered now. Migrants and their descendants are increasingly part of mainstream society; we find them also among entrepreneurs, artists, scientists, and politicians.

We also see that the transnational networks between regions of origin and destination are changing in part due to the social mobility of the migrant population. Together with a bottom-up diaspora policy aimed at the regions of origin that has been developing out of the migrant populations, we see a concomitant new migration dynamic forming since the economic crisis in the EU. A number of people with a migration background, particularly second and subsequent generations, aspire to return to their country of origin, of which a significant number do effectively return. These developments also have an impact on migration aspirations in the regions of origin. People are now better informed and are more selective in planning a migration project. Moreover, prospective migrants are often discouraged from immigrating by people in their community who have already established themselves in the region of destination.

Despite the increasing integration of people with a migration background, it appears there are still obstacles to smooth participation in society. The policy with respect to immigrants is being further professionalized at this stage but the categorical approach is being abandoned in favor of socially inclusive policies. The "Integration Policy" is being launched specifically for newcomers, and aims to allow the so-called third-country nationals to take part as quickly as possible in society.

In this phase, the phase of the late chain migration, we see that the research field of migration is undergoing a metamorphosis. It integrates itself more and more in all areas of social science research and increasingly follows the laws that apply in these areas. The research is also better supported theoretically, more analytical in nature and more strongly anchored in the international research context. The collaboration with policy will be continued and even institutionalized, as for example through the establishment of the Policy Research Centres. Research continues to focus on major current issues (employment, education, policy) but new research niches are also emerging (Islam, media, transnationalism, mobility). Studies are emerging that examine the changing migration and integration contexts (Vranken, Timmerman, van der Heyden, 2001; Bousetta & Martiniello, 2003; Khader, Martiniello, Rea, Timmerman, 2006; Foblets, Maes, Vanheule, 2011; Timmerman, Lodewyckx, Vanderwaeren, Vanheule, 2011; Zemni, 2010; Verhaeghe, Van der Bracht, Van de Putte, 2012; Levrau, Piqueray, Goddeeris, Timmerman, 2014; Timmerman, Martiniello, Rea, Wets, 2015).

Migration and integration policy meanwhile have themselves also become the subject of scientific research and observations (Blommaert, Verscheuren, 1992; Adam, 2010; Levrau, Loobuyck, 2013; Van Puymbroeck, 2014). Considerable research is also still produced on classical themes such as work (Cuypers, 1992; Scheepers, Speller, Willems, 1991; Geets, 2010; Glorieux, Laurijssen, 2009; Okkerse, Termote, 2004; Vandezande, Fleischmann, Baysu, Swyngedouw, Phalet, 2008; Vertommen, Martens, Ouali, 2006; Corluy, Marx, Verbist, 2011). In the field of health, on the other hand, significantly less has been published (De Munck, Peeters, 1994; Ferrant, Hermans, 1991; Verrept, Timmerman, 2001).

Education, especially with respect to the second and subsequent generations, has received a lot of attention since the '90s. Many of these studies are comparative and integrated into the international research context. We also see a lot of attention to this topic from anthropology (Leman, 1991; Roosens, 1995; Timmerman, 1999; 2000; Timmerman, Vanderwaeren, Crul, 2003; Duquet, Glorieux, Laurijssen, Van Doorselaer, 2006; Groenez, Van den Brande, Nicaise, 2003; Hermans, 2006; Hirtt, Nicaise, De Zutter, 2007; Lacante, Almaci, Van Esbroeck, Lens, De Metsenaere, 2007; Braeye, Hermans, 2011; Timmerman, Clycq, Segaert, 2012). In recent years several studies have focused on the educational situation of ethnic minority students in Flemish education, and again most of this research focused on Moroccan and Turkish origin students. The findings show that the experiences and performance of these youngsters can differ dramatically from those of Flemish native students (Clycq, et al., 2014). Studies have shown that a sense of futility in the school but also among teaching staff can have negative impact on this situation (Agirdag, et al, 2012) and that the root cause of the perceived difficulties are often situated by educators outside of the school environment, and in particular in the home environment (Clycq, et al., 2014). In more recent work, the issue of identity becomes paramount (Baysu, et al., 2011) and the lack of valuing diversity and in particular multilingualism is discussed (Timmerman, et al, 2016; Pulinx, et al., 2016). The context of the school often becomes a high cost context that is not 'identity safe' for these students and wherein stereotype threat effects can have an important negative effect on feelings of belonging and educational performance (Nouwen & Clycq, 2016).

Scholars have also looked at the political attitudes of migrants (Phalet, Swyngedouw, De Rycke, 2005; Jacobs, Swyngedouw, 2006; Fleischmann, Phalet, Swyngedouw, 2013) as well as their legal status (Foblets, 2000; Hebberecht, 2011; Vandenhole, De Clerck, Verhoeven, Timmerman, Mahieu, Ryngaert, Carton de Wiart, 2011; Foblets, Vanheule, 2012).

A theme that has gained particular popularity since the 90's is Islam in relation to migration (Dassetto, 1990; Platti, 1990; Leman, 1992; Leman, Renaerts, Van Den Bulck, 1992; Janssens, 1993; Clycq, 2011; Agirdag, Loobuyck, Van Houtte, 2012; Debeer, Loobuyck, Meier, 2010; Kanmaz, 2007; Timmerman & Vanderwaeren, 2008; Rondelez, Bracke, Fadil, 2013; H'madoun, 2013; Benyaich, 2013). The relevance of Islam in the Belgian research agenda will be discussed more in detail in the next chapter 'The study of Islam and Moroccan migration in Belgium' by Nadia Fadil. The anthropologically inspired research tradition of culture and ethnicity has also been advanced (Hermans, 1994; Roosens, 1994; Roosens, 1995; Timmerman, 1999; 2000; Phalet, De Rycke, Swyngedouw, 1999; Timmerman, Vranken, 2001; Fadil, 2002; Saaf, Sidi Hida, Aghbal, 2009; Clycq, 2009; Smets, 2013; Hesters, 2013).

What is new in this phase is that research pays attention to various forms of migration and different aspects of it, such as marriage migration, student mobility, feedback mechanisms (Wets, 1999; Deschamps, 2005; Timmerman, 2006; Descheemaeker, Heyse, Wets, 2009; Timmerman, Lodewyckx, Wets, 2009; Desmet, Leys, Ronsijn, 2011; Casier, Heyse, Clycq, Zemni, Timmerman, 2013; Van Mol, Timmerman, 2013; Timmerman, De Clerck, Hemmerechts, 2014; Van Mol et all, 2014); but also to transnationalism and diaspora (Wets, 2002; Perrin, Martiniello, 2011; Michielsen, Notteboom, Lodewyckx, 2012; De Bruyn, Develtere, 2008; Mahieu, 2014; 2015).

The question is when Belgium will land in the fifth and final phase, the stage of **'stagnation and decline'**. We note that there are fundamental changes in different explanatory levels of the migration process. Firstly, we see that on the macro level, some rather dramatic changes are taking place which affect the dynamics of migration in Belgium, among other places. Since 2008, an economic crisis has raged throughout Europe, resulting in an increase of job scarcity, insecurity, inequality and polarization. Migration has been gaining force during these years. At the same time, we note that a number of other regions are doing relatively well: the BRIC countries, but also Turkey, one of the major 'source countries' for Belgian immigration. However, the recent political tensions and embeddedness within the turmoil of the Middle East may negatively affect Turkey's socio-economic position in the future. This turmoil feeds also significant flows of asylum seekers towards Europe, which has become one of the major challenges the EU is facing now. The changing face of Europe compared to the rest of the world thus has repercussions on the migration aspirations of potential migrants. They may opt for destinations other than Europe, or just choose to stay at home. As was already discussed, migration aspirations are shaped by many factors that have to do with the regions of origin and destination and the networks developing between them. It is not only the economic situation of these regions, but also the overall situation in the fields of democracy and human rights which is taken into consideration when people make migration plans. There are also a number of internal migration dynamics that can have an inhibiting effect: the socio-economic mobility, integration and geographical distribution of the established migrant populations in Belgium could weaken transnational ties with the regions of origin. These factors along with the growing negative attitude and stricter policies on migrants, as well as the unfavorable economic climate could lead to established migrants dissuading prospective migrants from immigrating to Europe.

Research for the future

For future research on migration, there are thus countless interesting challenges. More than ever, scholars will have to examine these themes from an international perspective. Research on changing migration dynamics, including the so called refugee crisis, the increasing importance of transnational networks and spaces, new forms of social cohesion in increasingly diverse cities, new ideological and religious movements that see the light in the wake of migration, are just some of the many research topics that deserve examination. The field will certainly continue to develop...

Note

1 For more information on the demographic dynamics of the Belgian Moroccans, see Quentin Schoonvaere (2014). *België-Marokko: 50 jaar migratie. Demografische studie over de populatie van Marokkaanse herkomst in België*, Federaal Migratiecentrum.

Bibliography

Adam, I. (2010). *Au-delà des modèles nationaux d'intégration? Analyse des politiques d'intégration des personnes issues de l'intégration des entités fédérées belges.* Doctoral thesis. Bruxelles: Départment des science politique.

Agirdag, O. Loobuyck, P. & Van Houtte, M. (2012). Determinants of Attitudes Toward Muslim Students Among Flemish Teachers: A Research Note. *Journal for the Scientific Study of Religion*, 51(2): 368-376.

Agirdag, O., Van Houtte, M., & Van Avermaet, P. (2012). Why does the ethnic and socioeconomic composition of schools influence math achievement? The role of sense of futility and futility culture. *European Sociological Review*, 28, 366-378.doi:10.1093/esr/jcq070.

Bastenier, A. et F. Dassetto, (1981). La deuxième génération d'immigrés en Belgique, *Courrier hebdomadaire* 907-908.

Baysu, G., Phalet, K., & Brown, R. (2011). Dual identity as a two-edged sword: Identity threat and minority school performance. *Social Psychology Quarterly* 74, 121-143. doi: 10.1177/0190272511407619

Benyaich, B. (2013). *Islambeleving & het radicalisme bij Marokkanen in Brussel*, VUB SERV.

Blommaert, J. en Verscheuren, J. (1992). *Het Belgische migrantendebat. De pragmatiek van de abnormalisering.* Antwerpen: International Pragmatics Association.

Bousetta, H. & Martiniello, M. (2003). Marocains de Belgique: du travailleur immigré au citoyen transnational. *Hommes et Migrations*, 1245(mars-avril), 94-106.

Braeye, S., Hermans, P. (2011). The educational achievement of Chinese and Moroccan students in Flanders: parents' and students' perspectives. *Canadian Issues / Thèmes Canadiens*(winter), 85-90.

Cammaert, M.F. (1985). *Migranten en thuisblijvers: een confrontatie. De leefwereld van Marokkaanse berbervrouwen.* Leuven, Universitaire Pers Leuven.

Casier M., Heyse P., Clycq N., Zemni S., Timmerman C. (2013). Breaking the in-group out-group: shifting boundaries in transnational partner choice processes of individuals of Moroccan, Tunisian, Algerian, Turkish, Punjabi Sikh, Pakistani and Albanian descent in Belgium. *The sociological review* 61(3), 460-478.

Clycq, N. (2009). *Van keukentafel tot 'God'?. Belgische, Italiaanse en Marokkaanse ouders over identiteit en opvoeding.* Antwerpen/Apeldoorn: Garant.

Clycq, N. (2011). *At Home in Europe. Muslims in Antwerp.* New York: Open Society Foundation.

Clycq, N., Nouwen, W., & Vandenbroucke, A. (2014). Meritocracy, deficit thinking and the invisibility of the system: Discourses on educational success and failure. *British Educational Research Journal,* 40, 796-819. doi:10.1002/berj.3109.

Corluy, V., Marx, I, Verbist, G. (2011). Employment chances and changes of immigrants in Belgium: the impact of citizenship. *International journal of comparative,* 52(4), 350-368.

Cuypers, C. (1992). Ik werk, jij werkt, werkt zij? Migrantenvrouwen op de arbeidsmarkt in Limburg. *Bareel,* 13, 15-6.

Dassetto F. (1990). Vingt ans d'islam belge, *Migrations* 2(7), 19-36.

De Bruyn, Tom, Patrick Develtere (2008), *Het potentieel van de diasporafilantropie, Onderzoek naar het geefgedrag van Belgische migranten,* Leuven: HIVA.

De Haas, H. (2010). The internal dynamics of migration processes: A theoretical inquiry. *Journal of Ethnic and Migration Studies,* 36(10), 1587-1617.

De Munck, A & Peeters, R (1994). *Hoe gezond zijn Ali en Fatima Tien jaar wetenschappelijk onderzoek over gezondheid van en gezondheid voor allochtonen.* ESOC: Universiteit Antwerpen.

Debeer, J., Loobuck, P. & Meier, P. (2010). *Imams & islamconsulten in Vlaanderen: hoe zijn ze georganiseerd?* Antwerpen, Hasselt: Steunpunt Gelijkekansenbeleid.

Deschamps, L. (2005). De internationalisering van de 'Vlaamse' huwelijksmarkt, een oriënterende schets'. In: F. Caestecker (red.). *Huwelijksmigratie, een zaak voor de overheid?* Leuven: Acco.

Descheemaeker L., Heyse P. & Wets J. (2009). *Partnerkeuze en huwelijkssluiting van allochtone mannen, Een kwantitatieve en kwalitatieve analyse van het partnerkeuzeproces en het huwelijk van Marokkaanse, Turkse en sikhmannen.* Brussel: Instituut voor gelijkheid van vrouwen en mannen.

Desmet, G., Leys, D., Ronsijn, W. (2011). *Partnermigratie van derdelanders naar Vlaanderen en Brussel.* Een kwantitatieve en kwalitatieve studie in opdracht van de Vlaamse Overheid en het Europees Integratiefonds.

Dumon, W (1982). *Het profiel van de vreemdelingen in België.* Leuven, Davidsfonds.

Duquet, N., Glorieux, I., Laurijssen, I. & Van Doorselaer (2006). *Wit krijt schrijft beter. Schoolloopbanen van allochtone jongeren in beeld.* Antwerpen: Garant.

Fadil, N. (2002). Tussen Marokkaanse en Moslim: over de etnische en religieuze identiteit van Marokkaanse adolescente meisjes. *Tijdschrift voor sociologie,* 23(2), 115-138.

Ferrant, L & Hermans, P (1991). Problemes de santé et expression de la plainte chez les Marocaines de Belgique, *Les Cahiers de GERM* 26, 219.

Fleischmann, F., Phalet, K., Swyngedouw, M. (2013). Dual identity under threat: When and how do Turkish and Moroccan minorities engage in politics? *Zeitschrift für Psychologie* 221(4), 214-222.

Foblets, M.C. (2000), Migrant women caught between Islamic family law and women's rights: the search for the appropriate 'connecting factor' in international family law. *Maastricht journal of European and comparative law* 7(1), 11-35.

Foblets, M.C., D. Vanheule & M. Maes. Dertig jaar vreemdelingenrecht. *Migratie- en migrantenrecht.* 14, 1-46.

Foblets, M.C., Vanheule, D. (2012). *Vreemdelingenrecht,* Brugge: Die keure.

Gailly, A. & Leman, J, (1982). *Onderwijs, taal- en leermoeilijkheden in de immigratie,* Leuven, Acco, 5-33.

Geets, J. (2010). *De arbeidsmarktpositie van (hoog)geschoolde immigranten. Een vergelijkende kwantitatieve studie van autochtonen en immigranten.* Steunpunt Gelijkekansenbeleid (SGKB).

Glorieux, I. & Laurijssen, I. (2009). *The Labour Market Integration Of Ethnic Minorities In Flanders. Summary of the main findings concerning the entry into the labour market of youth of migrant descent.* Brussel: Vrije Universiteit Brussel (VUB).

Groenez, S., Van den Brande, I. & Nicaise, I. (2003). *Cijferboek sociale ongelijkheid in het Vlaamse onderwijs. Een verkennend onderzoek op de Panelstudie van Belgische huishoudens.* Leuven: Steunpunt LOA.

H'madoun, M.(2013). *Religion and economic preferences.* Antwerpen: Universiteit Antwerpen, Faculteit Toegepaste Economische Wetenschappen, Departement Algemene Economie, 2013.

Hanotiau B., *Les problèmes de sécurité sociale des travailleurs migrants.* Larcier, Bruxelles, 1973.

Hebberecht, P (2011). Het levensverhaal van jongeren van Turkse en Marokkaanse origine met een instellingsverleden. Hun ervaringen met en hun opvattingen over politie, justitie, bijzondere jeugdbijstand en welzijnswerk. In: Crombez, J. en De Wachter, E. (eds.), *Kansen voor kinderen. Een weg voor het jongerenwelzijn in Vlaanderen.* Antwerpen/Apeldoorn, Garant, 2011, 169-180.

Hermans, P (1985). *Maatschappij en individu in Marokko, Een Antropologische benadering.* Brussel: Cultuur en migratie.

Hermans, P. (1994). *Opgroeien als Marokkaan in Brussel. Een antropologisch onderzoek over de educatie, de leefwereld en de "inpassing" van Marokkaanse jongens.* Brussel: Cultuur en Migratie.

Hermans, P. (2006). Counternarratives of Moroccan parents in Belgium and The Netherlands: answering back to discrimination in education and society. *Ethnography and Education,* 1(1), 87-101.

Hesters, D. (2013). *De etnische identiteit van de tweede generatie van Marokkaanse afkomst in Brussel en Antwerpen. Naar een kwalitatieve, comparatieve onderzoeksstrategie in onderzoek naar etnische minderheden.* Leuven: KU Leuven.

Hirtt, N., Nicaise, N. & De Zutter, D. (2007). *De school van de ongelijkheid.* Berchem: EPO.

Jacobs, D. & Swyngedouw, M. (2006). La vie associative marocaine et turque dans la Région de Bruxelles-Capitale. In Khader, B., Martiniello, M., Rea, A. & Timmerman, C. (eds.) *Penser l'immigration et l'intégration autrement. Une initiative belge inter-universitaire.* Brussels: Bruylant, 135-158.

Janssens, R. (1993). Migratie, religiositeit en modernisme. Een onderzoek naar de religiositeit van Turkse migrantenvrouwen en de invloed ervan op een aantal waarden, normen en opinies. *VUB: Working Papers Series "Etnische minderheden in België",* nr. 1993-5.

Kanmaz, M. (2007). *Moskeeën in Gent. Tussen Subcultuur en Sociale Beweging. Emancipatiedynamieken van Moslimminderheden in de Diaspora.* PhD thesis. Gent: Universiteit Gent, Faculteit Politieke en Sociale wetenschappen.

Khader, B., Martiniello, M., Rea, A. & Timmerman, C. (eds.) (2006). *Penser l'immigration et l'intégration autrement. Une initiative belge inter-universitaire.* Brussels: Bruylant.

Koninklijk Commisssariaat voor het Migrantenbeleid (1989). *Integratie: een werk van lange adem,* Brussel (III Delen).

Lacante, M., Almaci, M., Van Esbroeck, R., Lens, W., & De Metsenaere, M. (2007). *Allochtonen in het Hoger Onderwijs Onderzoek naar factoren van studiekeuze en studiesucces bij allochtone eerstejaarsstudenten in het hoger onderwijs.* Eindrapport OBPWO 03.03. Bruxelles/Louvain: VUB & KUL.

Leman, J. (1991). The Education of Immigrant Children in Belgium. *Anthropology and Education Quarterly* 22, 140-53.

Leman, J. (1992). Ontmoeting op het terrein met moslims in België. *Cultuur en Migratie* 2, 7-24.;

Leman, J., Renaerts, M. en Van Den Bulck, D. (1992). De rechtspositie van de islamitische praxis in België. *Cultuur en Migratie* 2, 43-84.

Leman, J., Gailly, A., Hermans, P. (1980). Mediterrane dorpskulturen: het sociaal-kultureel verleden van de gastarbeiders in België en Nederland. *Kultuurleven: tijdschrift voor cultuur en samenleving* 47(9), 820-840.

Levrau François, Piqueray Edith, Goddeeris Idesbald, Timmerman Chris. (2014). Polish immigration in Belgium since 2004: new dynamics of migration and integration? *Ethnicities*, 14(2), 303-323.

Levrau, F., Loobuyck, P. (2013). Is multiculturalism bad for social cohesion and redistribution? *The political quarterly*, 84(1), 101-109.

Mahieu, R. (2014). Chapitre 8. Les Marocains et les Belgo-Marocains de Belgique. In: *Marocains de l'Extérieur*, Fondation Hassan II pour les Marocains Résidant à l'Etranger & IOM, 219-262.

Mahieu, R. (2015). Feeding the ties to home: diaspora policies for the next generation. *International Migration* 53(2), 397-408.

Martens, A. & Moulaer, F. (1985). *Buitenlandse minderheden in Vlaanderen en België: wetenschappelijke inzichten en overheidsbeleid*, Antwerpen: De Nederlandse Boekhandel.

Martens, A. (1969). Pourquoi les travailleurs étrangers ne dorment-ils pas derrière leur machine après le travail? *Frères du Monde* 61-62, 147-156.

Michielsen, J. Notteboom, E. & Lodewyckx, I. (2012). *Diaspora en ontwikkelings samenwerking. Een onderzoek naar de rol van de diaspora uit Congo, Ghana en Marokko*. Antwerpen: Stad Antwerpen.

Nouwen, W. & Clycq, N. (2016). The role of teacher-pupil relations in stereotype threat effects in Flemish secondary education, *Urban Education*, 1-30, doi:10.1177/0042085916646627

Okkerse, L. & Termote, A. (2004). *Singularité des étrangers sur le marché de l'emploi. À propos des travailleurs allochtones en Belgique*. Bruxelles: Direction Generale Statistique et Information Economique.

Pauwels, K. en Deschamps, L. (1989). *De vreemdelingenpopulatie in Vlaanderen en in de 19 Brusselse gemeenten*. Centrum voor Bevolkings- en Gezinsstudiën.

Perrin, N. & Martiniello, M. (2011). *Les pratiques transnationales des migrants en Belgique. Vecteur d'integration ou de repli communautaire?* Fondation Roi Baudouin.

Phalet, K., De Rycke, L., Swyngedouw, M. (1999). Culturele waarden en acculturatievormen bij Turken en Marokkanen in Brussel. In: Swyngedouw M., Phalet K., Deschouwer K. (eds), *Minderheden in Brussel. Sociopolitieke houdingen en gedragingen*. Brussels: VUB Press, 19-40.

Phalet, K., Swyngedouw, M., De Rycke, L. (2005). Sociaal-politieke oriëntaties van Turken en Marokkanen in Brussel. In: Swyngedouw M., Delwit P., Rea A. (eds), *Culturele diversiteit en samenleven in Brussel en België*. Leuven: Acco, 127-143.

Platti E. (1990). Les musulmans et l'Etat en Belgique, *Islamochristiana*, 16, 183-199.

Poulain, M. en Eggerickh, T. (1990). De demografische kenmerken van de vreemde bevolking in de Belgische steden (1983-1988). *Bevolking en Gezin*, 1, 77-92.

Pulinx Reinhilde, Van Avermaet Piet & Agirdag Orhan (2016). Silencing linguistic diversity: The extent, the determinants and consequences of the monolingual beliefs of Flemish teachers. *International Journal of Bilingual Education and Bilingualism* 20(5), 542-556, DOI:10.1080/13670050.2015.1102860.

Rondelez, E., Bracke, S., Fadil, N. (2013). *Islam, secularisering, en sociologie.* Leuven: Acco.

Roosens, E. (1989). *Creating Ethnicity. The Process of Ethnogenesis.* Newbury Park-London-New Delhi: Sage Publications.

Roosens, E. (1994). The primordial nature of origins in migrant ethnicity. In Vermeulen, H. and Govers, C. (eds). *The Anthropology of Ethnicity. Beyond Ethnic Groups and Boundaries.* Amsterdam: Het Spinhuis, 81-104.

Roosens, E. (1995). How Multicultural is the School in "multicultural society"? A Belgian Case. In: Roosens, E. (Ed.). Rethinking Culture, "Multicultural Society" and the School. International Journal of Educational Research, 23, 11-22.

Roosens, E. (1995). Interests Groups with a Noble Face. In Costa, J. and Bamossy, G. (eds). *Marketing in a Multicultural World: Ethnicity, Nationalism and Cultural Identity.* Newbury Park-London-New Delhi: Sage Publications, 126-41.

Saaf, A., Sidi Hida, B. & Aghbal, A. (2009). *Belgo-Marocains des deux rives. Une identité multiple en évolution. Une identité multiple en évolution.* Bruxelles: Fondation Roi Baudouin.

Scheepers, P., Speller, T. en Willems, A. (1991). De arbeidsmarktpositie van werkzoekenden na scholing: een vergelijking van allochtonen met autochtonen. *Sociologische Gids* 38, 162-73.

Schillemans, L (1989). De migrant in de eerstelijns gezondheidszorg. *Huisarts nu* 18:497-507.

Smets, K. (2013). *Diasporic film cultures: a structural and audience study among Turkish and Moroccan communities in Antwerp (Belgium),* Antwerpen: Universiteit Antwerpen, Faculteit Politieke en Sociale Wetenschappen, Departement Communicatiewetenschappen.

Timmerman C., Hemmerechts K., De Clerck H., (2014). The relevance of a culture of migration in understanding migration aspirations in contemporary Turkey. *Turkish studies* 15(3), 1-19.

Timmerman C., Lodewyckx I., Wets J. (2009). Marriage at the intersection between tradition and globalization: Turkish marriage migration between Emirdag and Belgium from 1989 to present. *The history of the family* 14(2), 232-244.

Timmerman C., Martiniello M., Rea A., Wets J. (2015). *New dynamics in female migration and integration.* London, Routledge.

Timmerman C., Vanderwaeren E., Crul M. (2003). The second generation in Belgium. *International migration review* 37(4), 1065-1090.

Timmerman C., Vranken J. (2001). Pluriforme samenlevingsconcepten: het particuliere gegrondvest in het universele. In Vranken, J., Timmerman, C., van der Heyden, K. (eds).

Komende generaties: wat weten we (niet) over allochtonen in Vlaanderen? Leuven: Acco, 43-58.

Timmerman C. (2006). Gender dynamics in the context of Turkish marriage migration: the case of Belgium. *Journal of Turkish studies* 7(1), 125-143.

Timmerman C. (1999). *Onderwijs maakt het verschil: socio-culturele praxis en etniciteitsbeleving bij Turkse vrouwen.* Leuven, Acco (Minderheden in de samenleving, 7).

Timmerman C. (2000). Secular and religious nationalism among young Turkish women in Belgium: education may make the difference. *Anthropology and education quarterly* 31(3), 333-354.

Timmerman C., Clycq N., McAndrew M., Balde A., Braeckmans L., Mels S., eds. (2016). *Youth in education: the necessity of valuing ethnocultural diversity.* London, Routledge.

Timmerman, C, Lodewyckx, I., Vanderwaeren, E., Vanheule, D. (2011). *MInteGRATIE: over nieuwe vormen van migratie en integratie.* Brussel, UPA.

Timmerman, C. & E. Vanderwaeren (eds.) (2008). *Islambeleving in de Lage landen.* Leuven/ Apeldoorn: Acco.

Timmerman, N. Clycq & B. Segaert (eds.) (2012). *Cultuuroverdracht en onderwijs in een multiculturele context.* Gent: Academia Press.

Timmerman, C., De Clerck, H., Hemmerechts, K., Willems, R. (2014). Imagining Europe from the Outside: the role of perceptions on human rights in Europe in migration aspirations in Turkey, Morocco, Senegal and Ukraine. In N. Chaban and M. Holland (eds.), *Communicating Europe in the Times of Crisis: External Perceptions of the European Union.* Palgrave-McMillan.

Van Loock, L. (1988). Les jeunes d'origine étrangère en Flandre. Formation professionnelle: pierre d'achoppement de l'insertion des jeunes immigrés en Flandre. *Tribune Immigrée* 24-25, 110-14.

Van Mol C., Timmerman C. (2013) Should I stay or should I go? An analysis of the determinants of Intra-European student mobility. *Population, space and place* 20(5), 1-15.

Van Mol, C., Mahieu, R., De Clerk, H. M. L. et al. (2014). Conducting qualitative research: dancing a tango between insider- and outsiderness. In Voloder, L. & Kipitchencko, L. *Insider Research on Migration and Mobility. International Perspectives on Insider Positioning.* Ashgate Publishing Limited.

Van Mol, Mark (1974). Marokkaanse immigranten en gezondheidszorg. *Kontakten*, 3-5.

Van Mol, Mark (1976). Aanpassingsproblemen van Marokkaanse vrouwen. *Kultuurleven*, 827-835.

Van Mol, Mark (1976). Houdingen van Belgen ten overstaan van migranten in Antwerpen. *Kultuurleven*, november, 854-857.

Van Puymbroeck, N (2014). Migratie en de politiek van stedelijk burgerschap: een vergelijkende analyse van vier Belgische steden (1974-2012).

Vandenhole W., De Clerck H., Verhoeven M., Timmerman C., Mahieu P., Ryngaert J., Carton de Wiart E. (2011). Undocumented children and the right to education: illusory right or empowering lever? *International journal of children's rights* 19, 613-639.

Vandezande, V., Fleischmann, F. Baysu, G., Swyngedouw, M. & Phalet, K. (2008). *De Turkse en Marokkaanse tweede generatie op de arbeidsmarkt in Antwerpen en Brussel. Resultaten van het TIES-onderzoek.* Leuven: CeSO (KUL).

Verhaeghe, P., Van der Bracht, K. & Van de Putte, B. (2012). *Migrant zkt. Toekomst. Gent op een keerpunt tussen oude en nieuwe migratie.* Antwerpen/Apeldoorn: Garant.

Verrept H., Timmerman C. (2001). Gezondheidsonderzoek bij allochtonen. In J. Vranken, C. Timmerman, K. van der Heyden (eds). *Komende generaties: wat weten we (niet) over allochtonen in Vlaanderen?* Leuven: Acco, 213-224.

Vertommen, S., Martens, A. & Ouali, N. (2006). *Topography of the Belgian labour market. Employment: gender, age and origin.* Brussels: Fondation Roi Baudouin.

Vranken J., Timmerman C., van der Heyden K. (eds) (2001). *Komende generaties: wat weten we (niet) over allochtonen in Vlaanderen?* Leuven: Acco (Minderheden in de samenleving, 10).

Wets, J. (1999). *Waarom onderweg? Een analyse van de oorzaken van grootschalige migratie- en vluchtelingenstromen.* KU Leuven, PhD thesis.

Wets, J. (2002). The Brain Business: Import and Export Assessed. In van Beurden J., de Graaf P., Meinema T. (eds.), *Bridging the Gap. Essays on economic, social and cultural opportunities at global and local levels.* Utrecht: Netherland Institute for Care and Welfare / NIZW, 59-69.

Zemni, S. (2010). *Belgische Marokkanen. Een stap verder.* Bruxelles: Fondation Roi Baudouin.

2. The study of Islam and Moroccan migration in Belgium

Nadia Fadil

This introduction attends to the importance given to Islam in the study of Moroccan migration in Belgian scholarship. As a predominantly Maliki and Sunni-oriented country, where the King is also regarded as the leader of the religious community (*amir al mûminin*), Islam figures as a foundational element in the Moroccan nationalist narrative (Hammoudi, 1997). The importance of Islam in the national imaginary is also reflected in the contours and shape of the Moroccan presence in Belgium. From the outset, Moroccan migrants, like other immigrant communities, have invested in the construction of mosques and the religious instruction of their children. Yet despite the importance given to Islam in the organisation of the community, this question will remain peripheral within the literature in the early years. The early phase of the research on Moroccan migrants was characterised by a more sustained attention given to labor (Martens, 1973) or social integration (Bastenier & Dassetto, 1981; Bastenier & Dassetto, 1982; Hermans, 1992). It is only in the second half of the nineties, with the exception of some early studies (Dassetto & Bastenier, 1984; Dassetto & Bastenier, 1987a; Dobbelaere & Billiet, 1974), that the focus on Islam will be more pronounced. A first quick look at the literature indicates a more prevalent attention for this religious question in the francophone scholarly field. Another important observation is the relative neglect of the role of ethnic and diaspora ties in understanding the organisation of the religious lives of Muslims in Belgium. Although some studies have examined the salience of ethnicity and the role it continues to have in processes of identification (Bastenier, 1997; Clycq, 2009; Kanmaz, 2009), a more explicit interest into how Islam was turned into an important (and new) identity marker has become more preponderant (Dassetto, 1996; Fadil, 2005), which echoes an international trend in the literature on Islam in Europe (Amiraux, 2012; Peter, 2006). The global rise and popularity of Islamic movements worldwide – also among Maghrebi migrants in Europe – lead to a growing concern among European analysts and scholars and which translated into the question whether one can speak of the emergence of a *European Islam* (Dassetto, 1996). Yet this concern around Islam's compatibility with the Belgian (and European) context occurs, we want to suggest, at the cost of a more careful investment into how these religious experiences continue to be structured and mediated by networks of the "home countries" and beyond.

The first Moroccan mosque in Leuven (source: Stadsarchief Leuven)

This chapter offers an overview of the way in which scholars working on (Moroccan) immigration in Belgium treated the presence of Islam (Fadil, El Asri & Bracke, 2015).[1] Because of this volume's emphasis on Moroccan migration, this review will restrict itself to the literature that has included this group in its empirical focus. But such restriction is largely artificial, for the reality of Islam in

Belgium is much more complex and cannot be restricted to the lived experience of Belgian Moroccans. However, when reviewing the literature, one quickly finds out that the Moroccan population has – albeit tacitly – often figured as the target group for many of the studies on Islam in Belgium, because of the size and public visibility of this group. In difference with the Turkish community, for instance, the Moroccan community has been much more the target of controversies on migration and often acted as public representative (Kanmaz, 2009). Although pragmatically driven, the focus on Moroccans in this review is thus also partially a reflection of the privileged political and scholarly focus on this group. The first part of this introductory section will give a general outline of the historical presence of Islam and Islamic movements within the Belgian-Moroccan community. The second and third part of this introduction will, on turn, be focussed on some key themes that have been addressed by Belgian scholars, i.e. the institutionalisation of Islam and the centrality of Islam in the organisation of the daily lives of Moroccan migrants in Belgium. In a final note a more general call will be formulated for a reinvestment into the complex realities of Belgian-Moroccan Muslims as European and transnational (religious) agents.

Belgian Moroccans/Muslims: a glocal community

Understanding the on-going religious dynamics among Belgian Moroccans through a local and Belgian lens is a challenging task, this at least for two reasons. The first reason has to do with the transnational imbrication of this community, which holds strong ties with the country of origin and with Moroccan migrants in other parts of Europe (such as France, the Netherlands, Spain, Italy or Germany) through ties of kinship, marriage or intra-European forms of mobility. Another important reason has to do with the transnational embedding of Islam, understood here as a tradition that informs and shapes the lives of Muslims in multiple and complex ways (Asad, 1986). The continuous reference to the *Umma*, as a global and trans-ethnic spiritual community, acts as an important moral imaginary for many Muslims in their religious practice. When looking for religious knowledge, Belgian Moroccans will rarely restrict themselves to local preachers or Imams but also look for knowledge abroad, either in Europe or in other parts of the Muslim world (Morocco, Egypt, Saudi-Arabia...). This globalisation of Islam has furthermore been spearheaded by the Internet, which has become a central space of moral deliberation in the recent years (Hirschkind,

2012; Mandaville, 2001; Roy, 2002). Although national authorities (such as Morocco or Turkey) have consistently sought to control the influence and spread of certain religious discourses, the reality of Islam remains nevertheless highly complex and decentralised and social actors continuously compete over the definition of the common good (LeVine & Salvatore 2005; Salvatore, 2004). Rather than speaking of a "Belgian Islam", it is thus more accurate to situate the religious experiences of Belgian Moroccans at the intersection of shifting theological and geo-political transformations that implicate the Moroccan state, European (i.c. Belgian) states, and other transnational agents from other parts of the Muslim world.

The late sixties and seventies have been an important turning point in this process. They corresponded with the massive growth and popularity of politicised and transnational Islamic movements within the Arab world (and beyond), also known as the Islamic revival (*al-sahwa al-islamiyya*). Reformist movements, that were since the 19th century competing over the definition of the contours of political modernity (Salvatore, 1997), were gaining unprecedented popular support after the gradual decline and demise of secular alternatives (such as Arab nationalism). It is around this same period that a number of countries repositioned themselves as global players in the organisation of the *Umma*. The Islamic Revolution in Iran and the establishment of the first Islamic Republic in the Middle East by Ayatollah Khomeini in 1979 revealed a global enthusiasm for this "*Islamic alternative*" (Nasr Hossein, 1964). Saudi Arabia profiled itself through the creation of two important institutions in 1969 that testified to the country's worldwide ambitions: the *Organisation of the Islamic conference* (OIC) and the *World Muslim league* (WML). The aspirations of Saudi Arabia also found its ramification in Belgium, as the institutions created under its auspices were also the main interlocutors of the Belgian state on Muslim affairs until the mid-eighties. In 1969, the Pavilion Oriental was donated to the Saudi King Faisal by the Belgian state, and will host the Islamic Cultural Center (ICC) that was established in 1968 (Kanmaz & Zemni, 2012; Panafit, 1999). Paralleling these ambitions by the Saudi state to extend its political and religious aura, the role of Arab and Muslim activists and intellectuals, who were escaping the repression of their native countries and landed in Europe as refugees, also needs to be stressed. This is particularly the case for intellectuals and activists linked to the banned Muslim brotherhood in Egypt or Syria and the party Ennahda in Tunisia. These new settlers played a crucial role in setting up Islamic organisations that would cater to the needs of – especially – a younger generations of migrants (often with a

Maghrebi background) who were looking for a proper way of apprehending their Islamic identity in a Belgian and European context (Marechal, 2008a; Marechal, 2008b; Maréchal, 2015). Other, more apolitical groups such as the *Salafi* or the *Tabligh*, also played an important infrastructural role in facilitating this turn to Islam among the first and second generations (Dassetto, 1988; Dassetto, 2000; Khedimellah, 2001; Touag, 2015). Moroccan based Islamic organisations and networks were also constitutive in the further expansion of this religious field and in nurturing the religious orientation of Belgian Moroccans. Islamist movements such as the popular '*adl wal ihsan* (justice and spirituality) have manifested their presence within he diaspora through the organisation of cultural festivals. Sufi movements, such as the influential *tariqa qadiriya boutchichiya*, will be more popular among the highly educated segments of the community.

This emergence and popularity of Islamic movements among the settled Belgian Moroccans will, however, also have an impact on the concerned states (i.c. Belgium and Morocco). In the case of the Belgian state, this visibility of Islam in the public sphere provoked a large series of debates from the late seventies onwards. Several commentators in especially the Francophone part of the country, highly influenced by the *laicist* discourse from France, saw in the presence of veils in Brussels alarming signs of "Muslim fundamentalism" (Dassetto, 2011; Dassetto & Bastenier, 1987b). The first "*affaire du foulard*" in Brussels also erupted shortly after the one in Paris in 1989 (Ouali, 2004: 38). These public anxieties around Islam also furthered the desire, by the Belgian state, to facilitate the creation of a representative body for Muslims that would mitigate these tensions and restrict the influence of foreign countries. These ambitions will materialise into the creation of the Executive for Muslims in Belgium in 1998 (Panafit, 1999; Kanmaz & Zemni, 2012).

The Moroccan state, on the other hand, had a more ambivalent position towards the mounting popularity of Islamic movements among its diaspora, which ranges from a relative indifference in the early years to a more pro-active and intervening role in the recent years. While Morocco offered a certain amount of support in the establishment of mosques or the organisation of religious instruction in the early period, its volume and reach cannot be compared to that of other states like Turkey who held a strong grip on the religious lives of Turks abroad (through the *Diyanet*). The more interventionist role of the Moroccan state was rather directed towards limiting the influence of (often left-wing) political activists (such as the RDM, UNEM, USFP) among the immigrant communities. This was done through the development of an elaborate and informal network of surveillance and through the creation of socio-cultural organisations such as the *widadiya* (amicales) (Bousetta, 2000; Frennet-De Keyser, 2011; Ouali, 2004). The Moroccan state also acted as a representative in Saudi-lead international organisations such as the IOC and the ICC and figured as an important interlocutor for the Belgian state on the religious instruction of Muslim pupils in public schools throughout its embassies. 9/11 will, however, become an important turning point, as concerns with international terrorism will reach global proportions and translate into a desire to gain more control over the existing religious discourses. In Morocco, the attacks in Casablanca on May 16th 2003 will announce an important shift in this regard and speed up the process of controlling the circulation of religious discourses (Zemni, 2006). In 2004, the *Conseil Superieur des Ulemas,* founded in 1981, will be renewed and its mission extended to developing a robust religious curriculum and controlling the spread of religious advices (*fatwa*).[2] In Europe, the *Conseil Européen des Ulemas Marocains* will be created in 2008, with its headquarters in Brussels. It was initially conceived as an answer for the need of properly trained imams and '*Ulema* according to the Maliki rite and who were also capable of addressing the specific problems encountered by Muslims in Europe. Yet in the recent years, this platform also increasingly came to address the question of "radicalisation", especially after it became clear that a significant amount of the European youngsters who left to Syria between 2013 and 2015 and the authors behind the attacks of Paris and Brussels in 2015 and 2016 had Moroccan roots.[3] These recent attempts by Morocco to set up a number of initiatives thus indicate a more outspoken desire by the state to extend its spiritual aura outside its national territory by promoting Malekism and Sûfism also amongst its diaspora.[4]

Constructing a Belgian Islam

The visibility of Islam in the Belgian public sphere and the gradual integration of this denomination into the institutional landscape will yield an important scholarly interest that would primarily focus on the institutional components of this reality (Dassetto, 1997; Dassetto & Bastenier, 1984; Debeer, Loobuyck & Meyer, 2011; Foblets & Van Overbeeke, 2002; Husson, 2012; Kanmaz & El Battiui, 2004; Maréchal & Bousetta, 2004; Panafit, 1999; Renaerts & Manço, 2000). This large focus on the institutional aspects can be understood in the light of the particular model of recognition in Belgium. In difference to its southern neighbouring country France, there exists no strict principle of separation in Belgium such as the model of *laïcité* that limits the interactions between religion and state. Rather, religious traditions are pro-actively recognised by the Belgian state (through the constitutional arrangements as stipulated in art. 181) and they also can benefit from a certain amount of state funding in their material organisation. Currently, there are seven officially recognised confessions (Catholicism, Judaism, Protestantism, Orthodox Church, Islam, Anglican Church and Secular denomination), and one has been in the process of being recognised for some time (Buddhism). The recognition of Islam in 1974 as an official denomination emerged firstly as a result of a growing need for proper religious instructors in state schools who had a growing cohort of Muslim pupils (Boender & Kanmaz, 2002; Dassetto & Bastenier, 1987a; Manço & Kanmaz 2006). Public schools are constitutionally obliged to arrange confessional education at the request of the parents and the organisation and administration of this question falls under the auspices of the representative body of the concerned denomination. The recognition of Islam in 1974 thus first comes to meet this need for a formal juridical framework to administer and organize this religious instruction in public schools. This recognition will, however also occur against the background of the tedious diplomatic ties with Saudi Arabia (after the oil crash of 1974), and a desire to formally acknowledge and institutionally imbricate the collaboration with foreign authorities such as Morocco and Turkey (Panafit, 1999).

The history of the institutionalisation of Islam, and especially of the instalment of the Executive for Muslims in Belgium in 1999, will become a key site of investigation for Belgian scholars, and several publications will attend to this long process (Kanmaz & Zemni, 2012; Leman, Renaerts & Van den Bulck, 1992; Renaerts & Manço, 2000). While the idea of a representative body emerged already in the early seventies, it is only in 1999 that the Executive for Muslims in Belgium (EMB) will be established, following a general election among the Muslim community in the fall of 1998. This brought an end to a long period of unsuccessful attempts to settle the question of representation, in which religious, secular actors and international actors confronted each other.[5] Several studies have documented these difficulties and sought to account for the main reasons behind it. Some have highlighted the confessional and ethnic divisions that they considered to stand in the way of a strong leadership (Dassetto, 2011: 78; Maréchal, 2003: 165), others have also reflected on the preconceptions imbricated within the Belgian law that is modelled on the hierarchical structure of the Catholic church and which is ill adapted to the heterogeneous composition of the Muslim community (Overbeeke & Foblets, 2002; Panafit, 1999; Kanmaz & Zemni, 2012). Other studies have invoked the political sensitivity of the question of Muslim representation and how this has consistently fueled a strong interventionism of political authorities (Manço & Kanmaz, 2006; Panafit, 1997). Examples such as the attempt by the federal state to organize a representative organ in 1985,[6] the non-recognition of elections organized by the ICC in 1991,[7] and the screenings of the elected candidates in 1998, of which some were removed on security grounds, are only few examples of such interventionist stands. Some other studies, finally, will look at the importance of mosques and religious authorities from a public sphere perspective. The focus is here on how these mosques emerge as spaces of agency for Muslims and as potential stakeholders in the interactions with the public authorities. Noteworthy are the studies of Meryem Kanmaz (2009) and Corinne Torrekens (2007; 2009), who describe the presence and role of the religious institutions in distinct urban settings, i.e. Ghent and Brussels. Their empirical studies show how these spaces emerge as alternative public spheres, which play an increasing role in the civic, political and public integration and participation of Muslims in urban settings.

From ethnicity to Islam

Whereas the institutional components of Islam in Belgium triggered a large amount of scholarly interest from the early years, this was lesser the case for the religious experiences of Moroccan migrants. Notwithstanding a few exceptions, a more systematic focus on the beliefs and practices of Belgian Moroccans emerges quite late in comparison to the other themes, and only at the turn of the new century. This has partially to do with the growing politicisation of this question in various European contexts at the end of the 20th century. This will translate into a growing interest into the lived practices of Muslims in Europe.

Nationwide controversies such as the first '*affaire du foulard*' in France, or the Rushdie affair in the UK in 1989 triggered heated debates on the proper role of Islam within the public space. Many of the early empirical researches were therefore explicitly oriented towards this societal interrogation on whether younger Muslims were developing forms of religiosity that were compatible with dominant liberal and secular values.[8] The first studies answered positively to this question by highlighting that Muslim practices were overall undergoing a process of secularisation among the younger generations, which they considered to be the result of an increased integration (Lacoste-Dujardin, 1994; Lesthaeghe, 1997; Lesthaeghe 2000; Manço 2000; Manço & Manço 2000). Subsequent findings will, however, increasingly problematize this trend of equating integration with a reduced importance given to Islam. A continued reference to Islam in the daily practice, so the argument goes, is neither the sign of a withdrawal from society nor an indication of an increased radicalisation but its significations can be complex. Most studies even suggest that a continued reference to Islam, in many cases go along with new forms of citizenship. This thesis will be at the heart of Felice Dassetto's (1996) influential study 'La construction de l'Islam European' (1996). In here, he develops the argument that the renewed assertions of Islam among the younger generations are part of a global religious revival that has found new points of articulation among migrants. Yet instead of viewing this "religious revival" as resulting simply from the 'manipulation' by transnational Islamist agents (see for instance Kepel, 1991 [1987]), Dassetto also situates this turn to Islam as an answer to a series of local and existential challenges. Islam becomes, in other words, a privileged source of identification that allows younger Muslims to position themselves in new ways into the European societies and to adopt a critical distance from the country of origin (Dassetto, 1996: 165). Subsequent studies on Muslim religiosity and identity will echo these findings and argue that a heightened assertions of one's identity as Muslim amongst the Belgian Moroccans often occurs at the cost of one's ethnic identification (Fadil, 2002; Kanmaz, 2002). In the line of other observations made elsewhere (Cesari, 1994; Khosrokhavar, 1997; Roy, 1999; Sunier, 1996), these researches will introduce a new outlook into what was often framed as a troubling "return to tradition". The importance of Islam among younger generations is no longer read as a form of disaffiliation from society, but in many cases seen as a sign of engagement with it (Fleischmann & Phalet, 2012; Güngor, Fleischmann & Phalet, 2011; Saaf, Sidi Hida & Aghbal, 2009; Timmerman & Vanderwaeren, 2012; Torrekens & Jacobs, 2016). Several studies will indeed describe how this privileging of Islam as an ethical and identity resource enables new forms of political participation or "Muslim civicness" (Fadil, 2006; Kanmaz, 2009; Pedziwiatr, 2010) or produces new critical interrogations of the tradition from a gender perspective (Djelloul, 2013; Fadil, 2011; Peleman, 2001; Vanderwaeren, 2005; Vanderwaeren, 2010).

The importance of the Muslim tradition, as an ethical resource, will lead to a rich scholarship that will attend to the ways in which Islamic norms impact and regulate the daily conduct of Muslims. Important to note is that although much of this scholarship is *de facto* concerned with Muslims with Maghrebi ethnic roots, little attention will be accorded to understanding how the ethnic background or the relationship with Morocco mediates this religious orientation. The presupposition is rather that this reference to Islam transcends the ethnic particularities, and that it is also continuously re-examined in the light of the collective and individual needs of Muslims in Europe. Researches will thus focus on how these religious norms are lived and re-examined in the daily practice of Muslims in Belgium and produce a new European Muslim subjectivity. The cases that will be examined range from the importance of dietary requirements such as halal slaughtering techniques and its changing significations across generations (Bonne & Verbeke, 2006; 2008), the evolving signification of religious knowledge in a number of Islamic institutions in Brussels (Groeninck, 2016; 2017; see also contribution in this volume), traditional forms of healing and religious norms (Touag, 2012) or the ways in which Muslim artists (such as hip-hoppers) negotiate restrictive Islamic norms on music in a European context (El Asri, 2015). Some studies have, however, also explicitly highlighted the presence and persistence of ethnicity in their findings. The studies of Van Den Branden (2006; Van Den Branden & Broeckaert, 2010), Ahaddour and Broeckaert (see also their contribution in this volume), for instance, examine how religious norms structure and guide the views on dying of Moroccan elderly in Antwerp. The work of Clycq looks at how the reference to Islam is at once also a marker of ethnicity and is actively invoked by Moroccan parents in the education of their children (Clycq, 2012; Clycq, 2015). Iman Lechkar's (Lechkar, 2012a; 2012b) work also explicitly accounts for the structuring and mediating role of ethnicity in her study on the conversion processes of Sunni Moroccan Muslims into Shi'ism as she describes how her interlocutors will put much effort in positioning this tradition within a larger Maghrebi-Islamic legacy (see also her contribution in this volume).

Yet this local revival of Islam among European Muslims is also met with frictions and tensions (Maréchal, Dassetto & Bocquet, 2014). Several studies and reports will therefore turn to the new forms of exclusions encountered by Muslims who visibly assert their faith such as veiled women (Brems et al., 2012; Brion, 2000; Ouald Chaib & Brems, 2012; Saroglou et al., 2009) or other forms of discriminations and Islamophobia (Clycq, 2011; Fadil, 2010; Mescoli, 2016; Zemni, 2011). Some researches will also look at how practices such as praying or other visible markers are negotiated and practiced in a professional context (Fadil, 2013; Lamghari, 2012). The recent attacks in Paris (2015, 2016) and

Brussels (2016) as well as the departure of hundreds of youngsters to Syria have also produced new studies that have sought to delve into the motivations of these Syria foreign fighters and to understand the problem of radicalisation (Brion et al., 2016; Dassetto, 2012; Laurent, 2016).

Conclusion

The importance of Islam has captured a significant amount of attention amongst scholars working on migration in Belgium in the recent years. One could indeed claim that the existing scholarship has tended to accompany this making of a transnational (*European) Muslim subject* by attending to the ways in which Islam has come to supersede other forms of identifications among ethnic minorities. Yet this focus on Islam, as an abstract entity, has often occurred at the cost of understanding the continued role the so-called "home countries" (i.c. Morocco), or of other non-European transnational agents, in accompanying these transformations. Little is indeed known on the active role countries of origin have played, and continue to play, in the institutionalisation process of Islam in Belgium. Nor are there studies on the recent promotion of Malekism as privileged *madhab* (religious school) among Moroccans in Belgium.[9] Our observations seem however to suggest that transnational religious networks catered by the Moroccan state, such as Sufi groups, or other socio-political groups from Morocco continue to capture an important audience abroad and to profoundly influence and shape the religious lives of Moroccan-Muslims in Belgium and Europe. The dramatic attacks of 2015 and 2016 in Paris and Brussels have, furthermore, reinforced the collaboration between the Belgian state and the "home countries" (such as Morocco) to contain discourses and practices deemed problematic.[10] Yet current scholarship has tended to neglect these transnational ties for a more sustained focus on the local Belgian and pan-European context. Although such emphasis on Belgium and Europe is understandable in the light of the on-going public anxieties around Islam and the negative appraisal of "foreign" interventions, it has come at the cost of a clearer understanding of how Belgian Moroccans (like other minority groups) constantly circulate in a European *and* Arab Muslim moral geography. An important track for future research should therefore be to re-invest this question by accounting for these on-going relationships. Such a perspective would not only allow for a better understanding of how Belgian Moroccans navigate between different fields and life-worlds in the structuring and organisation of their ethical lives, but it could also show that inhabiting multiple and highly complex (and at times contradictory) social worlds has become a central ingredient for what it means to be European and Belgian today.

Notes

1 This chapter partially draws on a chapter published earlier as Fadil, Nadia, Farid El Asri, and Sarah Bracke. 2015. "Islam in Belgium. Mapping an emerging interdisciplinary field of study." Pp. 222-61 in *The Oxford Handbook of European Islam*, edited by Jocelyne Cesari. Oxford: Oxford University Press

2 Laabi, Chafik "Etat et Religion. Comment lire les changements annoncés" in *La Vie Economique*, 07/05/04

3 The CEUM has consistently discouraged youngsters from 2013, through several religious advises (*fatawa*), to take part to the *jihad* in Syria. It has also condemned all attacks that were perpetuated in 2015 and 2016. Its Secretary General, Khalid Hajji, is an often-solicited public speaker on religious co-existence and the question of radicalization.

4 An example can be found through the promotion and support of cultural festivals on Sûfism and Sufi music in Fes such as "Le Festival des musiques sacrées du Monde" (generally held in April) or "Le Festival de Fes de la culture Soufie" (generally held in October) and which are largely advertised among the diaspora. Some Belgian based Muslim organizations or preachers have also come to explicitly profile themselves as Maliki in the recent years. These developments point towards a renewed investment by the Moroccan state in its diaspora as is also shown in the contribution by Mahieu et al. in this volume.

5 Important here is to refer to the role played by the (Saudi funded) *Centre Islamique Culturel* – Islamic Cultural Centre (ICC) of Brussels, which was appointed as interlocutor by the Belgian state in 1968 yet whose legitimacy was challenged by several (mostly secular) Muslims from the seventies and eighties on. This resulted in various attempts at establishing a representative organ, initiated either by Muslim actors (such as the elections for a Higher Council for Muslims in Belgium organized by the ICC in 1991) or by Belgian authorities (such as the Temporary Council of the Wise in 1996) (see Maréchal, 2003: 164 and Kanmaz & Zemni 2012).

6 The '*Conseil Superieur des Musulmans de Belgique*', which was established by a Royal Decree set out by the Minister Jean Gol, was, however, declared non-constitutional by the State Council that same year (Réa, 1999: 269)

7 The background to those elections was the ICC's fear of losing its position of leadership, as it felt threatened by initiatives taken by the Royal Commission for Migrant Policy. On the 13th of January 1991, the ICC organized elections and 26.000 Muslims (or 18% of the

adult Muslims) casted their vote. The Higher Council for Muslims in Belgium (*Hoge Raad van Moslims van België*) was established, composed by 17 members. The Belgian Minister of Justice however refused to recognize this body, while Turkish and Moroccan authorities called for a boycott of these elections (Kanmaz & Zemni 2012).

8   For a further exploration on how the societal gaze determines the researchers' orientation, see Amiraux, Valérie. 2002. "Academic Discourses on Islam(s) in France and Germany: Producing Knowledge or Reproducing Norms?", pp. 111-38 in *Islam and the West: Judgement, Prejudices, Political Perspectives*, edited by Werner Ruf. Münster: Agenda Verlag.

9   Malikism is then understood as a variant of Islam that sits in the line of ancestral forms of religiosity as transmitted by the parents and which is tolerant. Notions of "traditionalism" are reclaimed in ways that sit in contrast with *Salafism* or other reformist tendencies (such as the brotherhood) and which are seen to rather put an emphasis on a rupture from "tradition". For a further analysis of how these accounts of continuity with the "traditional Islam" are evoked in the case of "secular" and "liberal" Muslims of Moroccan background in Belgium, see Fadil Fadil, Nadia. 2015. "Recalling the Islam of the parents. Liberal and secular Muslims redefining the contours of religious authenticity." *Identities: Global Studies in Culture and Power* 22(6):1-18.

10 The most visible cooperations that have been at the level of security and surveillance through for instance the protocols signed between Belgium and Morocco on the exchange of information on criminal networks and terrorism and which have been updated in early 2016 or the crucial role Moroccan intelligence played in tracing the authors of the November attacks in Paris in 2015.

Bibliography

Amiraux, V. (2002). Academic Discourses on Islam(s) in France and Germany: Producing Knowledge or Reproducing Norms? In *Islam and the West: Judgement, Prejudices, Political Perspectives*, edited by Werner Ruf. Münster: Agenda Verlag, pp. 111-38.

Amiraux, V. (2012). Etat de la littérature. L'islam et les musulmans en Europe: un objet périphérique converti et incontournable des sciences sociales. *Critique Internationale* 56(3):141-57.

Asad, T. (1986). *The Idea of an Anthropology of Islam*. Washington: Georgetown University. Occasional Papers Series. Center For Contemporary Arab Studies.

Bastenier, A. & Dassetto F. (1981). La deuxième generation d'immigrés en Belgique. *Courrier Hebdomadaire du Crisp*, 2(907-908) (1982).

Bastenier, A. & Dassetto, F. (1982) *Aspects particuliers de la pathologie dans le milieu migratoire* Louvain-la-Neuve: UCL. Groupe d'étude des migrations.

Bastenier, A. (1997). Conscience ethnique et islam. In *Facettes de l'islam belge*, edited by Dassetto F. Louvain-la-Neuve: Bruylant Academia, 47-67.

Boender, W. and Kanmaz, M. (2002). Imams in the Nethlands and Islam Teachers in Flanders. In: Shadid W.A.R. and Van Koningsveld P.S. (eds) *Intercultural relations and Religious Authorities: Muslims in the European Union.* Leuven: Peeters 169-180

Bonne, K. and Verbeke, W. (2006). Muslim consumer's motivations towards meat consumption in Belgium: qualitative exploratory insights from means-end chain analysis. *Anthropology of food (online)* 5: http://aof.revues.org/index90.html.

Bonne, K. and Verbeke, W. (2008). Religious values informing halal meat production and the control and delivery of halal ceredence quality. *Agriculture and Human values* 25: 35-47.

Bousetta, H. (2000). Institutional Theories of immigrant ethnic mobilisation. Relevance and Limitations. *Journal of Ethnic and Migration Studies* 26(2): 229-45.

Brems, E., Janssens Y., Lecoyer K. et al. (2012). *Wearing the Face Veil in Belgium: Views and Experiences of 27 Women Living in Belgium concerning the Islamic Full Face Veil and the Belgian Ban on Face Covering.* Ghent: Human Rights Center, Ghent University (report).

Brion F. (2000). Des jeunes filles à sauver aux jeunes filles à mater: identité sociale et islamophobie. In: Manço U. (ed.) *Voix et voies musulmanes de Belgique.* Bruxelles: Publications des facultés universitaires de Saint-Louis, pp. 115-149

Brion, F., Coolsaet R., de Kerchove, G., et al. (2016). *La Belgique face au radicalisme. Comprendre et agir,* Louvain-la-Neuve: Presses Universitaires de Louvain.

Cesari, J. (1994). *Être musulman en France.* Paris/Aix-en-Provence: Karthala/Iremam.

Clycq, N. (2009).'*Van Keukentafel tot God'. Belgische, Italiaanse en Marokkaanse ouders over identiteit en opvoeding,* Antwerpen: Garant.

Clycq, N. (2011). *Muslims in Antwerp. Open Society Foundation. At Home in Europe Project.* New York – London: Open Society Foundation.

Clycq, N. (2012). 'My daughter is a free woman, so she can't marry a Muslim': The gendering of ethno-religious boundaries. *European Journal of Women's Studies* 19(2):151-71.

Clycq, N. (2015). 'You can't escape from it. It's in your blood': Naturalizing ethnicity and strategies to ensure family and in-group cohesion, *Ethnography,* 16: 373-393.

Dassetto, F. and Bastenier, A. (1984). *L'Islam transplanté: vie et organisation des minorities, musulmanes de Belgique,* Berchem: EPO.

Dassetto, F. and Bastenier, A. (1987-a). *Enseignants et enseignement de l'Islam au sein de l'école officielle en Belgique.* Louvain-la-Neuve: CIACO.

Dassetto, F. and Bastenier, A. (1987-b). *Medias U Akbar.* Louvain-la-Neuve: CIACO.

Dassetto, F. (1988): L'organisation du Tabligh en Belgique. In *The New Islamic Presence in Western Europe* edited by Gersholm, T. and Y.G. Lithman, Y.G., London & New York Mansell.

Dassetto, F. (1996). *La Construction de l'Islam Européen. Approche Socio-Anthropologique*, Paris: L'Harmattan.

Dassetto, F. (1997). Islam en Belgique et en Europe: Facettes et questions. In *Facettes de l'islam belge*, edited by Felice Dassetto. Louvain-La-Neuve: Bruylant-Academia, pp. 17-34

Dassetto, F. (2011). *L'iris et le croissant. Bruxelles et l'islam au defi de la co-inclusion*. Louvain: UCL Presses Universitaires de Louvain.

Dassetto, F. (2012). 'Sharia4 . . . all'. Éléments d'analyse et de réflexion à propos d'un groupe extrémiste. In *Essais et Recherches en ligne, CISMOC*. Louvain-la-Neuve: UCL, 31.

Debeer, J., Loobuyck, P. and Meyer, P. (2011). *Imams en Islamconsulenten in Vlaanderen. Hoe zijn ze georganiseerd?* Steunpunt Gelijke Kansen Beleid. Antwerpen: Universiteit Antwerpen / Universiteit Hasselt.

Djelloul, G. (2013). *Parcours de féministes musulmanes belges – De l'engagement dans l'islam aux droits des femmes*. Bruxelles/Paris: Academia/L'Harmattan.

Dobbelaere, K. and Billiet J. (1974). *Godsdienst in België: een sociologische verkenning*. Leuven: Sociologisch onderzoeksinstituut.

El Asri, F. (2015). *Rythmes et voix d'islam. Une socioanthropologie d'artistes musulmans européens* Louvain-la-Neuve: Presses Universitaires de Louvain.

Fadil, N. (2002). Tussen Marokkaanse en Moslim: over de etnische en religieuze identiteit van Marokkaanse adolescente meisjes. *Tijdschrift voor Sociologie* 23: 115-138.

Fadil, N. (2005). Individualizing Faith, individualising identity. Islam and Young Muslim Women in Belgium. In Cesari J and McLoughlin S (eds) *European Muslims And the Secular State*. London: Ashgate, 143-154.

Fadil, N. (2006). We should be walking Qurans. The making of an Islamic political subject. In Amiraux V and Jonker G (eds) *The Politics of Visibility. Young Muslims in European Public Spaces*. Bielefeld: Transcript Verlag, 53-78.

Fadil, N. (2010). Breaking the Taboo of Multiculturalism. The Belgian Left and Islam. In *Thinking Through Islamophobia. Global Perspectives*, edited by Abdoolkarim Vakil and Salman Sayyid. New York: Columbia University Press, 235-50.

Fadil, N. (2011). On not/unveiling as an ethical practice. *Feminist Review* 98: 83-109.

Fadil, N. (2013). Performing the Islamic prayer (salat) at work. Secular and pious Muslims negotiating the contours of the public in Belgium. *Ethnicities*, 13 (6), 729-750.

Fadil, N. (2015). Recalling the Islam of the parents. Liberal and secular Muslims redefining the contours of religious authenticity. *Identities: Global Studies in Culture and Power* 22: 1-18.

Fadil, N., El Asri, F. and Bracke, S. (2015). Islam in Belgium. Mapping an emerging interdisciplinary field of study. In Cesari J (ed) *The Oxford Handbook of European Islam*. Oxford: Oxford University Press 222-261.

Fleischmann, F., and Phalet, K. (2012). Integration and second generation religiosity: individual and institutional perspectives. *Ethnic and Racial Studies* 35: 320-341.

Foblets, M.C. & Overbeeke, A. (2002). State Intervention in the institutionalisation of Islam in Belgium. In Shadid W & van Koningsveld S (eds) *Religious Freedom and the Neutrality of the State. The Position of Islam in the European Union*, Leuven: Peeters, 113-128.

Frennet-De Keyser, A. (2011). *Histoire du Regroupement Marocain*, Bruxelles: Carhima asbl.

Groeninck, M. (2016). The Relationship between Words and Being in the World for Students of Qur'anic Recitation in Brussels. *Contemporary Islam* 10: 249-266.

Güngor, D., Fleischmann, F. and Phalet, K. (2011). Religious identification, belief, and practices among Turkish Belgian and Moroccan Belgian Muslims: Intergenerational continuity and acculturative change. *Journal of Cross-Cultural Psychology* 42: 1356-1372.

Hammoudi, A. (1997) *Master dan Disciple. The Cultural Foundations of Moroccan Authoritarianism*, Chicago: The University of Chicago Press.

Hermans, P. (1992). *De inpassing van Marokkaanse migrantenjongeren in België: een vergelijkend antropologisch onderzoek bij geslaagde en niet-geslaagde Marokkaanse jongens*, Leuven: K.U.Leuven (dissertation).

Hirschkind C. (2012). Experiments in devotion online: the Youtube Khutba *International Journal for Middle Eastern Studies* 44: 5-21.

Husson, J.F. (2012). Le financement public de l'islam, instrument d'une politique publique? In Maréchal B and El Asri F (eds.) *Islam Belge au Pluriel*. Louvain-La-Neuve: Presses Universitaires de Louvain, 241-257.

Kanmaz, M. (2002). Onze nationaliteit is onze godsdienst. Islam als 'identity marker' bij jonge Marokkaanse moslims in Gent. In: Foblets, M-C and Cornelis, E. (eds) *Migratie, zijn wij uw kinderen?* Leuven: Acco, 115-133.

Kanmaz, M. and El Battiui M. (2004). *Moskeeën, Imams en Leerkrachten in België. Stand van zaken en uitdagingen*. Brussel: Koning Boudewijn Stichting.

Kanmaz, M. (2009). *Islamitische ruimtes in de stad*. Gent: Academia Press.

Kanmaz, M. and Zemni, S. (2012). Moslims als inzet in religieuze, maatschappelijke en veiligheidsdiscours. De erkenning en institutionalisering van de islamitische eredienst in België. In: Timmerman C and Vanderwaeren E (eds) *Diversiteit in Islam. Over verschillende belevingen van het moslim zijn*. Leuven: Acco/Apeldoorn, 109-156.

Kepel, G. (1991) [1987]. *Les banlieues de l'Islam. Naissance d'une religion en France*. Paris: Editions du Seuil.

Khedimellah, M. (2001). Jeunes prédicateurs du mouvement Tabligh. La dignité identitaire retrouvée par le puritanisme religieux. *Religiosités comtemporaines* 10, URL: http://socio-anthropologie.revues.org/document155 (accessed 25 october 2016)

Khosrokhavar, F. (1997). *L'Islam des Jeunes*, Paris: Flammarion.

Lacoste-Dujardin, C. (1994). Transmission religieuse et migration: l'islam identitaire des filles de maghrébins immigrés en France. *Social Compass* 41: 163-170.

Lamghari, Y. (2012). *L'islam en entreprise. La diversité culturelle en question.* Louvain-La-Neuve: L'Harmattan Academia.

Laurent, P-J. (2016). *Tolérances et radicalismes: que n'avons-nous pas compris? Le terrorisme islamiste en Europe.* Mons: Couleur Livres.

Lechkar, I. (2012-a) Quelles sont les modalités d'authentification parmi les chiites belgo-marocains?. In Maréchal B and El Asri F (eds) *Islam Belge au Pluriel.* Louvain-La-Neuve: Presses Universitaires de Louvain, 113-126.

Lechkar, I. (2012-b). *Striving and Stumbling in the Name of Allah. Neo-Sunnis and Neo-Shi'ites in a Belgian Context.* Leuven: K.U.Leuven (dissertation).

Leman, J., Renaerts, M. and Van den Bulck, D. (1992). De Rechtspositie van de Islamitische Praxis in België. *Cultuur en Migratie* 2: 43-84.

Lesthaeghe R. (1997) *Diversiteit in Sociale verandering. Turkse en Marokkaanse vrouwen in België*, Brussel: VUB Press.

Lesthaeghe R. (2000). Transnational Islamic communities in a multilingual secular society. In Lesthaeghe R (ed) *Communities and Generations. Turkish and Morrocan populations in Belgium.* Brussels: VUB-Press, 1-55.

Manco, U. and Kanmaz, M. (2006). From Conflict to Co-operation Between Muslims and Local Authorities in a Brussels Borough: Schaerbeek in *Journal of Ethnic and Migration Studies* 31: 1105-1123.

LeVine, M. and Armando S. (2005). Socio-Religious Movements and the Transformation of 'Common Sense' into a Politics of 'Common Good'. In *Religion, Social Practice and Contested Hegemonies. Reconstructing the Public Sphere in Muslim Majority Societies*, edited by Armando Salvatore and Mark LeVine. London: Palgrave MacMillan.

Manço, U. (2000). *Voix et voies musulmanes de Belgique.* Bruxelles: Publications des Facultés universitaires Saint-Louis.

Manço, U. and Manço, A. (2000). Religiosité et intégration d'hommes musulmans. In *Voix et voies musulmanes en Belgique*, edited by Manço Ural. Bruxelles: Publications des Facultés universitaires Saint-Louis, 167-88.

Manço, U. and Kanmaz, M. (2006). From Conflict to Co-operation Between Muslims and Local Authorities in a Brussels Borough: Schaerbeek. *Journal of Ethnic and Migration Studies* 31(6):1105-23.

Mandaville, P. (2001). *Transnational Muslim Politics: Reimagining the Umma* London: Routledge

Maréchal, B., Dassetto, F. and Bocquet, C. (2014). *Musulmans et non musulmans à Bruxelles. Entre Tensions et Ajustements réciproques.* Bruxelles: King Baudouin Foundation (report)

Maréchal B. (2003). Institutionalisation of Islam and Representative Organisations for Dealing with European States. In Maréchal B, Allievi S, Dassetto F et al. (eds). *Muslims in the enlarged Europe. Religion and Society.* Leiden: Brill 151-182.

Marechal, B. (2008-a). Courants Fondamentalistes en Belgique. *Journal d'étude des relations internationales au Moyen-Orient* 3(1):65-78.

Marechal, B. (2008-b). *The Muslim Brothers in Europe. Roots and Discourses*, Leiden: Brill

Maréchal B. (2015). The Historical and Contemporary Sociology of the European Muslim Brotherhood Movement and its Logics of Action. *Journal of Muslims in Europe* 4: 223-257.

Martens A. (1973). *25 jaar wegwerparbeiders: het Belgisch immigratiebeleid na 1945.* Leuven: KUL Sociologisch onderzoeksinstituut. Afdeling Arbeids- en Industriele Sociologie

Mescoli, E. (2016). *Forgotten Women. The impact of Islamophobia on Muslim women in Belgium.* Brussels: European Network Against Racism.

Nasr Hossein, S. (1964). *An Introduction to Islamic Cosmological Doctrines.* Cambridge: The Belknap Press of Harvard University Press.

Ouald Chaib, S. and Brems, E. (2012). Doing Minority Justice Through Procedural Fairness: Face Veil Bans in Europe. *Journal of Muslims in Europe* 2: 1-26.

Ouali, N. (2004). *Trajectoires et dynamiques migratoires de l'immigration marocaine de Belgique.* Louvain-la-Neuve: Academia Bruylant.

Panafit, L. (1997). Les problématiques de l'institutionalisatoin de l'islam en Belgique (1965-1996). In *Facettes de l'islam belge* edited by Felice Dassetto. Louvain-La-Neuve: Bruylant Academia, 253-76.

Panafit, L. (1999). *Quand le droit écrit l'Islam. L'Integration juridique de l'islam en Belgique,* Louvain-La-Neuve: Bruylant Academia.

Pedziwiatr, K. (2010). *The New Muslim Elites in European Cities. Religion and Active Social Citizenship Amongst Young Organized Muslims in Brussels and London.* Saarbrücken: Verlag Dr. Müller.

Peleman, K. (2001). Moeizame onderhandelingen. Marokkaanse vrouwen in Borgerhout op zoek naar ontmoetingsplaatsen. *Migrantenstudies* 17: 20-38.

Peter, F. (2006). Individualisation and Religious Authority in Western European Islam. A review essay. *Journal of Islam and Christian-Muslim Relations* 17(1):105-18.

Renaerts, M. and Manço, A. (2000). Lente institutionnalisation de l'islam et persistance d'inégalités face aux autres cultes reconnus. In: Manço U (ed) *Voix et voies musulmanes de Belgique.* Bruxelles: Publications des Facultés universitaires Saint-Louis, 83-111.

Roy, O. (1999). *Vers un Islam Européen*. Paris: Éditions Esprit.

Roy, O. (2002). *L'Islam Mondialisé*. Paris: Seuil.

Saaf, A, Sidi Hida, B. and Aghbal, A. (2009). *Belgische Marokkanen. Een dubbele identiteit in ontwikkeling*. Brussel: Koning Boudewijn Stichting (report)

Salvatore, A. (1997). *Islam and the Political Discourse of modernity*. Reading: Ithaca Press.

Salvatore, A. (2004). Making Public Space: Opportunities and Limits of collective Action among muslims in Europe. *Journal of Ethnic and Migration Studies* 30(5):1013-31.

Saroglou, V., Lamkaddem, B., Van Pachterbeke, M. et al. (2009). Host society's dislike of the islamic veil. The role of suble prejudice, values and religion. *International Journal of Intercultural Relations* 33: 419-428.

Sunier, T. (1996). *Islam in Beweging. Turkse jongeren en islamitische organisaties*. Amsterdam: Het Spinhuis.

Timmerman, C. and Vanderwaeren E. (2012) *Diversiteit in Islam. Over verschillende belevingen van het moslim zijn*. Leuven: Acco/Apeldoorn.

Torrekens, C. and Jacobs, D. (2016). Muslims' religiosity and views on religion in six Western European countries: does national context matter? *Journal of Ethnic and Migration Studies* 42: 325-340.

Torrekens, C. (2007). Concentration des populations musulmanes et structuration de l'associatif musulman à Bruxelles. *Brussels Studies* 4(5 Mars 2007): 16.

Torrekens, C. (2009). *L'Islam a Bruxelles*. Brussels: Editions de l'Université de Bruxelles.

Touag, H. (2012). Géurir par l'Islam: l'Adoption du Rite Prophétique – Roqya – par les salafistes en France et en Belgique. In Maréchal B and El Asri F. (2012) *Islam Belge au Pluriel*, Louvain-La-Neuve: Presses Universitaires de Louvain, 201-217.

Touag, H. (2015). Exit, Voice and Loyalty. Les trois engagments de l'engagement salafiste en Belgique. *Cahiers de la sécurité et de la justice* 30: 109-116.

Van Den Branden, S. (2006). *Islamitische Ethiek aan het levenseinde. Een theoretisch omkaderde inhoudsanalyse van Engelstalige soennitisch bronnenmateriaal en een kwalitatief empirisch onderzoek naar de houding van praktiserende Marokkaanse oudere mannen in Antwerpen*. Leuven: Faculteit Godsgeleerdheid KU Leuven.

Van Den Branden, S. and Broeckaert, B. (2010). Necessary Interventions. Muslim Views on Pain and Symptom Control in English Sunni e-Fatwas *Ethical Perspectives* 17: 626-651.

Vanden Branden, S. (2006). *Religie en ethiek aan het levenseinde. Een onderzoek naar de invloed van religieuze en levensbeschouwelijke affiliatie en wereldbeeld op de houdingen tegenover beslissingen omtrent het levenseinde*. Leuven: Faculteit Theologie en Religiewetenschappen, KU Leuven (dissertation).

Vanderwaeren, E. (2005). *Moslima's aan de horizon*. Ethiek en Maatschappij 7: 94-111.

Vanderwaeren, E. (2010). *Vrouwen doen aan 'ijtihad: hybriditeit als creatieve ruimte bij interpretaties van Islam.* Antwerpen: Universiteit Antwerpen (dissertation).

Zemni, S. (2006). Islam between Jihadi threats and islamist insecurities? Evidence from Belgium and Morocco. *Mediteranean politics* 11(2):231-53.

Zemni, S. (2011). The shaping of Islam and Islamophobia in Belgium. *Race and Class* 53: 28-44.

3. Historical research on Moroccan migration in Belgium

Karim Ettourki, Sam De Schutter & Idesbald Goddeeris

Moroccan immigration in Belgium has had a major impact on Belgian society. In demographic terms, it has made the population younger. On the political level, it was initially a matter of migration and integration policy, as well as one of anti-migration discourse on the right, and subsequently played a role in policy making. The rich world of Moroccan associations also ensured embeddedness in Belgium's socio-cultural civil society. Last but not least, the role of Moroccans in the country's religious history cannot be forgotten: they make up more than fifty percent of the Islamic population in Belgium. In other words, Moroccan immigrants form an integral part of Belgian history.

Yet, Belgian historians still treat them like stepchildren. On the 'Contemporary History Day' (*Dag van de Nieuwste Geschiedenis*) – a study day organized every two years by the 'Belgian Association for Contemporary History' (*Belgische Vereniging voor de Nieuwste Geschiedenis*), held on 29 April in 2016 – Frank Caestecker showed that the topic of migration to date receives little attention in important overviews of Belgian history (Vandendriessche & Jouan, 2016). Already more than a decade earlier he had called for efforts toward migrant mainstreaming and for a revision of the nation's past by 'recognizing the place of ethnic minorities in national histories' (Caestecker, 2003).

One of the main reasons that this revision has yet to happen is that historical research into Moroccan migration in Belgium is still in its infancy. This article will attempt to illustrate and explain this. First, it gives an historical overview of studies on Moroccan migration in Belgium, situating research within the general views of migration history as well as studies into Moroccan migration in Belgium. Afterwards, it discusses a few important, and for the most part untapped, primary sources, in addition to the most recent developments in archival acquisitions and projects concerning oral history.

Historical research on Moroccan migration in Belgium

Real efforts at historical research on migration to Belgium began in the 1970s. From the 1980s onwards and certainly in the 1990s, as a result of an intensifying political debate on migration, historians' interest in the subject grew (Caestecker, 2003; Beyers & Venken, 2006). On the one hand, they studied migration from a top-down perspective. The work of Frank Caestecker, in particular, has been indispensable for understanding Belgium's policy towards all categories of 'aliens', be it immigrants, refugees or guest workers (e.g. Caestecker, 2000). On the other hand, a bottom-up perspective from historians detailing specific migrant groups has complemented this policy angle. This 'specialization' often offered a starting point for considering migrants as actors with their own agency, rather than subjects undergoing policies.

Anne Morelli, for example, studied Italian immigration in Belgium, focusing on, among other things, the political activism of the Italians in Belgium and on the role of women in the Italian diaspora (Morelli, 1980a, 1980b, 1987, 2000, 2002). Idesbald Goddeeris has written extensively on Polish migrants in the 19th and 20th century (Goddeeris, 2005, 2013). Historians like Frank Caestecker, Lieven Saerens, Jean-Philippe Schreiber and Rudi Van Doorslaer have scrutinized Jewish migration in Belgium (Caestecker, 1993; Dratwa, Gotovitch, & Van den Wijngaert, 1994; Saerens, 2000; Schreiber, 1996, 2002; Van Doorslaer, 1995; Van Doorslaer & Schreiber, 2004). Wim Coudenys wrote on the history of Russian immigration (Coudenys, 2004). The same is true for Sara Cosemans and Hannelore Roos in regards to South Asian migrants (e.g. Cosemans & Roos, 2013) and Tina De Gendt and Mazyar Khoojinian on Turks in Belgium (Khoojinian, 2006; De Gendt, 2014).

Moroccan migration has also received the attention of historians. After a brief overview in Anne Morelli's pioneering volume on migration in Belgium (Attar, 1993), the 40th and the 50th anniversaries of the alleged start of Moroccan migration to Belgium in 1964 generated new academic output (Frennet-De

Keyser, 2003, 2004; Ouali, 2004; Loriaux, 2005; Ettourki & El Morabiti, 2014; Raats, Leonard & Vandebroek, 2014; Schoonvaere, 2014). In her doctoral thesis, Jozefien De Bock also researched Moroccan immigration from the local angle of the city of Ghent (De Bock, 2013), while Norah Karrouche obtained her doctorate with a dissertation on Berber activism in Belgium, the Netherlands and Morocco (Karrouche, 2013). In 2014-2015, some within the Moroccan community itself wrote sweeping overviews of fifty years of Moroccan migration in Belgium, elaborating on a wide variety of aspects, such as religion, civil society and political activities (Dakira, 2014; Medhoune et al.; 2015). In addition, several students tackled the history of local Moroccan communities in interesting MA theses (Bare, 1994; Azzouzi, 2002; Vanhaecke, 2008; Ben Abbou, 2009; Ben Taib, 2013; Benotmane, 2014; Roofthoofd, 2014; Van Bastelaer, 2015).

All of this research has resulted in a number of interesting views. First of all, we should question 1964 as the 'start of Moroccan migration'. While Nouria Ouali points to contacts and travels dating back to the 12th century (Ouali, 2004b), more extensive research centers attention upon the interwar period, where the first traces of a more or less steady Moroccan migration can be found. In her overview of Moroccan migration to Belgium, Anne Frennet-De Keyser refers to Moroccan miners in Belgium from 1922 till 1927, and again after 1936. From that moment onwards there has been a continuous presence of Moroccans on Belgian soil (Frennet-De Keyser, 2004b).

The interwar period has thus far received little attention. In his MA thesis at the Université Libre de Bruxelles, Driss Bare explored the North African workforce in the Belgian coalmines between the two World Wars, showing how the presence of Moroccans in the mines and their reception by both employers and unions, was heavily dependent on the economic climate (Bare, 1994, 2004). Élisabeth Martin, researcher at the Université Catholique de Louvain, worked out a case study on Maghribian immigration in Châtelineau, a heavily industrialized town in the French-speaking part of Belgium, in the 1920s. She particularly noted the significant differences with the post-1964 wave of Moroccan migration. In contrast to these more recently arrived groups, the migrant population of the 1920s consisted almost exclusively of unskilled men, who were very mobile and stayed in Belgium for an average of only eight weeks. Characteristics of the Moroccan migration after 1964: permanence, family reunification, and the important influx of female migrants, were thus absent in these earlier migrations (Martin, 2012).

Other works have elaborated on the last fifty years of Moroccan presence in Belgium. Anne Frennet-De Keyser, historian and collaborator at Carhima (see below), has studied the bilateral agreement of 1964 between Belgium and Morocco, which stipulated the recruitment of workers for the Belgian coalmines and construction industry. Referring to documents from the ministries of Foreign Affairs and Employment and Work and from the Coal Federation of Hasselt, she contends that this bilateral agreement was not the basis for a massive migration wave, but merely an attempt to provide a legal framework for an already existing practice. Even after this agreement, many Moroccan workers kept coming to Belgium without a permit and were regularized after their arrival (Frennet-De Keyser, 2003, 2004a; see also the contribution of Albert Martens to this volume). This is an interesting point, as it forces us to shift our focus from the arena of government regulations and policies to the more informal ways in which migration took place. Preliminary research shows that informal networks were an important aspect in finding a place to work in Belgium (De Bock, 2012; Benotmane, 2014).

Networks were primarily developed on the local level, and in recent years new research has taken place into these local communities and the reception of them. It shows that during the 1960s and 1970s, initial assistance and support for migrants very often came from Catholic groups. In Brussels, for example, Paul Steels from the religious community *Redemptor Hominis* started a campaign in support of guest workers' children in 1969. As a result of the ambitious 'Manhattan Project', the youth centre moved from Brussels' Noordwijk to its Molenbeek district in 1973 (Lievens et al., 1975; Vanden Eede & Martens, 1994). The organization has since grown into the 'Foyer Regional Integration Centre' (*Regionaal Integratiecentrum Foyer*). In Mechelen, too, support initially came primarily from Catholic sources. They developed the Maria Assunta neighborhood campaign in the Klein Begijnhof-Heembeemd district, where many Moroccan migrants were living. The Catholic Student Action (*Katholieke Studentenactie*) set up a special working group for guest workers in 1969 (Roofthoofd, 2014). In Kortrijk similar efforts occurred, and priests and nuns contributed to establishing the NPO 'Integration for Migrants' (*Opbouwwerk voor Migranten*) in 1978 (Benotmane, 2014). Pluralistic undertakings also sprouted local initiatives, such as the 'Centre for Foreign Employees' (*Centrum voor Buitenlandse Werknemers*, or CBW), which was set up in Borgerhout in 1972 by a group of committed individuals who occupationally or voluntarily interacted with Moroccan migrants (Janssen & Rutten, 1992). After a long history of professionalization and mergers with

Inhabitants of the Brussels Noordwijk district protesting against the Manhattan project
(source: KADOC)

other migrant campaigns, this CBW grew into the 'Antwerp Integration Centre "de8"' (*Antwerps Integratiecentrum de8*).

With the passage of time, the reception and integration of guest workers also became a concern for various government authorities. The 'Provincial Reception Services for Guest Workers' (*Provinciale Onthaaldienst voor Gastarbeiders*, or POG) originated in Limburg in 1965, and the 'Flemish Consultative Committee on the Integration of Migration' (*Vlaams Overlegcomité Opbouwwerk Migratie*, or VOCOM) saw the light of day in 1977, in order to streamline the various neighborhood campaigns. Even so, an overall integration policy was a long time coming. The Flemish government approved the first Migrant Policy paper in March 1989. The guidelines for it were drawn up by the 'Royal Commission for Migrant Policy' (*Koninklijk Commissariaat voor het Migrantenbeleid*, or KCM), which was established by the federal government. In the wake of the KCM, diverse initiatives arose to bring about the social integration of migrants (De Vos, 2001). Across Flanders, a network emerged of local and regional integration centers, which were put under the umbrella of the 'Flemish Centre for the Integration of Migrants' (*Vlaams Centrum voor de Integratie van Migranten*, or VCIM). These centers have grown organically through the years. In Antwerp, for example, they often resulted from campaigns concerning Moroccan and Turkish women.

These developments resulted from important political debates in the second half of the 20th century, which of course have been subject to historical research. This also relates to another important aspect of the history of Moroccan migration: public opinion on migration in Belgium. From the 1970s onwards, the image of the so-called 'guest worker' as one who takes advantage of the social security system gained more prominence in the public opinion. Moreover, discussions about Islam came to the fore. The debate on headscarves in schools took off at the end of the 1980s and the extreme-right political party Vlaams Blok scored its first victories in the same years. Since Moroccans and Turks were Muslims and numerically the biggest groups among guest workers, they increasingly became the target of negative public opinion (Billiet, Carton & Huys, 1990; Blommaert & Verschueren, 1994; Zemni, 2009).

Nevertheless, many Moroccans stayed in Belgium. This permanence forces us to focus on the formation of a Moroccan community and the impact of its long-term presence on Belgian society. The many Moroccan associations that have mushroomed since the 1960s are an important aspect of this community formation. As Moroccan migration originally had a labor character, it is not surprising to see the creation of associations around labor issues in cooperation with Belgian union movements. One example was the *Groupement de travailleurs marocains* in 1974, which was linked to the French Maoist *Mouvement des travailleurs arabes* (Khoojinian, 2014). A very influential association was the *Regroupement démocratique marocain*, founded by Mohamed El Baroudi, and resulting from a collaboration between Moroccan workers and political refugees and Belgian intellectuals and unionists (Frennet-De Keyser, 2011; Leduc, 2014). But associations have been formed on all kinds of grounds: in addition to political, religious and cultural associations, there were also youth and women's organizations (Ouali, 2004a; Bentaleb, 2007). They all have contributed to the increasing 'sedentarization' and integration of Moroccans in Belgium, while simultaneously maintaining transnational ties with the home country (Surkyn, 1995; Bousetta & Martiniello, 2003).

Overall, it is clear that historical research on Moroccan migration in Belgium has taken off. Yet, one should not overestimate its results. As a matter of fact, the research is not very well developed compared to that on other migration flows, in spite of the fact that Moroccan immigration is one of the most important migratory flows in Belgium's recent history. Many of the above-mentioned findings come from studies on themes broader than just Moroccan migration. There are no doctoral dissertations yet on the history of the Moroccan presence in Belgium, or any established historians of Moroccan migration. Research is often published in non-academic journals (e.g. the *Cahiers du Fil Rouge*) and remains somewhat outside of mainstream academia.

One can only speculate as to the cause of this neglect. It could be a consequence of the underrepresentation of students and researchers with a Moroccan background in Belgian academia, especially in history departments. Moreover, there is no real institutional or disciplinary background to support research on Moroccan migration history (as for example Slavic studies has been for the research on Polish or Russian migration). Finally, migration history itself also evolved. Whereas it initially focused on migration policy (Caestecker) or on ethnic groups, it gradually shifted from these angles and aspired to transcend ethnic boundaries. A younger generation of contemporary historians included Moroccans in their research, such as Leen Beyers, who worked on interethnic relations in Zwartberg (Beyers, 2007). However, this turn away from the ethnic paradigm has made research on Moroccan migration less visible. Another new evolution is that migration historians, such as Anne Winter, increasingly elaborate on more distant periods, such as the 19th century and earlier, during which immigration from North Africa was marginal.

Primary sources for new research

Even this book has few genuine historical contributions: fundamental historical research into Moroccan migrants is still limited, and as yet their history is being written primarily by sociologists, political scientists and anthropologists. Naturally, studies by these social scientists are also about the past. And yet there is a difference. Historians look through different lenses and work with primary sources that were previously inaccessible.

In recent years a few important efforts have been made at unlocking and inventorying sources concerning the history of the Moroccan presence. In particular, the NPO Carhima is worth mentioning. This association initially had as its primary goal preserving the cultural heritage of Maghrebian and Arab associations as well as making that legacy accessible (Vicari, 2014); in the meantime, though, it has broadened its scope to include the entire legacy that derives from migration. In 2012 the organization published a *Guide des sources pour l'histoire de l'immigration maghrébine et arabe en Fédération Wallonie-Bruxelles* (Carhima, 2012). Additionally, it has collected works and periodicals that relate to Moroccan migration. The first steps have been taken toward unlocking sources for the history of the Moroccan presence in Belgium. The emphasis lies on civil society, but there are still other sources that are important for writing this history. The following overview will shed light on a few valuable collections.

Initial important sources are the files on aliens from the 'Public Safety' (*Openbare Veiligheid*) office. They contain information, in theory, about all aliens who were registered on Belgian territory. In total there are more than two million chronologically ordered dossiers (from 1835 to 1951), but not all have been preserved. Individual files opened after December 1951 are kept by the 'Immigration Office' (*Dienst Vreemdelingenzaken*, or DVZ), the successor to the 'Aliens Police' (*Vreemdelingenpolitie*) since 1977. For more recent decades these dossiers are not yet accessible, but for further research into Moroccan migration before 1964, they constitute a very valuable source (Caestecker, 2009). The same is true for the files on aliens created by various municipal administrations. The 'Felix Archives' (*Felixarchief*) in Antwerp and the city archives for Brussels both possess extensive collections of files on aliens. Naturally, in addition to these dossiers, other sources such as municipal council reports as well as arrival and departure registries can furnish interesting information.

Just as valuable are sources from diplomatic and economic agencies. In 1964 Belgium and Morocco concluded a bilateral accord on the employment of Moroccan guest workers in Belgian industry. The talks between the two countries started in Rabat in 1963, and led to the signing of bilateral agreements on 17 February 1964 in Brussels. The 'Belgian Coal Federation' (*Fédéchar*) had already opened a recruiting office in Casablanca by April 1963. The impact of those recruitment campaigns can be found in documents preserved at the National Archives in Hasselt, which, surprisingly, have remained for the most part untouched for research. They hold a wealth of information. The *Fédéchar* representative in Casablanca kept records of virtually all the application letters; made graphs of the number of applications as well as accepted and rejected candidates; drew up lists of names with address information and qualifications, and so forth. In addition to quantitative and biographical data on the (potential) guest workers, the archives also contain references to wages and issues concerning payment of child benefits, as well as moving reports of Moroccan parents or spouses desperately awaiting some sign of life from family members thought to be lost in Belgium. The National Archives of Hasselt also have archival documents

Recruitment statistics (1963) from the Fédéchar archives (source: State Archives of Belgium-Hasselt)

from local coal mining companies. They contain requests to hire foreign employees, information about cafeterias or boarding houses, and correspondence with *Fédéchar* about diverse work-related subjects.

It goes without saying that the archives of *Fédéchar* and the various mining companies constitute a unique source for further exploring the initial years of official labor recruitment. The Belgian-Moroccan accord was not limited to the mining industry. Labor contracts were also offered for the building sector, the metals and textiles industries, and even a glass company. The National Archives in Beveren preserve the personnel files of the *Union Cottonière* (Ettourki & El Morabiti, 2014), which was one of the most important employers of Moroccan immigrants in the province of East Flanders. In the archives for the Kortrijk textiles company *Linière de Courtrai*, there are dossiers about foreign workers (Benotmane, 2014). The archives of other companies who hired Moroccans can be tracked down by means of various source guides (Coppejans-Desmedt, 1975; Coppejans-Desmedt et al., 1998; Buntinx, 2001; Devos et al., 2002; Dehaeck & Derwael, 2008; Dehaeck & Vancoppenolle, 2011).

The archives of workers' and labor unions' movements in their turn offer a captivating angle for approaching the topic of labor. In the archives for the 'General Christian Confederation for Labor' (*Algemeen Christelijk Werknemersverbond*, or ACW) and the 'General Christian Trade Union Confederation' (*Algemeen Christelijk Vakverbond*, or ACV) – preserved at KADOC, the Documentation and Research Center for Religion, Culture and Society of the KU Leuven (KADOC, *Documentatie- en Onderzoekscentrum voor Religie, Cultuur en Samenleving*) – the problems of migrant laborers regularly come up for discussion. The ACV's archives contain, for example, information about the status of the guest workers; documents about migrants' right to vote; reports and memos from the 'ACV Migrant Employees Service' (*ACV-dienst der Migrerende Werknemers*); documentation about migrant policy; and a series of papers in national languages, such as *Le travailleur arabe* (Aerts & Martens, 1978). In other documentation and research centers one can turn to similar collections, albeit from other ideological angles, such as the socialist one in the Amsab-'Institute for Social History' (*Instituut voor Sociale Geschiedenis*, or ISG) in Ghent, which preserves the archives of the 'General Belgian Trade Union Confederation' (*Algemeen Belgisch Vakverbond*, or ABVV), or the *Institut d'histoire ouvrière, économique et sociale* (IHOES) in Seraing (Khoojinian, 2012).

Accessible for research, too, are quite a few of the many local, regional and national actors involved with the reception of newly arrived migrants. A number of years ago, KADOC supported the Foyer Regional Integration Centre in Brussels' Molenbeek district in the organization and safe preservation of its heritage collection. The POG's archives are preserved in situ as well, in the provincial government building in Hasselt. The documents of the VOCOM and the VCIM, on the other hand, can be consulted at the Amsab-ISG in Ghent, while those of the NPO *Welkom*, the former integration centre in Turnhout, can be consulted at KADOC.

Additionally, local and regional newspapers also provide important perspectives. Mechelen's *De Mechelaar*, for example, regularly covered migration (Roofthoofd, 2014). National newspapers and journals, too, reported on Moroccans with clock-like regularity. Television archives provide supplementary insights as well. From time to time, various in-depth news journals and human-interest programs on public television – including *Couleur Locale, Echo, NV De Wereld, Panorama* and *Babel* – broadcasted documentaries of Moroccan migrants and the world in which they lived.

Certain periodicals were explicitly oriented toward the topic of migration. A good example is the journal *Bareel* (1978-1996), which was set up by the independent NPO of the same name in order 'to provide insight into the migration

Le Travailleur arabe, the periodical of the Arab section of the Christian Labor Union
(source: KADOC)

issue' and to narrow the information gap [about this phenomenon], which 'still existed after dozens of years of immigration of foreign laborers'. The journal was oriented toward everyone interested in the topic of migration for professional or personal reasons (s.n., 1978a). It regularly cast light on Moroccan migrants, not only in connection with current topics – like the appointment of Grand Imam Alouini in Belgium (Michiels, 1978), or the delay in the construction of the mosque in Kortrijk (Vandenberghe, 1978) – but also in reports and interviews on certain aspects of the Moroccan community: education (s.n., 1982), youth (Rachib, 1982), women (s.n., 1978b), the world of Moroccan associations (Van Loock, 1986), and so on. A similar approach was employed by 'The House of Palmyra' (*Het Huis van Palmyra*, 1995-2001), a periodical from the 'Intercultural Centre for Migrants' (*Intercultureel Centrum voor Migranten*, or ICCM), which was set up as a foundation to support allochtonous civil society organizations in 1993.

It is striking that Moroccans themselves have left behind few journals of their own – as opposed to the Poles or Italians, for example. With the exception of a few relatively recent initiatives – like the e-newspaper *Dounia News* by Sarie Abdeslam (beginning in 1999); *Le Maroxellois*, which describes itself as '*le magazine des Bruxellois d'origine marocaine et des autres*' (beginning in 2009); and a few other, no longer extant periodicals of federations, like *De Wegwijzer* (from the VOEM federation), *Akhbar* (from FMDO) and e-newsletters like *Kalima* (from FMV) – few periodicals are known. Most likely their minimal number is related to the oral cultural tradition or even the low level of schooling of the first generation.

Moroccan sources for research into religious activities are also lacking. Although migrants founded Islamic places of prayer from starting in the late 1960s, and although the Belgian government officially recognized Islamic religious services in 1974, Moroccan mosques have few historical documents available. Since they are, unlike the Catholic Church, not hierarchically structured, little communication or response is required and a 'culture of written reporting' to the faithful is absent. Government archives about Islam will not be accessible for a few more decades; yet private archives can already assist today in studying the history of Islam in Belgium. The archives of Johan Leman, which KADOC received for preservation in 2012, provide captivating points of reference for analyzing the difficult history of the recognition of Islam in Belgium. The topic

Het Huis van Palmyra, a periodical published by the Intercultural Centre for Migrants
(source: KADOC)

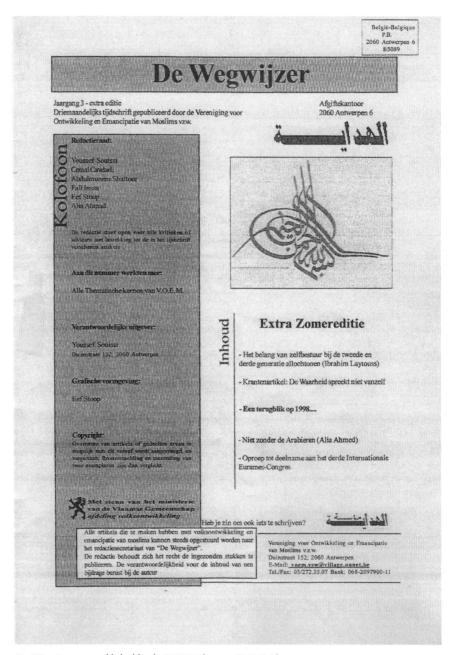

De Wegwijzer was published by the VOEM (source: KADOC)

is prominently present in the documents of the working group for Islam within the 'Royal Commission for Migrant Policy' (*Koninklijk Commissariaat voor het Migrantenbeleid*, or KCM) (Weyns, 2013).

Islam also regularly comes up for discussion in the archives of Wilfried Duyver, who worked for the Pedagogical Bureau of the 'Flemish Secretariat of Catholic Education' (*Vlaams Secretariaat van het Katholieke Onderwijs*, or VSKO) and was a member of diverse working groups, such as the 'Inter-confederation Advisory Group for Education with Migrants' (*Interverbonden Adviesgroep voor het Onderwijs met Migranten*). His papers – also kept in KADOC – hold information about the position of 'Catholic education' vis-à-vis the migrant issue. These private archives are best consulted together with those of the Secretariat (VSKO), which contain a specific dossier on Islam and broach the question of religion lessons, among other things. These archives can further add depth to research into the embeddedness of migrant children in the Flemish educational system, for example, by closely examining the pedagogical projects and standpoints of the various educational networks regarding Islam and migrants from a comparative perspective.

The archives of individual Moroccan migrants could also be very interesting, but none yet are known to have been placed anywhere for preservation. The archives of Sarie Abdeslam, for example, who shared responsibility for the campaign of the Arab section of the ACV from 1977 to 1997, and was additionally involved in a series of organizations – on the local, national as well as European level – are kept in part at his home and in part in Brussels at the 'Federation of Moroccan and World Democratic Organizations' (*Federatie van Marokkaanse en Mondiale Democratische Organisaties*).

Those who want to study the organizational structures of the Moroccan community close up are better off using the archives of associations that have survived the ravages of time. In that context, from 2008 to 2013 Amsab and KADOC launched the project 'Survey map of the civil society organizations of migrants and their legacy in Flanders and Brussels' ('*Stafkaart van het migrantenmiddenveld en zijn erfgoed in Vlaanderen en Brussel*'). It was intended to create a directory of the civil society organizations of migrants, that is, also organizations established by individuals with a Moroccan background, as well as a reference work for the (cultural) heritage collections assembled by them. The information collected was entered into the online database ODIS (Creve & Ettourki, 2011; Ettourki, 2013). These endeavors for the Moroccan community are being continued in the heritage project 'Dakira/Memory: 50 years of

Moroccan migration' ('*Dakira-Herinnering, 50 jaar Marokkaanse migratie*') – an initiative carried out by the 'Federation of Moroccan Associations' (*Federatie van Marokkaanse Verenigingen*), in close collaboration with KADOC. The survey map project made it clear that over the course of history archives have been either seriously neglected or lost. Some echoes of those bustling civil society organizations can be found, though, in the *Moniteur Belge/Belgisch Staatsblad*, the Belgian 'official gazette' in which all NPOs have been recorded. A number of datasets can be derived from this government journal – such as names, address information as well as date and place of birth for the founders and administrators, in addition to the objectives of these organizations. Even here, however, some caution is advised. For example, the objectives formulated in the registered bylaws are – as is the case with many associations – often merely formal descriptions and frequently responses to the (subsidy) policy for any given time period.

Better preserved are the archives of those migrants' federations that were established in the framework of the decree of 19 April 1995, in relation to subsidizing associations for community education programs, although their roots sometimes go back to the 1980s. Within this context, three federations with a Moroccan background originated: the 'Federation of Moroccan Associations' (*Federatie van Marokkaanse Verenigingen*, or FMV); the 'Association for the Education and Emancipation of Muslims' (*Vereniging voor Ontwikkeling en Emancipatie van Moslims*, or VOEM); and the 'Federation of Moroccan Democratic Organizations' (*Federatie van Marokkaanse Democratische Organisaties*, or FMDO). In the first instance these federations support organizations dealing with specific issues themselves in Flanders and Brussels, though they additionally elaborate their own projects for meeting the needs of their communities (Ettourki & El Morabiti, 2014).

All this material provides insight into the world of organizations for Moroccan migrants in Belgium. It not only allows for the visualization of these structures and their development but also for studying the forces driving them and their networks, as well as for researching around which topics and with which social cultural and political objectives people associate with one another. On top of that these documents provide insight into the challenges and problems confronted by certain segments of the Moroccan community, as well as insight into the responses they attempted to give to those issues. The disadvantage of these resources is that they are not yet sufficiently accessible for scholarly research. As yet the archives of these federations are preserved in situ – those

The Iqra school in Antwerp founded by the Federation of Moroccan Associations (source: KADOC)

for the FMV in Borgerhout, those of the VOEM in Antwerp, and those of the FMDO in Brussels – and there is little talk of any mechanisms for making them accessible. At the moment, though, the FMV is working out a plan to transfer its archives to KADOC over the long term. The first part of its documents has been moved to the archive centre in May 2017. The FMDO and FMV themselves are connected with the 'Forum for Ethnic and Cultural Minorities' (*Forum van Etnisch-Culturele Minderheden*), which transferred its archives to KADOC in 2016 (Ettourki, 2016).

Last but not least, oral history is also an important angle for the study of Moroccan migration (De Wever, 2009; Bleyen & Van Molle, 2012). Oral sources offer the chance to write a nuanced history in which Moroccan migrants themselves take center stage. As opposed to a top-down approach, or even a stance in which organizations and collectives constitute the focal point, oral history can offer insight into the individual experiences and personal opinions of those involved. A good example is the project 'Guests in Ghent' (*Gentse Gasten*) by the NPO Nakhla from 2007, in which various interviews were recorded with Moroccan migrants who arrived in Ghent in the 1960s and 1970s. In the expo project *Dakira*, too, more than twenty oral sources were used to tell the story of fifty years of Moroccan migration in Flanders. In Brussels the researchers for

Pictures from the Dakira exhibition in Leuven (source: KADOC)

'Collective Memory' (*Geheugen Collectief*) integrated this source into the book, 'We're here: the first generation of Moroccan and Turkish migrants in Brussels, 1964-1974' (*On est là, de eerste generatie Marokkaanse en Turkse migranten in Brussel, 1964-1974*), commissioned by the Foyer Regional Integration Centre.

Conclusion

All these recent initiatives concerning archival depositories and oral history show that the administrators of cultural heritage, archivists, Moroccan migrants, and other actors are becoming more and more conscious of the necessity to preserve historical sources concerning Moroccan migration. Only in this way can history be written, not only at the national level but also with regard to, for example, how provinces and municipalities delineated their own policies as well as placed their own priorities in those protocols, how the Flemish perceived all of this, and how Moroccans experienced it. For all these questions the sources are accessible. Now it is up to the historian to use them and to conduct new studies, for the further formation of theses and syntheses alike.

Bibliography

Aerts, M. & Martens, A. (1978). *Gastarbeider, lotgenoot en landgenoot*. Leuven: Kritak.

Attar, R. (1993). De geschiedenis van de maghrebijnse immigratie in België. In A. Morelli (Ed.), *Geschiedenis van het eigen volk: de vreemdeling in België, van de prehistorie tot nu*. Leuven: Kritak, 297-316.

Azzouzi, K. (2002). *Les mineurs marocains en Belgique dans les années 60: cas étudiés à travers l'exemple liégeois*, Brussels: unpublished Master thesis, ULB.

Bare, D. (1994). *Contribution à l'histoire de l'immigration: la main d'oeuvre nord-africaine dans les charbonnages belges (1920-1940)*. Brussels: unpublished Master thesis, ULB, Hedendaagse geschiedenis.

Bare, D. (2004). Les marocains dans les charbonnages belges dans l'entre-deux-guerres. In N. Ouali (Ed.), *Trajectoires et dynamiques migratoires de l'immigration marocaine de Belgique*. Louvain-la Neuve: Bruylant-Academia, 171-214.

Benotmane, A. (2014). *"Het is maar tijdelijk...": een geschiedenis van de Marokkaanse gemeenschap in Kortrijk*. Leuven: unpublished Master thesis, KU Leuven, onderzoekseenheid Geschiedenis.

Ben Abbou, G. (2009). *L'implantation, la localisation et les mutations sociales de l'immigration marocaine à Molenbeek Saint-Jean de 1964 à 1974*. Brussels: unpublished PhD thesis, ULB.

Ben Taib, H. O. (2013). *Pionnières de l'immigration marocaine dans la commune de Molenbeek-Saint-Jean. Parcours de femmes entre 1964 et 1974*, Brussels: unpublished PhD thesis, ULB.

Bentaleb, M. (2007). L'organisation des travailleurs immigrés marocains en Belgique: Des hommes dans leur siècle. *Cahiers du Fil Rouge* 7-8, 26-35.

Beyers, L., & Venken, M. (2006). Geschiedenis van integratie? Een historische kijk op vestigingsprocessen na migratie. *Mededelingenblad van de Belgische Vereniging Voor Nieuwste Geschiedenis* 28(4), 13-20.

Beyers, L. (2007). *Iedereen zwart. Het samenleven van nieuwkomers en gevestigden in de mijncité Zwartberg, 1930-1990*. Amsterdam: Aksant. p. 340.

Billiet, J., Carton, A. & Huys, R. (1990). *Onbekend of onbemind?: een sociologisch onderzoek naar de houding van de Belgen tegenover migranten*. Leuven: KU Leuven – Sociologisch onderzoeksinstituut.

Bleyen, J. & Van Molle, L. (2012). *Wat is mondelinge geschiedenis?* Leuven: Acco.

Blommaert, J. & Verschueren, J. (1994). *Antiracisme*. Antwerp: Hadewijch.

Bousetta, H., & Martiniello, M. (2003). Marocains de Belgique: du travailleur immigré au citoyen transnational. *Hommes & Migrations* 1242, 94-106.

Bousetta, H., Gsir, S. & Martiniello, M. (2005). Les migrations marocaines vers la Belgique et l'Union européenne. Regards croisés. Actes de la journée d'étude organisée dans le cadre du Pôle d'Attraction Interuniversitaire (PAI) par le CEDEM le 17 février 2004.

Buntinx, J. (2001). *Gids van bedrijfsarchieven in Vlaams-Brabant*. Brussels: Algemeen Rijksarchief.

Caestecker, F. (1993). *Ongewenste gasten. Joodse vluchtelingen en migranten in de dertiger jaren*. Brussels: VUB Press.

Caestecker, F. (2000). *Alien Policy in Belgium, 1840-1940: The Creation of Guest Workers, Refugees and Illegal Aliens*. New York: Berghahn.

Caestecker, F. (2001). De geschiedenis van grensoverschrijdende migraties uit en in Vlaanderen, weinig grensverleggend onderzoek. In J. Vranken, C. Timmerman, & K. Van der Heyden (eds.), *Komende generaties: wat weten we (niet) over allochtonen in Vlaanderen?* Leuven: Acco, 71-98.

Caestecker, F. (2003). Historiografie van de migratie, mainstream geschiedschrijving of onderzoek in de marge? *Mededelingenblad van de Belgische Vereniging Voor Nieuwste Geschiedenis* 25(2), 12-16.

Caestecker, F., Strubbe, F. & Tallier, P-A. (2009). De individuele vreemdelingendossiers afkomstig van de Openbare Veiligheid (Vreemdelingenpolitie), 1835-1943. *Zoekwijzer* 15. Available at <www.arch.be>

Coppejans-Desmedt, H. (1975). *Gids van de bedrijfsarchieven bewaard in de openbare depots van België*. Brussels: Algemeen Rijksarchief.

Coppejans-Desmedt, H., Luyckx, C. & Van Overstraeten, D. (1998). *Archives d'entreprises accessibles au public en Belgique: supplément au Guide des archives d'entreprises conservées dans les dépôts publics de la Belgique/Bedrijfsarchieven toegankelijk voor het publiek in België: supplement op de Gids van de bedrijfsarchieven bewaard in de openbare depots van België*. Brussels: Algemeen Rijksarchief.

Coudenys, W. (2004). *Leven voor de tsaar: Russische ballingen, samenzweerders en collaborateurs in België*. Leuven: Davidsfonds.

Creve, P. & Ettourki, K. (2011). Vreemd van ver. Prospectie en registratie van het erfgoed van het migrantenmiddenveld. *Meta* 2, 8-13.

De Bock, J. (2012). Alle wegen leiden naar Gent. Trajecten van mediterrane migranten naar de Arteveldestad (1960-1980), *Brood & Rozen* 3, 47-75.

De Bock, J. (2013). *Mediterranean Immigrants in the City of Ghent, 1960-1980. A historical Study of Immigration, Settlement and Integration processes*. Firenze: PhD thesis, European University Institute.

De Gendt, T. (2014). *Turkije aan de Leie. 50 jaar migratie in Gent*. Tielt: Lannoo.

Dehaeck, S. & Derwael, J. (2008). *Gids van bedrijfsarchieven in de provincie West-Vlaanderen*. Brussels: Algemeen Rijksarchief.

Dehaeck, S. & Vancoppenolle, C. (2011). *Gids van bedrijfsarchieven in de provincie Oost-Vlaanderen*. Brussels: Algemeen Rijksarchief.

De Marokkaanse Vrouw Tussen Schip En Wal, (1978). *Bareel* 1(1), 8.

Devos, G., Coppieters, G. & Lemayeur, B. (2002). *Gids van bedrijfsarchieven en archieven bij werkgevers-, werknemers- en beroepsverenigingen in de provincie Antwerpen: resultaten van twee enquêtes gehouden door het Centrum voor bedrijfsgeschiedenis, UFSIA, Universiteit Antwerpen*. Brussels: Algemeen Rijksarchief.

Devos, J. (2001). Minorisering of emancipatie, een kijk op het Vlaams integratiebeleid. <www.flw.ugent.be/cie/jdevos/index.htm>

De Wever, B., Rzoska, B. & Steffens, S. (2009). Mondelinge bronnen. In Koninklijke Commissie voor Geschiedenis. *Bronnen voor de studie van het hedendaagse België*, 1413-1427.

Dratwa, D., Gotovitch, J., & Van den Wijngaert, M. (1994). *Les Juifs de Belgique: de l'immigration au génocide 1925-1945*. (R. Van Doorslaer, Ed.). Brussels: Centre de recherches et d'études historiques de la seconde guerre mondiale.

Een Schooltje in Borgerokko, (1982). *Bareel* 5(19), 7.

Ettourki, K. (2013). Made in Flanders, organisaties van etnisch-culturele minderheden en hun erfgoed. *KADOC Nieuwsbrief* 4, 14-20.

Ettourki, K. & El Morabiti,Y. (eds.). 2014. *Dakira. 50 Jaar Marokkaanse Migratie*. Herent: Federatie van Marokkaanse Verenigingen.

Ettourki, K. (2016). Het archief van het Minderhedenforum. Een bron van emancipatie. *KADOC-nieuwsbrief* 2, 16-23.

Frennet-De Keyser, A. (2003). La convention belgo-marocaine du 17 février 1964 relative à l'occupation de travailleurs marocains en Belgique. *Courrier Hebdomadaire Du CRISP* 18(1803), 5-46.

Frennet-De Keyser, A. (2004a). La convention belgo-marocaine de main d'oeuvre: un non-événement? In N. Ouali (Ed.), *Trajectoires et dynamiques migratoires de l'immigration marocaine de Belgique*. Louvain-la Neuve: Bruylant-Academia, 215-250.

Frennet-De Keyser, A. (2004b). L'immigration marocaine en Belgique. In A. Morelli (Ed.), *Histoire des étrangers et de l'immigration en Belgique de la préhistoire à nos jours*. Brussels: Couleur livres, 329-354.

Frennet-De Keyser, A. (2011). *Histoire du Regroupement Démocratique Marocain*. Brussels: Carhima asbl.

Goddeeris, I. (2005). *De Poolse migratie in België 1945-1950: politieke mobilisatie en sociale differentiatie*. Amsterdam: Aksant.

Goddeeris, I. (2013). *La Grande Emigration polonaise en Belgique (1831-1870): elites et masses en exil à l'époque romantique*. Frankfurt am Main: Lang.

Guide des sources pour l'histoire de l'immigration maghrébine et arabe en Fédération Wallonie-Bruxelles, (2012). Carhima. < http://www.carhima.be/spip.php?article131>

Janssen, P. & Rutten, K. (1992). CBW20. Een verslag van 20 jaar migrantenwerk aangevuld met enkele impressies.

Karrouche, N.F.F. (2013). *Memories from the Rif. Moraccon-Berber Activists Between History and Myth*. Rotterdam: PhD thesis, Erasmus Universiteit.

Khoojinian, M. (2006). L'accueil et la stabilisation des travailleurs immigrés turcs en Belgique (1963-1980), *CHTP-BEG* 17, 73-116.

Khoojinian, M. (2012). Op zoek naar migranten in de syndicale archieven, *Brood & Rozen* 3, 76-95.

Khoojinian, M. (2014). Le rôle des organisations syndicales dans la régularisation des clandestins de 1974-1975. *Les cahiers du Fil Rouge* 20, 37-43.

Leduc, A. (2014). En l'absence de politique publique d'accueil, une expérience associative dans la mouvance de la FGTB de Bruxelles (1968-1989). *Les cahiers du Fil Rouge* 20, 24-36.

Lievens, J., Brasseur, N. & Martens, A. (1975). *De grote stad een geplande chaos? De Noordwijk van krot tot Manhattan*. Davidsfonds, Leuven.

Loriaux, F. (2005). L'immigration Marocaine En Belgique (1964-2004). CARHOP, http://www.carhop.be/images/Immigration_marocaine_F.LORIAUX-2005.pdf.

Martin, É. (2012). *Les premiers Maghrébins de Belgique. Analyse descriptive de l'immigration maghrébine en Belgique, dans les registres des étrangers de Châtelineau, pendant l'Entre-deux-guerres* (Document de Travail No. 4). Louvain-la-Neuve: Centre de recherche en démographie et sociétés.

Medhoune, A., Lausberg, S., Martiniello, M. & Rea, A., eds. (2015). *L'immigration marocaine en Belgique. Mémoires et destinées*. Mons: Couleur livres.

Michiels, L. (1978). Marokkanen en Turken gaan niet akkoord met het beleid inzake islam. *Bareel*, 1(1), pp. 5-7.

Morelli, A. (1987). *Fascismo e antifascismo nell'emigrazione italiana in Belgio, 1922-1940*. Rome: Bonacci.

Ouali, N., ed. (2004). *Trajectoires et Dynamiques Migratoires de L'immigration Marocaine de Belgique*. Collection Carrefours 4. Louvain-la Neuve: Bruylant-Academia.

Ouali, N. (2004a). Le mouvement associatif marocain de Belgique: quelques repères. In N. Ouali (ed.). *Trajectoires et dynamiques migratoires de l'immigration marocaine de Belgique*. Louvain-la-Neuve: Bruylant-Academia, 303-326.

Ouali, N. (2004b). Quarante ans de présence marocaine en Belgique. In N. Ouali (ed.), *Trajectoires et dynamiques migratoires de l'immigration marocaine de Belgique*. Louvain-la Neuve: Bruylant-Academia, 19-62.

Raats, J., Leonard, I. & Vandebroek, H. (2014). *"On est là". De eerste generatie Marokkaanse en Turkse migranten in Brussel (1964-1974)*. Antwerp: Garant.

Rachib (1982). Interview met een Marokkaanse jongen van Antwerpen. *Bareel*, 5(19), 22.

Reniers, G. (1999). On the History and Selectivity of Turkish and Moroccan Migration to Belgium, *International Migration*, 37(4), 679-713.

Roofthoofd, N. (2014). *Glad terrein. Het Mechelse migrantenbeleid en de Marokkaanse migratie tussen 1964 en 1994*. Leuven: unpublished Master thesis, KU Leuven, onderzoekseenheid Geschiedenis.

Roos, H., Cosemans, S. (2013). Een reis langs vele wegen: de Indiase diaspora in België. In: Goddeeris I. (Eds.), *Het wiel van Ashoka. Belgisch-Indiase contacten in historisch perspectief.* Leuven: Lipsius Leuven/Leuven University Press, 213-231.

Saerens, L. (2000). *Vreemdelingen in een wereldstad: een geschiedenis van Antwerpen en zijn joodse bevolking 1880-1944*. Tielt: Lannoo.

Schoonvaere, Q. (2014). *België-Marokko: 50 jaar migratie. Demografische studie over de populatie van Marokkaanse herkomst in België.* Centre de recherche en démographie et sociétés (UCL) & Federaal Centrum voor de analyse van de migratiestromen, de bescherming van de grondrechten van de vreemdelingen en de strijd tegen mensenhandel.

Schreiber, J.-P. (1996). *L'immigration juive en Belgique du Moyen Age à la Première Guerre mondiale*. Brussels: Éditions de l'Université de Bruxelles.

Schreiber, J.-P. (2002). *Dictionnaire biographique des Juifs de Belgique: figures du judaïsme belge (XIXe-XXe siècles)*. Brussels: De Boeck.

Surkyn, J. (1995). *Turkse en Marokkaanse gezinnen in migratie.* Brussels: Centrum voor Sociologie, Working Papers 'Etnische Minderheden in België', VUB.

Tirez, S. (2013). *Alterisering van migranten via het beeld: onderzoek naar de relatie tussen materiële cultuur, identiteit en stereotypering.* Leuven: unpublished PhD thesis, European Studies – KU Leuven.

Van Bastelaer, I. (2015). *Allemaal Mechelaars. Het migrantenbeleid van de stad Mechelen (1989-2006)*. Leuven: unpublished Master thesis, KU Leuven, onderzoekseenheid Geschiedenis.

Vandenberghe, L. (1978). Kristenen en Moslims in gebedsstonde te Kortrijk. Maar voor wanneer die moskee? *Bareel*, 1(4), 8.

Vandendriessche, J. & Jouan, Q. (2016). De Belgische historici in de internationale wandelgangen, *Contemporanea*, 38-2.

Vanden Eede, M. & Martens, A. (1994). *De Noordwijk. Slopen en wonen*, Berchem: EPO.

Van Doorslaer, R. (1995). *Kinderen van het getto: Joodse revolutionairen in België 1925-1940.* Antwerp: Hadewijch.

Van Doorslaer, R., & Schreiber, J.-P. (Eds.). (2004). *De curatoren van het getto: de Vereniging van de joden in België tijdens de nazi-bezetting.* Tielt: Lannoo.

Vanhaecke, B (2008). *Van aan de minaret tot onder de peperbus. De eerste jaren van Marokkaanse arbeidsmigratie naar Lokeren (1964-1974)*. Ghent: Unpublished PhD thesis, UGent, Vakgroep Nieuwste Geschiedenis.

Van Loock, L. (1986). De Marokkaanse Gemeenschap. *Bareel* 9, 4-10.

Weyns, K. (2013). Naar een coherent Belgisch migrantenbeleid. Archief Johan Leman, *KADOC-nieuwsbrief* 2, 16-20.

Zemni, S. (2009). *Het islamdebat*. Berchem: EPO. p. 220.

Part 2
Movement and Settlement

4. Moroccan migration in Belgium's labor policy and labor market

Albert Martens

Moroccan immigration to Belgium began as a labor related migration: the first Moroccans arrived as 'guest workers' for the Belgian coal mines. In 1974, the Belgian government issued a migration halt and new Moroccan immigrants could only settle via family reunification. This does not mean that labor issues had been solved. On the contrary, new generations of Moroccans, some having obtained Belgian citizenship, entered the job market over the following decades. This did not happen smoothly, however, and coincided with a great deal of discrimination.

This article discusses the Moroccan migration to Belgium from a labor perspective. It will analyze the employment of Moroccans – both the first generation and subsequent ones, some of whom became Belgians ('new Belgians' or 'Belgians of allochthonous origin', contrary to 'autochthonous' Belgians, who were born from Belgian parents) and others who did not (and remained 'foreigners'). It will do so by means of statistical data, most importantly of the labor cards (i.e. work permits) awarded to civilians from North African countries (since 1950) and from the Moroccan Kingdom (since 1969).

After a discussion of sources and their methodological challenges, we give an overview of the different phases of immigration and the evolution of the quantitative data related to work permits. This is in order to place the Moroccan or North African workers within the history of postwar immigration to Belgium. In the third section, we focus on Moroccan immigration and discuss the evolution of work permits, both before and after 1974. The fourth section argues that the

Belgian labor market is stratified according to ethnic lines and that people of Moroccan descent are overrepresented in particular sectors. The fifth section demonstrates by means of new statistical tools that things have not changed fundamentally in 2015. A final balance sheet points out the major economic and social effects of Moroccan immigration.

Quantitative analysis of foreign workers' first work permits

The most obvious way to analyze the numbers of labor migrants is by means of their first work permits. However, this is not an easy task. First, these quantitative data only mirror the official and regulatory side of the labor market. They were set up when an employer requested a foreign laborer or when a foreign laborer (or a member of his family) explicitly asked for a labor card. Undoubtedly, not all employed foreigners were official or legal, and it is difficult to estimate the number of those who remained in the shadows. They only appear in certain situations, for instance during 'regularization' measures.

Second, these quantitative data relate to either the same person in different situations or different persons. The same person may have received different kinds of permits at different moments. For instance, he may have initially received a 'B Permit with immigration' and a couple of years later an 'A Permit without immigration'. In fact, there were four types of permits. The A Permits were distributed for an unlimited period; B Permits for a determined and temporary period (mostly a year, but renewable). When the future foreign laborer still resided outside of Belgium, he or she received a permit to immigrate, i.e. a 'permit with immigration'; when he already resided for a period of time in Belgium, he obtained a 'permit without immigration'. Figure 1 gives an overview of the four different cases. It also includes a fifth type: the C Permit, which concerns people working with several employers (e.g. bartenders or waiters).

The arrows in figure 1 indicate the passages and shifts that may take place from one category to another in the course of a foreign worker's career. A typical example of labor migration starts when an employer who received the authorization to employ a foreigner invites him to come to work in Belgium (stage 1). The foreign worker receives a B Permit with immigration and is allowed to move to Belgium and to stay there for a limited period, usually for a year (stage 2). If his permit is annually renewed for a number of years (three to five years, depending on the case) (stage 3), he can benefit from a (first) permit of unlimited length, i.e. an

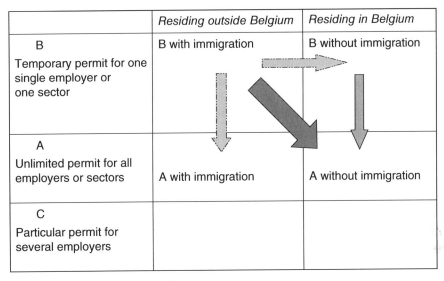

	Residing outside Belgium	*Residing in Belgium*
B Temporary permit for one single employer or one sector	B with immigration	B without immigration
A Unlimited permit for all employers or sectors	A with immigration	A without immigration
C Particular permit for several employers		

Figure 1: Types of work permits or cards

A Permit (without immigration, since he has already been authorized to stay in Belgium for several years) (stage 4).

This worker's wife and children are also permitted to come to Belgium. They are also considered foreigners and have to apply for a labor card if they want to work. As long as this worker has not yet received an A Permit, his wife and children can only receive a B Permit (without immigration, since they already reside in Belgium) (stage 5). When the worker receives his A Permit, he can transmit this privilege to all family members living under the same roof (stage 6).

This system of family reunion accordingly generates an immigration of new workers. The effect of this 'deduced' immigration, however, becomes manifest only after a certain time, for instance after the children (both the ones born in Belgium and abroad) reach the age to work (14 or 18 years).

This example represents the classical case of labor immigration after 1945. Yet, there are numerous exceptions. The most notorious exception took place between 1962 and 1964, when workers came to Belgium with a tourist visa and were hired without having obtained a work permit abroad. They then could benefit from an on-location 'regularization'. Moreover, legislation has changed regularly over the past decades. Foreigners of some nationalities are no longer obliged to get a labor card if they want to work in Belgium.[1] As a result, they do not show up in the statistics. Also the calculation of the relative importance of one group versus another one can be significantly modified. In addition, some foreigners became

Belgian nationals and also disappeared from the statistics, although this did not happen frequently before the 1980s.

For all these reasons, caution is required for a quantitative analysis of work permits and one should, for instance, not use them to compute the total amount of immigrated workers. Our attention will be placed primarily on the first permits with immigration of workers from Morocco and other North African countries. But first, we will place this immigration in a broader history of labor migration after 1945.

Work permits A and B (source: Federation of Moroccan Associations)

Successive immigration phases after the Second World War

One should not underestimate the importance of the context in which the immigration of foreign workers unfolded in the wake of the Second World War (Martens, 1976). By creating the 'status of coal miner' in 1945-46, the government made great efforts to attract Belgian workers to the mines and to guarantee coal production, which was indispensable for the 'national reconstruction'. However, unlike the years of German occupation, when many Belgians sought work in mines in order to escape forced labor in Germany, Belgian workers began leaving the mines en masse. The new status and all the material and moral advantages it offered could not change this. Between 1943 and 1947, about 25,000 underground miners left the coal mines, and by doing so jeopardized the economic recovery. The new privileges seemed unsatisfactory, but the government was unwilling to pay a higher price to find the urgently needed labor force. It therefore first requisitioned former Belgian miners, a measure that proved both difficult and unpopular. Afterwards, it asked the occupation troops in Germany to provide approximately 64,000 German prisoners of war, of whom more than 40,000 began working in the underground coal mines. As a result, coal production not only stabilized, it grew by more than a third (Sunou, 1980).

This system, however, was unsustainable. After a year, Germany had signed its capitulation and Belgium had to set its POW's free. Just as before the war, it was forced to rely on a foreign labor force, which became a significant and indispensable element of Belgium's employment policy after 1946. We can distinguish five key moments of immigration to Belgium, each with its own particularities.

The first phase saw the immigration of about 70,000 Italians (who arrived in numbers of about 2,000 per week starting in 1945) and approximately 23,000 displaced persons recruited by Belgium in German camps. These DP's, especially Poles and Ukrainians, had been taken into captivity by the Germans, were liberated by the Allies, but did not want to return to their fatherlands that had become part of the Eastern Bloc. They therefore hoped to start a new life in Belgium (Goddeeris, 2005).

The second immigration wave took place during the economic revival in the early 1950s. It was comparable to the first and primarily consisted of Italians. During a third phase in the years 1955-58, the recruitment countries diversified, largely due to the mine catastrophe of Marcinelle in 1956 that killed 262 miners, of which 136 were Italian. After protesting the government against unsafe conditions in the Belgian coalmines, the Italian government refused the delivery of documents to Italians who wanted to work in Belgian mines. To escape this restriction, the Belgian mine industry recruited workers from Spain and Greece, and was joined by recruiters from other sectors including metallurgy, construction, and domestic work.

The economic revival and boom of the golden sixties, especially from 1962-67, led to a new phase of migration. This period not only saw an overall greater volume of foreign workers arriving, but more countries were represented: next to Italy, Greece and Spain, now also Morocco, Turkey and Yugoslavia. Furthermore, foreign workers were being employed in professional sectors outside of mining, namely commerce, public transport, and cleaning.

The new growth of economic activities in the years 1970-74 sparked a fifth phase of foreign employment. It resembled the previous phase, but with one major difference. In addition to newly arrived immigrants, foreigners who already resided in Belgium were being employed in a wide range of economic sectors. Over the course of 1974, the recruitment of foreign workers residing abroad was once again strictly regulated. Touristic immigration (arriving with a tourist visa and later being regularized in Belgium) was banned. Although 1974 is often considered a migration halt, regular immigration continued afterwards, following the legal possibilities and limitations of the time.

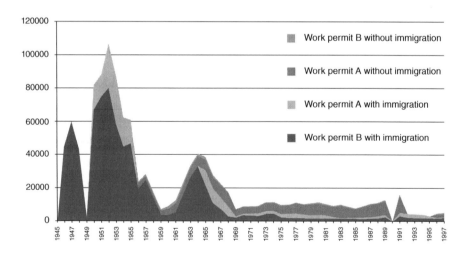

Figure 2: Numbers and types of first work permits, 1945-97 (source: Labor Ministry)

Figure 2 demonstrates the different immigration phases beginning in 1945. Up until 1974, it shows great oscillations between periods of recruitment and periods of migration halts. The high number of B Permits mirrors the importance of recruitments. We also observe how A Permits without immigration were distributed after a couple of years, not only to those who had previously received a B Permit with immigration, but also to those who in the frame of family reunification lived with the family chief (who had previously received a B Permit with immigration and afterwards an A Permit without immigration).

The graph reveals that the successive immigration phases had a three-part expansion. First, the number of recruited workers increased until 1968. Second, the spectrum of professional sectors hiring foreigners broadened: starting almost exclusively with coal mining, but later other sectors including textile manufacturing, heavy industry, and service jobs in addition to the other previously-mentioned examples. Third, the countries of emigration expanded: initially only Italy, then the North Mediterranean (Spain, Greece), and finally the Maghreb countries and Turkey.

Immigration from North Africa

The first waves of immigration from North Africa began in 1950. Initially counted under the umbrella 'Africa' (1950-64) and later 'North Africa' (1965-68), countries of origin such as Morocco, Algeria, and Tunisia were only mentioned explicitly from 1969 onwards. This is years after these countries became independent and were able to conclude international treaties on labor, social security, etc. (Morocco and Tunisia in 1956; Algeria in 1962).

The chart below shows the evolution of the annual numbers of first given work permits. Between 1963 and 1967, more than 21,000 first B Permits with immigration were awarded to North African workers, mostly Moroccan. This historical period was characterized by considerable economic growth, very low unemployment (less than 4% of the active population), and strong tension on the labor market. Fearing that the cost of low or non-qualified labor would increase significantly, the patronage, trade unions, and government collectively decided to suspend the obliged authorization required for a foreign worker. This was the beginning of the so-called touristic migration, which is a fitting euphemism for the pure and simple acceptation of immigrants non-conforming to the law and accordingly illegal. A foreign worker could come to Belgium with a tourist passport and, if after a medical exam, he was able to find employment, his employer could easily regularize the worker's situation. During those five years, more than 124,000 first work permits were given, among which a fifth – 21,000 – went to workers from Maghreb countries.

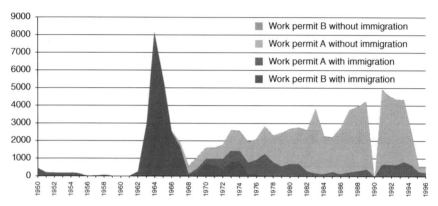

Figure 3: First work permits for North African workers (1950-68) and Moroccans (1969-1997)
(source: Labor Ministry and proper calculations)

It was only in 1968 that one again only allowed 'regular' immigration and unconditionally demanded an authorization. The number of first B Permits with immigration immediately dropped significantly, but rose again between 1970 and 1974 – years of certain economic growth – and fell down more radically after 1974. Although the government in that year solemnly proclaimed a halt to migration, we have to note that this measure only concerns the first B Permits with immigration for non-qualified workers. The other permits, resulting from previous immigration, continued to be awarded.

We indeed see that the number of A Permits without immigration is considerably higher, if not twice the number of B Permits with immigration. This confirms the importance of family reunification, a greater demographic reproduction among the Moroccan community, or a greater demand among the Moroccan community to participate in the labor market. In order to highlight the role of deduced immigration, figure 4 compares the total number of first permits given to these workers before 1970, 1981, and 1991 (thrice the left column) with the Maghreb population in those years, divided into different age categories.

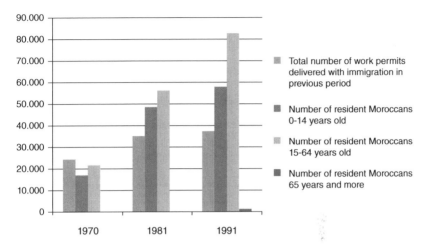

*Figure 4: Number of first permits and demographic structure of the Moroccan population
(source: Population Censuses and Labor Ministry)*

The immigration of labor (the left columns for each period) initially caused a growth of the age category of 0-14 years, and later contributed to the growth of the 15-64 year old category. This evolution of demographic composition of labor immigrants was not without consequences. After a number of years of residence (certainly for those who were born in Belgium) the possibility to acquire the Belgian nationality was much easier. Whereas between 1946 and 1986 hardly 1.6% of the naturalized Belgians were from Moroccan origin, their share of the total number of naturalizations grew to 27% (131,700 on 491,289: see Ouali 2004: 43). As a result, in demographic and labor statistics these new Belgians were considered Belgian nationals, and not foreigners or Moroccans. This situation makes it impossible to conduct quantitative research on the occurrence of discrimination in the social field (e.g. employment, accommodation, education, health, etc.).

The ethno-stratification of the labor market

It is not a coincidence that the question of this presence was brought to the forefront starting in the 1990s. Hedged off in the previous years within very particular job sectors (mining, steel industry, metallurgy) and within specific regions, the next generation entering the job market was no longer subject to these restrictions. A new generation was – at least in principle – also able to enter a larger job market.

Most of the public felt this access to the labor market did not pose major problems, nor should it have been subject to restrictions. Many people thought that these Moroccans had already lived in Belgium for a long time and had been able to assimilate. Indeed, some were born and schooled in the country and/or had been able to apply for Belgian citizenship. It was not considered a problem for them to find work, even in the public sector.

Although several studies at the time already provided different information, and notably revealed the existence of manifest discrimination in the workplace (Haex e.a., 1976; Nayer e.a., 1991; Martens & De Nolf, 1993), it was only after an inquiry by the International Labor Organization (Bovenkerk, 1992; Arrijn, 1997) that the vastness of the discrimination young Belgians of Moroccan origin ('allochthonous' Belgians) experienced came to light. But how could one lay bare discriminatory practices? Only first-hand tests could prove that an employer's preference systematically went to 'autochthonous' Belgians (Belgians who were born of Belgian parents).

This debate led to the development of statistical analysis tools that brought to light discrimination against 'Belgians of allochthonous origin', and demonstrated that their work situation (selection, remuneration, unemployment, etc.) was clearly less favorable than that of 'autochthonous' Belgians (Martens, 2012). In this way, the combined use of two administrative databases – of the Social Security and of the National Registration – provided pertinent information, partially for the year 1997 and more complete for the years 2000 and 2007 (Martens, Verhoeven, 2006).[2] One hoped to expose inequalities and to statistically validate and confirm the hypothesis of the 'ethnostratification' of the labor market.

The different proportions of new or 'allochthonous' Belgians and foreigners are clearly evident in figure 5. Italians and North, West and South Europeans form a significantly larger share of foreigners. The new Belgians represent respectively 6%, 35% and 24% of their total populations. Within the other origin groups, in contrast, we note an over-representation of new Belgians, on average 62%. People with a non-EU origin thus acquire the Belgian nationality to a relatively greater extent.

More importantly, this approach allowed a measurement of the spread (and its evolution) between 'autochthonous' and 'allochthonous' Belgians. Figure 6 lists the five largest sectors of employment for people of Moroccan origin in Belgium – both Moroccan citizens ('foreigners') and 'new Belgians'.

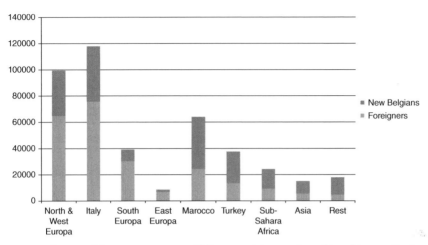

Figure 5: Belgians and foreigners, 18-55 years old (June 2001) (source: Central Social Security Bank (CSSB), operations by the Center of Sociological Research (CeSR), Univerity of Leuven (KU Leuven) (Vertommen & Martens, 2005)

The figure consists of primarily blue-collar jobs. Among men, the public sectors do not even appear in the top five. Less than 5% of male new Belgians of Moroccan origin have a job in the 'public administration sector'. This is much lower than among North, West and South Europeans, of whom 10% are employed in this sector. For the Moroccan women, 'public administration' is still in the top five but also here, it employs only half the share compared to other European women. The share of Moroccan women in 'education' is also much smaller. 'Health and social work' remains very popular. Last but not least, few Moroccans, men nor women, are represented in high-wage sectors such as 'post and telecommunications', 'financial intermediation', 'advice and services to business' and 'electricity, gas, steam and hot water supply'.

Conversely, the hierarchy of sectors that employ many Moroccans shows a somewhat different picture than the one of European employees. The sectors 'industrial cleaning', 'hotels and restaurants' and 'temporary employment' have a very large share of Moroccan employees: on the average 25% of the new Belgians and 40% of the foreigners. The high concentration indexes demonstrate the strong over-representation of Moroccan employees in these sectors. Compared to native Belgians, Belgian Moroccan men are 24 times more likely to work in 'industrial cleaning', and Belgian Moroccan women 9.6 times more. These indexes amount to respectively 41.2 and 22.8 for non-Belgian Moroccans. The indexes of 'hotels and restaurants' and 'temporary employment' are more moderate,

Men – New Belgians	%
Construction	9.1
Land transport	8.7
Hotels and restaurants	7.4
Temporary employment agencies and employment	7.1
Industrial cleaning	6.5

Men – Foreigners	%
Temporary employment agencies and employment	14.1
Industrial cleaning	11.1
Hotels and restaurants	10.2
Construction	10.0
Agriculture	5.7

Women – New Belgians	%
Health and social work	21.1
Retail trade, except motor vehicles; repair of personal and household goods	10.4
Industrial cleaning	10.1
Public administration and defense; compulsory social security	8.6
Hotels and restaurants	8

Women – Foreigners	%
Industrial cleaning	24.0
Health and social work	17.5
Hotels and restaurants	11.6
Temporary employment agencies and employment	8.5
Public administration and defence; compulsory social security	6.0

Figure 6: The five largest sectors of employment for Moroccans in Belgium (June 2001)
(source: Central Social Security Bank (CSSB), operations by the Centre of Sociological Research (CeSR), Univerity of Leuven (KU Leuven)

but still significantly larger. In the case of the foreigners (men and women), the 'agriculture-indexes' are also quite high. It goes without saying that sectors where Moroccans are active are characterized by low wages, poor job security and bad working conditions (secondary market) (Vertommen & Martens, 2005).

The situation in 2015

Since 2007, it has been possible to check the ethnic stratification of the labor market at a given moment and to analyze the evolution of the share of different nationalities and ethnic origins in job categories. This has allowed the Interfederal

Center for Equality of Chances to compile two studies of the socio-economic situation of workers of other nationalities and ethnic descent, and of the impact of acquiring Belgian citizenship, of birth in Belgium, of the length of stay in Belgium, etc. on employment and wages. The latest report (Centre, 2015) clearly demonstrates that the ethno-stratification of the labor market remains a factor, certainly for the Moroccan population. The latter group, by now, is very diverse. Figure 7 shows that almost three quarters have Belgian nationality, but that this group consists of people born in Belgium – from Belgian or non-Belgian parents – as well as of people having obtained Belgian nationality either recently or more than five years ago. Strikingly, 19% consist of Moroccan civilians who for the first time registered in the national database over the past five years.

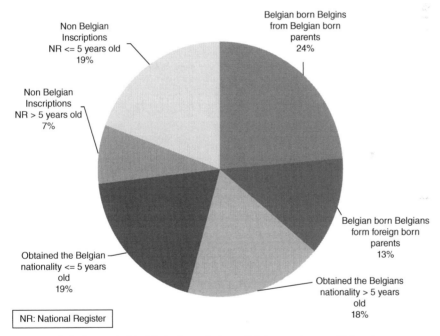

Figure 7: The background of the Maghreb population in Belgium, 18-60 years old (2012)
(source: Centre 2015 and proper calculations)

All of these people of Moroccan descent – whether of Belgian or of Moroccan nationality – keep being hedged off within particular sectors of the labor market and continue to work in circumstances inferior to the ones of 'autochthonous' Belgians. Even obtaining the Belgian nationality does not necessarily afford significant social mobility. Some data from the 2015 report, listed in figure 8, are quite telling.

	Autochthonous		
	Belgians %	Moroccans %	Difference points %
Active population			
Men	80,8	68,3	-12,5
Women	75,1	54,7	-20,4
Employment rate			
20-60 years old	76,6	44,5	-32,1
Unemployment	8,5	25,5	17,00
Men	5,6	23,7	18,1
Women	6,3	28,3	22
Professional status			
Blue-collar worker	29,07	50,63	21,56
White-collar worker	48,24	30,37	-17,86
Public services	16,66	3,25	-13,41
Other	6,03	15,75	9,71
Wages			
Low wage	26,1	53	26,90
Low wage: men	20	46,3	26,30
Low wage: women	32,2	63,6	31,40
High wage	30	8,7	-21,30

Figure 8: Some comparisons of Moroccans' and 'autochthonous' Belgian's position in the Belgian labor market (source: Centre 2015 and proper calculations)

In sum, the report of 2015 confirms that the jobs relatively common among Moroccans are unsecure and precarious (short-term contracts) and are isolated in sectors such as cleaning, gardening, domestic care, loading, and interim service in enterprises. Most of them lack upward mobility.

A balance sheet

Could one make a general balance sheet of Moroccan immigration to Belgium? If so, one certainly has to distinguish between an economic and a social assessment.

Regarding the economy, Moroccan immigration had three major and undeniable effects. First, it contributed to a decreasing of the wage tension on the labor market between 1963 and 1968. This kept the production in low salary sectors, such as textile, catering, service industry (both interim and low-qualified jobs), construction, loading, cleaning, etc. It also reduced the benefits of other, better-paying jobs such as underground mining. Indeed, from 1969 onwards, the advantages that had been awarded to miners immediately after the Second World War (approximately 25% of average salaries) gradually disappeared and were acquired in other sectors, such as utility work and petrol refining.

Second, Moroccan immigration – just as all other migration – has maintained the salary hierarchy between qualified and non-qualified jobs and sectors. The permanent influx of Moroccan labor has saved sectors and jobs that are well protected and unionized (public sector, utility work, etc.), from significant tension.

Third, these less organized, less demanding workers paid considerable costs during industrial re-organization. As temporary workers, they do not benefit from 'outplacement' and other sectoral benefits. Less unionized, they also lack strong union support. As a result, the reconversion costs were lightened considerably: companies could in case of reconversion always refuse the reconversion of a work permit.

Regarding social effects, there are also at least three important points. First, there is the growth of job segmentation due to the ethno-stratification of job sectors. The ethnic division, in addition to the division between sexes, has contributed to increasing division in the labor market. Discrimination – both in the access to jobs and in promotion, formation, etc. – is often based on race and ethnicity. The salary market is largely dominated by sexual and ethnic discrimination, in parallel with the overall job market.

Second, the presence of an under-qualified, and thus cheap, labor force is consistently replicated due to the link between poor education and lower wage employment. In the first period, Belgium easily recruited workers who were immediately available (and therefore saved on social costs related to health and education). Later, Belgium was able to retain this cheap labor force by systematically underinvesting in education, professional development, and housing.

Third, the gradual shift from old industrial centers to urban agglomeration across the country led to greater concentrations of Moroccan and other immigrants in certain urban districts. This increase in numbers combined with their different culture and religion made them much more conspicuous.

Notes

1   The obligation to issue labor cards was abolished in 1959 for Benelux (Belgium, the Netherlands and Luxemburg), in 1968 for EEC (France, FRG, and Italy) nationals, in 1973 for Irish, Danish and UK citizens, in 1988 for Greeks, in 1992 for Spanish and Portuguese, in 1994 for Austrians, Swedes, Norwegians and Fins, and in 2003 for all foreigners who had obtained a lifetime permit.

2   To reveal possible ethno-stratification, we will also detect over- and under-representation of origin groups in certain sectors by means of concentration indexes. A concentration index equals the share of employees of a specific origin group in a sector over the share of native Belgian employees in that sector. An index equaling one signifies an equal representation in a sector, one greater than one signifies over-representation and an index smaller than one signifies under-representation.

Bibliography

Arrijn, P, Feld, S, Nayer, A., Smeesters, B. (1997). *Discrimination à l'embauche*. Bruxelles: SSTC.

Bovenkerk, F. (1992). *A manual for international comparative research on discrimination on the grounds or "race" and ethnic origin*. Geneva: ILO

Coenen, M.T. (dir.) (1999). *Les syndicats et les immigrés. Du rejet à l'intégration*, Bruxelles: EVO-CARHOP-FEC.

Centrum voor Gelijkheid van Kansen en voor Racismebestrijding (1997). *Etnische dicriminatie bij aanwerving. Belgische deelname aan het internationaal vergelijkend onderzoek van het Internationaal Arbeidsbureau*, Brussel: DWTC.

Centre Interfédéral pour l'Egalité des chances et la lutte contre le racisme (2015). *Monitoring socio-économique 2015 Marché du travail et emploi*. Bruxelles. See: www.diversite.be and www.emploi.belgique.be

Feld, S., Nayer, A., Arryn, P. (1997). *La discrimination à l'embauche en raison de l'origine ethnique*. Bruxelles: Centre pour l'égalité des chances et de lutte contre le racisme – Services fédéraux des affaires scientifiques, techniques et culturelles.

Goddeeris, I. (2005). *De Poolse migratie in België 1945-1950: politieke mobilisatie en sociale differentiatie*, Amsterdam: Aksant.

Haex, J., Martens, A., Wolf, S. (1976). *Arbeidsmarkt, discriminatie, gastarbeid*. Leuven: S.O.I.-reeks. Sociologische studies en documenten.

Martens, A (1976). *Les immigrés. Flux et reflux d'une main-d'oeuvre d'appoint. La politique belge de l'immigration de 1945 à 1970*. Louvain: Presses Universitaires de Louvain et Editions Vie Ouvrière.

Martens, A., Denolf, L. (1993). Inégalité sociale sur le marché de l'emploi: la détermination ethnique, *Critique régionale 19, L'emploi des immigrés. Intégration et différenciation sociale.* Cahiers de sociologie et d'économie régionales, Bruxelles: Institut de Sociologie, 39-55.

Martens, A., Ouali, N., Van de maele, M., Vertommen, S., Dryon, Ph., Verhoeven, H. (2005). *Discriminations des étrangers et des personnes d'origine étrangère sur le marché du travail de la Région de Bruxelles-Capitale.* Recherche dans le cadre du Pacte territorial pour l'emploi des Bruxellois. Rapport de synthèse. Bruxelles: Observatoire Bruxellois du marché du travail et des qualifications. ORBEM.

Martens, A, & Verhoeven, H. (2006). Les minorités ethniques sur le marché de l'emploi en Belgique. In: Khader, B., Martinielleo, M. Rea, A., Timmerman, C. (eds.), *Penser l'immigration et l'intégration autrement. Une initiative belge inter-universitaire* (pp. 271-297). Bruxelles: Bruylant.

Martens, A. (2012). La recherche sur les discrimination en perspective historique. *Baromètre de la diversité –Emploi.* Bruxelles: Centre pour l'Egalité des Chances et de Lutte contre le Racisme, 130-138.

Martens, A. (2015). Immigrer pour travailler... et repeupler. In Medhoune, A., Lausberg, S., Martiniello, M., Rea, A. (dir.) *L'immigration marocaine en Belgique. Mémoires et destinées.* Mons: Couleur livres. (57-65).

Ouali, N. (2004).Trajectoires et dynamiques migratoires des Marocains de Belgique. Louvain-La-Neuve: Bruylant-Academia.

Nayer, A., Beauchesne, M-N., Nys, M., Zinbi, T. (1991). *La discrimination dans l'accès à l'emploi et l'intégration professionnelle en Région Bruxelloise.* Bruxelles: CeRP, Institut de Sociologie.

Sunou, Ph. (1980) *Les prisonniers de guerre allemands en Belgique et la bataille du charbon 1945-1947.* Bruxelles: Musée Royale de l'Armée. Centre d'Histoire Militaire.

Vertommen S., Martens, A. (2005). Ethnicity on local labour markets: facts and figures. *Interuniverisitary consortium an immigration and integration.* Brussels: King Baudewijn Foundation 5/12/2005.

5. Partner migration in the Moroccan community: a focus on time and contextual evolutions

Emilien Dupont, Bart Van de Putte, John
Lievens & Frank Caestecker

Introduction

Through time, there were several routes migrants of Moroccan origin could use to enter the country, such as labor and partner migration (Reniers, 1999; Schoonvaere, 2014). Previous studies on the history of Moroccan migration to Belgium reported three subsequent, partly overlapping waves that are largely influenced by the prevailing migration policy and legislation at that time (Schoonvaere, 2014; Surkyn & Reniers, 1997). Marriage migration is situated within the third wave.

Notwithstanding the presence of residents of Moroccan origin before 1960, the bulk of Moroccan migration waves took off from the 1960s onwards. The first wave of labor migration from Morocco to Western Europe was part of a wider project to attract foreign labor, in order to cope with the worker shortage in particular sectors of the economy, such as the textile, metal, and the coal industry (Schoonvaere, 2014). This was formalized through bilateral agreements (Morocco: 17 February1964) between the governments of the respective countries (Reniers, 1999). Both the Belgian government and the guest workers conceived this as a temporary arrangement; at the end of their contracts, the workers were supposed to return to Morocco.

To cope with the economic strain following the oil crisis in 1973, the Belgian government adopted restrictive migration policies, which resulted in the end of labor migration in 1974. This drastically reduced the amount of labor migrators and led the way to the second wave of migration, family reunification. Because of these restrictive policies that greatly reduced the possibilities to enter Belgium, families shifted from a temporary settlement to a more permanent one as the remaining family arrived in Belgium (Reniers, 1999). While the labor migrants consisted predominantly of men, their wives and children began entering the country in large numbers.

The third wave of partner migration started in the early 1980s and remained one of the few ways to enter Belgium after immigration policies became even stricter (Reniers, 1999). Entry was only granted to asylum seekers, students, and spouses of those Moroccans legally residing in Belgium. Through this new dynamic of family formation immigrants joined their partners in Belgium. This type of migration could only occur because of the strong bonds and resulting networks between Moroccan communities in Belgium and Morocco. These networks have been facilitating and canalizing new migrations (chain migration), mostly in the form of new partnerships. This has resulted in on-going streams of migration and "transplanted" communities despite the strict regulative migration legislation in Belgium (Reniers, 1999). Nowadays partner migration still remains the most important route for residents of Moroccan origin to enter Belgium (Myria, 2015).

Partner migration has recently been considered particularly relevant for migration policies and dominates public debates because marrying a spouse from the country of origin could potentially hinder or even fully inhibit the integration process. Mixed partnerships (partnerships with another nationality) on the other hand are seen as manifestations of assimilation (Waters & Jiménez, 2005). Preferring a partner from the country of origin could express a longing for a more traditional way of life (Lichter, Carmalt & Qian, 2011). However, other scholars question the view of intermarriage as litmus test for assimilation (Song, 2009; Waters & Jiménez, 2005). Choosing a partner from the country of origin should not always be considered an expression of being more stuck to the homeland, but can also be instigated by modern motives, such as a way of emancipating oneself (Lievens, 1997).

Because of the relevance of partner migration in social policy and public debates, we want to investigate the evolution in partner migration for the whole Moroccan community while simultaneously disentangling classical assimilation effects, such as generation and age, and contextual influences. We only focus on intra-ethnic partnerships to fully examine the factors shaping the choice of partner migration instead of a partner within the local ethnic community. Mixed partnerships make up 15% of all partnerships of Moroccan migrants in Belgium between 2001 and 2008, but are not taken into account due to their distinct character. Furthermore, the prevalence of mixed partnerships has remained stable during this period.

Social scientists researching migration in Belgium often focus on residents of Moroccan and Turkish origin because they are the two largest groups of residents of non-European origin in Belgium and are well established (see Eeckhaut et al., 2011; Reniers, 1999; Timmerman, Vanderwaeren, & Crul, 2003). Furthermore, there are strong similarities between these groups (period of arrival, legal conditions, and cultural characteristics (Reniers, 1999)). However, since there is more literature on Turkish migrants than on Moroccan ones, we will sometimes draw parallels between these two groups to contextualize our assumptions. The most significant difference between these groups is the presence of weaker ties between sending and receiving Moroccan communities in comparison to the strong ties between Turkish communities (Surkyn & Reniers, 1997). This is mainly due to the more individualistic, socio-cultural and innovative character of Moroccan migration, which makes it more fragmented in terms of geographical dispersion, marital status, educational level, religious-political orientation, and socioeconomic status (Reniers, 1999; Surkyn & Reniers, 1997).

This article consists of six chapters. After this introduction, we first list our data and methods. In the fourth section, we discuss the individual level time trends, i.e. period effects, intergenerational changes, and age effects. Afterwards, we analyze contextual effects, namely the community size and the sex ratio. Finally, we summarize our most important findings in the conclusion.

Data

Our data on residents of Moroccan origin consist of an extraction from the Belgian national register. This extraction focuses on marriages and legally registered cohabitations, conducted between 1 January 2001 and 12 December 2008. Two conditions had to be met: at least one partner is (1) a resident in Belgium before the partnership, and (2) has a nationality at birth from a third country, i.e. a country outside the European Economic Area and Switzerland. All registered partner choices among first and second generation migrants originating from 97 third countries and living in Belgium are comprised. We selected Moroccan migrants based on their nationality at birth. Only intra-ethnic partnerships were selected. Furthermore, our focus lies on first partner choices to retain a homogenous group that is not biased by previous partner choices. Both marriages and legally registered cohabitations are included. In sum, we counted 24,712 Moroccan partner choices.

However, the automatic naturalization of ethnic minorities, including Moroccans, in Belgium from the early 1990s onwards results in a slight inaccurateness regarding the size of the second generation group. When one parent has the Belgian nationality, children born in Belgium automatically receive the Belgian nationality at birth. Although they are technically a part of the second generation group, these naturalized minorities are omitted from it. However, we do not expect this resulting underrepresentation of minorities from the second generation to be a substantial problem, as the changes in the Belgian nationality legislation that enabled minorities of the second generation to apply en masse for Belgian citizenship occurred only in the early 1990s. Because one has to be at least 18 to get married, the very large majority of second generation Moroccans born in the 1980s were still born with the Moroccan nationality and are therefore part of our sample.

Because our dataset is an extraction from the Belgian national register, our dataset includes the complete population of non-EU migrants. However, there are also some limitations. First, there is no socio-economic information available at the individual level, such as educational attainment, employment status, and income. Furthermore, the Belgian national register also lacks data on unregistered cohabitations. Lastly, the focus on nationality at birth to discern the Moroccan group ignores ethnic differences (for example Berbers and Arabs) within Morocco.

Method

We analyzed the effects of individual level time trends (period, generation, and age) and contextual effects (community size and sex ratio). The basic descriptive analyses can be found in table 1. The theoretical background, as well as the construction and effects of these variables will be discussed in the following sections.

To deal with the simultaneous analysis of age, period and cohort effects (Yang & Land, 2006) we use a cross-classified design supplemented with a Hierarchical Age Period Cohort model, with four different levels: the individual level, the

Table 1 Descriptive analyses

	Men		Women	
	Range	N (%) Mean (Std. Dev.)	Range	N (%) Mean (Std. Dev.)
Individual				
Dependent				
Partner choice				
Partner migration	0/1	6949 (54.5%)	0/1	6138 (51.3%)
Local intra-ethnic	0/1	5807 (45.5%)	0/1	5829 (48.7%)
Time				
Partnership year	1 - 8	4.548 (2.258)	1 - 8	4.643 (2.277)
Generation				
First	0/1	2877 (22.6%)	0/1	1332 (11.1%)
1.5	0/1	1102 (8.6%)	0/1	774 (6.5%)
Second	0/1	8771 (68.8%)	0/1	9856 (82.4%)
Birth cohort	2 - 19	14.821 (1.989)	7 - 20	16.507 (1.661)
Age	17 - 71	28.089 (5.564)	14 - 55	23.101 (4.553)
Contextual				
Community size	11-54991	26584.912 (19334.614)	11-54991	25223.179 (19299.673)
Sex ratio	58.335-188.889	102.453 (15.935)	57.709-172.350	103.047 (16.300)
Control				
District size	41103-1048491	812148.331 (289152.300)	41103-1048491	799948.494 (294799.136)
Diversity level	0.555-0.988	0.722 (0.162)	0.555-0.986	0.734 (0.164)

birth cohort, the district, and the year of the partnership (=period). To properly estimate the age and period effects we use informative Bayesian priors on birth cohort and presume no effect (Bell & Jones, 2014, 2015).

The *individual level* is the level of the individual partner choices. Furthermore, each *birth cohort* spans a three-year interval. With a range from 1934 until 1992, this provides us 20 potential birth cohorts of which 19 are used. Moroccan migrants within our dataset live in 41 *districts*. There are 43 Belgian districts in total, which constitute the administrative level between municipalities and provinces in Belgium. The metric variable *partnership year* is based on the year when the partnership was formalized into a marriage or a legal cohabitation. It allows us to assess the overall evolution for the whole Moroccan community independently of changes within subgroups, such as generations. We choose the first possible partnership year (2001) as the reference point to which the other partnership years are compared.

Because we only have information on partnerships established between 2001 and 2008, we have to cluster these 8 *partnership years* within districts to enlarge the sample size of partnership years to 267 units (Stegmueller, 2013). This enables us to assess (1) the variation of effects through time within a certain district and (longitudinal); and (2) to examine differences between districts, irrespective of temporal variations (cross-sectional) (Fairbrother, 2013). This construction assumes that changes through time are happening within districts. Because of the geographical clustering of Moroccan communities, we assume this construction to be legitimate (Surkyn & Reniers, 1997; Reniers, 1999). The final construction of the resulting cross-classified design of our multilevel model can be found in figure 1.

We use binary logistic cross-classified multilevel analyses.[1] Table 2 and 3 display the results of these analyses in odds-ratios. In these tables, the choice of partner migration (1) is compared to the choice of a local co-ethnic (0). To interpret the effects of the sex ratios, separate analyses were performed for men and women. Four models were obtained. First, the null-model tested the different levels of our model (individual level, partnership year, birth cohort, and district). Furthermore, the first model includes the individual time variables (partnership year, generation, birth cohort and age at partnership) at the individual level that makes the birth cohort both a level in our model and a variable at the individual level. The second model adds an interaction effect between partnership year and generation. The third and final model ads the longitudinal as well as the cross-

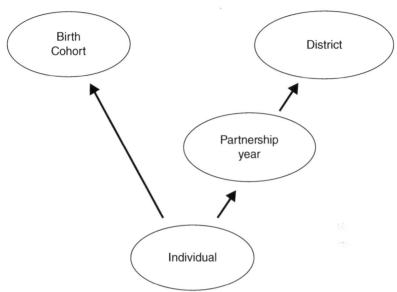

Figure 1: Cross-classified multilevel design.

sectional higher level variables and controls the district size and the diversity level.

The district size reflects the total numbers of inhabitants of a district. Because larger districts often have larger ethnic communities, this variable controls this effect. This is the only contextual variable without a longitudinal component, as district sizes are less likely to fluctuate heavily, especially within such a short period of time (2001-2008). The second control variable, the degree of diversity within a district, is conceptualized in terms of nationality and was calculated using the Herfindahl index. When applied to diversity, this index measures the sum of quadrats of the percentages of all nationalities residing in every district. A higher degree reflects a more homogeneous ethnic composition in a district, which in these data most likely indicates a district that largely consists of ethnic Belgians.

The cross-sectional effects of the community size, the level of diversity and the sex ratio as well as the district size were transformed with their natural logarithm to correct for skewness.

We calculated the Intraclass Correlation Coefficients on the basis of the higher level variance found in table 2 and 3, to assess how much of the total variance each level accounts for.[2] Within the male Moroccan group, the higher levels explain 31.39% of the total variance (birth cohorts: 23.94%, districts: 6.30%, and

Table 2 Results of longitudinal cross-classified multilevel analyses of choosing partner migration (1) vs. a local co-ethnic partner (0) for men

	Null model		Model 1		Model 2		Model 3	
	Coef.	Std. Error	Coef.	Std. Error	Coef.	Std. Error	Coef.	Std. Error
Intercept	4.693***	(0.276)	1388.529***	(1.079)	447.197***	(0.713)	248699.346***	(0.657)
Individual								
Time								
Partnership year			0.901***	(0.024)	0.877***	(0.019)	0.878***	(0.020)
Generation								
1.5 Generation			1.511***	(0.074)	1.267*	(0.127)	1.281*	(0.123)
First generation			0.861**	(0.049)	0.518***	(0.092)	0.518***	(0.089)
Birth cohort[a]			1.000	(0.001)	1.000	(0.001)	1.000	(0.001)
Age partnership			0.557***	(0.062)	0.662***	(0.076)	0.663***	(0.020)
Age partnership^2			1.011***	(0.001)	1.008***	(0.001)	1.007***	(0.001)
Interaction with								
Partnership year								
1.5 Generation					1.050	(0.032)	1.048	(0.031)
First generation					1.154***	(0.022)	1.153***	(0.021)
Contextual								
District								
Community size							0.825*	(0.076)
Sex ratio							0.351***	(0.165)

Partnership year (PY)								
Community size							1.000	(0.001)
Sex ratio							0.998	(0.002)
Control								
District size							1.037	(0.074)
Diversity (district)							0.802	(0.851)
Diversity (PY)							17.814	(3.517)
Variance								
Birth cohort	1.148	(0.596)	17.108	(9.353)	4.148	(6.245)	0.139	(0.265)
District	0.302	(0.117)	0.328	(0.120)	0.331	(0.126)	0.238	(0.093)
Partnership year	0.055	(0.021)	0.007	(0.006)	0.008	(0.008)	0.004	(0.004)
DIC	16725.380		16495.969		16500.016		16511.005	

*p < .05; **p < .01; ***p < .001; Final model: $N_{individual} = 12,750$; $N_{birthcohort} = 18$; $N_{district} = 40$; $N_{partnershipyear} = 255$

[a]Informative prior, mean: 1.000, standard deviation: .001

Table 3   Results of longitudinal cross-classified multilevel analyses of choosing partner migration (1) vs. a local co-ethnic partner (o) for women

	Null model		Model 1		Model 2		Model 3	
	Coef.	Std. Error	Coef.	Std. Error	Coef.	Std. Error	Coef.	Std. Error
Intercept	2.018**	(0.234)	15568.423***	(0.699)	10331.988***	(0.653)	318379,708***	(1.856)
Individual								
Time								
Partnership year			0.939***	(0.016)	0.915***	(0.016)	0.904***	(0.020)
Generation								
1.5 Generation			1.970***	(0.084)	1.806***	(0.170)	1.800***	(0.167)
First generation			1.616***	(0.064)	0.782	(0.135)	0.776	(0.131)
Birth cohort[a]			1.000	(0.001)	1.000	(0.001)	1.000	(0.001)
Age partnership			0.516***	(0.053)	0.537***	(0.047)	0.542***	(0.050)
Age partnership^2			1.011***	(0.001)	1.010***	(0.001)	1.010***	(0.001)
Interaction with_								
Partnership year								
1.5 Generation					1.024	(0.038)	1.024	(0.037)
First generation					1.201***	(0.030)	1.202***	(0.029)
Contextual								
District								
Community size							1.021	(0.062)
Sex ratio							0.892	(0.352)

	Model 1	Model 2	Model 3	Model 4
Partnership year (PY)				
Community size				1.000 (0.001)
Sex ratio				1.000 (0.002)
Control				
District size				0.784* (0.099)
Diversity level (district)				1.519 (0.770)
Diversity level (PY)				1.317 (3.607)
Variance				
Birth cohort	0.473 (0.277)	0.053 (0.096)	0.043 (0.068)	0.038 (0.052)
District	0.237 (0.107)	0.240 (0.097)	0.234 (0.094)	0.195 (0.089)
Partnership year	0.208 (0.050)	0.006 (0.006)	0.005 (0.005)	0.005 (0.004)
DIC	15952.409	15599.966	15564.207	15567.538

*p < .05; **p < .01; ***p < .001; Final model: $N_{individual}$ = 11,962; $N_{birthcohort}$ = 14; $N_{district}$ = 38; $N_{partnershipyear}$ = 231

a Informative prior, mean: 1.000, standard deviation: .001

partnership years: 1.15%). Within the female group, this is 21.82% of the total variance (birth cohorts: 11.24%, districts: 5.63%, and partnership years: 4.94%). This highlights the importance of including higher level measures to explain partner choices among residents of Moroccan origin in Belgium.

Individual level time trends

Generally, people prefer certain characteristics in potential partners and are searching a partner who resembles them (McPherson, Smith-Lovin, & Cook, 2001). This mostly applies to similarities in age, socio-economic status, and the cultural background. Cultural similarities are often associated with a certain ethnic background, which could explain the strong preference for ethnically similar partners. This part discusses several time trends situated on the individual (or micro) level, namely: period effects, intergenerational changes, and age effects that could influence individual preferences.

Period effects

Recent quantitative and qualitative research in Belgium note a declining preference for a partner from the country of origin within the Turkish migrant group (Van Kerckem et al., 2013). The most often cited rationales are the risk perception and problem awareness related to partner migration, a higher acceptance of premarital relationships with local co-ethnics, and a declining parental involvement. Descriptive analyses (not shown) reveal that also within the Moroccan group there is a more general decline in partner migration, as its prevalence was notably higher in 2001 (around 59%) compared to 2008 (around 45%).

However partner migration was and still is the dominant partner choice, even within the second generation (Timmerman, 2008; Van Kerckem et al., 2013). Descriptive analyses (table 1) show that for first partner choices, the prevalence of partner migration is 54,5% for women and 51,3% for men. This dominance can partially be explained by the unpopularity of local partners. Youngsters from the second generation in Belgium often have a bad reputation within Belgian communities and are considered 'too western' and therefore unsuitable future partners (Timmerman, 2008). Potential mates from the country of origin, in contrast, are perceived as better partners. Most of the youngsters furthermore believe that the advantages of partner migration outweigh the disadvantages, such as dependency of the migrating partner (Teule, Vanderwaeren, & Mbah-Fongkimeh, 2012; van Kerckem et al., 2013). Men could prefer a woman from their country of origin because of her supposedly subordinated position, especially in comparison with the more emancipated women in Belgium (Beck-Gernsheim, 2007; Lievens, 1997). Women on the other hand could choose a man from their country of origin. This offers freedom and autonomy since she knows the language, customs, and traditions.

We find partial support for this declining preference for partner migration. The odds ratios indicate a negative correlation between the partnership year and the choice of partner migration (table 2 and 3). This finding reflects a pronounced overall period effect: more recently formed couples opt less for partner migration and more for a local partner.

Migrant generation

Generational differences can be understood from the combined perspective of the socialization and the assimilation theory. These two theories state that a longer socialization period in the country of destination is coupled to a more engrained integration (Alba & Nee, 1997; Lievens, 1997). The first generation in our dataset (migrated above the age of 16) consists predominantly of students, people who migrated because of humanitarian reasons, and presumably a few early labor migrants (Myria, 2015). Since we only include first partnerships, migrated wedding partners are excluded. Despite the diversity within the first generation, they all have been primarily socialized within Morocco, making the socialization and assimilation theory also applicable. The 1.5 generation migrated between 6 and 15 years old and the second generation migrated before the age of 6, or was born in Belgium.

Following the socialization and assimilation theory, we expect that further generations will behave less in line with the values in Morocco and more in line with the prevailing values in Belgium (Lievens, 1997). This could impact the partner choice as well as the possibilities and opportunities of finding an eligible partner (Carol et al., 2014). Overall, second generation migrants could be more assimilated because they grew up and went to school in Belgium, and acquired the language. Furthermore, we can assume that the ties between the migrant and the country of origin are growing weaker with the following generations (Surkyn & Reniers, 1997). We therefore expect that the second generation has a lower likelihood of choosing partner migration compared to the 1.5 and first generation.

Our analyses, which compare the 1.5 and first generations to the second generation group, reveal an important gender difference. The 1.5 generation and women from the first generation opt more for partner migration than those from the second generation as was expected (table 2 and 3). Men from the first generation however are more likely to choose a local partner compared to the second generation. In other words, Moroccans who grew up in Morocco tend to marry a Belgian Moroccan, while the next generation, i.e. Moroccans who were born in Belgium, are keen on marrying a wife migrated from Morocco.

Another conclusion is that this trend is weakening over time for all generations. Our results indeed indicate that the inclusion of the interaction effect eliminates the gender difference and nuances our findings (table 2 and 3). In 2001, all Moroccan migrants from the 1.5 generation have a higher likelihood of choosing partner migration compared to the second generation while the likelihood is lower for first generation men (women: not significant). However, from 2001 until 2008, the likelihood of partner migration is rising for the whole first generation while the likelihood within the second generation declines.

Age at the establishment of the partnership

Age has been associated with '(…) changes, accumulation of social experiences and/or role- or status changes' (Yang & Land, 2006, p.76). Age at partnership is sometimes conceptualised as a proxy for the parental influence on the partner choice (Lievens, 1997). Parents often desire a partner with the same ethnic origin, preferably form the country of origin for their children (Lievens, 1997). Therefore, a greater parental influence can accompany a higher likelihood of marrying a partner from the country of origin. However, this influence weakens as children grow older and become more independent (van Zantvliet, Kalmijn, & Verbakel, 2014). Other studies in various countries have reported a higher likelihood of mixed partnerships, and therefore a lower likelihood of partner migration at a higher marriage age, as well as a declining social support for marriage migration over time (Kalter & Schroedter, 2010).

In our analyses, we conceptualize the correlation between the age at the partnership and the partner choice as curvilinear (figure 2). The graph shows a decline that commences from the youngest persons, until those who are approximately 47 years old at the partnership. From then onwards the line rises again. However, the group of Moroccan migrants above 47 years does not comprise even 1 percentage of the whole group. As expected, we can conclude that for almost all Moroccan migrants, the likelihood of partner migration is declining with age.

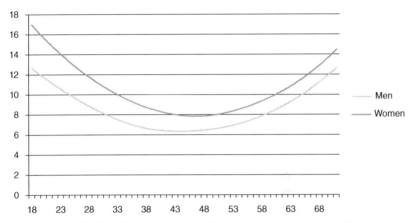

Figure 2: Predicted likelihood (intercept + effect) of choosing partner migration for all ages, by sex

Contextual effects

The partner choice among residents of Moroccan origin may also be affected by structural conditions, such as the community size and the sex ratio in a district. To fully grasp them, we depart from Blau's opportunity theory (1977, 1994), which states that structural conditions at the macro level within a specific context regulate the relationships between groups and persons within that context. These structures could explain partner choices that seemingly contradict individual interests and preferences (Blau, 1994). The marriage market and its contact opportunities and constraints are shaped by structural conditions (Kalmijn, 1998).

All of our contextual variables are based on data derived from Statistics Belgium (n.d.) and have both a longitudinal (evolution from 2001–2008 within a district) and a cross-sectional (district average) component. We refer to Fairbrother (2013) for the method of calculating both components. We believe that the district is an acceptable representation of the marriage market, since approximately 80% of all partnerships are formed with a partner living within the same district (analyses not shown).

Community size

Contacts with other ethnic groups decline when the size of the own group increases (Blau, 1994). When a Moroccan community expands in a given district, the opportunities increase to meet a Moroccan partner within that local community (Teule et al., 2012). Logically, when there are more potential partners available, the likelihood of meeting a partner and cohabiting or marrying increases. We expect a community size to be an important and relevant factor, as the Moroccan community is still expanding due to the on-going migration inflow (Schoonvaere, 2014).

We conceptualize the community size as the size of the Moroccan community in a certain district. We investigated whether the likelihood of choosing partner migration is indeed lower within larger communities (cross-sectional), and whether a growing Moroccan community is accompanied by a declining likelihood of partner migration (longitudinal). Our results however show that only for men the likelihood of choosing a local partner is higher when communities are larger (table 2 and 3).

Sex ratio

A shortage of men or women with the same ethnic background in a given district forces people to adapt their partner choices (Blau, 1994; McPherson et al., 2001). Partners have to then be found outside a local ethnic community (Kalmijn & van Tubergen, 2006). Furthermore, the balance of men and women is contingent on the phase of migration and usually goes from an unbalanced to a balanced situation (Castles & Miller, 2003), which is also the case within the Belgian context (Schoonvaere, 2014).

Within our analyses, we conceptualized the sex ratio as the number of Moroccan women per 100 men in a district. We only considered opposite sex partnerships because of the low prevalence of same sex partnerships (0.02%). Our analyses reveal that only men choose a partner from Morocco when there is a shortage of women (table 2 and 3). Women on the other hand do not prefer a partner from Morocco when men are lacking within their district.

Conclusion and discussion

This paper investigates the intra-ethnic partner choices in Belgium among residents of Moroccan origin with a focus on time as well as contextual influences. Time variables include partnership year, generation and the age at partnership. Contextual influences include: the sex ratio and the size of the Moroccan community. We used an extraction of the Belgian national register, of which 24,712 partner choices of residents of Moroccan origin were retained in our final analyses. All migrants in our analyses were nested in 19 birth cohorts, 267 partnership years (nested in districts), and 41 Belgian districts.

Partner migration loses importance for the whole Moroccan group in Belgium. This decrease could be attributed to potential risks and uncertainties that can accompany the choice of partner migration. Risks and uncertainties include important cultural differences (Eeckhaut et al., 2011; Surkyn & Reniers, 1997), economic dependency, and the limited amount of time the partners get to know each other before the formal establishment (Van Kerckem et al., 2013). This decline remains prominent after controlling classical assimilation effects and contextual influences even though these also have an effect on the partner choices of Moroccan migrants.

First, we note some important generational differences. The 1.5 and female first generation prefer partner migration more than the second generation. This is in line with the socialization and assimilation theory that states that a longer socialization period in the country of destination is coupled to a more engrained integration (Alba & Nee, 1997; Lievens, 1997). However, first generation men have a higher likelihood of choosing a local partner compared to the second generation. The explanation for this finding may lie in the diversity within the first generation, consisting predominantly of the early labor migrants, students and people who migrated for humanitarian reasons (Myria, 2015). Our descriptives indicate that the male first generation is twice as big as the female one (approx. 23% vs. 11%). Men may be more likely to migrate because of humanitarian reasons or arrive here as students, which may account for this difference in size. To obtain permanent residence, these groups have to marry locally, which results in a higher likelihood of choosing a local partner for Moroccan men.

The inclusion of the interaction effect eliminates the gender difference and nuances these findings. The likelihood within the second generation to choose partner migration declines over time, whereas the likelihood rises within the first generation. Since the second generation is by far the largest group (men: 68%, women: 82%), it is especially this group that accounts for the declining importance of partner migration.

Furthermore, our results show a declining preference for a partner from Morocco when migrants are older. This could indicate a parental influence on the partner choice, as parents generally prefer a partner with the same ethnic background and from the country of origin (Lievens, 1997). As children grow older, the parental influence is likely to weaken (van Zantvliet et al., 2014).

In addition to these evolutions through time, the place of residence influences the partner choice of men since it can limit the chances of finding a potential partner (Blau, 1994; Kalmijn, 1998). Residing within larger communities enhances the likelihood of finding a local partner. Moreover, a shortage of local Moroccan women stimulates men to choose a partner from Morocco.

In April 2011, the Belgian government severely tightened the conditions for partner migration (Lievens, Van de Putte, Van der Bracht, & Caestecker, 2013). Since then, it tries to strictly regulate partner migration, influencing the partner choice among all non-European country nationals and Belgians (Carol, Ersanili, & Wagner, 2014). Yet, a declining trend was already present before 2011 within the Moroccan migrant group. This decline is happening in addition to generational changes and ageing processes. Therefore, more recent generations who grow older could be the catalysts for change. Even though an important shift between age groups and generations exists, at the same time a more general shift towards a more local partner choice is occurring within the whole Moroccan community in Belgium. This decline remains unaffected after accounting for structural conditions.

Notes

1 Our models are estimated by applying Markov Chain Monte Carlo (MCMC) estimation procedures using MLwiN 2.24 and were first fitted using MQL1 estimation procedures before applying MCMC procedures.

2 The variance at the individual level was fixed at $\pi^2/3$ because of the nature of logistic models.

Bibliography

Alba, E. & Nee, V. (1997). Rethinking assimilation theory for a new era of immigration. *International Migration Review* 31(4), 338-351

Beck-Gernsheim, E. (2007). Transnational lives, transnational marriages: A review of the evidence from migrant communities in Europe. *Global Networks* 7, 271-288.

Bell, A., & Jones, K. (2014). Another 'futile quest'? A simulation study of Yang and Land's Hierarchical Age-Period-Cohort model. *Demographic research*, 30(11), 333-360.

Bell, A., & Jones, K. (2015). Bayesian informative priors with Yang and Land's hierarchical age–period–cohort model. *Quality & Quantity* 49(1) 255-266.

Blau, P. M. (1994). *Structural context of opportunities*. Chicago: University of Chicago Press.

Carol, S., Ersanilli, E., & Wagner, M. (2014). Spousal choice among the children of Turkish and Moroccan immigrants in six European countries: Transnational spouse or co-ethnic migrant? *International Migration Review*, 48(2), 387-414.

Castles, S., & Miller, M. J., (2003). *The age of migration. International population movements in the modern world*. New York: Guilford Publications.

Eeckhaut, M., Lievens, J., Van de Putte, B., & Lusyne, P. (2011). Partner selection and divorce in ethnic minorities: Distinguishing between two types of ethnic homogamous marriages. *International Migration Review* 45, 269-296.

Fairbrother, M. (2013). Two multilevel modeling techniques for analyzing comparative longitudinal survey datasets. Geraadpleegd op http://seis.bris.ac.uk/~ggmhf.

Kalmijn, M. (1998). Intermarriage and homogamy: Causes, patterns, and trends. *Annual Review of Sociology* 24, 395-421.

Kalmijn, M. & van Tubergen, F. (2006). Ethnic intermarriage in the Netherlands: confirmations and refutations of accepted insights. *European Journal of Population/Revue europeenne de demographie* 22, 371-397.

Kalter, F., and Schroedter, J.H. (2010) Transnational marriage among former labour migrants in Germany. *Zeitschrift fur Familienforschung* 22 (1), 11-36.

Lichter, D., Carmalt, J., & Qian, Z. (2011). Immigration and intermarriage among Hispanics: Crossing racial and generational boundaries. *Sociological Forum* 26, 241-264.

Lievens, J. (1997). Kenmerken van gezinsvormende migratie. In Lesthaeghe, R. (ed.), *Diversiteit in sociale verandering: Turkse en Marokkaanse vrouwen in België*. Brussels: VUB Press, 73-104.

Lievens, J., Van de Putte, B., Van der Bracht, K., & Caestecker, F. (2013). Trends in partnerkeuze van eerste en tweedegeneratiemigranten in België: partnerkeuze van personen woonachtig in België met een migratieachtergrond, 2001-2008. Met bijzondere aandacht voor de bevolkingsgroep van Marokkaanse en Turkse herkomst in België.

McPherson, M., Smith-Lovin, L., & Cook, J.M. (2001). Birds of a feather: homophily in social networks. *Annual Review of Sociology*, 27, 415-444.

Myria, Federaal Migratiecentrum (2015). *Migratie in cijfers en in rechten 2015*.

Reniers, G. (1999). On the history and selectivity of Turkish and Moroccan migration to Belgium. *International Migration* 37(4), 679-713.

Schoonvaere, Q. (2014). België-Marokko: 50 jaar migratie. Demografische studie over de populatie van Marokkaanse herkomst in België. Nota. *Federaal Migratie Centrum*

Song, M. (2009). Is intermarriage a good indicator of integration? *Journal of Ethnic and Migration Studies* 35, 331-348.

Statistics Belgium (n.d.). FOD Economie, SPF.

Stegmueller, D. (2013). How many countries for multilevel modeling? A comparison of frequentist and bayesian approaches. *American Journal of Political Science*, 57(3), 748-761.

Surkyn, E., & Reniers, G. (1997). Selecte gezelschappen. Over de migratiegeschiedenis en de interne dynamiek van migratieprocessen. In Lesthaeghe, R. (ed.), *Diversiteit in sociale verandering: Turkse en Marokkaanse vrouwen in België.* Brussels: VUB Press, 41-72.

Teule, J., Vanderwaeren, E., & Mbah-Fongkimeh, A. (2012). *Marriage migration from Emirdağ to Brussels.* King Baudouin Foundation. Geraadpleegd op http://www.kbs-frb.be

Timmerman, C. (2008). Marriage in a 'culture of migration'. Emirdag Marrying into Flanders. *European Review* 16(04), 585-594.

Timmerman, C., Vanderwaeren, E., & Crul, M. (2003). The second generation in Belgium. The *International Migration Review* 37(4), 1065-1090.

Van Kerckem, K., Van der Bracht, K., Stevens, P. A. J., & Van de Putte, B. (2013). Transnational marriages on the decline: Explaining changing trends in partner choice among Turkish Belgians. *International Migration Review* 47(4), 1006-1038.

van Zantvliet, P. I., Kalmijn, M., & Verbakel, E. (2014). Parental involvement in partner choice: The case of Turks and Moroccans in the Netherlands. *European Sociological Review*, 30(3), 387-398.

Waters, M. C. & Jiménez, T. R. (2005). Assessing immigrant assimilation: New empirical and theoretical challenges. *Annual Review of Sociology* 31, 105-125.

Yang, Y., & Land, K. C. (2006). A mixed models approach to the age-period-cohort analysis of repeated cross-section surveys, with an application to data on trends in verbal test scores. In R. M. Stolzenberg (ed.), *Sociological Methodology* 36, 75-97. Malden: Wiley-Blackwell.

6. Household division of labor and family formation among Moroccan couples at the turn of the 21st Century

Jonas Wood[1], Layla Van den Berg & Karel Neels

Introduction

The second half of the 20th century in Europe was characterized by substantial changes with respect to households' organization of economic activity and childrearing. Whereas the prevalence of the male breadwinner model in Europe peaked during the 1950s and early 1960s (Cooke & Baxter, 2010), more recent decades are characterized by increasing female labor force participation. Amongst other factors, higher female educational attainment and rising earning potential, the expansion of the service sector, and the stagnation or decline of real wages are each responsible for this rise in women's economic activity. In addition, the expansion of work-family reconciliation policies such as subsidized childcare, and outsourcing policies such as service vouchers have facilitated the combination of childrearing and economic activity, particularly for women. Belgium is a vanguard country in this respect as it is characterized by a long history of reconciliation policies. It is, alongside France and Scandinavian countries, regarded as a society in which work and family are relatively compatible (Gornick, Meyers, & Ross, 1997). Since the 1970s formal childcare has been continuously extended, and as a result Belgium is included in a short list of countries that meet the Barcelona target of 33 per cent childcare enrolment for children aged 0-3 (Population Council, 2006). In addition, Belgium is also a forerunner with respect to the subsidized outsourcing of household work (e.g. service vouchers) (Raz-Yurovich, 2014). Couples increasingly use the strategy of outsourcing household work and childrearing tasks in order to combine the dual earner model with childrearing in Belgium.

Since the increased labor force participation of women during the second half of the 20th century coincided with the postponement of motherhood and the decline of fertility levels in Europe, most scholars in the 1980s associated declining fertility with rises in women's labor force participation. Whereas economists explained the negative relation between female labor force participation and fertility with enhanced opportunity costs of non-market activities (Becker, 1981), sociologists related declining birth hazards with women's increasing economic autonomy, rising individualism, and the increased quest for self-realization (Lesthaeghe & Van de Kaa, 1986). However, recent evidence indicates a turnaround in the relation between women's economic position and fertility. At the macro level, the cross-country correlation between female labor force participation and fertility has turned positive since the mid-1980s (Ahn & Mira, 2002). At the micro level, recent research increasingly opposes the assumption of a negative relation between women's socio-economic position and childbearing (Matysiak & Vignoli, 2008; Wood & Neels, 2016). Hence both male and female labor force participation have increasingly become a prerequisite to childbearing, in countries supporting work-family combination such as Belgium.

In comparison to the wealth of research that studies the interrelation of work and family transitions for the general population, our understanding of migrant households' labor force participation in relation to childbearing decisions remains limited (Andersson & Scott, 2007; Lundström & Andersson, 2012). This gap in knowledge is remarkable given that migrant groups – especially those with a non-European background – in Western European countries are found to witness fewer labor market opportunities (Corluy, 2014) and also potentially exhibit different preferences with respect to work-family combination compared to majority populations (Bernhardt, Goldscheider, & Goldscheider, 2007; Idema & Phalet, 2007). As a result of these differential opportunities and attitudes, one would expect migrant groups to exhibit different household employment and fertility dynamics. This chapter addresses this issue by comparing Belgian couples to couples in which at least one partner has a Moroccan background with respect to their economic activity and the transition to parenthood. The Moroccan minority population constitutes the largest non-European migrant group in Belgium.

Besides studying the employment-fertility link for a group that has hitherto not received much attention, this study is also innovative as it adopts a couple perspective (Matysiak & Vignoli, 2008). In contrast to previous research on work-family dynamics for migrant groups based on individual-level data (Andersson & Scott, 2007), the use of couple data allows for a more comprehensive study of how work and family are related at the couple-level. A couple approach is required particularly in the study of migrants' fertility and labor market activity, as the ethnic composition of couples exhibits strong variability. Available literature shows that besides partnerships between two Moroccan individuals, mixed partnerships between a Belgian and a Moroccan person increasingly occur. In addition, considerable numbers of second generation Moroccans partner with a first generation Moroccan instead of a second generation peer. Although the dynamics of partner choice among migrant groups have been studied (Gonzalez-Ferrer, 2006; Lievens, 1999) and are also discussed in this volume, the subsequent effect on breadwinner models and fertility outcomes remains largely unknown.

Background

Migrant groups and breadwinner models

Due to the fact that migration from Morocco started in the post-WWII period, large groups of descendants of these first generation Moroccan immigrants currently reside in Belgium. As a result of varying partner choices among migrants' descendants (Lievens, 1999), strong variation in the ethnic composition of couples occurs. Previous research for Flanders for instance (Corijn & Lodewijckx, 2009) indicates that large proportions (around 40 per cent among men and more than 50 per cent among women) of second generation Moroccans choose to partner with a Moroccan resident. In addition, among second generation Moroccan men there is also a considerable proportion that partners with someone with a non-Moroccan background (mostly Belgian). This chapter compares Belgian couples (two partners of Belgian origin) to mixed Belgian-Moroccan couples and ethnically homogenous Moroccan couples. With respect to ethnically homogenous migrant couples, we also consider heterogeneity in terms of generation. Moroccan migrant groups are expected to differ considerably with respect to household breadwinner models due to differences in labor market opportunities and attitudes toward gender roles.

With respect to varying labor market opportunities, available literature shows that the Moroccan minority group in Belgium exhibits lower levels of educational attainment. In addition, this group also witnesses fewer opportunities in the labor market regardless of educational attainment and is more likely to seek employment in lower wage sectors (Corluy, 2014; Neels & Stoop, 2000). Compared to first generation migrants, their descendants have been found to exhibit educational and employment patterns more similar to the majority population. However, regardless of whether generation is taken into account, non-European minority groups consistently display educational and employment disadvantages in Belgium (Phalet, 2007; Timmerman, Vanderwaeren, & Crul, 2003). One of the reasons suggested in the literature is that foreign origin groups, such as Moroccan minorities, are discriminated in recruitment procedures (Smeesters, Nayer, Saddouk, & Schingtienne, 1997; Van den Cruyce, 2000). First generation migrants can experience additional disadvantages due to a lack of country-specific human capital, which may impede their chances of socio-economic integration in the host country. Compared to first generation migrants, second and higher generations are more likely to be fluent in the host country's language, have attended school in the host country, and are more likely to have contact with natives (Gonzalez-Ferrer, 2006). In addition, migrants' employment opportunities are more strongly determined by their social network (Bernhardt et al., 2007). Given the fact that post-WWII labor migrants and their descendants have been typically employed in male-dominated secondary sectors of the economy, relying on social networks in order to achieve employment can be easier for men than for women (Surkyn & Reniers, 1997).

With respect to attitudes toward household gender roles, own calculations on Generations and Gender Survey data (see appendix) for Belgium indicate that especially first generation Moroccan migrant groups exhibit less favourable attitudes toward female labor force participation and more strongly emphasize women's role of childrearing. The results for second generation Moroccans suggest attitudes more similar to those of Belgians, though findings are mixed. Yet, a study by De Valk (2008) conducted in The Netherlands indicates that the attitudes toward breadwinner models of second generation Moroccan adolescents are gendered. Whereas the attitudes toward female labor force participation of female second generation adolescents are fairly similar to Dutch natives, male Moroccan adolescents have a stronger preference for a traditional male breadwinner household.

Different attitudes between the majority population and especially first generation Moroccans can be related to the context of the origin country and to selective migration mechanisms. First, Morocco shows a cultural and institutional climate that is geared towards the male breadwinner model. Although one may argue that migrants' descendants have little or no first-hand experience with the culture of the origin country, it is likely that parental attitudes and family networks will act as a source of origin-specific values for these groups (Idema & Phalet, 2007; Marks, Chun Bun, & McHale, 2009). Second, selective migration mechanisms are also assumed to entail different attitudes among migrant groups in Belgium. While Moroccan immigration was fairly heterogeneous, a large proportion of Moroccan guest workers was predominantly recruited from low-educated rural areas (Reniers, 1999). To the extent that low education is related to more traditional gender roles (Marks et al., 2009), this may have affected the cultural norms of the resulting Moroccan population in Belgium. In addition, we note that as male migration was intrinsically intertwined with labor market participation, the group of male migrants in Belgium is likely to highly emphasize the male role of providing for the family. After the migration stop in 1974, family reunion was the only legal ground to enter the country for non-European migrants (Reniers, 1999; Surkyn & Reniers, 1997). As a result the migration flows of Moroccan women in the context of family reunification were, in contrast to male guest workers, to a lesser extent associated to employment opportunities. This selection of migrants and its potential influences on their descendants (Idema & Phalet, 2007; Marks et al., 2009) may entail particular favourable attitudes toward the male breadwinner model.

With respect to second generation migrants in particular, the occurrence of mixed-origin couples may reflect a weakening of the boundaries between migrant and native origin groups (Coleman, 1994) and it is expected that these couples will exhibit household breadwinner models more similar to Belgian couples. Similarly, second generation migrants' choice to partner with a second rather than a first generation migrant may be interpreted as a stronger degree of assimilation to the home country. However, with respect to second generation Moroccans partnering with first generation co-ethnics, previous research (Lievens, 1999) indicates that whereas second or higher generation Moroccan male migrants are found to argue that women from their origin group are too modern, second generation Moroccan female migrants mention that men in their origin group are too traditional.

As a result of the aforementioned differences in opportunities and preferences we expect that Moroccan minority groups in Belgium will deviate from the dominance of the dual earner model for majority groups. Due to fewer labor market opportunities, the proportion of households with no breadwinner is assumed to be larger for Moroccan couples. We also expect a greater share of male breadwinner households among Moroccan couples due to lower opportunities for migrant women and relatively unfavourable attitudes toward female labor force participation, especially among the first generation. Whether Moroccan couples will exhibit lower or higher shares of female breadwinner models compared to Belgian couples is unclear. Whereas less favourable attitudes toward female employment may yield fewer female breadwinner households, weak labor market prospects among men may strengthen the economic necessity of the female breadwinner model.

In addition, we also expect differences within the Moroccan population. Since second generation Moroccans possess a higher degree of country-specific human capital compared to marriage migrants, and are influenced by the majority population's attitudes, we expect couples consisting of two second generation migrants to be more similar to Belgian couples with respect to household labor force participation. Since earlier research has pointed out that motives for marrying a partner from the origin country are gendered (Lievens, 1999), we expect couples consisting of a female Moroccan descendant and a first generation Moroccan man to exhibit breadwinner models more similar to the majority population. For couples consisting of a first generation Moroccan woman and a second generation Moroccan man the contrary is expected.

Transition to parenthood

The question of how different breadwinner models relate to family formation yields various responses depending on the theoretical assumptions made and on the context considered. In the 1980s, many scholars associated declining fertility with rises in women's labor force participation. Whereas the second demographic transition theory relates women's rising economic autonomy to declining birth hazards through changing values and the increased quest for self-realization (Lesthaeghe & Van de Kaa, 1986), Becker's new home economics (1981) explain the negative relation between female labor force participation and fertility with enhanced opportunity costs. Hence, both theories assume that the male breadwinner model is best suited for childbearing (Matysiak & Vignoli, 2008).

However increased work-family compatibility, higher contributions of men to childcare and lowering real wages in Western Europe cast doubt on this assumption. First, many Western European countries have extended reconciliation policies that enhance work-family compatibility. Belgium is a forerunner with respect to formal childcare arrangements (Population Council, 2006) and the subsidized outsourcing of household work (e.g. service vouchers) (Raz-Yurovich, 2014). Second, contemporary evidence indicates that men's contribution to childcare and housework has increased in recent decades (Sullivan, Billari, & Altintas, 2014) and that these changes associate positively with female employment and fertility (Goldscheider, Bernhardt, & Branden, 2013; Torr & Short, 2004). Third, real wages have stagnated or declined and labor market uncertainty has increased, especially for men (Oppenheimer, 1994; Verick, 2009). In a context with high labor market uncertainty and low real wages, strong reliance on the male-breadwinner model may be a particularly risky and inflexible household strategy (Oppenheimer, 1997). In line with these contextual changes in Western Europe, recent findings increasingly reject the assumption that female employment yields lower fertility (Matysiak & Vignoli, 2008).

This chapter assumes a positive association between the dual breadwinner model and the transition to parenthood. However, the effect of breadwinner models on the transition to parenthood is likely to differ for Moroccan origin groups due to aforementioned differences in opportunities and attitudes. With respect to Belgian couples, we expect that the dual breadwinner model is positively associated with having a first child. From an economic point of view, this breadwinner model lowers income uncertainty whereas opportunity costs are limited due to the high availability of reconciliation policies. In addition, the dual breadwinner model conforms to prevalent attitudes and norms for this group. For Moroccan groups the relation between household breadwinner models and first births is expected to deviate from the pattern of the majority population. Given the aforementioned lower wage potentials, the cost of outsourcing childrearing and household tasks may approximate or exceed the additional household income related to labor force participation and as a result the dual breadwinner model may not be the economically most attractive model for family formation. Being uninformed on the use and availability of reconciliation strategies may also prevent Moroccan couples from choosing to combine labor force participation and parenthood (Keuzenkamp & Merens, 2006). In addition, in the occurrence of limited labor market opportunities, individuals are expected to emphasize other roles such as being a caregiver (Friedman, Hechter, & Kanazawa, 1994). Hence it is more likely that one of both partners will take responsibility for childrearing tasks. Given the relatively favourable attitudes toward female childrearing roles and male provider roles, especially among Moroccan men, we expect a positive association between the male breadwinner model and the transition to parenthood among Moroccan minority groups. The female breadwinner model, on the contrary, is expected to be perceived as an unsatisfactory household situation for the transition to parenthood. This expectation is in line with previous literature that shows that men with conservative gender attitudes are more likely to display low well-being and low relationship quality when being part of a female breadwinner household (Coughlin & Wade, 2012; Vitali & Arpino, 2015). Similarly to the majority population, the occurrence of a household without a breadwinner is assumed to be perceived as an unfavourable situation for childbearing. However, as both first and second generation migrant groups structurally face stronger limitations in the labor market, these groups may adapt to these lower labor market opportunities. To the extent that limited opportunities in the labor market entail more emphasis on alternative roles (Friedman et al., 1994), the negative impact of having no breadwinner in the household may be more limited for Moroccan minority groups.

Data and methods

Data

This study draws on the 2001 Belgian census data[2] combined with birth registrations from 2002 to 2005. The 2001 Belgian census provides detailed information of all individuals legally residing in the country, including fertility histories, employment status, education, nationality, and marital status. At the household level, the 2001 census contains detailed information on household composition (Deboosere & Willaert, 2004). The individual microdata from the 2001 census have been linked to data from the National Register, which provides information on changes in household composition in the period 2002-2005. This study adopts a prospective research design to assess whether household breadwinner models in 2001 are differentially related to the transition to a first child in 2002-2005 by the households' ethnic composition. The foremost limitation of the data is that employment status is only known for 2001. Hence employment histories for 2002-2005 are not available. We focus on a total of 176,048 co-residential couples of Belgian, Moroccan, or mixed Belgian-Moroccan origin (574,813 couple-years) consisting of a man and a woman both aged 15-49 and not enrolled in education at the time of the census. In cases where couples divorce or one of the partners dies before a first birth occurs, the data is omitted.

Method

The main independent variable of interest is the household's breadwinner model in 2001. This variable consists of four categories: (I) DBW: dual breadwinner model (both partners participate in the labor force), (II) MBW: male breadwinner model (only the male partner participates in the labor force), (III) FBW: female breadwinner model (only the female partner participates in the labor force) and (IV) NBW: no breadwinner (both partners do not participate in the labor force). To study whether the effect of the household's breadwinner model varies by origin group we include the household's ethnic composition. *Ethnic composition* distinguishes seven types of couples which are labelled as "origin woman_origin man": (I) BEL_BEL: both partners are of Belgian origin, (II) BEL_MOR: Belgian woman and Moroccan man, (III) MOR_BEL: Moroccan woman and Belgian man, (IV) MOR2_MOR2: both partners are second generation Moroccans, (V) MOR2_MOR1: second generation Moroccan woman and first generation Moroccan man and (VI) MOR1_MOR2: first generation Moroccan woman and second generation Moroccan man. Given that origin based on the parents' and the respondents' birth country is not available, origin group is operationalized using both the respondents' birth nationality and their parents' birth nationality. In case both the individual and her/his parents were born with the Belgian nationality, the individual is categorized as Belgian. Individuals born with a foreign nationality are classified as first generation migrants, whereas individuals born as a Belgian citizen, with at least one parent born with a non-Belgian nationality, are identified as second generation migrants.

In addition, we examine a number of other covariates. First, the number of years since the woman's graduation is included as a cubic function. The cubic function – a linear, quadratic and cubic term –captures the fact that first birth probabilities typically increase during the first few years after graduation and decrease more gradually at older ages. This variable is interacted with household educational attainment and household ethnic composition to control for differing first birth schedules. Second, her age at graduation indicates the age of the woman when leaving education. Third, household educational attainment in 2001 distinguishes low education (all levels below higher secondary education) from medium education (higher secondary education) and high education (all post-secondary levels of education) for both partners. All nine couple combinations of educational levels are included in the models. Fourth, marital status in 2001 distinguishes married couples from non-married couples. Finally, the age difference between partners equals the man's age minus the woman's age. Table 1 displays the distribution of couple-years with respect to our (in)dependent variables.

Table 1   Distribution of couple-years over main covariates

	N	%	
Origin			
. BEL_BEL	566,326	98.52	
. BEL_MOR	3,335	0.58	
. MOR_BEL	1,898	0.33	
. MOR2_MOR2	662	0.12	
. MOR2_MOR1	2,079	0.36	
. MOR1_MOR2	513	0.09	
Breadwinner model			
. DBW	495,183	86.15	
. MBW	51,612	8.98	
. FBW	16,993	2.96	
. NBW	11,025	1.92	
Education			
. Low_Low	50,253	8.74	
. Low_Mid	30,553	5.32	
. Low_High	8,332	1.45	
. Mid_Low	57,730	10.04	
. Mid_Mid	116,771	20.31	
. Mid_High	40,278	7.01	
. High_Low	27,940	4.86	
. High_Mid	83,932	14.60	
. High_High	159,024	27.66	
Married			
. No	300,598	52.29	
. Yes	274,215	47.71	
	Mean	**Min**	**Max**
Age at graduation (woman)	19.766	10	47
Age difference	2.028	-29	30

(source: Belgian 2001 census & register data, calculations by authors)

In the descriptive section of this chapter, simple cross tabulation yields an overview of the prevalence of different breadwinner types by ethnic background. In the multivariate analysis, two discrete-time event-history models are estimated. Model 1 assesses the effect of breadwinner models in 2001 on first birth hazards in 2002-2005, whereas model 2 studies the interaction between breadwinner models and household ethnic composition. Given that the impact of labor force participation has been found to vary by level of education (Kreyenfeld & Andersson, 2014), we also include an interaction between breadwinner model and education in both models. This prevents contamination of the origin-specific effects of breadwinner types due to composition effects of educational attainment. Given that the occurrence of a birth is a binary outcome, a logit link function is used. We will present exponentiated parameter estimates that can be interpreted as odds-ratios. The latter represent the ratio between the odds of having a first birth for a certain group compared to the reference group. Hence unity represents no effect, all estimates above unity signal a positive effect, and odds-ratios below one indicate negative effects. The odds are the ratio of the probability that a couple has a first child in a certain year relative to the probability that a couple does not have a first child in that year. Hence if the odds are higher for a given category, the corresponding probability will also be higher.

Results and discussion

Descriptive results

With respect to the prevalence of different breadwinner models, descriptive results (Figure 1) show that among Belgian couples the overwhelming majority (86.65 percent) exhibits a dual breadwinner model. The remaining Belgian households predominantly display a male breadwinner model whereas the shares of households in which the woman is the only breadwinner or no breadwinner is present are very small. This pattern of household breadwinner models differs strongly from the pattern for couples with at least one partner of Moroccan origin. Couples in which one or both partners are of Moroccan origin exhibit much lower shares of dual earner households, and much higher shares of male breadwinner models, female breadwinner models, or households without an earner.

In addition to the differences between migrant groups, comparisons between couples with at least one Moroccan partner indicate important differences in the distribution of breadwinner models. Among these couples, mixed origin couples exhibit a pattern more alike to Belgian couples compared to ethnically homogenous couples. However, mixed couples with a Belgian female and a Moroccan male (BEL-MOR) have a considerably lower incidence of male breadwinner models compared to couples consisting of a Moroccan female and a Belgian male (MOR-BEL). Within ethnically homogeneous Moroccan couples, couples consisting of two second generation migrants are most similar to Belgian or to mixed couples with respect to the household division of paid work. Ethnically homogeneous couples in which a first generation migrant is present show stronger deviations from the ones with at least one Belgian partner. It is noteworthy that couples in which the woman is the first generation migrant (MOR1_MOR2) show the strongest deviation from the Belgian pattern, with large shares of male breadwinner models.

With respect to differences between Belgian and Moroccan couples, the larger shares of one-earner households or households without an earner seem in line with lower labor market opportunities for Moroccan migrant groups. Although the higher shares of female breadwinner models among migrant groups seem to contradict prevailing gender role attitudes, we note that this finding may be related to less favourable labor market prospects for Moroccan men (Vitali & Arpino, 2015). The relatively large proportions of female breadwinner couples among households with a Belgian woman and a Moroccan man seem to support this assumption.

Concerning differences between different types of couples with at least one partner of Moroccan origin, results support the hypothesis that mixed-origin couples reflect weakening differences between majority population behaviour and migrant group behaviour (Coleman, 1994; Milewski, 2010). The high share of the male breadwinner model for couples consisting of a first generation Moroccan female and a second generation male can be related to the fact that higher-generation men import marriage partners in order to form a more traditional household (Lievens, 1999). This gendered motivation for importing marriage partners is further supported by the higher prevalence of dual breadwinner models among couples consisting of a second generation Moroccan woman and a first generation man.

Multivariate results

The results of the multivariate analysis are expressed in odds ratios (OR) that represent the odds of having a first child for a specific category compared to the reference category.

Concerning the impact of breadwinner models on the transition to parenthood, our results (Table 2, model 1) indicate that the dual breadwinner model yields the highest odds of parenthood. Compared to dual earner couples, male breadwinner couples exhibit ((1-.920)*100) 8 per cent lower odds of witnessing

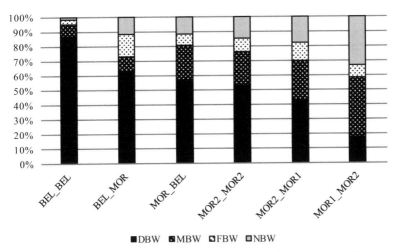

Figure 1: Distribution of couple-years by origin group and breadwinner model, Belgium 2002-2005 (source: Belgian 2001 census & register data, calculations by authors)

a first birth. Couples adhering to a male breadwinner model are thus less likely to have a first child compared to dual breadwinner couples. The occurrence of a female breadwinner model or the absence of an earner lowers the odds of first birth by 15.6 and 19.1 per cent respectively. Hence this chapter finds that dual earner couples exhibit the highest first birth odds.

Table 2, model 2 shows that these associations between breadwinner models and parenthood mask considerable variation between Belgian couples and couples with at least one Moroccan partner (Δdf: 15, Δ-2LL: 34.76, sig < .01). Model 2 presents differential effects for couples that consist of at least one partner with a migrant background. In addition, effects by origin group and breadwinner model are presented in Figure 2. The former allows us to assess whether the effects of breadwinner models on the transition to parenthood differ significantly between Belgian and Moroccan couples, whereas the latter has the advantage of grasping the group-specific effect of having a first birth for all ethnic compositions and breadwinner models.

For Belgian couples, Figure 2 indicates odds-ratios below unity for all breadwinner models. Hence, among Belgian couples, the male breadwinner model, the female breadwinner model and couples without an earner are less likely to have a first child compared to dual earner couples. For couples with at least one partner with a Moroccan background, a clearly different picture emerges. Whereas differential effects of the female breadwinner model or the

Table 2   Exponentiated coefficients (odds-ratios) from discrete-time event-history models of first birth, Belgium 2002-2005

	Model 1					
	MBW		**FBW**		**NBW**	
	OR	**sig**	**OR**	**sig**	**OR**	**sig**
Main effect						
. Main effect	.920	**	.848	**	.769	***
	Model parameters					
-2LL	297599.4					
df	87					
BIC	298753					
	Model 2					
	MBW		**FBW**		**NBW**	
	OR	**sig**	**OR**	**sig**	**OR**	**sig**
Main effect						
. Main effect	.883	***	.843	**	.770	***
Differential effects						
. BEL_MOR	1.486	*	1.187		1.230	
. MOR_BEL	1.373		1.358		1.161	
. MOR2_MOR2	2.150	**	1.290		1.415	
. MOR2_MOR1	1.496	**	1.027		1.052	
. MOR1_MOR2	1.284		.937		.863	
	Model parameters					
-2LL	297564.6					
df	102					
BIC	298917.3					

Controlling for: baseline (linear, quadratic, cubic), origin (6 household ethnic compositions), baseline*origin, education (9 educational attainments), baseline*education, education*breadwinner model, age difference between partners, marital status.

Significance levels: NS (-), p < .10 (*), p < .05 (**), p < .01 (***)

(source: Belgian 2001 census & register data, calculations by authors)

lack of an earner in a couple are not significant, convincing positive differential effects for the male breadwinner model are found for all couples with at least one partner of Moroccan origin. This indicates that the negative effect of the a male breadwinner as opposed to a dual breadwinner model for Belgian couples

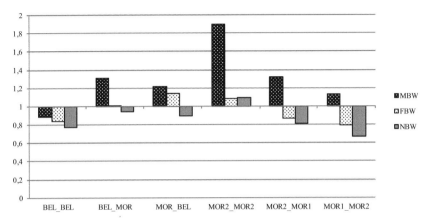

Figure 2: Odds-ratios (Model 2) by household ethnic composition and breadwinner models (dual breadwinner model as reference category), Belgium 2002-2005.
(source: Belgian 2001 census & register data, calculations by authors)

is weaker and possibly turns positive for couples with one or two Moroccan partners. The positive differential effect (table 2) of having a male breadwinner model is especially strong and significant among couples consisting of two second generation Moroccan descendants. In addition, the positive effect of the male breadwinner model is also significantly stronger for couples consisting of a Belgian woman and a Moroccan male and for couples consisting of a second generation woman and a male marriage migrant. Hence, these groups deviate significantly from the pattern observed among Belgian couples and show a different link between breadwinner models and the transition to parenthood. The group-specific effects displayed in figure 4 confirm these findings. For all couples having at least one partner of Moroccan origin, the male breadwinner model yields the highest odds of entry into parenthood. Hence, whereas among Belgian couples the dual earner model yields the highest first birth odds, the male breadwinner model plays this part for Moroccan couples.

Conclusion

Due to considerable changes in households' organization of employment, and since the second half of the 21st century, the issue of how work and family are related has become a frequently revisited topic. However, the relation between employment and fertility for migrant groups has rarely been examined (Andersson

& Scott, 2005, 2007; Lundström & Andersson, 2012). This is remarkable given the documented differences with respect to labor market opportunities (Corluy, 2014; Neels & Stoop, 2000), family formation (Corijn & Lodewijckx, 2009), and attitudes toward gender roles and the division of paid work (Bernhardt et al., 2007; De Valk, 2008; Lesthaeghe & Surkyn, 1996). This chapter studies differences in the division of paid work and the transition to parenthood between Belgian couples, mixed origin Belgian-Moroccan couples, and Moroccan couples. Hence this study provides a detailed comparison between Belgian couples and couples with at least one person with a Moroccan background with respect to how work and family formation is organized.

Our findings – of models that do not take different employment-fertility links by origin group into account – confirm the hypothesis that in Belgium dual breadwinner couples display the highest probability of having a first child. This positive effect is assumed to reflect both the economic and cultural advantage of the dual earner couple. Having two earners protects couples from income instability (Oppenheimer, 1994) and, in a context with relatively high work-family compatibility like Belgium, the opportunity costs of childbearing are expected to be limited (Gornick et al., 1997). Single earner breadwinner models and especially couples without an earner may face more income uncertainty. From a cultural perspective, the dual breadwinner model is in line with prevalent norms and attitudes toward gender roles in Belgium.

In addition, this study shows that the general association between breadwinner models and the transition to parenthood masks considerable variation between Belgian couples, mixed origin Belgian-Moroccan couples, and Moroccan couples. Whereas Belgian couples display a positive relation between the dual earner model and first births, this breadwinner type does not necessarily entail the highest first birth probabilities for couples with at least one partner with a Moroccan background. The results for couples with at least one partner of Moroccan origin indicate that the male breadwinner model yields the highest first birth probability. Hence, for couples with at least one partner with a Moroccan background, a positive relation between the male breadwinner model and parenthood is observed. This diverging pattern for the Moroccan community in Belgium is assumed to reflect both economic and cultural differences. From an economic perspective the outsourcing of childrearing and household tasks may be too costly for these groups due to lower wage potentials (Raz-Yurovich, 2014; Van Lancker & Ghysels, 2012). Furthermore, it is likely that among groups who perceive difficult access to rewarding career tracks will emphasize other pathways of identity formation such as developing the role of a mother (Friedman et al., 1994). From a cultural perspective, Moroccan groups – particularly first generation migrants and men – are also more likely to exhibit less favourable attitudes toward female labor force participation (De Valk, 2008). Although the later decades of the 20th century have experienced the rise of the dual earner model, and work-family reconciliation policies were introduced to facilitate the combination of this new model and childrearing especially in Western European countries such as Belgium, it is crucial to keep in mind that these general trends mask a strong degree of variation within populations.

Appendix

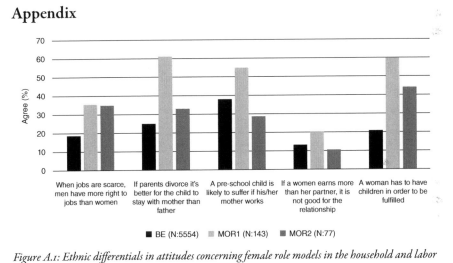

Figure A.1: Ethnic differentials in attitudes concerning female role models in the household and labor market, Belgium (Source: Belgian GGS Wave 1, 2008-2010).
note: The origin groups in this figure are BE (respondent and both parents are born in Belgium), MO1 (respondent born in Morocco), MO2 (respondent born in Belgium, one or both parents born in Morocco.

Notes

1   J. Wood(✉), Centre for Longitudinal and Life-course Studies (Cello), University of Antwerp, Sint Jacobstraat 2, 2000 Antwerp, Belgium. e-mail: Jonas.Wood@ua.ac.be.
2   See http://statbel.fgov.be/ for more information.

Bibliography

Ahn, N., & Mira, P. (2002). A note on the changing relationship between fertility and female employment rates in developed countries. *Journal of Population Economics*, 15(4), 667-682.

Andersson, G., & Scott, K. (2005). Labour-Market status and first-time parenthood: The experience of immigrant women in Sweden, 1981-97. *Population Studies*, 59(1), 21-38.

Andersson, G., & Scott, K. (2007). Childbearing dynamics of couples in a universalistic welfare state: The role of labor-market status, country of origin, and gender. *Demographic Research*, 17(30), 897-938.

Becker, G. (1981). *A Treatise on the Family*. London: Harvard University Press.

Bernhardt, E., Goldscheider, F., & Goldscheider, C. (2007). Integrating the second generation: Gender and family attitudes in early adulthood in Sweden. *Zeitschrift für Familienforschung*, 19(1), 55-70.

Coleman, D. A. (1994). Trends in fertility and intermarriage among immigrant populations in Western Europe as measures of integration. *Journal of Biosocial Science*, 26(1), 107-136.

Cooke, L. P., & Baxter, J. (2010). Families in International Context: Comparing Institutional Effects across Western Societies. *Journal of Marriage and Family*, 72(3), 516-536.

Corijn, M., & Lodewijckx, E. (2009). De start van gezinsvorming bij de Turkse en Marokkaanse tweede generatie in het Vlaamse Gewest. Een analyse op basis van Rijksregistergegevens. *Studiedienst van de Vlaamse Regering*, 6.

Corluy, V. (2014). *Labour market outcomes and trajectories of immigrants in Belgium*. Antwerp: University of Antwerp.

Coughlin, P., & Wade, J. C. (2012). Female breadwinner families. Their existence, persistence and sources. *Journal of Sociology*, 41(4), 343-362.

Crompton, R., & Lyonette, C. (2005). The new gender essentialism – domestic and family 'choices' and their relation to attitudes. *The British Journal of Sociology*, 56, 601-620.

De Valk, H. (2008). Parental Influence on Work and Family Plans of Adolescents of Different Ethnic Backgrounds in The Netherlands. *Sex Roles*, 59(9), 738-751.

Deboosere, P., & Willaert, D. (2004). *Codeboek algemene socio-economische enquête 2001*. Working Paper 2004-1. Steunpunt Demografie Vakgroep Sociaal Onderzoek (soco) Vrije Universiteit Brussel. Brussels.

Drago, R., Black, D., & Wooden, M. (2005). Female breadwinner families. Their existence, persistence and sources. *Journal of Sociology*, 41(4), 343-362.

Friedman, D., Hechter, M., & Kanazawa, S. (1994). A Theory of the Value of Children. *Demography*, 31(3), 375-401.

Goldscheider, F., Bernhardt, E., & Branden, M. (2013). Domestic gender equality and childbearing in Sweden. *Demographic Research*, 29(40), 1097-1126.

Gonzalez-Ferrer, A. (2006). Who Do Immigrants Marry? Partner Choice Among Single Immigrants in Germany. *European Sociological Review*, 22(2), 171-185.

Gornick, J., Meyers, M., & Ross, K. (1997). Supporting the employment of mothers: Policy variation across fourteen welfare states. *Journal of European Social Policy*, 7(1), 45-70.

Heath, A. F., Rothon, C., & Kilpi, E. (2008). The second generation in Western Europe: Education, unemployment, and occupational attainment. *Annual Review of Sociology*, 34, 211-235.

Idema, H., & Phalet, K. (2007). Transmission of gender-role values in Turkish-German migrant families: The role of gender, intergenerational and intercultural relations. *Zeitschrift für Erziehungswissenschaft*, 19(1), 71-105.

Keuzenkamp, S., & Merens, J. G. F. (2006). *Sociale atlas van vrouwen uit etnische minderheden.* Den Haag: Sociaal en Cultureel Planbureau.

Kravdal, O., & Rindfuss, R. R. (2008). Changing Relationships between Education and Fertility: A Study of Women and Men Born 1940 to 1964. *American Sociological Review*, 73(5), 854-873.

Kreyenfeld, M., & Andersson, G. (2014). Socioeconomic differences in the unemployment and fertility nexus: Evidence from Denmark and Germany. *Advances in Life Course Research*, 21, 59-73.

Lesthaeghe, R., & Surkyn, J. (1996). Aisha is Fatma niet. Culturele diversiteit en fragmentatie van de moderniteit bij Turkse en Marokkaanse vrouwen in België. *VUB Working Paper 1996-1.*

Lesthaeghe, R., & Van de Kaa, D. (1986). Twee demografische transities? In R. Lesthaeghe & D. Van de Kaa (Eds.), *Bevolking: groei en krimp.* Deventer: Van Loghum Slaterus.

Lievens, J. (1999). Family-Forming Migration from Turkey and Morocco to Belgium: The Demand for Marriage Partners from the Countries of Origin. *International Migration Review*, 33(3), 717-744.

Lundström, K. E., & Andersson, G. (2012). Labour market status, migrant status, and first childbearing in Sweden. *Demographic Research*, 27(25), 719-742.

Marks, J., Chun Bun, L., & McHale, S. M. (2009). Family patterns of gender role attitudes. *Sex Roles*, 61(3-4), 221-234.

Matysiak, A., & Vignoli, D. (2008). Fertility and Women's Employment: A Meta-analysis. *European Journal of Population*, 24, 363-384.

Milewski, N. (2010). *Fertility of Immigrants: A Two-Generational Approach in Germany.* University Rostock, Rostock.

Neels, K. (1998). Migratiegeschiedenis en Schoolloopbaan. Onderwijspositie van Turkse en Marokkaanse mannen in België op basis van UIAP-Surveydata. *Vrije Universiteit Brussel, Working Paper 1998-1.*

Neels, K. (1999) Education and the transition to employment: the experience of young Turkish and Moroccan adults in Belgium. *Vol. 1999:3. Interuniversity papers in demography series*: Vrije Universiteit Brussel.

Neels, K., & De Wachter, D. (2010). Postponement and recuperation of Belgian fertility: how are they related to rising female educational attainment? *Vienna Yearbook of Population Research*, 8, 77-106.

Neels, K., & Stoop, R. (1998) Social mobility and equal opportunities: the case of Turkish and Moroccan immigrants in Belgium. *Interuniversity papers in demography series*. Brussels: Vrije Universiteit Brussel.

Neels, K., & Stoop, R. (2000). Reassessing the ethnic gap: employment of younger Turks and Moroccans in Belgium. In R. Lesthaeghe (Ed.), *Communities and Generations*. Brussels: VUB University Press.

Oppenheimer, V. K. (1994). Women's Rising Employment and the Future of the Family in Industrial Societies. *Population and Development Review*, 20(2), 293-342.

Oppenheimer, V. K. (1997). Women's Employment and the Gain to Marriage: The Specialization and Trading Model. *Annual Review of Sociology*, 23, 431-453.

Phalet, K. (2007). *Down and out: the children of immigrant workers in the Belgian labour market*: Oxford University Press.

Population Council. (2006). Policies to Reconcile Labor Force Participation and Childbearing in the European Union. *Population and Development Review*, 32(2), 389-393.

Raz-Yurovich, L. (2014). A Transaction Cost Approach to Outsourcing by Households. *Population and Development Review*, 40(2), 293-309.

Reniers, G. (1999). On the history and selectivity of Turkish and Moroccan migration to Belgium. *International Migration*, 37(4), 679-713.

Schmitt, C. (2012). A Cross-National Perspective on Unemployment and First Births. *European Journal of Population*, 28, 303-335.

Smeesters, B., Nayer, A., Saddouk, C., & Schingtienne, L. (1997). Etnische discriminatie bij aanwerving (pp. 244): Federale Diensten voor Wetenschappelijke, Technische en Culturele aangelegenheden.

Sullivan, O., Billari, F. C., & Altintas, E. (2014). Fathers' Changing Contributions to Child Care and Domestic Work in Very Low–Fertility Countries The Effect of Education. *Journal of Family Issues, 35*(8), 1048-1065.

Surkyn, J., & Reniers, G. (1997). Selecte gezelschappen. Over de migratiegeschiedenis en de interne dynamiek van migratieprocessen. In R. Lesthaeghe (Ed.), *Diversiteit in sociale verandering. Turkse en Marokkaanse vrouwen in België*. Brussels: VUBPress.

Timmerman, C., Vanderwaeren, E., & Crul, M. (2003). The second generation in Belgium. *International Migration Review*, 37(4), 1065-1090.

Torr, B., & Short, S. (2004). Second Births and the Second Shift: A Research Note on Gender Equity and Fertility. *Population and Development Review*, 30(1), 109-130.

Van de Kaa, D. (2002). *The Idea of a Second Demographic Transition in Industrialized Countries*. Paper presented at the Sixth Welfare Policy Seminar of the National Institute of Population and Social Security, Tokyo.

Van de Kaa, D., & Lesthaeghe, R. (1986). *Bevolking, groei en krimp*. Van Loghum Slaterus.

Van den Cruyce, B. (2000). *Statistische discriminatie van allochtonen op jobmarkten met rigide lonen*. Leuven: PhD thesis, Katholieke Universiteit Leuven.

Van Lancker, W., & Ghysels, J. (2012). Who benefits? The social distribution of subsidized childcare in Sweden and flanders. *Acta Sociologica*, 55(2), 125-142.

Verick, S. (2009). *who is hit hardest during a financial crisis the vulnerability of young men and women to unemployment in an economic downturn*. Paper presented at the IZA Discussion Paper no.4359, Bonn.

Vitali, A., & Arpino, B. (2015). *Who brings home the bacon? The influence of context*. Paper presented at the Annual Meeting of the Population Association of America, San Diego.

Wood, J., & Neels, K. (2016). First a job, then a child? Subgroup variation in women's employment-fertility link. *Advances in Life Course Research*.

Wood, J., Neels, K., & Kil, T. (2014). The educational gradient of childlessness and cohort parity progression in 14 low fertility countries. *Demographic Research*, 31(46), 1365-1416.

Wood, J., Vergauwen, J., & Neels, K. (2015). Economic Conditions and Variation in First Birth Hazards in 22 European Countries between 1970 and 2005. In K. Matthijs, K. Neels, C. Timmerman, J. Haers & S. Mels (eds.), *Population Change in Europe, the Middle-East and North Africa. Beyond the Demographic Divide*. Farnham England, Burlington Vermont: Ashgate.

Part 3
Politics and policy

7. Towards a comprehensive integration policy: a critical analysis of how social imaginations underpin Flemish integration policies

Noel Clycq & François Levrau

The intertwined idioms of nationhood, peoplehood, and citizenship—like the idioms of race, religion, rights, and revolution—are eminently flexible and adaptable. They can be used to legitimate a polity but also to challenge its legitimacy, to demand a new polity, or to claim autonomy or resources within an existing polity. And the abstract category of nationhood or peoplehood can be imagined in a variety of ways: the nation can be understood to be grounded in citizenship, history, language, descent, race, religion, way of life, or shared political experience (Brubaker, 2015: 9).

Introduction

As the title of this edited volume reveals, the first official Moroccan labor migrants set foot on Belgian soil some 50 years ago. During these five decades, the 'Moroccan community' has grown to be one of the largest ethnic minority communities in Belgium and Flanders. During this period, a new policy agenda and discourse on the 'integration' of foreigners, migrants, newcomers, and even allochthones emerged as a response to continuing migration flows and settlement processes. Rather than discussing the history of Moroccan migration, which is covered in chapter 8 by Van Puymbroeck, in this chapter we focus on Flemish integration policies from a more theoretical point of view. We explore several imaginations of what the Flemish nation is or represents and how they (might) underpin the Flemish integration policies. What are the dominant stories of Flemish peoplehood that migrants and minorities, and Moroccans in particular, are confronted with or are expected to integrate into? Are the integration policies primarily concerned with finding a common identity within a context of increasing diversity, or are they rather invoked in order to exclude the 'cultural, ethnic or religious other' and hence to build/maintain a kind of fixed and pre-existing identity?

By answering these and related questions, we demonstrate how the multiplicity of integration discourses and politics is built upon a specific image of belonging together. This imaginary, constituted by influential representations of 'a people' and 'a mainstream society', helps to explain why 'integration', in its day-to-day language and political reality, is mainly concerned with the inclusion and exclusion of people (Schrover & Schinkel, 2013). If the image of 'a peoplehood' functions as the proverbial gravitational field or nodal point for integration policies, the implication is that people can be described as 'insiders' or 'outsiders'.

So, if we want to understand the integration of (Moroccan) immigrants, we should not only focus on structural integration processes in the domains of education, the labor market and housing; we also need to consider broader societal and cultural processes as they form the broader (implicit as well as explicit) imaginary and identity context into which this structural integration can take place. After all, it is only within this dialectical relation between the 'structural' and the 'cultural' that one can fully grasp integration processes and policies (Alba & Foner, 2015).

We start this chapter with an explanation of why we focus on Flemish (instead of Belgian) integration policy, and thereby present some of the main motives found throughout the designing and implementation of these policies in the past decades. This will contextualize the subsequent paragraphs that deal more in-depth with some of these issues. In the second paragraph we discuss what we mean with 'social imaginaries' and 'peoplehood' in the context of integration policy. We continue with illustrating how different types of peoplehood stories have been proposed in these policy discourses as ideological ways to increase feelings of a shared sense of belonging. In the next paragraph we discuss the social imagination of Flanders and consider some definitions of the Flemish nationhood that have been proposed by the political elite. In the following paragraph we provide a brief outline of what a future integration policy may look like. Insofar as integration policies can be understood as concrete illustrations of the social imaginations of Flanders, we argue that an inclusive narrative must underpin integration policies. The implication is that a just and cohesive Flemish society should not only deal with newcomers, but also with the autochthones and society's basic structure and core democratic institutions. Throughout the chapter, the migration and integration of individuals of Moroccan background is employed as a case study.

Why a Flemish integration policy and what are its central features?

As already discussed in the introduction of this book, the immigration stop in 1973-1974 marks an important date in the policy development on migration and integration processes. However, shortly after the introduction of this migration stop, politicians became aware that the labor migrants did not (want to) return to their home countries, as many had started building up a life in Belgium and Flanders. Thus, from the early 1980s onwards the enduring presence of former labor migrants became an element in policy making. Several major policy shifts occurred. From the 15th of December 1980 onwards, foreigners were allowed to settle legally in Belgium and due to the state reform of the 8th of August 1980, the competencies for the reception and integration of migrants were transferred from the federal state to the Communities (Van den Broucke, et al. 2015). Next to the legal and judicial aspects of this transfer, it is important to note that these competencies are transferred to the 'cultural' community level and not to the 'economic' regional level. Newcomers are expected to integrate into the Flemish cultural community rather than into the federal Belgian one. Moreover, this shows that integration policy from the beginning has already been imagined as being essentially concerned with the cultural and linguistic dimensions of the (Flemish) community. This is much more so the case in Flanders compared to the French community, since the integration policies of the latter focused less on cultural integration. Flanders is much more interventionist when it comes to cultural integration, both in terms of multicultural and assimilationist policies. Wallonia, on the other hand, implements a laissez-faire policy in the domain of cultural integration (Adam, 2013; Jacobs, 2004; Loobuyck & Jacobs, 2009). According to Adam (2013), the difference between the two policy perspectives is to be explained mainly through the differing histories of the Communities: Flanders constructed its own subnational identity primarily in contrast to the then dominant Walloon-Belgian identity. In a salient and ongoing nation-building process, of which Flemish cultural and linguistic identity is [now] considered to be one of the most defining features, it is to be expected that this tension also remains present in Flemish relations vis-à-vis newcomers as well as the Walloon 'other'. In Wallonia, on the other hand, the emphasis is mainly placed on socio-economic integration. The assumption is that those who have work in Wallonia will automatically become culturally integrated. Newcomers do not need a kind of policy push. The idea that is prevalent in the French-speaking side of Belgium is that using a cultural integration policy actually reinforces the differences instead of bringing groups together (Adam, 2013). This difference in thinking is partly influenced by the fact that Flanders reflects and elaborates on the Anglo-Saxon and Dutch multicultural policy model, while Wallonia focuses more on the French Republican state model (Jacobs, 2004). Another reason why Flanders implements another type of integration policy has to do with the electoral success of the right-wing party Vlaams Blok, currently Vlaams Belang. In the French-speaking part of Belgium, 'integration' has only been politicized marginally—i.e., the extreme right party Front National has never been successful—so in Wallonia, there is not a lot of support for investing time and money into integration policies (Adam, 2013). Yet, as touched upon above, part of the explanation has to do with the fact that a part of Flemish population sees Flanders as a nation-in-becoming. The separation or confederalization is a much debated issue in Flemish politics, while in Wallonia, pro-separation or confederalization voices are much weaker. Adam (2013) emphasizes that a nation-in-progress needs to be internally legitimized by its own citizens. This legitimacy can be gained by implementing as many policies as possible in order to demonstrate its competency. As mentioned, this broader political current of separatism or further regionalization is much less prominent among the Walloons, since the region is imagined as primarily a part of Belgium. A nation-in-progress, however, also needs external legitimacy. This could be achieved by demonstrating to Europe/the world that the region is pursuing a multicultural policy and thus rejecting racist and intolerant convictions (Adam, 2013). However, it seems that the current notion of a 'good nation-state' is increasingly considered to be a state that abandons 'naïve' multicultural policies, but implements strong civic integration policies. It is no coincidence that—as we will illustrate—Flanders has indeed implemented strong civic integration policies. This is not to say that Flanders has implemented some 'naïve multicultural strategies' in the past, but it is a common rhetoric to think that integration has failed due to multicultural policies that have given too much freedom to minority groups. Flanders, as most other countries, has simply not sufficiently invested in a thorough and all-encompassing integration policy. Presumably based upon the assumption that 'integration' is merely a matter of time and adaptation. What has been rather neglected is that dealing with diversity implies a fundamental acknowledgement that both tailored integration policies and general recognition strategies are needed. After all, all individuals need to get used to the changing demographics of societies in the 21th century.

Integration: Maintaining national ties and/or excluding the other?

In his bestselling book *'Imagined communities'*, Benedict Anderson (1991: 6) studied the nation-formation processes and argued that imagination takes up a pivotal role in these processes. 'The nation (...) is an imagined political community—and imagined as both inherently limited and sovereign. It is imagined because the members of even the smallest nation will never know most of their fellow-members, meet them, or even hear of them, yet in the minds of each lives the image of their communion.' Like Anderson, Charles Taylor emphasized the idea of the imaginary, but whereas Anderson focused on the nation, Taylor applied the realm of the imaginary to 'the ways people imagine their social existence, how they fit together with others, how things go on between them and their fellows, the expectations which are normally met, and the deeper normative notions and images which underlie these expectations' (Taylor, 2004: 23). These 'social imaginaries', these images, stories, ideals, narratives and legends function as 'social glue' since they provide the lenses through which one perceives the social world with its many practices, rituals, interactions, as more or less self-evidently coherent and meaningful (Brubaker, 2004).

From this perspective, the social community is always to a large extent imagined in the minds of its presumed members. However, in order to delineate communities and nation-states, concrete criteria are needed to decide who can become a member. Apart from all kind of institutions, states also invoke certain images that are considered and felt to be the 'natural' representation of the group. As such, these images take up the function of 'quilting points' that exercise— often in an unconscious way—adhesive forces upon the members of a group (Brubaker, 2004). People, especially when nationalistic rhetoric and politics are invoked, might internalize the social construction of peoplehood to the extent that they feel the nation is a living, natural and hence vulnerable entity that needs to be protected against outsiders or enemies. Considered from this perspective, it becomes understandable that many individuals in Flanders (but not exclusively in Flanders, as similar feelings can be found across the world) feel that in the last decades, the 'imagined national communities' are increasingly challenged or even threatened by immigration and associated integration processes (Alba & Foner, 2015). After all, integration is always concerned with a deep imagination of 'the group' into which other individuals and/or groups integrate (Schinkel, 2013). Although the imagining of a group can be constructed along different lines (see the introductory quote by Brubaker), from the very moment that a (restricted) national group is created, antagonisms in the form of out-groups are invoked. And, as people with (supposedly) different lifestyles, convictions, traditions, customs, backgrounds enter the imagined unity of the nation, many people will assume the societal glue is loosening, or, at the very least, the question 'What does it mean to be a member of a national group?' will come to the fore. What was always presumed to be obvious— however, one also needs to acknowledge the often eager effort to forget recent and deep-rooted nation-internal conflicts and tensions—seems no longer that obvious. Taking this perspective on the 'imagination of the nation' helps to explain some of the current tensions and crises of the nation-state.

For example, various countries face so-called 'identity crises' as they feel they are forced to explain what they stand for, especially when designing civic integration policies for newcomers. Think of the popular political credo of the failed multicultural policies launched around 2010-2011 by prominent politicians such as Angela Merkel, Nicolas Sarkozy and David Cameron: the credo made clear that several countries wanted to turn away from their (supposedly) multiculturalist policies and wanted to exchange it for policies that emphasized the national culture and the central role of liberal values. Various discussions emerged from this dialectic between, on the one hand, the focus on a strong national culture, and on the other, on 'universal' liberal values. In the past decades, we saw several attempts to construct a so-called inclusive narrative of 'the nation' that ultimately got stranded in a rather exclusive imagination. David Cameron (prime minister of the UK from 2010 to 2016), for example, coined the term 'muscular liberalism': 'Frankly, we need a lot less of the passive tolerance of recent years and a much more active, muscular liberalism. A passively tolerant society says to its citizens, as long as you obey the law we will just leave you alone. It stands neutral between different values. But I believe a genuinely liberal country does much more; it believes in certain values and actively promotes them. Freedom of speech, freedom of worship, democracy, the rule of law, equal rights regardless of race, sex or sexuality. It says to its citizens, this is what defines us as a society: to belong here is to believe in these things. Now, each of us in our own countries, I believe, must be unambiguous and hard-nosed about this defense of our liberty' (Cameron, 2011). This 'muscular liberalism' comes closer to the 'comprehensive liberalism' à la Okin (1989), than the 'political liberalism' as outlined by Rawls (1993). Political liberalism does not make any claim on how life should be lived. People are free to live their lives according to their own conception of the good life. Political liberalism wants citizens to live according to liberal principles in the public realm, but in the private realm, people can choose to live otherwise.

However, it is difficult to satisfactorily explain what the nation stands for if it is indeed to a large extent an imaginary construction. The idea that the national heart – around which the symbolic society with its institutions, laws and policies, is built – might be nothing more than an image or phantasm, could be upsetting to us. To the extent that the 'other' points at the fictive heart of the nation, he becomes a threat to the self-evident unity of the nation and invokes anger in the 'autochtones'. It is often in the image and construction of the 'other' that one finds meaning for what 'we' stand for (e.g. Catholic tradition, white, not 'lazy', etc.). This, however, is only an ideal portrayal as it camouflages the internal diversity.

What becomes clear from everyday life in Flanders is that this role of 'the other' and the 'threat to the nation' is often accorded to 'the Moroccan', and by extension, 'the Muslim'. And, even though migrant and integration policies are in principle focused on all migrants, newcomers and their descendants, particularly North Africans (to a large extent of Moroccan origin) are still singled out by policy makers as one of the main groups suffering from exclusion. This has been the case since the 1980s (Vrielink, 2010), which is remarkable, especially since recent research indicates that on important indicators for cultural integration such as Dutch language proficiency, Moroccans often seem 'well-integrated' (Van Craen & Vancluysen, 2008; Clycq, et al, 2014). This is the so-called 'integration-paradox' whereby the efforts of immigrants to integrate well are not 'rewarded' by the autochthonous majority. This suggests that being well integrated does not necessarily imply that one also gets incorporated into the imaginary realm, annexing the tenacious image of the 'heart' of the nation. Put differently, structural and even 'cultural' integration does not automatically lead to imaginary integration. Therefore, what is needed is another narrative, an inclusive story that speaks to the heart and mind of *all* citizens. We return to this conclusion in the final paragraph of this chapter.

Besides this 'integration paradox', there is another paradox that clearly illustrates how 'integration' implies the tenacity of the imaginary conception of who belongs to the nation. A good example is the second generation Moroccans (cf. youth with a Moroccan origin born in Belgium). Having been born in Belgium or Flanders, they are part of the Belgian and Flemish people, yet they are paradoxically often represented as not fully integrated in 'explanations' of their problematic educational or labor market trajectories. In these discussions, 'native born' individuals are still represented as 'not integrated', creating a bizarre imagination of the 'outsider within society' (Schinkel, 2013). The argument of jus soli 'being born in Belgium makes you a genuine Belgian citizen' is thereby still corrupted by the adherence to the 'jus sanguinis' tenet, the idea that these second generation individuals are 'by blood' not genuine Belgian (native) citizens. This is a catch 22 situation that prevents the construction of an inclusive narrative to underpin integration policies. As we will argue, if one wants to keep the expression of 'being well/not integrated', it should also be applied to autochthonous people.

Different stories of peoplehood as ideological tools underpinning integration policies

As societies are becoming increasingly diverse, the conviction has become widespread that social cohesion is threatened, solidarity is in decline and that primarily ethno-cultural diversity is to blame for it (Putnam, 2007). This is the so-called 'heterogenity-redistribution trade-off' (Banting & Kymlicka, 2006), also called the progressive dilemma (Goodhart, 2004; Pearce, 2004). Either one opts for cohesive societies and hence for a decrease of diversity; or one opts for diverse societies and hence should be willing to pay the price of social cohesion. Put differently, due to an influx of newcomers, the imaginary unity is challenged. In fact, the loss of societal cohesion has become one of the most prominent 'fears' in 'Western societies' and the question of how to create 'unity in diversity' is one of the most discussed topics in political science (see e.g. Schaeffer, 2014; but also Levrau, 2015; Levrau & Loobuyck, 2013a & 2013b). The fear of a loss of (national) unity has been tempered by different political strategies. While these strategies differ in kind, they have in common that they rely on imaginary stories of peoplehood. Below, we discuss six 'stories of peoplehood' that have been proposed as ideological ways to increase a shared sense of belonging together. We also briefly illustrate how they have been invoked (or not) in the context of Flanders/Belgium.

(1) Ethnic nationalism. Extreme right politicians advocate forms of 'ethnic nationalism' where nationhood is defended on the basis of a common racial/ethnic descent and common territory. The imagination of autochthony—the idea of 'we were here first'—is said to be found in societies all over the world (Geschiere, 2009; Roosens, 1998). This 'blood and soil' ideology excludes immigrants and ethnic minorities because they are not 'natives' and because diversity is assumed to be detrimental for social cohesion and feelings of belonging

together. This often goes hand in hand with the imagination that one's descent is 'naturally' linked to a common religion, common language, common history, etc. Immigrants therefore cannot become 'real' citizens of a nation, unless they were to assimilate fully. Those who defend assimilation see integration as a strict one-way strategy: 'When in Rome, do as the Romans do.' In Flanders, this position is defended by the extreme right political party *Vlaams Belang*. If we indeed allow immigration, there are, however, several reasons why this 'far right' model could be criticized. Assimilation sees integration as a one-way process, whereby the receiving country has no obligation to help the integration of newcomers, as the latter are solely responsible for their integration. This is problematic, since every society is arranged in such a way that the dominant autochthonous group is the primus inter pares, meaning that the 'others' are disadvantaged when it comes to access to the main institutions. In a just, and therefore neutral, society, people should not be disadvantaged when it comes to their basic rights (such as freedom of religion) and their access to the main institutions should be guaranteed in an even-handed way. Assimilation, however, also leads to illiberal and perfectionist policies that demand that newcomers adjust to the dominant cultural patterns of the majority. As said, all people should be able to enjoy their fundamental rights to the same extent, and should be able to live according to their own conceptions of the good. Hence, a neutral policy may not impose nor privilege one way of living. Assimilation does not fully take into account the constitutive bindings of people. By asking to put aside ethnic-cultural or religious connections, it does not respect the thick identities of people (Parekh, 2000).

(2) Liberal value consensus. Liberal thinkers propose that a shared belief in the principles of liberal-democratic justice is sufficient to ensure solidarity. A reference to a 'national culture' is unnecessary (e.g. Rawls, 1980). The assumption here is that people act in solidary ways because there is public agreement on the appropriate principles of a liberal-democratic political order. Immigrants and natives should therefore agree with the basic freedoms and equalities. A good example is the Report of the Commission that Bossuyt (2006) developed to become the fundament of Flemish (civic) integration policy. In the Preface of the Report, it is said that the task given to the Commission was to articulate the common values and standards of Flemish society today in order for newcomers to become familiar with the Flemish society. Ultimately, the report was built around five key values, namely freedom, equality, solidarity, respect and citizenship; and three systems of values and standards: democracy, the rule of law and pluralism. Remarkably, these 'common values' are by many felt and claimed to be universal

(see e.g. the universal declaration of human rights) and hence it seems that Flemish society has no specific characteristics, history, customs, traditions. Another telling example is the Belgian 'Newcomers Declaration'. The federal government of Belgium—by way of its Secretary of State, Theo Francken from the right-wing Flemish nationalist and separatist party N-VA (New Flemish Alliance) who is responsible for amongst others Asylum and Migration policy—has invoked a Declaration of the main values of Belgium. Francken wanted this Declaration to be signed by all newcomers. Here again, what people should actually sign are the universal human rights, which are by definition not unique to Belgium at all. This Declaration and the liberal consensus approach has some pitfalls. First, as Francken's political party repeatedly argues, Flanders and Wallonia supposedly have completely different democracies and cultures. But, if that is the case, it seems odd that both Belgian regions seem to share these fundamental values and principles. If both regions share the same values, how can they be that different? Here, it should be clear that the liberal value consensus approach misses the point. After all, why should we feel more solidarity towards our co-citizens than to other people who also share the same liberal-democratic values? There is a logical gap between a belief in universal values, and a felt solidarity towards co-citizens (Banting & Kymlicka, 2015). Second, quite recently, the 'Council of State' (in line with political liberalism à la Rawls, see above) has criticized this Declaration on the grounds that a government cannot force citizens to believe in certain values (by signing this Declaration). This might be expected since freedom of thought is a key value or principle, yet this would be breached by obligating people to sign the Declaration and by arguing that a refusal to sign would be documented and might negatively impact their future (e.g. in their asylum procedure).

(3) Constitutional patriotism or republican/civic nationalism. Another ideological position is provided by those who believe that 'bounded nationhood' emerges from the active participation in collective liberal-democratic decision-making processes. As it has been defended by amongst others Habermas (1992), the patriotic attachment does not solely constitute attachment to abstract universal values, but to the specific way they are codified within particular constitutions. Hence, according to this 'constitutional patriotism', immigrants need to take part in the political game. This position can take a republican form in the sense that through a shared engagement in liberal-democratic procedures, people come to see themselves as 'co-authors' of the laws and institutions, and hence see the political order as an expression of the collective will. An example cited often is France, and by extension, the Walloons in Belgium—insofar

as they are orientated towards France and not, like Flanders, to the Anglo-Saxon tradition—where there is supposed to be no multicultural focus on and recognition of different identities, but rather a strict focus on structural and political integration. However, as argued by several scholars, when politicians articulate this 'civic' or 'republican' concept of nationhood, ethnic and cultural elements are often used to describe its particularity. This was also apparent in the public and political discussion on French national identity launched by former president Sarkozy, which also relied on cultural and ethnic notions of what it means to be French (Alba & Foner, 2015).

(4) Liberal nationalism. This position lays the emphasis on an inter-generational national community with a common history of living together on a shared territory, reflected in national language, institutions, policies and patrimony (Tamir, 1993). Contrary to the 'blood and soil nationalism', the liberal national story of peoplehood is more open to diversity. Requiring a shared blood, a shared religion, and a shared ethnic culture is exclusionary of immigrants, but requiring a shared language, knowledge of national history, public culture (reflected in public national media, symbols, museums) does not have to be. This is why the liberal nationalistic story can easily be complemented by multicultural policies that give public recognition to ethno-cultural diversity within a shared national identity as well as by civic integration policies that help immigrants to find their way in the society (Kymlicka, 2001). While Flanders has not always emphasized the equal importance of liberal nationalism, multiculturalism and civic integration, some argue that a mixture of these three policies is a good way to describe the Flemish integration policies of the last decades (see also Loobuyck & Jacobs, 2009).

These four options stress the importance of the imaginary of the nation as the locus for cohesion. However, there are also other contexts that could create feelings of belonging together. Some scholars and politicians focus on European and/or cosmopolitan frameworks. Others emphasize the importance of local identity dynamics. Both options are invoked because it is believed that the nation is too exclusive and guarantees only limited openness towards (specific) immigrant groups. By applying these macro and micro approaches, it is thought that it would be easier to deal with the challenges that go along with the increasing diversity.

(5) Europeanization and cosmopolitanism. European identity is by definition imagined as 'unity in diversity' and is therefore by definition an 'intercultural' identity taking into account the various social, cultural and historical differences

that are related to the imaginations of nationhood (Delanty, 2013). It is therefore argued that this inherently diverse identity should be at the core of European identity construction (Jenkins, 2008). However, several scholars are also discussing the difficulty of European identity construction, especially in the wake of the financial crisis that shook the European Union (Delanty, 2013; Jenkins, 2008; Pasture, 2015). They argue that European nation states are currently repositioning themselves in relation to Europeanization and globalization processes as well as in relation to the European Union. The nation often remains the nodal point for identity construction for everyday life, as most citizens do not believe that their 'European identity' is their core identity (Arts & Halman, 2014). When discussing the difficulties of imagining the nation, it is relevant to take into account that many political parties arguing for the existence of a unique national identity underlying their integration policies often refer to an intercultural European identity. Marc Jongen, vice president of the German right-populist party *Alternative für Deutschland*, who argues that the German values are European, is exemplary in this: 'The most important [values] are European: the traditions of the Enlightenment, the Christian heritage, humanism. Roman law and Greek philosophy and Greek concept of democracy. There are also properties in which Germans distinguished diligence, order, thoroughness, accuracy' (Jongen, in Leijendekker, 2016). Another example is the above-mentioned Belgian Declaration for Newcomers, as it does not apply to European newcomers because it is believed that they all share the same European value framework (Francken, 2016). However, although the European identity might be imagined as intercultural, nowadays, it seems to be based predominantly on political and economic rationales. Brexit is the most recent example of the difficulties with which the EU struggles, with the case of Greece during the EURO crisis lingering as well. Although ancient Greece is portrayed as the cradle of Europe and European (or even universal-cosmopolitan) identity, nowadays, there are voices advocating the exclusion of Greece from the European Union because of its economic and financial situation and their negative effect on constructing a cohesive European identity (Triandafyllidou, Gropas & Kouki, 2013). And, when it comes to (cultural) identity, the imaginary of Europe (and the EU) certainly also has exclusionary aspects. Take the example of Turkey. Although the Ottoman empire has for centuries dominated (some) parts of Europe and as such has contributed to the construction of European culture, Turkey is not (yet?) a member state because it is argued that its values do not fully match those of the EU (Aydin-Düsgit, 2012).

Moreover, in these discourses, reference is often made to Islam as an alien feature of European culture. An important question that arises is what this implies for the approximately 10 million citizens of Turkish descent living in Europe who predominantly identify as Muslim. Can they be genuine citizens and members of a so-called European society? This question has come to the fore as Recep Tayyip Erdoğans governing style has become increasingly reliant on religious rhetoric and some of his policies clearly reflect a shift towards religious and authoritarian politics. Since 'many European Turks' supported his policy in the referendum of 2017 that mainly dealt with the expansion of the president's power, concern was raised across Europe as to whether these 'European Turks' were truly 'European' citizens. Against this backdrop, it remains remarkable that the large numbers of Europeans supporting undemocratic extreme-right political parties—e.g., the French presidential elections with Le Pen, or the elections in the Netherlands with Geert Wilders, and Belgium with the Vlaams Belang—are seldom seen as less European or badly integrated citizens.

(6) *Local communities.* Others have turned to the micro level and have emphasized cities, neighborhoods or small-scale communities as the new loci of politics and peoplehood (e.g. Holston, 1999). This is particularly important as metropolitan areas around the world—also in Flanders—are experiencing a rapid diversification of their population. This means that while Flanders used to be a region with only a few big minority groups, due to the bilateral agreements that the government made in the 60s with countries like Italy, Morocco, Turkey, in the near future it will be characterized by a wide umbrella of ethnic, cultural and religious diversity. In the coming years many cities will see the traditional ethnic majority group (native Flemings for example) turn into a minority next to other minority groups (Crul & Mollenkopf, 2012). Cities will then be portrayed as the new arenas of citizenship and, for example, by means of intercultural policies, people might connect and form city-citizenship. Some scholars argue that in order to deal with 'superdiversity', globalization and the potential loss of social cohesion, we need local and common places, solutions, contacts and identities (Oosterlynck, et al. 2016). Moreover, to address these complex transformations, some cities have constructed municipal or city identity cards making 'illegal' individuals 'legal' within the territory of the city (de Graauw, 2014). However, this would imply a further localization of competencies and policies that hitherto have remained on the national or regional levels.

These six different scenarios of peoplehood illustrate that integration is deeply concerned with the social imagination of a community, most often the nation.

Integration assumes that the 'other' (i.e. migrants, refugees, newcomers, non-natives, refugees, Muslims, etc.) needs to be included within an already existing community or at least within a shared identity-in-progress. In this regard, all sorts of integration policies are designed to facilitate the process of participation in society. Insofar as these policies are exteriorizations of the social imaginaries of a nation, however, they are infused with narratives, images, feelings and representations about who we are, about who the other is, and about what has to be done to create a sustainable community where people can live in harmony. As such, examining these policies can shed light on the dominant social imaginaries and the way the nation is conceived.

The imaginary society as a moving equilibrium

According to Taylor (2004), the social imaginary constitutes the horizon for a particular community and sets the parameters for what is deemed meaningful in that community. One can portray it as a 'moving equilibrium'. It is an 'equilibrium' because it represents the taken-for-granted vision of things in a community. It is therefore difficult to question its legitimacy without calling into question the entirety of its interconnected social, political, and religious elements. As Taylor (2007: 173) maintains, a social imaginary 'is in fact that largely unstructured and inarticulate understanding of our whole situation, within which particular features of our world whole up for us in the sense they have.' And, although the social imaginary is contingent and revisable, it is presented as universal and normative. Taylor (2004: 17) suggests that the social imaginary has become 'so self-evident to us that we have trouble seeing it as one possible conception among others.' This is exactly why it is so difficult to grasp or formulate a thick national identity of Flanders and hence the central story in which immigrants should take part in. Either the story is a too encompassing and homogenizing imagination that does not reflect nor incorporate the diversity of the Flemish natives, or it is too thin in the sense that the difference with other nations is not clear. The social imaginary, however, is a 'moving' equilibrium in the sense that is not static or self-enacting. Although it has a deep historic dimension, it does not simply bubble up, but rather represents social constructions that can, at least partly, be molded by politicians, media, etc.

The civic integration policies are probably the best illustration of how Flanders has asked its newcomers to adjust to its nationhood. Already from the onset, it was clear that 'culture' is pivotal. The liberal 'values' are the core of (civic) integration policies (Commission Bossuyt, 2006) and are hence put forward to give meaning and content to the cultural imagination of Flanders. These values are treated as the main building blocks for fostering cohesion and the sense of belonging together. As the former minister of civic integration, Marino Keulen, argued in the introduction to the Bossuyt-report: 'culture and origin strongly influence the way we interact with each other' (Commission Bossuyt, 2006: 7).

Although many eagerly refer to these values as the bedrock of Flanders, there is no empirical evidence that all autochthonous Flemish citizens live in full accordance with these values. On the contrary, given the various discriminatory practices and discourses that are reported to and documented by organizations such as the UNIA—the Interfederal Centre for Equal Opportunities—certain core values are not held in highest regard by many Flemish natives. If in their daily lives, people do not live in full accordance with the imaginations of these fundamental values, this implies that people's social ethos does not reflect the same egalitarian and liberal principles that form the ground upon which the main institutions are built. Up till now this has not encouraged leading Flemish politicians to claim that Flemish autochthonous people also need to internalize the so-called Flemish values, let alone that these people need to sign a Declaration in which they confirm that they uphold the values. If 'integration', however, is indeed a matter of adherence to liberal values, it means that the 'autochthonous population' also needs to confirm and prove their attachment to these core (Flemish) values. One is not 'by nature' gifted with liberal values but has to learn, appreciate and internalize these values, so that one can also live up to these values in one's daily life and in the many private and public choices that one must make.

Of course, this is a mere thought exercise, since the signing of such a statement is not mandatory, and since what a liberal state can expect from its citizens is simply that they respect and practice these values in public life (and to a certain extent also in private life). As the liberal rights and liberties are said to be the foundation of the Flemish society, it means that all people must equally enjoy these rights and freedoms. Muslim women, for example, should therefore be allowed to wear a headscarf, even if the majority of the people hold negative opinions or even attitudes towards Islam and the wearing of headscarves. This is precisely why the Declaration cannot solely focus on specific groups in society. If such a Declaration were of any value, it would be directed towards all citizens and would hence in principle benefit all citizens in Flanders. 'Foreign newcomers', 'future born newcomers' and 'autochthonous residents' need to understand what certain democratic principles and values imply, even if one were to (in private life) disagree with the content. Hence, (also) the autochthonous Flemish majority group has to understand what freedom of religion implies and that multicultural recognitions are not unfair advantages, but instead ways to equalize laws and to compensate for unfair disadvantages. Moroccans, for example, can formally have religious freedom, but in practice, they can be prevented by work commitments or holiday arrangements from actually enjoying that freedom. Respecting that 'formal freedom' could mean, to give just one example, that the work calendar be adjusted so that Moroccans can take time off when there is an Islamic feast. This has already been implemented in a few organizations, and is actually one of the specific actions proposed by the report 'Roundtables of Interculturality' (2010).

Towards an all-inclusive integration policy

As argued above, integration policies nowadays all too often assume or imagine that Flemish citizens automatically adhere to the liberal values and hence that it is the 'other' who has to openly confirm and prove their will to integrate and to adhere to the core values of Flanders. If 'integration' is indeed a matter of adherence to liberal values, however, it means that the 'autochthonous population' also needs to confirm and 'prove' their attachment to these core (Flemish) values. In that sense, integration is a continuous process whereby all citizens can be integrated to a greater or lesser degree. The concrete implications for an all-inclusive integration policy are at least threefold.

First, 'integration' needs to be redesigned in a way that involves all citizens. It is [should be] unacceptable that the third generation Moroccans be treated differently and/or be still less entitled to 'Flanders' than a newborn Belgian autochthone. They are both Belgian citizens and hence should be treated as equal.

Second, as the Flemish society is becoming increasingly diverse, society's core institutions (such as education, labor marked, history, media) need to be adjusted so that they better reflect the demographic diversity. This is a plea for multiculturalism as advocated by liberal-multiculturalists like Kymlicka (1995) and Modood (2007).

Third, 'autochthones' need to understand that a monocultural society is an anachronism and hence that they will eventually become—due to this rapid diversification and similar to other societies throughout the world—a minority next to other minorities. This means that integration politics will be oriented to all citizens, insofar as they are all minorities, and that they need to learn as well how to live in a diverse society. This can be reinterpreted as a plea for the stimulation of a stronger 'egalitarian and multicultural logos, pathos and ethos'. By 'logos' we mean a fuller acknowledgement by all citizens of what living in diverse and liberal-democratic societies implies. 'Pathos' implies a stimulation among all citizens of feelings of empathy and solidarity with each other, in order not to rapidly hunker down. 'Ethos' refers to the fact that all citizens need to live their daily lives more in line with the multicultural/egalitarian logos (cognitions) and pathos (emotions).

Thus, the adherence to liberal values is not something that can be expected only from 'the newcomer' and the Flemish core institutions. It needs to be supported as much as possible by all citizens. This can be realized in a society in which the hearts and mind of people are committed to equal treatment of all regardless of skin color, religion, ethnocultural background, etc. A liberal society open to diversity is one in which people internalize norms of equality and are prepared to act accordingly. What is needed is an 'all-inclusive integration policy and movement' that involves changes in the hearts and minds of all citizens, and not just in a particular structure of legal rules. We need egalitarian principles for institutions and a corresponding ethos for the citizens. The former is concerned with the principles that ought to guide institutions or policies and applies to individuals only in their role as political actors with a responsibility to support just and democratic institutions. The latter is concerned with principles for individuals in the sense that they impose only a limited duty. One cannot, for example, force autochthones to meet up with people with a Moroccan background or to engage in intercultural dialogues, but one should not flee from it due to fear of the other, egocentric motives or stereotyped assumptions. As such, the egalitarian ethos functions as a social mechanism: it is an effective set of informal social norms pointed at living together in diversity, with equal respect and concern for all citizens (Carens, 2014).

Conclusion

In this text we have illustrated how the social imagination has deeply molded the way in which Flemish nationhood took form. This became visible in particular in the integration policies that have been implemented in the last decades. Newcomers were asked to integrate in the so-called national/cultural unity of Flanders. A closer look at this unity reveals that recently the propagated bedrock is formed by liberal, democratic and in fact European/universal values. Good illustrations thereof can be found in the civic integration policies and in the recent Declaration for newcomers. However, if these values do indeed, at least partly, form the Flemish anchor points, the question arises to what extent newcomers should be singled out to ensure that they respect the values. As we have illustrated, what is needed is a comprehensive integration policy where (1) integration is understood as a dynamic process that involves all citizens, (2) majority institutions are multiculturalized and (3) all citizens respond to a multicultural and egalitarian logos, pathos and ethos.

Bibliography

Adam, I. (2013). *Les entités fédérées belges et l'intégration des immigrés. Politiques publiques comparées.* Brussels: Éditions de l'Université de Bruxelles.

Adam, I. & Torrekens, C. (2015). *Marokkaanse en Turkse Belgen: een (zelf)portret van onze medeburgers.* Brussel: Koning Boudewijn Stichting.

Aydin-Düzgit, S. (2012). *Constructions of European identity debates and discourses on Turkey and the EU.* London: Palgrave Macmillan.

Alba, R. & Foner, F. (2015). *Strangers no more. Immigration and the challenges of integration in North America and Western Europe.* Princeton, New Jersey: Princeton University Press.

Anderson, B. (1991). *Imagined communities. Reflections on the origin and spread of nationalism.* London: Verso.

Arts, W. & Halman, L. (2014). *Value contrasts and Consensus in Present-Day Europe.* Leiden: Brill.

Banting, K. & Kymlicka, W. (2006). *Do multicultural policies erode the welfare state?* Oxford: Oxford University Press.

Banting, K. & Kymlicka, W. (2015). *The political sources of solidarity in diverse societies.* EUI Working Paper RSCAS 2015/73

Blommaert, J. & Verschueren, J. (1998). *Debating Diversity.* Oxford: Routledge

Bocquet, C., Maréchal, B., Van Den Abbeele, S., Dassetto, F. & Fadi, I. (2015). *Moslims en niet-moslims in België: inspirerende praktijken bevorderen het samenleven.* Brussel: Koning Boudewijnstichting.

Brubaker, R. (2004). *Ethnicity without groups?* Cambridge: Harvard University Press.

Brubaker, R. (2015). *Grounds for difference.* Cambridge, Massachusetts, London: Harvard University Press.

Cameron, D. (2011). PM's speech at Munich Security Conference, 5 February. https://www.gov.uk/government/speeches/pms-speech-at-munich-security-conference

Carens, J. (2014). The egalitarian ethos as a social mechanism. In Kaufman, A. (ed.) *Distributive justice and access to advantage: G.A. Cohen's egalitarianism*. Cambridge: Cambridge University Press, 50-78.

Civic Integration Policy (2003). Decreet betreffende het Vlaamse integratie- en inburgeringsbeleid. http://www.codex.vlaanderen.be/Portals/Codex/documenten/1023121.html

Commission Bossuyt (2006). EINDVERSLAG Commissie ter invulling van de cursus maatschappelijke oriëntatie. http://www.inburgering.be/sites/default/files/Eindverslag%20Commissie%20Waarden%20en%20Normen.pdf

Crul M. & Mollenkopf, J. (2012). *The changing face of world cities. Young adult children of immigrants in Europe and the United States*. New York: Sage.

de Graauw, E. (2014). Municipal ID Cards for Undocumented Immigrants Local Bureaucratic Membership in a Federal System, *Politics & Society* 42(3): 309-330.

Delanty, G. (2013). *Formations of European modernity. A historical and political sociology of Europe*. London: Palgrave Macmillan.

Francken, T. (2016). Poolse bouwvakker past perfect in ons waardenpatroon. *De Standaard*, 31 maart 2016.

Geschiere, P. (2009). *The perils of belonging: Autochthony, citizenship, and exclusion in Africa and Europe*. Chicago, London: The University of Chicago Press.

Goodhardt, D. (2004). Too diverse. *Prospect*, 30-37.

Habermas, J. (1992). Citizenship and national identity: Some reflections on the future of Europe. *Praxis International* 12 (1): 1-19.

Habermas, J. (2001). Why Europe needs a constitution. *New Left Review* 11, 5-26.

Holston, J. (Eds.) (1999). *Cities and citizenship*. Duke & London: Duke University Press.

Jacobs, D. (2004). Alive and kicking? Multiculturalism in Flanders. *International Journal on Multicultural Societies* 6(2): 280-299.

Kymlicka, W. (1995). *Multicultural citizenship*. Oxford: Oxford University Press.

Kymlicka, W. (2001). *Politics in the vernacular: Nationalism, multiculturalism, and citizenship*. Oxford: Oxford University Press.

Leijendekker, M. (2016). 'Duitsland ja, Wilders nee'. Interview Marc Jongen, Alternative Für Deutschland. *De Standaard* (4 February 2016).

Levrau, F. (2015). De multiculturele herverdelingsstaat: over gelijkheid en solidariteit in de multiculturele samenleving, *Res Publica* 57 (3): 269-294.

Levrau, F. & Loobuyck, P. (2013a). Is multiculturalism bad for social cohesion and redistribution?, *The Political Quarterly* 84 (1): 101-109.

Levrau, F. & Loobuyck, P. (2013b). Should interculturalism replace multiculturalism? A plea for complementariness. *Ethical Perspectives* 20 (4): 605-630.

Loobuyck, P. & Jacobs, D. (2009). Migration and integration policy in Belgium and Flanders in Belgian society and politics 2009 – The diversity challenge for the Left. *Annual Review* 3: 19-27.

Modood, T. (2007). *Multiculturalism. A civic idea.* Cambridge: Polity Press.

Okin, S.M. (1989). *Justice, gender, and the family.* New York: Basic Books

Oosterlynck, S., Loopmans M., Schuermans, N., Vandenabeele, J. & Zemni, S. (2016). Putting flesh to the bone: Looking for solidarity in diversity, here and now. *Ethnic and Racial Studies* 39(5): 764-782.

Parekh, B. (2000). *Rethinking multiculturalism. Cultural diversity and political theory.* Basingstoke: MacMillan.

Pasture, P. (2015). *Imagining European Unity since 1000 AD.* New York: Palgrave Macmillan.

Pearce, N. (2004). Diversity versus solidarity. A new progressive dilemma? *Renewal, A Journal of Labour Politics* 12(3): 79-87.

Putnam, R. (2007). E pluribus unum: Diversity and community in the twenty-first century. *Scandinavian Political Studies* 30(2): 137-174.

Rawls, J. (1980). Kantian constructivism in moral theory, *Journal of Philosophy* 77 (9): 515-572.

Rawls, J. (1993). *Political liberalism.* New York: Columbia Press.

Richard J. (2008). The ambiguity of Europe, *European Societies,* 10(2): 153-176.

Roossens, E. (1998). *Eigen grond eerst? Primordiale autochtonie: dilemma van de multiculturele samenleving.* Leuven: Acco.

Schaeffer, M. (2014). *Ethnic diversity and social cohesion: Immigration, ethnic fractionalization and potentials for civic action.* Farnham: Ashgate.

Schinkel, W. (2013). The imagination of 'society' in measurements of immigrant integration. *Ethnic and Racial Studies* 36(7): 1142-1161.

Schrover, M. & Schinkel, S. (2013). Introduction: the language of inclusion and exclusion in the context of immigration and integration. *Ethnic and Racial Studies* 36(7): 1123-1141.

Tamir, Y. (1993). *Liberal nationalism.* Princeton: Princeton University Press

Taylor, C. (2007). *Secular age.* Cambride: MA Belknap Press.

Taylor, C. (2004). *Modern social imaginaries.* Durham: Duke University Press.

Triandafyllidou, A., Gropas, R. & Kouki, H. (eds.) (2013). *The Greek crisis and European modernity.* London: Palgrave.

Van Craen, M. & Vancluysen, K. (2008). *Voorbij wij en zij? De sociaal-culturele afstand tussen autochtonen en allochtonen tegen de meetlat.* Brugge: Vanden Broele.

Van den Broucke, S., Noppe, J., Stuyck, K., Buysschaert, P., Doyen, G. & Wets, J. (2015). *Vlaamse Migratie- en Integratiemonitor 2015*. Antwerpen/Brussel: Steunpunt Inburgering en Integratie/Agentschap Binnenlands Bestuur.

Vrielink, J. (2010). *Van haat gesproken? Een rechtsantropologisch onderzoek naar de bestrijding van rasgerelateerde uitingsdelicten in België*. Antwerpen/Apeldoorn: Maklu

8. Moroccan Migration and its (Unique) Pattern of Self-Organizations? Comparative Reflections on Antwerp and Ghent

Nicolas Van Puymbroeck

Introduction

It is common practice in migration studies to classify migrant groups on the basis of their national descent and host nation (see for instance Gaudier & Hermans, 1991; Bousetta et al., 2005; Medhoune et al., 2015). This book also uses 'methodological nationalism' (Wimmer and Schiller, 2003) to define Moroccan migrants and their descendants who came to Belgium over the last fifty years. There are many good reasons to use a national lens to understand migration processes. Political legislation, language, and cultural customs are often nationally distinct. At the same time, authors like Schiller and Caglar (2013) have argued that societal distinctions such as gender or class, might however complicate national migration patterns. For instance, migrants from very different countries can still experience similar migration processes. Likewise, within host societies, the effects of migration can take widely different forms.

This chapter takes issue with methodological nationalism and investigates sources of variation in the pattern of Moroccan self-organizations in Belgium. It asks whether the Moroccan population has indeed developed an own unique organizational infrastructure which is different in kind from other migrant populations and which gives shape to a specific sense of belonging abroad. Immigrant self-organizations, i.e. formalized non-profit associations established by people from foreign descent with a distinctly migrant target audience, can be considered as highly symbolic expressions of group belonging in migration processes.

The chapter will reflect on the uniqueness of the organizational pattern, drawing on comparative data of Moroccan as well as Turkish organizations in two Flemish cities, Antwerp and Ghent. These data will be approached from an 'interactional' theoretical perspective on organizational genesis which looks at characteristics of immigrant groups as well as local host society conditions. My main argument is that while the Moroccan organizational infrastructure tends to take highly different local manifestations, this does not mean that it is exactly identical with the pattern of Turkish organizations. In fact, the pattern of Moroccan organizations as it was established in Antwerp and Ghent arose from intricate combinations of group factors and local conditions.

A theoretical note on migrant organizations

Common wisdom has it that immigration and the establishment of organizations are closely related. Whenever international population movements occur, more or less formalized connections tend to engraft onto the immigration experience (Schrover & Vermeulen, 2005). They happen to arise because of the drastic changes geographical relocation can entail for the immigrants themselves, as well as for the countries they leave behind and the host societies where they settle. It would therefore be very surprising if immigration from Morocco to Belgium, firstly initiated on a large scale now fifty years ago, would not have been accompanied by migrant organizations of some sort.

This basic feature of any collective immigration still leaves ample room for many different expressions of the process of migrant 'self' organizing. Commonly, scholarship distinguishes instrumental motivations, such as providing informational brokerage or material solidarity, from identity-related reasons, such as cultural reproduction (Rijkschroeff & Duyvendak, 2004; Van Puymbroeck et al., 2014). The function, number, size, density, and networks of migrant organizations can vary drastically over time and a lot of research has therefore developed an interest in accounting for the genesis of their wide range (Babis, 2014). Very often this topic is connected to the beneficial or detrimental effects of migrant organizations on so-called structural or cultural 'integration' of people from immigrant descent. Penninx and Schrover (2001) nicely capture the idea that self-organizations can be 'bastions' which separate migrants from the native population or 'binders' which act as a stepping-stone to the entire society.[1]

This chapter asks whether people who migrated from Morocco, as well as their descendants, established a unique pattern of organizations in Belgium. The aim is to describe and explain qualitative developments of the organizational tissue. I refrain from claims about the quantitative importance of migrant organizations and the number of Moroccan immigrants who are actually involved in them. Instead, this chapter takes the existence of migrant organizations at face value, approaching their existence as a symbolic expression in its own right. The focus will be on identity-related organizations because they hold most promise of being established on grounds of national and ethnic belonging.

Explanations of organizational genesis usually draw attention to group characteristics of the migrant population (such as personal networks, shared sense of belonging, and prosperity) or to host society conditions (such as entry restrictions, citizenship traditions and welfare provisions). Scholarship on Moroccan self-organizations in Belgium is still in its infancy, but two exemplary studies by Ouali (2004) and Bousetta (2001) can illustrate this difference in theoretical approach.

On the one hand, Nouria Ouali (2004) has studied migrant organizations from the perspective of group characteristics. She argues that there is a 'singular' pattern of Moroccan organizations which can be found in her case study on Brussels, but also in other destination cities and countries of the Moroccan diaspora. Among the basic characteristics of the 'associational movement', as she calls it, firstly the syndical and political activism of Moroccan organizations stands out. A second characteristic is the enthusiasm of Moroccan women to establish own self-organizations, often in opposition to male-dominated ones. Thirdly, the Moroccan second-generation would be engaged in a form of antagonist struggle for cultural and religious recognition.[2] The explanations for this pattern are believed to lie in group characteristics, such as the migration of political refugees from Morocco, the presence of some higher-educated female Moroccan students, and a lower-educated second-generation.

On the other hand, Bousetta (2000) has approached the organizational genesis from the point of view of host society conditions, so-called 'political opportunities'. Drawing on a comparative study of Moroccan migrant organizations in four cities, he comes to the conclusion that "the ecological and institutional environment of cities structure the field of post-immigration politics" (Bousetta, 2001, p.364). Institutional provisions, such as subsidy channels and consultation procedures, are said to explain the rise and demise of Moroccan organizations, and as such outweigh presumably unique national origins. For instance, the proliferation of many organizations catering to the needs of Moroccan women is considered a direct consequence of the open and beneficial opportunity structure in many Western countries that promote gender issues.

The discrepancy between both approaches does not need to be very sharp. In passing, both Ouali and Boussetta have also made reference to institutional provisions and group characteristics respectively. This echoes the need for what Michon and Vermeulen (2013) have called an 'interactional' approach which considers both explanations simultaneously. They recognize the importance of existing institutional channels, but deny that they necessarily mainstream migrant incorporation. Group characteristics are also not unimportant, but their expression is always embedded in a larger socio-political and historical context.

In their own way, both Ouali (2004) and Bousetta (2001) complicate methodological nationalism. On the one hand, while Ouali makes the case that Moroccan associations are unique and unlike others, her research still shows a splintered pattern of the Moroccan associational movement. Many fault-lines concerning education, gender, and class, seem to crisscross and intersect. Far from being a coherent movement, which derives its unity from a common national descent, organizations by Moroccans do not necessarily engage in a shared project at all. On the other hand, Bousetta's research shows that national origins of migrant groups are not the determining factor to explain organizational genesis. Simultaneously, he argues that research should study the local variations in political opportunities for self-organizations rather than limiting itself to national host society conditions.

Even though the chances are small that a pattern of migrant organizations will ever be exclusive to one nationality, it can still be a good idea to start from national migration histories. People who migrate from the same country often share a common immigration status, talk the same language, and have a similar cultural frame of reference. Self-descriptions of migrant organizations also frequently refer to national origins. Having said this, especially in a context of post-migration, it might become less clear what third and fourth generations exactly understand to be 'Moroccan' (Lamghari et al., 2016). Different geographical categories, some supra-national like the Maghreb or sub-national like the Rif, as well as cultural-religious boundaries, such as Amazigh or Arabism, complicate group identities.

A great challenge awaits future scholarship to continue describing and explaining the genesis of migrant organizations. This chapter argues that figuring out patterns of incorporation requires careful comparative research in which both national origins and institutional contexts are set out against each other in order to find similarities and differences. It constitutes an exploratory attempt, drawing on twenty-four in-depth interviews of representatives of migrant organizations and key experts, for two national groups, in two cities. Nine out of twelve interviews with people from Moroccan descent were held in Antwerp. Eight out of twelve Turkish interviews were conducted in Antwerp. Secondary sources were used to reconstruct the political opportunities in Antwerp and Ghent (Van Puymbroeck, 2014).

Reconstructing organizational developments and associational patterns proved very difficult due to very limited 'paper trails' and little secondary literature. Because a limited number of organizations had extensive archives, the genesis of organizations, including 'factual' information about their activities and target audience, were reconstructed during the interviews. I asked respondents in which immigrant organizations they had been active, what kind of function they had, why they became involved, how their organization was different/similar compared to others, ... This type of 'oral history' deals with problems of validity because recollections of the past can be seriously distorted. Also issues of reliability come into play because only a small subset of all people who had actually been involved in self-organizations could be interviewed. While the descriptions below do not include references to each of the separate interviews for reasons of space and anonymity, they should therefore be treated with caution given the difficult process of data-gathering.

A (unique) pattern of moroccan organizations?

The limited scope of this chapter does not allow a detailed and exhaustive overview of all Moroccan organizations which were found in the respective case cities. By way of alternative, I first ask whether the singular pattern identified by Ouali in Brussels can also be found in Antwerp and Ghent. Secondly, this chapter will put the national hypothesis to the test by asking whether the pattern of Moroccan associations shows resemblances with Turkish organizations. Before doing so, a preliminary concern about the role of mosques needs to be addressed. Mosques were missing in Ouali's account whereas they are the most numerous and visible migrant organizations established by Moroccans and Turks. Importantly, Dassetto and Bastenier (1984) remark that Islam was institutionalized differently in Morocco and Turkey, suggesting also potential disparities in Belgium. Nonetheless, they also note a "constant tension between the pure and simple reproduction and attempts of adapting the organizational model to a new context" (Dassetto & Bastenier, 1984, p.9-10), a perspective adopted by many other scholars who have conducted research on mosques in Belgium over the last years (see for instance Kanmaz, 2007 or Debeer et al., 2011). Drawing on their findings, the expected pattern is that Moroccan mosques are not well structured internally and externally, which leads to few institutionalized contacts with state authorities. Turkish mosques by contrast, would be structured extremely well.

Different cities, similar pattern?

In this first section, I employ a so-called 'divergent' comparison which varies the contextual opportunities of Antwerp and Ghent, while holding the immigrant group 'constant' (Fauser, 2012). If associational patterns are similar across different cities, then this type of comparison indicates that group characteristics rather than contextual opportunities influence organizational dynamics. If not, then specific opportunities of a city seem to have an impact on how migrant organizations develop.

Host society conditions that can have a potential impact on organizational genesis are the result of complex vertical articulations between different levels of government and the horizontal relations between state and civil society. Surely, many of the political opportunities are similar in Antwerp and Ghent: both fall under the same immigration law, take part in the same welfare model, and are also subject to the same regional Flemish integration policy. Still, drawing on my archival research on the political opportunities for immigrant self-organizations, I came to the conclusion that local differences existed. Firstly, the period of beneficial opportunities provided by the local authorities for immigrant organizations seems to have started earlier and also lasted longer in Ghent (between 1989 and 2008) than in Antwerp (between 1994 and 2003) (see also Heyse, 2008). For instance, categorical subsidies for immigrant organizations were already established by the end of the eighties in Ghent, while Antwerp only installed them in the early nineties. Secondly, these opportunities have however been more extensive in Antwerp than in Ghent. For instance, Antwerp authorities have extended their support to religious institutions as well, whereas Ghent restricted itself to secular organizations.

Below I will ascertain whether Moroccans in Antwerp and Ghent organized in a manner similar to Ouali's pattern observed in Brussels. It is important to acknowledge that she defined a historical dynamic of the Moroccan associational movement. Syndical and political activism of Moroccan organizations took place in the sixties and seventies, women's organizations came in the eighties, and second-generation mobilization followed in the late eighties and nineties. Mosques are an exception, in the sense that the first mosques originated as poorly structured organizations during the late sixties and early seventies, but have continued ever since and have especially grown in number without proper organizational links. Evidently, the host society opportunities have likewise evolved. This chapter cannot discuss the process of their institutional evolution, but tries to see whether the expected organizational trends in the Moroccan associational movement are influenced by coinciding local and regional opportunities.

One important caveat of this chapter concerns the important changes in the geopolitical context which have occurred during the past fifty years. Migration, especially from Islamic countries, has become a hotly contested issue due to its connection with illiberal regimes and the threat of terrorism. Surely, this global dynamic must have its bearing on how Moroccan and Turkish immigrants manifest their identity in cities, amongst others by establishing their own organizational (transnational) networks. It goes however beyond the scope of this chapter to investigate how these macro-trends are translated differently on the actual terrain of organizational genesis. I assume that despite these overarching contextual factors, more local interactions explain detailed patterns of associations.

Taking Ouali's associational pattern as reference point, the first question is whether we see syndical and political activism of Moroccan organizations in Antwerp and Ghent, just like in Brussels. A number of authors has identified especially left-wing Moroccan activism such as the *'Regroupement Démocratique Morocain'* in Brussels (Frennet-De Keyser, 2011) and the *'Komitee Marokkaanse Arbeiders in Nederland'* in Amsterdam (Van der Valk, 2001). During the late sixties and seventies, these movement-like organizations typically rallied for a democratic revolution of the Moroccan regime on their return. Simultaneously, they strove for equal treatment in their temporary host societies. In Brussels for instance, they supported hunger strikes of clandestine laborers to obtain legal working permits. Generally, these organizations upheld good relations with socialist labor unions, which often gave them infrastructural support (Leduc, 2014).

Interestingly, interviewees did not recall the existence of similar organizations in Antwerp nor Ghent.[3] An exception was the *'Regroupement Sportif Marocain'*, a rather informal left-wing organization which originated in Hoboken-Antwerp around 1974. Its founder had fled Morocco for political reasons and joined his father who came to Antwerp as guest worker. Rather than continuing his studies in Belgium, the young intellectual also became enrolled in factory labor. His organization brought together like-minded youth, but they only engaged in sports, not political activism.

The syndical connection was however not entirely absent. For instance, in 1978 the Christian Labor Union set up the *'Centrum voor Marokkaanse Arbeiders'* in Antwerp. Apart from a football team, the organization aimed at strengthening the position of Moroccan laborers by providing language lessons. Its activities were less contentious in political terms and aimed to strengthen working conditions from within the factories. In Ghent, where far less Moroccans resided at the time, labor unions were mostly dominated by South-European guest workers, and it remains unclear how many Moroccans were syndicated. It stands without a doubt however that both cities did not experience contentious manifestations by Moroccans during the initial migration period. This obviously departs from Ouali's expected pattern, but how to explain it?

'Guest workers' employed in the construction industry (source: KADOC)

It is well-known that the Amicales, which were organizations financially supported by the Moroccan regime, put a check on political activities of Moroccans abroad and also dismissed their labor union membership. The two Amicales of Antwerp and the one of Ghent will surely have had their effect on mobilization, yet Amicales were also very much active in cities like Brussels (OGB, 1976). The prime reason for the observed anomaly seems to reside in the different composition of the Moroccan population in Antwerp and Ghent, which attracted far less politically conscious immigrants. Moroccans were unevenly distributed over Belgian cities due to contextual opportunities. In particular, French-speaking universities in the capital attracted more young intellectuals, which generated a beneficial climate for avant-garde political activism.

According to Ouali, the rise of Moroccan women's organizations is, secondly, also connected to the specific composition of the immigration stream. She writes that "the presence of female university students from Morocco and their encounter with Moroccan families contributed to a focus on the invisible reality of women in migration, which gave rise to their organization" (Ouali, 2004, p.307). While this might have been the case for Brussels, the situation in Antwerp and Ghent was completely different given the lack of higher educated Moroccan women. The spouses who migrated due to family reunification came from rural regions, had received little or no education, and were often illiterate. Despite these disadvantageous group characteristics, still a large number of women organizations would develop.

In Antwerp, women's organizations initially started within the ambit of the catholic pillar. They were not strictly self-organizations, as they were mostly coordinated by Belgian women, but their target-audience was predominantly Moroccan. With the help of a range of volunteers often well-known for their role in charitable parish work, sisters like Andrea Meire or Trees Castelein, would set up organizations such as 'Flora', 'Ed Dayera' and 'Nowwar' around the late seventies and the beginning of the eighties. They operated most importantly as social gathering places to prevent the social isolation of women. Activities included drinking tea and cooking, knitting, and occasional language lessons (WOM, 1983).

The organizational tissue of the Christian pillar in Ghent did not pick up the needs of Moroccan women because it was strongly focused on the Turkish group, which was more numerous. During the second half of the eighties however, community development organizations in Ghent would also take on board Maghrebi women. For instance 'El Ele' broadened its target audience and developed a more empowering approach than the Christian organizations (Creve, 2014). In Antwerp, a similar development gave rise to new Moroccan organizations like 'Nadi Echams', which had grown out of neighborhood centers.

Nadia Merchiers, the socialist alderwomen for immigrant affairs in Ghent, would support women's organizations particularly early, whereas their Antwerp counterparts were often struggling to find funding. By 1991 however, the Flemish regulation on Local Integration Centers funded most of these women's organizations on structural grounds. The Janushead of this beneficial opportunity entailed that they were forced to open up to other (parts of) immigrant groups as well. A number of spin-off Moroccan women organizations like 'Nahkla' in Ghent or 'Dar El Salaam', 'El Nour' and 'Maa-Ezahr' in Antwerp emerged as a consequence (CBW, 1994). Their success and continuity depended strongly on better educated second-generation women taking the lead.

Consistent with the research of Bousetta, the existence of Moroccan women's organizations seems more influenced by political opportunities (ranging from pillarized structures, specific subsidies provided by female politicians, and general Flemish legislation) than by group characteristics. Therefore, Ouali's expectation that female university students would take the lead in organizing on the basis of gender seems more like a Brussels' exception than a general rule.

A third presumed characteristic of the Moroccan associational movement was the rise of independent second-generation organizations from the late eighties onwards. Ouali (2004, p.311) draws attention to group characteristics and explains how "failed employment and difficulties of professional insertion of youth shifted their demands to identity and culture". One expression of this would be "the proliferation of faith-based associations around the mosques" (Ouali, 2004, p.315). Another supposed consequence was the insistence on aspects of heritage and belonging in a struggle for recognition as equal citizens.

While there are no reasons to assume that the second-generation fared any better in Antwerp nor in Ghent, the organizational dynamic seems different, indicating also institutional effects. One powerful motivation for second-generation initiative was a critique on the institutionalized integration sector. Youth houses for Moroccans like 'Mdiq' in Antwerp or 'El Paso' in Ghent, which originated in the early eighties, had been run by the 'white majority' (Baeckeland and Vanderslycke, 1987). With the coming of age of the second generation, this implicit form of enlightened paternalism was no longer tolerated. A battle was fought over who should represent Moroccans and who should receive the subsidies. The outcome was a gradual shift of funding to new migrant organizations like *'Marokkaans Socio-Cultureel Centrum Ahlan'* in Antwerp and the *'Riff Boys'* in Ghent during the early nineties.

Another driver for mobilization was the rise of the extreme-right. The *'Vlaams Blok'* reached unprecedented electoral heights in Antwerp during the nineties, which spurred a boom of political awakening. In a matter of a few years, organizations like *'Vreemd maar Vriend'*, *'Vereniging voor Integratie en Participatie'*, *'Safina'* and *'El Wafa'* emerged in Antwerp. Amongst others, they organized debates about the political developments and about the future outlook of the second-generation. Corresponding to the extensive multiculturalism under Alderman Wellens (1994-2000), these organizations received active support from the Antwerp authorities. A number of them joined forces and established the *'Federatie van Marokkaanse Verenigingen'*. In comparison, the success of the extreme-right was far less strong in Ghent. Unsurprisingly, no similar politically motivated (umbrella) organizations came into existence.

In Ghent, mosques played a very pivotal role in the Moroccan associational tissue and would indeed develop some additional roles apart from the purely religious one. In Antwerp however, part of the motivation to establish innovative organizations was that the repertoire of activities developed by the mosques remained too limited. Notwithstanding some exceptions, most Moroccan mosques were only places of prayer that also offered Islam classes. Apart from the secular organizations, some faith-based organizations came about which had a very clear goal. For instance, the *'Vereniging Islamgodsdienst Leerkrachten Vlaanderen'* was set up to direct Islamic teaching in public schools, until it turned into a much broader umbrella-like organization called *'Vereniging voor Ontwikkeling en Emancipatie van Moslims'*. Over time, Moroccan faith-based associations in Ghent would also join this network.

Overall, the differences between Brussels, Antwerp and Ghent, despite the structural agreement in terms of disadvantaged position of the Moroccan second-generation, indicate that political opportunities need to be taken into account to explain the genesis of the organizational boom. While the pattern overlaps more or less with the expectations formulated by Ouali, its causes seem to lie elsewhere. In particular, the presence of a beneficial subsidy structure and a polarized climate of extreme-right mobilization incited organizational mobilization.

A room for Arabic classes in the Mosque of Mechelen (source: KADOC)

The last feature of the associational pattern concerns the establishment of mosque organizations. Before the sixties, hardly any Muslims resided in Belgium, which explained the general absence of mosques. The lack of places of worship was experienced as one of the most important differences with Morocco. By consequence, many more mosques than secular organizations would be established. Moroccan Islam is characterized by the non-separation of religion and state. In accordance, it is said that Amicales were closely involved in controlling Moroccan mosques in Belgium, especially by limiting their function to religious affairs (Dassetto & Bastenier, 1984, p.67). They did not however financially support Moroccan mosques, making them dependent on voluntary contributions instead. Therefore, they supposedly remained poorly structured internally and externally.

Was Moroccan Islam indeed transplanted to Belgium independently from host society conditions? At least formally, Islam was recognized as a religion in 1974, which enabled it to organize freely. However, non-profit legislation which interdicted organizations with an entire foreign board until 1984, hampered the execution of this fundamental right. Initially, Moroccan Muslims typically found shelter in church buildings both in Brussels, Antwerp and Ghent. Over time, pillarized Catholic organizations would provide them with separate places of worship, indicating the critical catalyzing role of host opportunities. Interestingly, in Ghent an attempt was made to establish one mosque for all Muslims in the city, regardless of their nationality (De Gendt, 2014, p.102). The experiment did however not last long, and Moroccan and Turkish Muslims each founded their own mosques.

In Antwerp, the number of Moroccan mosques would indeed accrue over time, mirroring exponential migration rates during the late seventies and eighties. Whereas the Amicales strictly controlled the religious function of the mosques, they could not prevent internal fissures on the basis of regional identities. In general, the Arabic minority amongst the Berber Moroccan majority withdrew and established its own mosques. Likewise, within Berber groups, familial and communal bonds created the incentive to further divide up existing mosques. This proliferation had its direct origins in group characteristics and can also be found (although to a lesser degree) in Ghent. This dynamic contributed to a poor internal structuration.

Concerning external relations with state authorities however, institutional opportunities did play a role. In Antwerp, Christian-Democrat Alderman Wellens decided to support the establishment of a Moroccan mosque umbrella, called 'Unie van Marokkaanse en Islamitische Moskeeën van Antwerpen'. Due to the splintered pattern of small neighborhood mosques, he wanted to have one interlocutor which could buffer relations with individual mosques relating issues such as the Feast of the Sacrifice or religious burials. Ghent's multiculturalism was less extensive on this account, holding on to a strict interpretation of secularism and therefore not recognizing an official intermediary religious partner organization. While individual informal contacts were upheld with far fewer Moroccan mosques in Ghent, this difference still shows the impact political considerations can have on patterns of institutionalization.

To summarize, a recurring observation is that host society conditions which vary locally often have important consequences for the way in which the Moroccan associational movement has developed. Opportunities as different from having French-speaking universities, pillarized catholic women's organizations and politicians favorable to feminism, extreme-right success and extensive non-secular multiculturalism, influence organizational genesis. Therefore, the Moroccan organizations are not only internally very heterogeneous, but they also seem to be not strictly Moroccan. Put differently, the singular pattern identified by Ouali does not entirely pass this first comparative test. In order to further tease out whether distinct features of Moroccan associations do exist, the following section draws comparisons with Turkish associational developments.

Interior of the Moroccan mosque Al Fath in Ghent (source: KADOC)

Different nationality, similar pattern?

This second section draws on the preceding conclusion that political opportunities count strongly in explaining organizational genesis. Therefore, one would expect to find very similar associational developments among different nationalities in the same city. I now combine a 'convergent' and 'divergent' comparison, thus varying both the national group by including people from Turkish descent, as well as distinguishing between Antwerp and Ghent. If Turkish and Moroccan groups display similar patterns in each city, then this would corroborate the thesis that the city environment dominates. As will be shown however, the research results indicate that migrant organizations do not entirely respond to host society conditions. Rather, institutional provisions tend to reinforce or weaken certain selected group characteristics.

Firstly, regarding left-wing activism, one would expect to find none in Antwerp nor Ghent among Turkish nationals because Moroccan left-wing organizations were also absent in both cities. This expectation is redeemed in Antwerp. Although some left-wing so-called *'Halk Evi's'* came about during the late seventies and early eighties, they did not engage in contentious politics. In

Ghent however, *'Demokratik Halk Kültür Dernegi'*, the very first Turkish migrant organization established in 1979, had an outspoken communist character and did not shy away from public manifestations. For instance, its members would hold marches against ultra-nationalist *'Grey Wolves'* organizations in the city. Interestingly, all key figures behind it belonged to a former Jugoslav minority in Turkey. Their minority status was connected to an above average level of education and stronger political consciousness. By chance, rather than by the attractiveness of Ghent's university for instance, a chain migration of like-minded left-wing Turkish intellectuals came to Ghent. These group characteristics were picked up by Ghent's predominantly socialist political class, who supported the gradual development of an entire network of leftist organizations grouped together under the umbrella *'Cagdas Dernekler Federasyonu'* in 1994.

Secondly, drawing on the beneficial opportunities for gendered organizations noted above, the expectation is to also find Turkish women's organizations in both cities. Quite remarkably, *'Kadenin Sesi'* was the only one found in Antwerp. It was developed comparatively late when neighborhood centers would diversify their target groups during the eighties. Unsurprisingly, the number of Turkish women's organizations in Ghent was higher. Apart from El Ele, the higher-educated left-wing Turkish elite established *'Gent Türk Kadinlar Birligi'*, a progressive organization which voiced concerns of equal gender roles, emancipation and cultural recognition. This mirrors nicely Ouali's mechanism observed for Moroccan women in Brussels, but it should be remembered that the Turkish women's organization also received financial help from alderwoman Merciers. This said, even in Ghent the number of secular organizations for Turkish women remained reasonably low.

Thirdly, expectations about second-generation organizations go two ways. Because of the difference in extreme-right success, it is expected to find a stronger Turkish mobilization in Antwerp compared to Ghent. However more integration centers in Ghent catered directly to the needs of the Turkish population, which raises expectations about fewer spin-offs in Antwerp. This ambiguity is translated in the organizational pattern. In 1992, Turkish organizations in Antwerp established the first immigrant umbrella of Flanders called the *'Unie van Turkse Verenigingen'* after the election results of Vlaams Blok in 1991. This initiative was not primarily driven by the second-generation but transcended a number of fault-lines, including age, gender, religion and political orientation (Clycq, 2011). In Ghent, many more second-generation independent youth houses split-off from integration centers, such as *'Posküder'* and *'Ozburun'*. Given the lack of urgency however, it took until 1998 before they established the *'Federatie van Zelforganisaties Vlaanderen'*, which emerged more out of competition to left-wing organizations than out of political motivation against the extreme-right.

Lastly, what about the establishment of Turkish mosques in Antwerp and Ghent? In Turkey the institutionalization of Islam is secularized. Although the state finances mosques, it is not involved in determining the content of religious practice. Over time, this group characteristic was transplanted to Belgium as well. Initially, Turkish Muslims received support by church communities in Antwerp and Ghent, before subsequently acquiring their own dwellings. Then *'Diyanet'*, the official Turkish state institution for religion, procured the mosques in exchange for the provision of an imam (Kanmaz, 2007). This transnational involvement went beyond the control function exercised by the Amicales.

Since the mid-eighties, also Turkish mosques would exponentially grow in number. However, the rationale was opposite to the dynamic among Moroccans. It was ideologically inspired, with especially *'Milli Gorus'* defending a political Islam. Without financial help from the Turkish authorities, Milli Gorus developed its own mosques that were even organized on a European level. A key feature of their success was a comprehensive list of connected faith-based organizations, like youth houses, football clubs, and women's organizations. Diyanet mosques, who initially only organized a place of worship, would copy this pattern and also established flanking organizations. By consequence, different Turkish confessions established well-organized associational networks regardless of the specific opportunity structure in their city. Therefore, Antwerp authorities saw no need to develop a buffer organization to represent Turkish mosques in their external contacts. In Ghent, also no institutionalized dialogue with Turkish mosques came about.

These results force us to adjust the conclusion that opportunities outweigh group characteristics. Despite some differences between Antwerp and Ghent, there are certain features which set Turkish associations aside from Moroccan ones. This is least the case for left-wing mobilization, but reveals itself clearly in the other three types of associations. Drawing on research by Jacobs (2006) amongst others, it is possible to hypothesize that family relations among the Turkish population are more dense, which partly inhibits the influence of opportunities for gendered organizations. A similar consideration is that generational divides seem to be less pronounced among the Turkish population, which has an impact on the ascendency of second-generation organizations. Lastly, ideology rather than geographical origin is a strong binding factor for Turkish Islamic networks, leading to more structured mosque networks. Overall, these hypotheses lead to the assumption that the Turkish population in Belgium fits better the image of constituting a 'migrant community', whereas Moroccans tend to be more loosely connected. Therefore the impact of institutional provisions is also more pronounced in the case of the Moroccan associational movement.

Conclusion

Do national groups develop 'unique' patterns of associational incorporation or do contextual provisions 'mainstream' expressions of belonging? The answer to this question is that both processes seem to apply. The first empirical section has shown that Moroccan associations developed differently according to the contextual provisions of their city environment. In the second empirical section, this conclusion was nuanced, indicating that it did not imply that the Turkish population would engage in exactly the same organizational pattern in Antwerp and Ghent respectively. Instead, specific group characteristics seem to interact with contextual local opportunities, which entails that both explanatory models should be studied simultaneously. This calls for an interactional comparison of the type employed here.

Methodological nationalism, I would argue, is useful as long as it is approached critically. This not only implies the need to actively look for interactions with host society conditions, but it also requires paying specific attention to different types of organizations established by one nationality group. The organizations studied here all belonged to the class of identity-related organizations. There were three assumptions guiding this selection. Firstly, this class is expected to be most numerous and important given the cultural differences between Belgium and the countries of origin. Secondly, local authorities seem to have most discretionary room to develop specific opportunities for these organizations. Thirdly, chances are considerate that migrant groups from different origins will develop own organizational patterns. Future research needs to extend the comparison by including instrumental organizations linked to the process of immigration, like repatriation organizations, or to material solidarity, like migrant housing corporations.

Within the class of identity-related organizations, important historical differences were noted. Left-wing activist organizations seem to depend strongly on the presence of politically motivated immigrants. Host society conditions, like universities, can indirectly influence the migrant composition of intellectual avant-gardists. Women's organizations tend to depend very strongly on contextual opportunities, like the existence of Catholic women organizations or feminist politicians. Still, the social cohesion of migrant minority groups can significantly disturb the reach of penetration of these opportunities to the core of their community, for instance when tight gender patterns interfere with host society opportunities to establish women's organizations. A similar consideration goes for the second-generation organizations, which are also more strongly related to subsidy structures and discursive political contexts, but which are also mediated by community cohesion. Lastly, mosques and faith-based institutions seem to be embedded strongly in transnational networks. Host society conditions therefore have only a limited effect on their institutionalization.

The analysis unfolded here was confined to migrant organizations established before the turn of the millennium. This implies it corresponds to the organizational dynamics of first and second generation migrants. One crucial question for future research is whether it is still valid to draw on methodological nationalist criteria for studying organizational patterns of third and fourth generations who have been socialized entirely in Belgium. Although many organizations existing today still hold on to national references in their name, the question is how people actually experience its meaning, especially in a context of far-reaching globalization. It is my hypothesis that a national pattern of organizations, which historically only existed to some extent, will become even less likely in the future, with more hybrid individual and group patterns replacing it.

Notes

1   These roles are not necessarily mutually exclusive because bastions can be a home-base for binding, although binder-bridges often tend to distort strong bonding capital.

2   Ouali (2004) also discusses a fourth trend, which consists in transnational development aid. Likewise, Bousetta (2000, p.297-299) singles out Amazigh associations as a distinct type. Chapter 4-1 by Karrouche discusses this issue.

3   According to Frennet-De Keyser (2011, p.12) the Regroupement Democratique Marocain also had a cell operating in Antwerp. It is unclear what the importance of this branch was for the local situation in Antwerp, but the hearth of the movement was definitely situated in Brussels.

Bibliography

Babis, D. (2014). Understanding Diversity in the Phenomenon of Immigrant Organizations: A Comprehensive Framework. *Journal of International Migration and Integration, forthcoming.*

Baeckeland, L., & Vanderslycke, D. (1987). *El Paso Stad Gent 4 Jaar Stratego: Een Kleine Sociale Geschiedenis van Jeugdcentrum El Paso.* Gent.

Bousetta, H. (2000). *Immigration, Post-Immigration Politics and the Political Mobilization of Ethnic Minorities. A Comparative Case-Study of Moroccans in Four European Cities:* Unpublished PhD Thesis.

Bousetta, H., Gsir, S., & Martiniello, M. (2005). *Les Migrations Marocaines vers la Belgique et l'Union Européenne. Regards Croisés.* Bilbao: HumanitarianNet.

CBW (CentrumBuitenlandseWerknemers) (1994). *Eigen Organisaties van Marokkanen en Turken.* Antwerpen: CBW.

Clycq, N. (2011). *Muslims in Antwerp.* New York: Open Society Foundations.

Creve, P. (2014). Cherchez la femme. Het archief van El Ele. *Brood & Rozen. Tijdschrift voor de Geschiedenis van Sociale Bewegingen*(1), 62-65.

Dassetto, F., & Bastenier, A. (1984). *L'Islam Transplanté. Vie et Organisation des Minorités Muselmanes de Belgique.* Antwerpen: EPO.

Debeer, J., Loobuyck, P., & Meier, P. (2011). *Imams en Islamconsulenten in Vlaanderen: Hoe zijn ze georganiseerd?* Steunpunt Gelijkekansenbeleid: Lithos.

De Gendt, T. (2014). *Turkije aan de Leie.* Tielt: Lannoo.

Fauser, M. (2012). *Migrants and Cities. The Accommodation of Migrant Organizations in Europes.* Farnham: Ashgate.

Frennet-De Keyser, A. (2011). *Histoire du Regroupement Démocratique Marocain.* Bruxelles: Carhima ASBL.

Gaudier, J.-P., & Hermans, P. (1991). *Des Belges Marocains. Parler à l'immigré / Parler de l'immigré.* Bruxelles: De Boeck Université.

Heyse, P. (2008). *Onderzoek naar de Structuur en Werking van Allochtone Vrouwenverenigingen.* Steunpunt Gelijkekansenbeleid.

Jacobs, D. (2006). La vie associative allochtone dans la Région de Bruxelles-Capitale. In P. Delwit, A.

Rea, & M. Swyngedouw (Eds.), *Bruxelles Ville Ouverte. Immigration et diversité culturelle au coeur de l'Europe* (pp. 181-194). Paris: L'Harmattan.

Kanmaz, M. (2007). *Moskeeën in Gent: Tussen Subcultuur en Sociale Beweging. Emancipatiedynamieken van Moslimminderheden in de Diaspora.* Universiteit Gent, Gent.

Lamghari, Y., Thys, R., Westerveen, L., Van Dijk, M., Torrekens, C., & Adam, I. (2016). *Marokkaanse en Turkse Belgen: een (zelf)portret van onze medeburgers.* Brussel: Koning Boudewijnstichting.

Leduc, A. (2014). *En l'absence de politique publique d'accueil, une expérience associative dans la mouvance de la FGTB de Bruxelles (1968-1989).* Bruxelles: Collectif Formation Société Education Permanente – Cohesion Sociale.

Medhoune, A., Lausberg, S., Martiniello, M., & Rea, A. (2015). *L'Immigration Marocaine en Belgique. Mémoires et Destinées.* Mons: Couleurs Livres.

Michon, L., & Vermeulen, F. (2013). Explaining Different Trajectories in Immigrant Political Integration: Moroccans and Turks in Amsterdam. *West European Politics, 36*(3), 597-614.

OGB (Onthaalcomité voor Gastarbeiders van de provincie Brabant). (1976). *Amicales: Verlengstuk van het Marokkaans Regime.* Brussel.

Ouali, N. (2004). Le Mouvement Associatif Marocain de belgique: Quelques Repères. In N. Ouali (Ed.), *Trajectoires et dynamiques migratoires de l'immigration marocaine de Belgique* (pp. 303-325). Louvain-la Neuve: Bruylant-Academia.

Penninx, R., & Schrover, M. (2001). *Bastion of Bindmiddel? De Organisatie van Migranten in een Lange-Termijn Perspectief.* Den Haag: NWO/NMPS.

Rijkschroeff, R., & Duyvendak, J. W. (2004). De Omstreden Betekenis van Zelforganisaties. *Sociologische Gids, 51*(1), 18-35.

Schiller, N. G., & Caglar, A. (2013). Locating Migrant Pathways of Economic Emplacement: Thinking Beyond the Ethnic lens. *Ethnicities, 13*(4), 494-514.

Schrover, M., & Vermeulen, F. (2005). Immigrant Organisations. *Journal of Ethnic and Migration Studies, 31*(5), 823-832.

Van der Valk, I. (2001). *Van migratie naar burgerschap, twintig jaar Komitee Marokkaanse Arbeiders in Nederland.* Amsterdam: Instituut voor Publiek en Politiek.

Van Puymbroeck, N. (2014). *Migratie en de Metropool, 1964-2013.* Leuven / Den Haag: Acco.

Van Puymbroeck, N., Van Dam, S., & Dierckx, D. (2014). Het Migrantenmiddenveld in Antwerpen: De Historische Contouren Geschetst (1964-2013). In G. Verschraegen, C. de Olde, S. Oosterlynck, F. Vandermoere, & D. Dierckx (Eds.), *Over Gevestigden en Buitenstaanders. Armoede, Diversiteit en Stedelijkheid* (pp. 121-141). Leuven / Den Haag: Acco.

Wimmer, A., & Schiller, N. (2003). Methodological Nationalism, the Social Sciences, and the Study of Migration: an Essay in Historical Epistemology. *International Migration Review, 37*(3), 576-610.

WOM (Werkgroep Overleg Migrantenvrouwen). (1983). *De Migrantenvrouw: Een Dubbele Discriminatie.* Antwerpen: CBW.

9. The shifting Moroccan policy paradigm regarding the integration of MREs[1] (Moroccans Living Abroad): reconciling transnational ties and migrant integration

Rilke Mahieu, Christiane Timmerman & Nadia Fadil

Introduction

Existing literature on diaspora policies has tended to pay attention to the ways in which countries of origin incite emigrants to sustain and cultivate transnational links to their 'homeland' (Gamlen, 2006; Dufoix, Guerassimoff & de Tinguy, 2010; Collyer, 2013). Studies have documented the wide spectrum of strategies origin states employ in order to secure their emigrants' transnational ties, including institution building (Gamlen, 2014), the granting of political rights (Lafleur, 2016) and language and cultural education. As such, these studies uncover the various ways in which emigrants' connections with 'home' seem to be a continuous point of concern by the countries of origin.

Yet what are we to make of cases in which diaspora policies not only seek to maintain transnational ties, but also to foster smooth integration in the country of residence? This case study of Moroccan diaspora policies seeks to show how, beyond maintaining transnational ties to the 'homeland', diaspora policy discourses increasingly address the expatriates as citizens of and subjects of integration in the receiving societies. Nowadays, notions such as *intégration* (integration) and similar terms, such as *enracinement* (the act of 'taking root'), are omnipresent in official Moroccan diaspora policy discourses, and are seen to relate positively to continued transnational ties to Morocco. This evolution is especially visible in the field of Moroccan cultural diaspora policies, which focus on the transmission of national culture and languages to the emigrants' descendants.

This evolution is remarkable for at least two reasons. First, it implies a total rupture with previous Moroccan diaspora policy discourses. A few decades ago, integration – and in particular, naturalization, as the most symbolically loaded expression of integration – of expatriate Moroccans in the receiving country was rejected completely, because it was deemed to undermine their homeland affiliation. On the contrary, current Moroccan diaspora policies do not merely tolerate but also promote integration, and embrace dual citizenship.[2] Secondly, the current Moroccan policy position goes against the grain of a widespread assumption that predominates in contemporary public and political debates on immigrant integration. This assumption states that there is a zero-sum game of attachment in which stronger integration implies weaker transnationalism and vice versa (Carling & Pettersen, 2014; Bouras, 2012). This viewpoint resonates with the assimilationist perspective on minorities' ethno-cultural accommodation which is, as Joppke (2007) argues, dominant in Western Europe. Accordingly, migrant origin states investing in their emigrants' transnational ties are regularly accused of 'meddling' in migrant populations affairs, thereby 'hindering' this population's integration in the receiving countries. The current Moroccan policy approach, reconciling the concepts of integration and transnationalism, seems to be defying these popular assumptions.

While receiving states' views and policies on integration of immigrants are generally well-investigated, analysis of how countries of origin regard or respond to the integration processes of their expatriate citizens is scarce. The aim of this chapter is therefore to describe and understand this new Moroccan policy interest in and appreciation of 'integration'. More in particular, how did integration, once considered to be fully inconsistent with Morocco's interests, evolve into a desirable outcome of Moroccan diaspora policies? This pertinent reorientation also raises the question how the notion of integration is understood in Moroccan policy discourses, especially in relation to transnational ties.

These questions relate to the academic debate about the tension between *integration* and *transnationalism* (see e.g. Erdal & Oeppen, 2013), concepts that broadly represent the relationship of emigrants (and their descendants) with their country of residence and their country of origin, respectively. In the next, second section of this article we explain how this debate provides us with a suitable analytic framework for studying the Moroccan state's approach to integration.

In order to understand Morocco's current policy focus on integration, it is necessary to take into account the historical trajectory leading up to this point. Therefore, in the third section of this article we outline the historical evolution of the Moroccan official stance regarding integration, drawing on literature, policy documents and political discourses.

In the fourth and main part of the article, we disentangle Moroccan diaspora policy makers' understanding of the interaction between transnationalism and integration, based on an analysis of in-depth interview material.

The integration-transnationalism nexus reconsidered: the origin state perspective

"We will continuously support your efforts to integrate in the countries of settlement (...)". (King Mohammed VI, Royal Speech of 20 August 2012)

Studies looking into diaspora policies tend to focus on the sending states' attempts to turn their emigrants into 'transnational subjects' (Smith & Guarnizo, 1998) and the wide range of strategies employed for this purpose (Gamlen, 2006). Strategies consist of the management and safeguarding of the transnational practices and identifications of emigrants regarding their 'homeland', for instance through emigrant-oriented investment and banking policies (to capture expatriate remittances) or language and cultural policies (to ensure expatriates' identification with the homeland). Accordingly, diaspora policy discourses cultivate the idealized image of the loyal emigrant, contributing to the homeland's economic and political interests. Therefore, diaspora policies can be regarded as the origin state's policy response to the reality of migrant transnationalism.

However, in our case study on Moroccan diaspora policy discourses, a matter emerged which cannot be understood through this transnational lens, since it seems largely unrelated to homeland issues and interests. Besides continuing homeland-oriented (transnational) concerns, we detected a growing policy interest on behalf of the Moroccan state regarding the issue of integration, that is, the adaptation and incorporation of the migrants into their respective receiving societies. In-depth empirical studies that investigate this policy dimension of diaspora policies are rare and usually do not take into account the origin state perspective.[3]

To make sense of this emergence of the notion 'integration' on the Moroccan diaspora policy agenda, we need a conceptual framework not only incorporating the notion of integration, but also taking into consideration its complex interaction with continuing transnational ties to the homeland. For this, we turn to the scholarly debate on the complex empirical relationship between migrant integration and transnationalism (Erdal & Oeppen 2013; Snel et al. 2006). While this debate is mainly confined to understanding the micro-level interaction between both processes in migrants' everyday lives, the conceptual framework of the 'transnationalism/integration nexus' is useful as well to frame the state of origin position regarding integration and the interrelation between emigrants' integration and their transnationalism. Particularly suitable for this purpose is the typology of Erdal and Oeppen (2013, 878) distinguishing three forms of interaction between integration and transnationalism. The first type of interaction is 'additive': here the result of the interaction between processes of integration and transnationalism equals the sum of the two, implying they are separate processes not influencing one another. The second type of interaction is 'synergistic', where the result of the interaction is greater than the sum of the two parts, meaning that integration and transnationalism processes stimulate each other. The third type of interaction is 'antagonistic'; here the outcome of the interaction is less than the sum of the two. This is the opposite of the synergistic interaction, because here integration and transnationalism processes thwart each other. While the case of antagonistic interaction supports the popular belief that migrant integration necessarily implies a loosening of ties to the homeland, the case of additive interaction does not support this hypothesis and the case of synergistic interaction even refutes it.

We argue that this basic typology, while in origin interested in describing empirical relationships between two dimensions of migrants' daily lives, can be used as an analytic lens to study shifting (state) discourses on integration and transnationalism. More precisely, this typology allows us to make sense of the emergence of 'integration' as a goal in the Moroccan state's diaspora policies, and makes clear how integration is conceptualized in relation to other, 'classic' homeland-related aims. A core question is to what extent we can observe in discourses a conceptual juxtaposition between integration on the one hand and loyalty to one's roots on the other hand, or reconciliation of both positions.

The Moroccan paradigm shift regarding emigrant integration: from rejection to promotion

Over the course of the last decades, the Moroccan state's position on the integration of its expatriate citizens in their countries of residence has evolved from outspoken hostility to warm embrace. The paradigm shift was not sudden, but the result of a gradual evolution in the official position occurring in two stages. First, in the 1990s, there was a shift from rejection to acceptance of integration, and more recently, there was a shift from acceptance to promotion. The first shift, documented by various scholars (de Haas, 2007; Brand, 2006; Iskander, 2010), implied that the Moroccan state started to recognize and tolerate that Moroccan expatriates were increasingly incorporated in all realms of the host society, that is, *de facto* integration was taking place. Moreover, the state acknowledged that this integration did not necessarily harm emigrants' transnational ties to Morocco. As a consequence, the Moroccan state no longer denounced its emigrants' integration, nor its main symbol, naturalization.

Based on our empirical examination of current Moroccan diaspora policies, we now argue that a second discursive shift has taken place: from mere acceptance to more active encouragement. Today, integration is not only tolerated by the Moroccan state, moreover, it has become a constitutive element of its official policy agenda. In addition, the state promotes the idea that continued transnational ties have a positive effect on integration. As this current paradigm has not been investigated yet, we will describe it more extensively than the first shift.

Using Erdal and Oeppen's (2013, 878) threefold interaction typology as analytic lens, we argue that over the course of the last three decades, the Moroccan official understanding of the relationship between integration and transnationalism has evolved from antagonistic to synergistic. This implies that the assumed relationship between integration and transnationalism, which also depends on a specific understanding of integration, has been redrawn.

The antagonistic perspective: integration as a threat to transnational ties
In the first decades of Moroccan mass emigration, durable integration of Moroccan migrants in the receiving countries was a non-issue for the Moroccan state, as well as for the receiving states. Moroccan labor migration was considered temporary and transitory (Benkirane, 2010; De Haas, 2007), an assumption supported by the circular character of Moroccan migration in the 1960s (Iskander, 2010).

However, the question of integration would soon enter the political agenda. Due to the wave of family reunification following the 1974 labor recruitment stop, the demographic composition of the expatriate communities started to shift, from male workers to families with children. As the profile of Moroccan emigrant communities shifted, transnational practices and homeland loyalties started to change too. As Brand (2006) notes, this was a matter of state concern because 'no longer could Rabat assume that these Moroccans would all eventually return home to retire, bringing with them their accumulated savings and expertise. Nor could it simply expect or assume that they would maintain their ties of loyalty to family, culture, religion, or, most importantly, king' (2006: 89).

A Moroccan family in the 1970s (source: KADOC)

While the dream of return was not abandoned completely, expatriate Moroccans were *de facto* integrating into their receiving societies. However, this reality was not recognized by the Moroccan state. On the contrary, the Moroccan monarchy and government strongly rejected and denounced any form of integration in the receiving countries up to the early '90s. For instance, emancipatory migrant movements advocating for Moroccan migrants' (political) rights in the receiving countries were fiercely condemned, just as the idea of naturalization. Exemplary here was the interview of late King Hassan II on national French television in 1989, in which he defended his anti-integration stance and imprinted on Moroccans in France not to participate in French politics:

"I am against it . . . for the simple reason that for me, there is no distinction between a Moroccan born in Morocco and raised in Morocco and a Moroccan born in France and raised in France. (...) I am against integration, in any sense of the term. (...) I told them [Moroccan emigrants], you shouldn't fill your head and your spirit, at night before going to bed, with electoral problems that do not concern you, that are not yours. Because you are definitely not French. They'll always court your voices but then they'll always forget you afterwards." (King Hassan II as quoted in Iskander, 2010: 324).

The main reason for this Moroccan reluctance regarding emigrants' integration and political participation in European countries was the fear that Moroccan dissidents would be politically empowered abroad and cause unrest in their homeland (Desiderio & Weinar, 2014). During the nation-wide French labor strikes in the 1970s in which French Moroccan labor migrants took a prominent role, Morocco grew concerned that these organized protests would spill over and destabilize the Moroccan political system (Iskander, 2010). In addition, the state worried that incorporation into the receiving country would decrease remittances (de Haas, 2007). In sum, during this period the Moroccan state considered emigrants' transnational loyalties to be irreconcilable with deeper entrenchment into the receiving countries, which attests to an antagonistic understanding of the interaction between integration and transnationalism.

The turning point: recognition of integration
However, by the end of the 1980s, this approach by the Moroccan state proved counterproductive, only increasing the sense of alienation of Moroccan emigrants and their descendants of the Moroccan state. As a result, the government's drive to keep emigrants from becoming enfranchised workers undermined the government's ambition to convert Moroccan labor into capital for the kingdom's economy (Iskander, 2010). Moreover, opportunities for migrants to participate in the receiving countries grew, irrespective of Morocco's approach. Increasingly, Western European states offered immigrants a range of opportunities for social and political participation, and in some cases, access to citizenship. These evolutions represented a direct threat to Hassan II's claim on its subjects, which triggered the Moroccan state to change its approach radically. From the late '90s on, the Moroccan state began to acknowledge that only by accepting the gradual integration of MREs into European host states, there would be a chance

of preserving ties of sovereignty. As such, the Moroccan state moved away from its former position, which rejected integration in order to hold on to its subjects (Brand, 2006).

As the demographic outlook of Moroccan expatriate communities shifted from male workers to emigrant families, the Moroccan government shifted its focus accordingly, from controlling workers' organizational activities to engaging with emigrant families in order to define their cultural relationship with Morocco. Within this new approach the officially promoted cultural identity for expatriate Moroccans, and accordingly, the official discourses on integration, showed a significant departure from previous state rhetoric. Return to the homeland or exclusive allegiance to the Moroccan state was no longer required for Moroccan cultural belonging, moreover, "in an abrupt about-face from the position the king had maintained vociferously for decades (...) the Moroccan regime was no longer against Moroccan emigrants' integration into their host societies" (Iskander, 2010: 174). While integration no longer implied weakening ties of loyalty to Morocco, the Moroccan state stressed however that Moroccan nationality was inalienable (de Haas, 2007). The indissoluble, perpetual nature of the connection to Morocco was further underlined as the relationship between expatriate Moroccans and the Moroccan King was reframed in filial terms (the King as father, the Moroccans abroad as his children) (Iskander, 2010).

In sum, the antagonist understanding was abandoned, making way for a more pragmatic position. Integration of Moroccan emigrants and their descendants in the receiving countries was tolerated, and was no longer considered to impact emigrants' transnational loyalties in a negative sense. Moreover, slowly the understanding emerged that structural integration could support MREs' transnational engagements such as the practice of sending remittances (de Haas, 2007). Brand (2006) understands this paradigm shift as a pragmatic move: a more limited form of sovereignty over expatriates was accepted "in order not to lose them entirely by joining what would certainly be a losing battle against the reality of growing integration" (2006, 83). However, at this stage, Moroccan policies did not consider integration to be an official policy goal in and of itself, nor was integration linked substantially to the idea of maintaining loyalty. Therefore, we propose to read this period as a transition period between two opposite paradigms: overt rejection of integration (an 'antagonistic' understanding of the integration-transnationalism nexus), on the one hand, and encouragement of integration (a 'synergistic' understanding of this nexus), on the other.

The synergistic perspective: promoting integration as a diaspora policy goal
Looking at Moroccan diaspora policies today, approximately two decades later, we initially seem to find similar notions as before: acknowledgement of the permanent settlement of Moroccan migrants and their descendants in the receiving societies. In the strategic plan of the leading Moroccan diaspora institution, the Ministry for Moroccans Residing Abroad and Migration Affairs (MCMRE),[4] the 'permanent installation' and the 'emergence of new generations' are recognized as major evolutions in Moroccan expatriate communities:

> "Integration of MRE in the receiving countries is irreversible; due to massive naturalization, the socio-economic insertion of the younger generations and political participation. (...) The integration of the Moroccan Community Residing Abroad in the countries of residence does not affect the consistency of their primary loyalty to the country of origin. The relationship with Morocco is an elementary socio-cultural and economic component of Moroccan emigration. It is situated at the origin of the migratory project (...)" (MCMRE, 2012/2013).

Clearly, integration is no longer defined as a threat for the expatriates' loyalty; on the contrary, strong ties with Morocco are presented here as an inherent characteristic of Moroccan migrant communities, unwavering across time and generations. The incorporation of expatriate Moroccans has also been legally enshrined: the new Constitution of 2011 recognizes the citizenship of expatriate Moroccans in their respective countries of residence.[5]

However, at the same time, current Moroccan diaspora policies increasingly frame integration not just as a reality to take into account, but also as a central policy goal. First signs can be found in the early years of the new millennium. In a 2003 government-supported strategic note, for instance, the Deputy Minister for the Moroccan community living abroad[6] aims:

> "To encourage integration and coexistence in the receiving societies, while preserving fully Moroccan national identity in its Muslim, Arab and Amazigh dimension (...) [and] to incite [the Moroccan community abroad] to assume responsibility as citizens, as well as membership in political, syndicalist and associative life [in the receiving societies]." (Deputy Minister for the Moroccan community living abroad, as quoted in Benkirane, 2010: 8).

By this time, expatriate Moroccans' integration is actively encouraged, and this notion is incorporated throughout state discourses. Especially since the reinstallation in 2007 of a fully-fledged Ministry for Moroccans Residing Abroad, this new approach seems to have gained momentum. According to the first minister in charge of this institution, Morocco seeks to develop diaspora policies 'embracing all aspects of the daily life of the community', replacing the narrow mercantile approach characterizing Morocco's diaspora policies up to the early '90s. This policy vision translates as a holistic, dual policy approach "supporting the integration of MRE in the host societies, while contributing to the consolidation and strengthening of ties with Morocco."[7] In the same vein, the first out of four objectives in the Ministry's 2008-2012 Strategic Plan is:

> "To assist the integration (*l'enracinement*)[8] of the new generations in the countries of residence without uprooting (*le déracinement*) their ties with the country or origin." (MCMRE, 2008)

Interestingly, integration and transnationalism are now conceived as intertwined processes. The subsequent 2012-2016 Strategic Plan further recognizes that the Moroccan diaspora institutions take on some 'new roles' vis-à-vis Moroccans living abroad; namely, the roles of: "representing the Moroccans Living Abroad, *promoting their integration* and defending their rights" [italics added].

Observing the widespread use of this notion in current Moroccan diaspora policy discourses, the question raises what actually counts as 'integration'. By and large, we find that when integration is mentioned, in the first place structural integration is meant, rather than more extensive interpretations including socio-cultural integration or even assimilation. For instance, one of the policy objectives of the 2008-2012 Strategic Plan clearly hints at structural integration only:

> "Favoring cultural proximity to Morocco, by offering the Global Moroccans an adapted cultural offer *coherent with the objectives of their socio-economic integration in the receiving societies*." [Italics added] (MCMRE, 2008)

More specifically, high value is placed on obtaining an educational degree and participating in the labor force, while language acquisition, naturalization[9] and political participation in the receiving country are acknowledged to facilitate these processes. Also, obedience to the laws and regulations of the host society is promoted.

There is however a clear limit to what 'integration' entails, as conceptualizations of integration that require 'loosening' or 'cutting' cultural, linguistic and religious ties with the country of origin are rejected. This position is illustrated in the MCMRE Minister's intervention on the Global Diaspora Conference in 2013:

> "The cultural enrichment the migrant brings to his two countries, contributes to the *rapprochement* of nations, to breaking up and fighting prejudices and stereotypes, and the promotion of tolerance, and to the rejection of discriminatory and xenophobic attitudes. In this sense, it is incumbent on all of us to *encourage models of integration that are uniting in a balanced manner the freedom and right of preservation of the cultural identity of the migrant,* while respecting the social values and civic and legal duties in the host country.[10]" [Italics added]

When it comes to ethno-cultural identity, expatriate Moroccans are expected to remain 'Moroccan at heart'. Desiderio & Weinar (2014) also note the Moroccan state's tendency to focus on functional, i.e. economic, civic and political integration. Smith & Guarnizo (1998) discern a similar pattern in various sending states: while states encourage their emigrants' instrumental accommodation to receiving society, simultaneously, these states inhibit the emigrants' cultural assimilation and promote their own national culture. Thus, while origin states (including the Moroccan state) incorporate the concept of 'integration' in their discourses, they can be seen to put forward a particular understanding of it that does not contradict other (transnational) claims.

The new Moroccan policy paradigm on integration is also reflected in the reframing of older policy programs dating back to the era during which integration was denounced completely. A good example here is the organization of education aimed at transferring national language(s) and culture (a program commonly referred to as ELACM – *Enseignement de la langue Arabe et de la culture Marocaine*) and religion to the 'next' generation (the emigrants' descendants). This education is at the heart of Moroccan cultural diaspora policies, and different diaspora institutions are involved in it. Previously, these programs were aimed at smoothening eventual return migration and the preservation of an 'umbilical cord' with the country of origin. According to de Haas (2007), they were actually the Moroccan state's attempt to prevent migrant descendants' integration in the receiving country and their alienation of the country of origin. However, in current policies, we see a different meaning being attached to these policies: they are presented as beneficial for integration. For instance, the Strategic Action Plan 2008-2012 (MCMRE, 2008) explains that education of the Arabic language and Moroccan culture for children with Moroccan background is organized in order to 'preserve their cultural identity, strengthen their ties with the motherland, and *realize the conditions necessary for their integration in the countries of residence'* (2008, 23) [italics added]. Also more recently developed cultural policy programs, such as the establishment of Moroccan cultural centers in various receiving countries (*Dar el Maghrib*) and the Summer Universities for young Moroccans living abroad, are inscribed into this logic: they are consistently presented as either 'fully coherent with' or 'contributing to' integration.

Similarly, Moroccan diaspora policies increasingly promote social cohesion and interaction between expatriate Moroccans and the other (non-Moroccan) citizens of receiving societies. Some exposure programs (like the Ministry's *Séjours Culturels*) involve bringing not only expatriate Moroccans to Morocco, but also their non-Moroccan peers, in order to improve the latter group's perception of Morocco and Moroccan culture. Other programs support Moroccan cultural events in the country of residence, actions that are equally aiming at harmonious intercultural relations and at reducing negative stereotypes about Moroccans. Again, policy actions that were previously conceptualized — in a 'transnational' logic — as preserving expatriate Moroccans' ties to Morocco are now understood from a different angle: they are seen to be improving social cohesion and intercultural understanding, and therefore, to be paving the way to integration. However, this does not imply full abandonment of older, 'transnational' claims. Rather, both viewpoints exist simultaneously. This characterizes the new synergistic understanding, in which integration and transnational ties go hand in hand.

Moroccan diaspora policies also increasingly aim at supporting structural integration of expatriate Moroccans in a more direct manner. For instance, the Ministry for Moroccans living abroad recently started paying attention to the issue of school failure among expatriate Moroccan students. In 2015, this attention translated into a pilot study on the subject across various residence countries. Among others, this study concluded that European education policies have failed to integrate Moroccan children. In response to the study's results, the Ministry launched a participative, project-based policy approach in close cooperation with Moroccan migrant organizations active in the field of education. This focus on school failure was framed as a new approach of the Ministry regarding the educational support for expatriate Moroccan children, complementing the existing educational programs.[11]

Clearly, this current approach to integration is more ambitious than previous approaches. The policy discourses display overt ambition to contribute to emigrants' integration. Through its diaspora policies, the Moroccan state appears to be claiming a position as a legitimate stakeholder in the integration process of expatriate Moroccans. This ambition is explicitly expressed in a media interview of the Moroccan ambassador in Belgium (2009), explaining the Moroccan state perspective regarding its expatriate communities to a Belgian audience:

"The reality is: there is a large Moroccan community (...) that has ties to Morocco. Our position is: one needs to make the difference between citizenship and identity. Too often, the Moroccan identity of Moroccans [living in Belgium] is denied; they want to make Belgians of them (...). Because of integration troubles, unfortunately, many Moroccan youngsters end up as petty criminals or in religious extremism. We need to control the situation, and this can be done more effectively in cooperation. We [the Moroccan state] can help you."[12]

One the one hand, this excerpt reveals how the Moroccan state, by offering the receiving state a 'helping hand' in dealing more efficiently with integration-related challenges, is claiming the legitimacy of its authority regarding Moroccan expatriate communities. The ambassador conveys the message that the Moroccan state is a significant stakeholder, capable of improving the integration of expatriate Moroccans in their receiving societies. On the other hand, the excerpt illustrates the critical view of the Moroccan state regarding the way many receiving countries – and most in particular, European countries – pursue and conceptualize integration. Especially assimilationist policies are denounced fiercely by Morocco. This point is repeatedly articulated, though usually in rather veiled terms. For instance, a Strategic Note of the Ministry (2008) states that

"Host countries of the Community of Moroccans Living Abroad are posing more and more openly the question of the integration of this population. This integration, if it is done according to the standards and policies of the countries of residence, risks, eventually, to separate this community from its country of origin, with all the consequences."[13]

In sum, the emergence of 'integration' on the diaspora policy agenda does not only imply that the Moroccan state is broadening its policy agenda; it also reinforces its authority regarding expatriate Moroccans' affairs. However, throughout the process of incorporating the notion of integration, we also witness how Moroccan state actors articulate a very particular understanding of integration that complies with Morocco's broader political (transnational) agenda. This point is discussed in the next section.

Transnational attachments as a lever for integration: underlying dynamics

> "Well, there is a Moroccan proverb, I don't know how to translate it, but it is saying that 'if we don't not know our roots, we cannot integrate easily in other countries'. So, we can say that it's integration without [uprooting]; it is putting down your roots without uprooting (...). Because someone who does not really know his roots or where he comes from, cannot integrate himself easily. Therefore, the objective [of our policies] is not only to have a Moroccan identity, it is to incite them to integrate more in the societies of the receiving countries." (Interview with civil servant C, MCMRE)

In the previous part, we outlined how the official Moroccan position on integration evolved throughout the last decades, and highlighted the radical shift in paradigms regarding integration. In this section, we look into the underlying implications of the current paradigm, which reconciles the notion of integration with continuing transnational ties.

The promotion of integration as an official policy goal implies that the Moroccan state is claiming a stakeholder position in the integration of Moroccans living abroad. As explained above, policy programs that were once conceived in order to maintain transnational linkages are now presented as 'supporting integration'. Broadly speaking, the recurring argument employed in Moroccan state discourses is that 'a strong transnational orientation is a fertile breeding ground for integration'. Resultantly, Morocco's cultural diaspora policies make a *dual* claim: not only do they claim to strengthen transnational ties, but also to support Moroccan expatriates' integration into the receiving country. A closer examination of this argument is necessary, as it explicitly contradicts the widespread, more skeptical belief that diaspora policies thwart emigrants' integration.

In order to disentangle this argument, we turn to in-depth interviews conducted with a range of officials employed or commissioned by Morocco's main diaspora institutions (MCMRE, FHII, CCME).[14] In the interviews, respondents were inquired extensively about the aims and strategies of cultural diaspora policies. The interviews were especially useful to get a deeper understanding of the concepts underlying more generalist public discourses. Besides interviews, we also consider publically available documents, such as media interviews with officials and the website content of various diaspora institutions.

In line with our research question, the analysis particularly focuses on how diaspora policy officials assume that their cultural diaspora policies have a positive effect on the expatriates' integration abroad. What kind of dynamics are these policies supposed to engender, relative to integration? Concretely, how is the transmission of culture, language and religion of origin considered to smoothen the integration of young expatriate Moroccans?[15] With respect to our analytic framework (see above), respondents' answers reveal how Moroccan state actors understand the synergy between transnationalism and integration in the Moroccan expatriates' lives and how they operationalize this understanding policy-wise.

The respondents' support for the idea that transnational cultural ties to Morocco offer a fertile breeding ground for integration is based on a combination of two distinctive arguments. The first is of a more general nature: it argues that preservation of the culture of origin is a condition for integration, since it is understood that the 'culture of origin' offers migrants and their descendants a 'point of reference' and a 'source of empowerment' in the receiving country society. Contrasting to this more general argument, the second line of reasoning draws on a particular characteristic of the Moroccan culture. Tolerance regarding diversity is portrayed as an inherent characteristic of the Moroccan culture, therefore, a stronger internalization of Moroccan culture by emigrants and their descendants is understood to facilitate integration. As will become clear, the distinction between both arguments mainly serves analytic purposes, as they are usually employed in an interwoven manner.

While the articulation and disentanglement of discourses may appear as a purely conceptual matter, it should be noted that state discourses may have a deep impact on the ground. By presenting the promotion of integration as a shared concern of both origin states and receiving states, opportunities open up for cooperation between diaspora policy actors and a broad range of actors in the receiving countries concerned with 'immigrant integration'. As Pécoud (2015) points out, the federative power of shared narratives should not be underestimated. Particularly when the issue at stake is highly sensitive — like migration — or the actors have little in common, the existence of shared narratives can constitute the cement of relationships that would not exist otherwise (Ibid., 2015). Therefore, as a result of the paradigm shift, local authorities or community organizations that promote minority incorporation in receiving countries may see the value of cooperating with Moroccan diaspora institutions.[16]

The culture of origin as a point of reference and a source of empowerment

"Besides maintaining the ties between the MRE and their motherland and promoting knowledge of the culture and languages of Morocco among the new generations, these cultural policies stimulate *a healthy integration in the country of residence, and bring solutions to the identity conflict some young MRE are confronted with* [Italics added] (Media interview with Minister of MCMRE)."[17]

Within Moroccan diaspora policy discourses, a major argument in favor of fostering transnational ties states that in immigration contexts, knowing and acknowledging your roots is essential for the development of a balanced identity and a strong personality. In these discourses, frequent reference is made to the persistence of ethnic, racial and religious identities in other minority groups (such as Jews and Afro-Americans), thereby implying that 'knowing your roots' is a universal need transcending the Moroccan context.

Academically, this argument resonates strongly with studies in various academic disciplines (i.a. sociology, social psychology, political philosophy) indicating that when immigrants are allowed to retain socio-cultural praxis and identifications of their 'country of origin', this eventually benefits their incorporation in the receiving societies (Roosens, 1998; Modood, 2007, Berry et al., 2007; Levrau et al., 2014). One of the explanations given is that such praxis and identifications have a positive impact on immigrants' self-esteem (Kivisto, 2001).

In a similar manner, the manager in charge of the extensive language and cultural education program of the Hassan II Foundation (FHII) frames the culture of origin as a necessary *point de repère* (point of reference) for Moroccan expatriate citizens, without which one could not adapt sustainably to a new environment — the society of residence.

> "Our actions aim at allowing these Moroccans [living abroad] to just know this [Moroccan] culture, because, if one does not know his own culture, he won't be able to comprehend or adapt there where he is living. (...) If we do not manage to situate ourselves, it will be difficult to position ourselves in relation to the country of residence. That's a bit the essence of our actions." (Interview with directing manager N, FHII)

However, as he points out, this policy perspective only arose when the return perspective of the initial Moroccan emigrants started to wither away and a new, post-migrant generation emerged:

> "We have tried to make this education today an element that offers something valuable to them, that helps these children to integrate. (...) To integrate, you have to situate yourself first, [you need] to have this point of reference. This education has evolved somewhat in this sense, from an education to facilitate return [to Morocco] to an education that contributed, more or less, to their integration in the receiving country. That's the evolution from the sixties on, and it still continues." (Interview with directing manager N, FHII)

However, the 'culture of origin' is here more than just a point of reference, it is also considered a source of empowerment. By increasing expatriate Moroccans' pride, knowledge and conscience about (the value of) their ethno-cultural roots, their self-confidence will rise. A particular cultural model seems to inform these views, which conceives of a strongly defined and valorized (ethnic) identity as a possible resource and cover against alienation. A fragmented and incoherent self-understanding is, on the other hand, perceived as a facilitator of social anomia and marginalization. Having a strongly demarcated Moroccan identity is, consequently, deemed to be an effective protection to withstand negative stereotyping regarding immigrants' ethno-cultural and religious background (like racism and Islamophobia) in the country of residence. Knowledge provides the 'ammunition' to shield immigrants from internalization of these stereotypes.[18]

The underlying dynamic here, that is, the empowerment of expatriate Moroccans by embracing their ethno-cultural background, is clarified passionately by one ministry official. He starts his argument by describing the harsh living conditions of young Moroccans growing up in Europe. Particularly problematic, according to him, is the everyday stigmatization young Moroccans experience due to their Arab and Muslim background, a phenomenon that is fueled by misinformation:

> "So, if a youngster, for instance in the suburbs of a European city, [faces] problems like exclusion, unemployment, delinquency, criminality, etcetera; if they keep repeating all day long 'you are a dirty Arab, you are a terrorist, your Qur'an incites murder, your prophet was [a murderer]', things that are not accurate; he feels unarmed, without means for answering to these things. He [this Moroccan youngster] will be convinced himself that indeed, he is coming from such a country. (...) The description of Arabic countries, Muslim countries, in certain societies is horrible; it shows zero degree of knowledge about this Arabic country, this Muslim country [Morocco]. These [Moroccan] youngsters need to know this Morocco where they are coming from." (Interview with policy advisor F, MCMRE).

He continues explaining how young Moroccans' should respond to stigmatization: by embracing their roots proudly and in an informed manner. One important strategy here is remembrance of the historic Arabo-Andalusian civilization, a Muslim civilization that was at the time more advanced than its non-Muslim counterparts on the European continent. By evoking this glorious past, contemporary stigmatization of Moroccans living abroad (who are framed as inheritors of this Arabo-Andalusian legacy) can be invalidated:

> "So, how can we make them understand, and what's the objective of making them understand? It is in order that they [would] know, they would be able to respond to those who are accusing them of coming from an underdeveloped country, a murderous country, a country of ... terror, of I don't know what, they need to know that in the Middle Ages, when Europe was still thinking about what language to speak, what art to use, what science etcetera, Muslims and Arabs, who were at that time living in Spain, already reached a cultural level that was evoking admiration of the Europeans." (Interview with policy advisor F, MCMRE).

Besides being undesirable, this ministry official also considers assimilation to be an illusion. Referring to Afro-Americans, he stresses the indissoluble connection with one's roots, even across generations:

"This notion of belonging to a civilization ... whether one likes it or not, they still have Arab blood in their veins, African blood in their veins. This remains, even if one lives three or four centuries in the country of residence. The slaves who gave birth to the American nation of today, the Africans, the Americans of African origin, they cannot strip themselves of their origins. (...) So it is an indissoluble element of one's personality. (...) Even when trying to assimilate in the receiving society, they always stay Moroccan, they always stay African, they always stay Muslim. Consequently, he needs to, to accept this belonging (...) so that he make it into a positive aspect of his personality, instead of a negative aspect." (Interview with policy advisor F, MCMRE).

Finally, the ministry official explains how this view informs the policy vision of the Moroccan diaspora policies, while also referring to royal speeches on the matter.

"[Immigration], it's an added value to the society ... it's for this reason that we try to make sure that the effort we make to maintain the Moroccan identity of the immigrant, remains equal to the effort we make to make him integrate the best as possible in his receiving society. We do not dissociate these elements. But, on the level of the [official] discourse – the most official one existing in Morocco being the discourse of His Majesty the King – [the King] incites the government to work in this sense. The constitution, the new constitution [of 2013] puts forward two objectives simultaneously: to maintain the ties with Morocco with its subjects [abroad] and to help them to integrate in their countries of residence. So these are not two contradictory things." (Interview with policy advisor F, MCMRE).

Following this line of argumentation, the persistent Moroccan focus on ethno-cultural transnational ties should not be interpreted as an attempt to ensure exclusive loyalty to and identification with Morocco. On the contrary, a balanced dual hyphenated identity, reflecting the emigrant population's affiliation with the country of origin as well as the country of residence, is presented as the ideal. For instance, one program coordinator commissioned by the Ministry explains:

"We encourage them to integrate in society. But integration in European societies, that does not mean that the ties with the country of origin really need to be *cut*, no. For me, both are complementary. (...) They need to integrate, [be] Moroccan for 100% and [be] Belgian for 100%. So these two, for me, they are complementary. And it is not because one integrates himself, that this implies forgetting [the country of origin] because I'm sure that someone who forgets his roots, has no future." (Interview with directing manager J, MCMRE).

At the Hassan II Foundation, the metaphor of the two chairs is recited frequently to indicate the value of a dual identity:

"Someone who knows his identity has a strong personality. If you don't know your identity, you feel insecure (...) someone who's sitting on two chairs simultaneously, bridging from the one to the other, is better off than someone who's sitting in between two chairs. In between two chairs, you cannot sit in a comfortable manner. But if you know, if you have a good knowledge of the [receiving society] culture, the [receiving country] language, you can achieve more, and if you know the Moroccan language, the Moroccan culture, the same applies." (Interview with civil servant E, FHII)

As El Asri (2012) observed, this embracement of dual nationality and multiple belongings is relatively new; until the '90s, Moroccan public policies aimed at maintaining a strong and exclusive national connection.

The argument that embracing one's identity of origin enables successful integration in the country of residence is often used in an inverted manner, that is, by pointing at negative examples. Expatriate Moroccans who ignore or undervalue their ethno-cultural roots are considered to be more susceptible to suffer an identity crisis, as they are 'footloose'. They get 'lost' more easily and they are more likely to fall prey to delinquency or 'harmful' (non-Moroccan) ideologies – like religious extremism.

Openness and tolerance as inherent Moroccan values

> "When a youngster is proud about [his] Moroccan identity, proud of his country of origin, when he has a good Moroccan culture, he can integrate easily in the receiving society. (...) The Moroccan culture is a culture of openness, and as such, it helps him to integrate in his country of birth [in Europe or elsewhere]." (Interview with program coordinator H, MCMRE)

Besides the more general claim about the value of knowing your culture of origin, a second context-specific element is mentioned by the respondents to explain how Moroccan cultural policies enhance the integration of expatriate Moroccans. It is the (assumed) open and tolerant nature of Moroccan society and culture. This *culture d'ouverture et de la tolérance* is regarded as the historical product of the country's location at the crossroads of different civilizations.[19] This notion is widely present throughout Moroccan official discourses and relates to various particular claims regarding the Moroccan historical and contemporary experiences with diversity. A central element to this claim is the religious diversity in Morocco, notably the historical presence of a large segment of Jews in the Moroccan population.[20] Further, Moroccan interpretations of Islam, grounded in the Maliki Sunni School, are commonly regarded as moderate and tolerant towards non-Muslims.[21] The claim of being an open and tolerant society is further supported by reference to various evolutions in the last decades, such as the increase of civil liberties, expanding rights for women and cultural recognition of the Berber minority.

This conceptualization of the Moroccan society and culture as open and tolerant is also employed in Morocco's state discourses regarding her emigrants. Expatriate Moroccans can benefit especially from the open and tolerant mind-set this entails, since they are confronted on a daily basis with different religions and cultures in their receiving societies. As such, the Moroccan 'culture of tolerance and openness' is considered to offer the perfect attitude to fit into a diverse society without forsaking one's own identity.

> "A youngster, who takes into account the richness and the strength of belonging to [the society of residence], but who at the same time belongs to a society like the Moroccan society, with her values, her inherent values, the values of tolerance, the value of respect for diversity, because

we are a country that respects diversity, the value of equilibrium, the value of openness … Well, frankly spoken, this can only result in added value for the [society of residence] *and* for the Moroccan society" (Interview with directing manager O, CCME)

Another illustration of the idea that Morocco can set an example of peaceful coexistence for young expatriate Moroccans was offered by the program coordinator of one of the major cultural visiting programs (the Summer Universities for young Moroccans living abroad):

"Here in Morocco, there are many ethnic groups: there are Berbers, there are Soussi, there are Arabs, there are Riffians. Even like that, we manage to live in peace, with peace. So, we show them [young expatriate Moroccans] *this reality*, that is, we try to make them *feel* [the effects of this diversity]. Resultantly, when they leave [Morocco and return] abroad, I believe that this will *help* them, as a sort of 'supplementary course'. This way, we try to give them the means to integrate well in Europe." (Program coordinator I, MCMRE)

The intention to promote and cultivate a tolerant attitude among Moroccans abroad is also expressed in the Moroccan king's royal speeches, which can be considered to constitute the blueprint for Morocco's diaspora policies.

"Just as I commend the members of the Moroccan community abroad for abiding by the laws and regulations of host countries, I am keen to ensure they preserve their distinctive cultural and religious identity, which is based on tolerance, respect for others and moderation as advocated by Islam." (King Mohammed VI, Royal Speech of November 6, 2006).

Accordingly, Morocco's cultural diaspora policies do not merely aim to transmit cultural *knowledge* to the Moroccan expatriate population, but equally aim to teach 'Moroccan' *values* of openness and tolerance. The underlying assumption is that young expatriate Moroccans, especially those born abroad, are ill informed about the true nature of Moroccan culture.

A particular variant of this argument relates to Morocco's dominant religion, Islam. Morocco tends to represent itself as the holder of a 'moderate' Islam (see also chapter of Fadil in this volume). Reconnecting with Moroccan Islam (as a constitutive part of Moroccan identity) is therefore considered to affect integration in the receiving country positively. As one official at the Ministry states, young generations of expatriate Moroccans need to know "what Moroccan Islam is: the tolerant Islam, the open Islam, the Islam not excluding intercultural and interreligious dialogue" (Policy advisor F, MCMRE). Moroccan Islam is therefore considered highly suitable for smooth integration and coexistence in the country of residence, in contrast to conservative or 'radical' approaches (especially Saudi-Arabia is accused of importing these radical approaches into the receiving countries).[22] As a result, educating young expatriate Moroccans about the values of Moroccan Islam (next to other values inherent to Moroccan culture) is seen to help their integration.

> "Throughout these [policy] actions, we build relationships, we can, you see, instill them with good, civilized manners but also even, the Islamic education, we are showing them that [Islam], it is completely different from extremism. [This is necessary] because — can you imagine! — immigrants are more extremist than people here. Why is this the case? Because [these immigrants] misunderstand Islam. They are not immunized against [wrong interpretations of Islam]. They are influenced by other cultures, where there are extremists. Islam in Morocco is a moderate Islam, an Islam of the middle ground, it is an Islam that is not extremist. (...) I took Islam or the religious dimension as an example, [but] it's the same story for other aspects. You see, I talked about religion; [but] there are other sides: the political, the social, that is, other aspects. So we, what we offer is support. Support in order that they integrate in an honorable manner, without causing troubles, neither for the receiving countries, neither for themselves".
> (Program coordinator G, MCMRE)

The example of religious homeland ties also illustrates how (first) general and (second) context-specific arguments about the importance of retaining Moroccan identity are mobilized in an intertwined manner. On the one hand, Moroccan Islam is more generally framed as one of the 'points of reference' for expatriate Moroccans to not get 'lost' in the receiving society; on the other hand, the particular nature of Moroccan Islam as moderate and tolerant contributes to smooth integration.

Conclusion

This chapter has shed light on the origin-state perspective on the integration of expatriates in the society of residence, a perspective migration scholars have tended to neglect so far. Based on our investigation of how the Moroccan state links the notion of integration to the promotion of the 'culture of origin' among their expatriates, we have demonstrated how contemporary Moroccan diaspora policies rely on an active promotion of the idea of 'integration'.

Drawing upon the integration-transnationalism interaction typology of Erdal & Oeppen (2013), we have argued that this discursive evolution — from rejection over acceptance to promotion of integration — can be considered as a succession of reinterpretations of the integration-transnationalism nexus by the state of origin. Over the course of the last three decades, the Moroccan state's understanding of the relationship between preserving transnational ties and integration has moved from an antagonistic to a synergistic understanding. Consistent with this paradigm change, the cultural programs in place have been reframed. A closer look at Moroccan state discourses further reveals a particular understanding of integration that is fully compatible with the maintenance of transnational ties.

To gain a deeper understanding of this embracement of 'integration' by the Moroccan state, this chapter has unpacked the underlying claim that a strong transnational orientation is a fertile breeding ground for integration. We observed two different but intertwined arguments used by state actors to support this claim. On the one hand, reverberating academic knowledge, Moroccan officials stress that preserving the culture of origin supports integration, since it serves as a point of reference and source of empowerment for expatriate Moroccans. On the other hand, the Moroccan culture is seen as an appropriate mind-set for integration, as it promotes the values of tolerance and openness. These arguments imply that, through its cultural diaspora policies, the Moroccan state claims a role in the integration process of its expatriate citizens.

Clearly, the paradigm shift on integration should not be interpreted as fading ambition on behalf of the Moroccan state. It shows, rather, the Moroccan state's capacity to adapt continuously to shifting circumstances, thus allowing it to pursue its ambitions further.

Notes

1 Marocains Résidant à l'étranger.

2 It should be noted here that there is no trade-off between naturalization in the receiving country and retaining the Moroccan nationality. Based on the principle of *ius sanguinis*, the Moroccan nationality is passed automatically, irrespective of other nationalities. Article 6 of the Moroccan Nationality Code stipulates that any child born of a Moroccan father or mother is a Moroccan citizen. Provided that it is allowed by the receiving country, dual citizenship is tolerated and, indeed, widespread among emigrants (Perrin, 2011).

3 In their explorative study, Desiderio and Weinar (2014) observed that 'the main origin countries of migrants residing in the European Union – such as Turkey and Morocco – have progressively moved away from rhetoric that stigmatises integration in the receiving society, and have instead started to encourage integration as an instrumental process for leveraging development returns to emigration'.

4 At the time of fieldwork and analysis of this chapter, the MCMRE was an independent ministry. However, in the new government presided by El Othmani, which was installed in April 2017, the migration portfolio was assigned to a minister-delegate to the Ministry of Foreign Affairs.

5 Article 16 stipulates "the Kingdom of Morocco works to protect the legitimate rights and interests of the Moroccan citizens (f/m) residing abroad, *while respecting the international law and the laws effective in the countries of residence* (...). It guards the strengthening of their contribution to the development of their fatherland, Morocco, and to the tightening of the friendship and cooperation ties with the governments and societies of the countries *where they live or where they are citizens too.*" [Italics added]

6 At that time, a fully-fledged Ministry for Moroccans living abroad was missing; instead a Minister-Delegate had been appointed to the Ministry of Foreign Affairs.

7 Press article "Les Marocains du monde et du Canada sont un gisement de compétences. Entretien avec Mohamed Ameur, Ministre Chargé de la Communauté MRE". Le Matin, 1/12/2010.

8 Literally, *enracinement* means 'taking root' while *déracinement* refers at 'losing your roots'.

9 See footnote 2.

10 International Dialogue on Migration 2013: Conférence Ministérielle sur la Diaspora Genève 18 & 19-6-2013. Session 3: Migration et Développement. Intervention de Mr Abdellatif Mâzouz Ministre Délégué auprès du Chef du Gouvernement chargé des Marocains Résidant à l'Etranger.

11 Press article "La performance scolaire des enfants MRE conditionnée par plusieurs facteurs (étude). Atlasinfo.fr (MAP) 29-02-2016.

12 Press article "Dossier Belliraj: Interview met de Ambassadeur van Marokko", 29-8-2009, MO* Magazine.

13 Note Synthétique Relative à La Stratégie de mobilisation en faveur de la Communauté Marocaine Résidant à l'Etranger. Ministère Chargé de la Communauté MRE. Undated, probably 2008.

14 15 interviews conducted in May 2013 and May-June 2014 in the Moroccan Ministry for Moroccans Living Abroad (MCMRE), Hassan II Foundation for Moroccans Living Abroad (FHII) and the Council for Moroccan Community Living Abroad (CCME). From the end of 2013, on, "Migration Affairs" was added to the MCMRE's name (referring to its new competency regarding the incorporation of immigrants in Morocco), but to avoid confusion, we employ the same acronym throughout the article. Interview citations have been anonymized upon request of part of the respondents.

15 The focus of Morocco's cultural diaspora policies are Moroccan children and youngsters born and raised outside of Morocco.

16 In other areas of the Moroccan diaspora policies, the inscription of Moroccan diaspora policies into broader, global policy agenda's has proven effective yet: for instance, its participation in the global agenda on migration and development generates a wide range of partnerships and corresponding funding.

17 Identité: l'offre culturel au profit des MRE se renforce. Le Matin, 20-11-2014.

18 Social psychology studies on minority adolescents indicate too how a strong ethnic identity increases self-esteem and may buffer the negative outcomes of discrimination (see e.g. Rivas-Drake, Hughes & Way, 2008).

19 For instance, the website of the MCMRE states 'the different civilizations which have followed on from each other in Morocco have each influenced our [current] identity. Which undoubtedly explains the tolerance and open-mindedness of Moroccans. There are no culture clashes here, just meetings and sharing.' http://www.marocainsdumonde. gov.ma/fr/culture/culture/histoire-du-maroc.

20 However, Boum (2013) notes ambivalence according to the audience: 'internationally, the government promotes Morocco as a nation of Jewish-Muslim historical symbiosis and contemporary tolerance. [On the contrary] nationally, the state has maintained a relative silence about its Jewish history and culture.' (2013: 130) Boum explains this ambiguity by pointing at the negative sentiments regarding Jews in the Moroccan popular opinion, which are due to the Israel-Palestine conflict. Externally, 'Moroccan Jewish heritage is emphasized to enhance the image of Morocco as a place of tolerance and therefore a positive destination for tourists.' (2013: 129).

21 For instance, drawing on their ethnographic fieldwork experience in Morocco, anthropologists Crawford and Newcomb make the assessment that 'while many Moroccans are religiously conservative, Moroccan society is friendly, open and tolerant' (2013).

22 A particular element underpinning the difference between 'moderate' and 'conservative' interpretations is the revised Moroccan Family Code of 2004 (*Moudawana)* that is among the more gender-equal ones in the Muslim world.

Bibliography

El Asri, F. (2012). *Migrations Marocaines. Les compétences marocains de l'étranger: 25 ans de politiques de mobilisation*. Rabat: Conseil de la Communauté Marocaine à l'étranger.

Benkirane, Y. (2010). Émigration et politique des émigrés au Maroc. Du dépassement de l'Etat 'proxénète' à la mise en place de l'Etat 'paternaliste': pérenniser l'allégeance, orienter l'investissement et 'désamorcer' la contestation. *Revue Averroès*, N°2, 1-16.

Berry, J. W. (2007). Acculturation strategies and adaptation. In: Lansford, J. E.; Deater-Deckard, K.; Bornstein, M. H. (Eds.), *Immigrant families in contemporary society*. Duke series in child development and public policy (pp. 69-82). New York: Guilford Press.

Boum, A. (2013). *Memories of absence. How Muslims remember Jews in Morocco*. Redwood City: Stanford University Press.

Bouras, N. (2012). *Het land van aankomst. Perspectieven op verbondenheid met Marokko, 1960-2010.* Hilversum: Verloren.

Brand, L. A. (2006). *Citizens Abroad. Emigration and the State in the Middle East and North Africa*. Cambridge: Cambrigde University Press.

Carling, J. & Pettersen, S. V. (2014). Return migration intentions in the integration-transnationalism matrix. *International Migration*, 52 (6), 13-30.

Crawford, D. & Newcomb, R. (2013) (eds.). *Encountering Morocco. Fieldwork and cultural understanding*. Bloomington: Indiana University Press.

Collyer, M. (ed.) (2013). *Migration Nations. Policies and Ideologies of Emigrant Engagement*. Hampshire: Palgrave Macmillan.

Desiderio, M. V. & Weinar, A. (2014). *Supporting immigrant integration in Europe? Developing the governance for diaspora engagement*. INTERACT Working Paper. Brussels: Migration Policy Institute Europe.

Dufoix, S., Guerassimoff, C. & de Tinguy, A. (eds.) (2010). *Loin des yeux, près du coeur. Les états et leurs expatriés*. Paris: Presses de SciencesPo.

Erdal, M. B. & Oeppen, C. (2013). Migrant Balancing Acts: Understanding the Interactions between Integration and Transnationalism. *Journal of Ethnic and Migration Studies, 39* (6), 867-884.

Gamlen, A. (2006). Diaspora Engagement Policies. *What are they and what kinds of states use them?* Working Paper n° 32. Oxford: COMPAS, University of Oxford. Reprinted in: Topic 19 March 2009 – Remittances, Diasporas, and States. Brooklyn NY: Social Science Research Council.

Gamlen, A. (2014). Diaspora Institutions and Diaspora Governance. *International Migration Review*, 48, S180-S217.

de Haas, H. (2007). *Between courting and controlling. The Moroccan state and 'its' emigrants.* Working Paper n° 54. Oxford: COMPAS, University of Oxford.

Ionecsu, D. (2006). *Engaging Diaspora as Development Partners for Home and Destination Countries: Challenges for Policy Makers.* IOM Migration Research Series n°26. Geneva: International Organization for Migration.

Iskander, N. (2010). *Creative State. Forty Years of Migration and Development Policy in Morocco and Mexico.* Ithaca & London: Cornell University Press.

Joppke, C. (2007). Beyond national models: civic integration policies for immigrants in Western Europe, *West-European Politics*, 30, 1-22

Kivisto, P. (2001). Theorizing Transnational Immigration: A Critical Review of Current Efforts, *Ethnic and Racial Studies*, 24 (4), 549-577

Lafleur, J.M. (2013). Transnational Politics and the State. The External Voting Rights of Diasporas. Abingdon: Routledge.

Levrau, F., Piqueray, E., Goddeeris, I. & Timmerman, C. (2014). Polish migration in Belgium since 2004: New dynamics of migration and integration? *Ethnicities,* 14 (2) 303-323.

Ministry for Moroccans Residing Abroad and Migration Affairs (MCMRE) (2008) *Strategic Action Plan 2008-2012.* Unpublished policy document.

Modood, T. (2007). *Multiculturalism: a civic idea.* Cambridge: Polity Press.

Pécoud, A. (2015). *Depoliticizing migration: Global Governance and International Migration Narratives.* Basingstoke: Palgrave Macmillan.

Perrin, D. (2011). *EUDO Citizenship report. Country report: Morocco.* Florence: European University Institute.

Rivas-Drake, D., Hughes, D. & Way, N. (2008) A Closer Look at Peer Discrimination, Ethnic Identity, and Psychological Well-being Among Urban Chinese American Sixth Graders. *Journal of Youth Adolescence,* 37, 12-21.

Roosens, E. (1998). *Eigen grond eerst? Primordiale autochtonie. Dilemma van de multiculturele samenleving.* Leuven & Amersfoort: Acco.

Smith, M.P. & Guarnizo, L.E. (1998). *Transnationalism from below.* New Brunswick & London: Transaction Publishers.

Snel, E., Engbersen, G. & Leerkes, A. (2006) Transnational involvement and social integration. *Global Networks,* 6(3): 285-308.

Part 4
Identity and ethnicity

10. Becoming Berber: ethnicity and identity politics among Moroccans in Belgium

Norah Karrouche

Introduction

"I am not an Arab. It's my country. I am Amazigh".[1] It's a sentence I've heard from many Moroccan Berber activists over the years, who were referring to their homelands as 'their country', a Berber nation and not an Arab one. Moroccan Berber activism denotes a particular form of cultural and political transnational activism, which opposes politics of ethnic and cultural categorization and assimilation. From Belgium, it remains directed towards Morocco as an 'imagined homeland' with which it maintains ties.

Migrant transnationalism heavily impinges upon the constitution and reproduction of identities (Glick Schiller-Fouron, 2001, Vertovec, 2004, 2009). As a form of identity politics, it becomes visible through social movements when migrant voices claim recognition and a right to difference, which is the basic message underlying Moroccan Berber activism in Belgium today. By emphasizing the unique character of the Berbers as an ethnic group and this group's sameness from within, as well as its difference vis-à-vis others – in this case, particularly Arabs – Berber activists in Morocco and Belgium aim at replacing 'old, possible solidarity bonds' with new bonds that are based on kinship, which are moreover rooted in history (Ferguson, 2009: 144-146). Hence, by making use of 'strategic essentialism' (Martin Alcoff, 2000: 320) Berber activists claim a fixed location in history, as is the case with ethnic minority activisms in general. In this way, their identity is perceived and presented as the result of a natural, historical process.

At the beginning of the nineties, a small network of Moroccan-born activists began founding associations both in Morocco and abroad, predominantly in urban settings. Traveling elites and migrating intelligentsia were the key driving forces behind the resurgence of a Berber cultural activism and Berber associations in Belgium, 'recovering' the Berber past of Morocco and Moroccan migration as a 'political archaeology', and carrying out the idea of a deep historical Berber nation to the masses; one that was and is different from an Arab and/or Islamic nation. The construction and dissemination of this particular view on Moroccan history in the diaspora was at the core of my dissertation research.

When I started interviewing Berber activists in Antwerp in 2008, and participating in their public events, I wanted to try and understand how and why these activists were stressing the ethnic component of their social and cultural identities. I also wanted to understand how and why, accordingly, they were attempting to engage with Moroccan national history and the history of migration towards Europe in new and meaningful ways. Shared understandings of the past forge collective identities.

The purpose of this chapter is to present an overview of the history of ethnic and cultural Berber activism in Belgium, with an emphasis on Flanders and Antwerp in particular. Whereas during the early nineties, some Moroccan Berbers attempted to establish associations in the cities of Ghent and Liège, most activities currently take place in the Antwerp region, which explains this geographical focus. The chapter is based on four years of ethnographic and archival research in Belgium, the Netherlands and Morocco. Throughout this period, I conducted life story interviews with forty activists in the Netherlands and Belgium, fifteen of which in Antwerp, interviewed fourteen representatives of other Moroccan (migrant) associations, attended associations' meetings and cultural festivals, and analysed their cultural production (e.g. published poetry, public history) and private archival records (e.g. reports of meetings and internal and external communication).[2] One of the main findings in this research was that the rise of Berber identity politics in Morocco and the diaspora could be explained by trends in both national (Moroccan, Belgian, Dutch) politics and (historical) migration patterns. However, the discourse of the Berber Movement can only be understood by also taking into account the legacy of French colonialism.

The roots of the Berber-Arab issue

Several scholars have argued that under colonial rule, French administrators and ethnologists stressed ethnic and cultural differences between Arabs and Berbers in order to facilitate their colonial mission (Aouchar, 2005, Burke, 2007, Gellner-Micaud, 1972, Guerin, 2011, Hammoudi 1997, Hart 1997, Pouessel 2010, Silverstein 2004). They stressed the importance of safeguarding indigenous Berber culture and regarded Arab culture – and Islam – as exogenous to the Maghreb. From the late nineteenth until the mid twentieth century, the French produced what Hammoudi (1997: 112) has called "a dense authoritative corpus" in the Maghreb. This "Moroccan Vulgate" (Burke, 2007), underscored by orientalist ideas and colonial ethnology, continues to shape the Berber Movement's perception of what it signifies to be Berber, with activists relying on historical and ethnological knowledge produced in the early twentieth century. In the long run, French colonial rule impacted the Berber speaking rural populations more than the Arab speaking urban populations (Gross-McMurray, 1993: 39-58). What French colonial discourse had denoted as 'Berber culture', and indigenous and also secular culture, survived well into the postcolonial era, when Morocco was reconfigured as a constitutional monarchy. Well into the nineties, support for the Berber cause was seen as support for policies having originated under the French colonialist regime (Maddy-Weitzman, 2007: 30). Even renowned scholar of nationalism, Ernest Gellner (with Micaud, 1972), predicted that Berber identity would not become a major issue in Moroccan politics and that Berber culture would be superseded by other common identifiers, such as Islam. The course of history, however, has proven that Gellner and Micaud were wrong on this account.

The Berber Movement from a historical and transnational perspective

In a recent volume on the history and current state of the Berber Cultural Movement in Morocco and Algeria, Bruce Maddy-Weitzman (2007) concluded that the more Morocco was challenged socially, economically and politically on both its interior and exterior fronts, the more predominant the role of the Berber Cultural Movement became (Maddy-Weitzman, 2007). Thus, the democratization and liberalization of the Maghreb on the one hand, and the development of Berber associations on the other, are linked. With the advent of mass labor migration, and the formation of diaspora cutting across several national contexts, this framework became increasingly transnational. Migration has had lasting effects on not only the ways in which Moroccan national identity and politics have been defined and challenged, but also on the development of Berber associative life. In particular since the nineties, these associations are relying on a discourse of human rights and indigeneity (Maddy-Weitzman, 2007: 44). Berber activism in Morocco and its diaspora has become a significant contributor in debates on minority, human and women's rights, and the ongoing discussions about democratization and secularization in Moroccan society.

Moroccan political Berberism – politicized 'ethnic' sentiment – originally arose out of the *Mouvement Populaire,* a political party with a primarily rural and Berber-speaking following that had been created as a counterweight to the Arab nationalist *Istiqlal* in 1959 and out of discontent with the marginalization of local notables. Though the *Mouvement Populaire* channeled opinions of '*Berberité*', the party supported the national, centralized state authority. The party encouraged the new king to make room for a Berber element in newly independent Morocco, suggesting the use of Berber or Tamazight in national education. However, Mohamed V ideologically operated in the middle of Arabism and Berberism and proclaimed a Moroccan identity based on Islam, Arabism and 'Moroccanism', solving the ethnic issue, yet only temporarily.

Following the death of Mohamed V, the authoritarian system of Hassan II functioned as a way to co-opt competitive and threatening elements into the state structure (Hammoudi, 1997). The seventies were characterized by general political instability. Two military coups marked the beginning of Morocco's state of oppression and persecution of political opponents in years to come. As a result of the coups of 1971 and 1972, 'Berbers' employed in finance, security and foreign relations were discharged. Two 'Berbers' were behind the coups: Mohamed Medbouh from the Rif and Mohamed Oufkir from the Middle Atlas. A 'Berber dimension' was easily added to both affairs. The decade following these coups counted severely oppressed uprisings, political trials, and the creation of secret detention center Tazmamart in 1977. The appointment of Driss Bassri, the feared Minister of the Interior, in 1979 additionally contributed to the maintenance of a reign of terror within a dictatorial regime (Maddy-Weitzman, 2011: 92). This was the political climate in which the Berber Movement gradually arose.

Demands made by Berber activists throughout the seventies and eighties, were ignored, if not condemned, by Hassan II. Moreover, any sign of Berber identity in public space was seen as an act undermining state authority and national identity. During these decades, known as le *années de plomb* (the 'Years of Lead') numerous members of the political opposition were kidnapped or imprisoned without a fair trial. Even though regarded illegal, the Berberist agenda was now organized outside of the political party system. In 1967 the two very first Berber associations were established, even though activists could not always freely meet. A group of Algerian and French intellectuals founded the *Académie berbère* (Berber Academy), soon renamed *Agraw Imazighen* (Berber Academy), in Paris. Originally, this association resembled more of an elitist society. It was also very much orientated towards cultural affairs and payed little attention to political questions.

During the seventies in Paris, several other associations were founded. Most of the activists that would develop the Movement in Morocco during the late sixties and seventies were in fact students in France and became inspired there, taking ideas back with them upon their return to Morocco. This element of exchange across national borders was vital from the start (Pouessel, 2010: 108).

The first Berber association in Morocco, the *Association Marocaine de Recherche et d'échange Culturelles* ('Moroccan Association of Research and Cultural Exchange', AMREC) was founded by a group of Berber speaking students in Rabat in 1967 as well. Most of them were students at the faculty of arts and history. These students sought recognition for their people's language and culture in Morocco. The association *al-Intilaqa* '('The Launching') in Nador was the first association outside of the capital of Rabat to advocate popular and oral culture. The association temporarily dissolved in 1981 under severe political pressure (Feliu, 2006: 275). Berber associations were – and still are – predominantly made up by mostly left-wing, secular intelligentsia. Berber activism as we have come to know it since the late eighties and early nineties in Morocco has its roots in political ideologies such as Marxism (Pouessel, 2010). This also applies to the founders of associations in the diaspora, who were mostly highly educated, first-generation migrants.

Through governmental institutions such as the *Amicales*, the *années de plomb* were equally felt in the diaspora. The last decade of Hassan II's reign was marked by some significant changes, attained in part by substantial interior and international pressure to bring about more respect for human rights. A landmark in the development of the *Amazigh* movement, the *Charte d'Agadir relative aux droits linguistiques et culturels* dissected Moroccan culture and languages from the perspective of the Berbers' human rights as an indigenous, albeit now 'minority' population. The concise document, written by prominent Berber activist Mohamed Chafik, appealed to the indigenousness of Berber languages and cultures in North Africa. All the while, it stressed the interaction of the Berbers with 'others' all throughout Moroccan history, stressing their ability towards intercultural exchange, an argument which is being made by activists in the diaspora in particular.

Though the last years of Hassan II's reign were marked by significant changes on a national level, the Berber movement increasingly profiled itself as an international and global movement, all the while struggling with local issues and internal differences of opinion. From 1997 onwards, when the first *Congrès Mondial Amazigh (CMA)*, was held, the *Amazigh* Movement had indeed become more internationalist, aspiring to unite all Berbers in North Africa and the diaspora for one common cause. Increasingly, activists sought out various international platforms where their voice could be heard and their rights in home countries and host societies defended. The *CMA* was founded in France in 1995 by some forty Berber associations, predominantly from Algeria, Morocco, and France (Kratochwil, 1999; Maddy-Weitzman, 2011: 133-139). Again, the role of the Berber diaspora was crucial.

Migration to Europe and the development of migrant associations

During the early sixties, Hassan II's investment in national and local economies had been far too scarce to initiate entry in the international economy. An active emigration policy was to relieve the country from domestic unemployment. Migration was thus aspired to in view of migrant remittances and thus, supported a mainly economic goal. Consequently, migration due to domestic unemployment became a structural asset of the economy. Besides France, a large body of emigrants was employed in Germany, the Netherlands and Belgium (Brand, 2008: 20-21). In particular the southern Souss and northern Rif regions provided the Moroccan state with a reservoir of migrants, whose first language was mostly Berber. According to some, especially migration from the Rif was fostered, and not just for economic reasons but political ones, too (Brand, 2008: 47; De Haas, 2007: 39-70; Reniers, 1999: 679-713). Bouras and Cottaar (2009), however, at least for emigration towards the Netherlands, argued that there is no evidence to support this thesis and asserted that in fact, all recruitment *bureaux* operated in the Atlantic coastal towns (Cottaar & Bouras, 2009: 35-37).

Few scholars in the Netherlands and Belgium have tackled the politics and discourses of Berber activism and the constitution of Berber identity among Moroccan migrants and post-migrants. Sociologists have studied identifications with Berber culture among Dutch-Moroccans and Flemish-Moroccans as part of studies on the integration and identifications of Moroccan migrants and their offspring. These studies were mostly based on surveys (Entzinger & Dourleijn, 2008; Crul & Heering, 2008). According to these studies, self-identification as Berber by way of mother tongue has increased to over sixty percent in urban areas among second-generation youth. Yet this identification does not obstruct self-identification as Moroccan. The role of new media in the construction of Berber identity and Dutch-Moroccan youth's rising interest in Berber culture on online discussion platforms such as maroc.nl, maghreb.nl and *Amazigh* websites at the turn of the 21st century was signalled and discussed by Brouwer (2006), Mamadouh (2001) and Merolla (2002, 2005).

The presence and development of Berber associations in the Netherlands and Flanders have been noticed and discussed by Bouras (2012) and Jacobs (2005) in their studies on the development of Moroccan migrant associations. Van Heelsum (2001; 2003; with Kraal 2002) studied the history and discourse of Berber associations in the Netherlands. Associative life of Moroccans in the Netherlands and Belgium developed from the onset but only started to flourish during the eighties when both the Dutch and Belgian government set up legal frameworks for family reunification. Berber cultural associations came in late and developed during the mid-nineties. Contrary to other migrant associations they were not founded by guest workers and their offspring, but mostly by new migrants, follow migrants, who came to the Netherlands and Belgium as students in higher education or in view of family unification during the early and mid-nineties, which may be explained by both migration patterns and policy shifts in Morocco itself.

Most historians studying migrant associations depended on the theory developed by Marlou Schrover and Rinus Penninx (2001), through which they could interpret the emergence and demise of migrant associations. They argued that during the earliest stages of the settlement of Moroccans in the Netherlands, organizations primarily attended to issues concerning their country of origin. Associations served practical purposes and offered aid with social security and working permits. This was followed by a stage where the focus on the specific needs and infrastructures for the migrants in the receiving country became more poignant. In this period, for instance, mosques were not merely religious associations as they began to act as social organizations, offering communal leisurely activities. Thirdly, as the heterogeneity of the Moroccan community grew more marked during the eighties and nineties, prompted by family reunification and family formation processes, associations became more aware of the changing demands and needs of their fellow members. This resulted in the growth of women's and youth's organizations.

The emergence of a Belgian-Berber diaspora

In Belgium, the Berber diaspora constitutes a pronounced Riffian community. The large majority of Berber activists boast a Riffian identity and maintain contacts with Berber activists in the Rif. As founders of associations, they were not guest laborers, but members of the so-called 'in-between' generation. They migrated towards Belgium as youth or young adolescents and most of them are highly educated lawyers, social workers or teachers. Emigration from Morocco towards Western Europe shows clearly defined, self-sustaining regional patterns (De Haas, 2007, 2009). The Rif was and still is a region where, once unemployment is high and the level of urbanization low, men are very likely to migrate as a way to opt out and start anew. Many times over, the activists in Belgium originating from the Rif area stressed during interviews that at the beginning of the nineties in the Rif area, Nador, Al Hoceima and Oujda as well, they were engaged in left-wing Marxist activism. Yet in the Rif, *al-Intilaqa* had already been a fixture in the Berber Movement from 1978 onwards, even though it had been temporarily forced to shut down its activities in 1981. It would, however, not be until 1990 when associative life in the Rif started to bloom. These associations were, and still remain, highly concentrated in the urbanized areas in between Nador and Al-Hoceima. In Nador *Ilmas* started out in 1990 with cultural activities, *Tanukra* ('Resurrection'), and *Taseghwnest* ('Fibula') followed in the first half of the decade. In Al Hoceima, *Numidia* was founded and Imzouren was home to *Nukur,* both names referring to 'ancient Berber kingdoms'. These associations were founded by an elite of alumni from the universities of Fez and Oujda, mainly lawyers, journalists and artists, sometimes with a past as activists in *Ilal Amam*, a Marxist-Leninist organization that was grounded in a secularist pan-Arab ideal. These associations organized cultural festivals, plays and poetry readings, next to conferences and debates on political themes regarding *Amazigh* culture, language and identity. They often cooperated with human rights associations in the vicinity of Al-Hoceima and Imzouren.

Riffian associations have showed very little interest in national action and collaborating with other Berber associations. The associations active in the vicinity of Nador united in *Tamunit* ('Union') in 1997. Local associations' profiles have been remarkably regionalist from the start. As argued by Kratochwil (2002), this exceptional Riffian regionalism contributed to the idea of a culturalist 'neo-*siba*', a Berber countryside opposing the *makhzen*. This substituted for the previous, and popular Marxist-Leninist opposition of the seventies and eighties. The Rif had always refused to channel its political opposition through political parties such as the *Parti Populair Socialist* and *Union Socialist des Forces Populaires* and the *Mouvement Populair*. This also means that, during the nineties at least, opposition to the *makhzen* in the Rif was organized along cultural lines, and no longer took place along the lines of class struggle. This reluctance to participate in national associations was also noted by van Amersfoort and van Heelsum (2007). While Riffians founded several local associations, simultaneously, Belgian Moroccan-Riffians were doing the same in their places of residence.

Hence, since the late eighties, Berber cultural associations in France, Germany and the Netherlands have been advocating the rights of Berbers in the Maghreb and its diaspora. These associations nowadays continue to strive for the recognition and dissemination of knowledge on Berber languages, history and culture both in Morocco and among Moroccan migrants and their offspring in the diaspora. Members of such transnational associations more than often position themselves as secular actors. As opposed to other Western-Europeans countries, Berber associations only became popular in Belgium during the early 2000's. Among Berber activists themselves, the lack of Berber ethnic sentiment among young Moroccans in Belgium has been due to the popularity of the Arab European League, in Antwerp in particular. Other activists stressed the relevance of Morocco's ties with its citizens abroad and explained that many Moroccans in Belgium were afraid of expressing themselves as Berbers well into the nineties, precisely because of Hassan II's repressive attitude towards the Berbers in their homeland. How and why have these associations then come to construct Berber identity in a Belgian diaspora context? In the following sections I describe and analyze the history of Berber associations and their members in Belgium, and Antwerp in particular, in a more detailed fashion against the backdrop of Moroccan labor and follow migration. I explain why and how these associations developed late in comparison to other Western-European countries and address their public lives and roles as secular actors in Flemish society, by scrutinizing the interviews I conducted with activists and representatives of other Moroccan (umbrella) organizations in Antwerp. In so doing, I take into account both local Belgian politics and transnational ties.

Rabat in Antwerp during the eighties and nineties: cultural diplomacy

The history of Berber identity politics in Flanders reaches back to 1986 in the region of Antwerp, when *Vreemd maar Vriend* ('Foreign but Friend'), bearing no reference to Berber identity whatsoever in its name, grew out of youth center Rzoezi in Mechelen. Some of the members of Rzoezi would become members of AEL (Arab European League) , yet before there was AEL, *Vreemd maar Vriend* took care of providing a platform for Berber identity. The founder of *Vreemd maar Vriend*, however, describes the association as a cultural association, and not explicitly as a Berber activist association. In a similar vein, Dutch association *Bades* equally does not wish to be perceived as a Berber association as such, at least when relating to local, Dutch issues of integration. At the time when *Vreemd maar Vriend* was established, the association's leading figure was still a student, and experimented with a few activities, which initially failed because of a lack of professional organizational experience on his part. In fact, the founder migrated to Flanders when he was only a child during the late seventies. In 1991, he restarted, this time with a Berber festival in Brussels. His motivation, different from the political reasons given by Dutch activists born in Morocco around the same time, for doing so was: '(...) an opportunity to come out with it, not towards Belgians, but especially towards Moroccans because I saw that most Moroccans did not know their history and also know little about *Amazigh* culture or the Berbers and then I thought that it would perhaps be a good thing to organize something like that'. He focused on both second- and first-generation Moroccans. The first generation in particular had received very little education and regarded Arab culture as a higher culture.

At first, the founder of *Vreemd maar Vriend* used music as a means to reach out to the Moroccan communities. The first edition, he recalls, was very successful because he was able to attract well-known and popular Berber musicians and bands. The songs of these bands were, however, politically charged. They sang about poverty among and oppression of the Berbers in Morocco. One year later, he expanded the program and added theatre and poetry readings in Berber. It was only natural to him that for the next editions, he invited speakers to touch upon topics such as Berber language, culture, tradition, history. Even today, this is one of the core activities practiced among Berber associations. Mostly students from Brussels attended these gatherings. As these Belgian Berber festivals in Brussels became more widely known, Berbers residing abroad started to attend. The founder recalls these foreign visitors were mainly Dutch Berbers. At that time, the popularity of Dutch Berber associations was on the rise. In 1997, Dutch newsletter *Adrar* noted the magazine that was being published by *Vreemd maar Vriend*, which was distributed in Antwerp, and spoke of the association in very positive terms: "*a broadly orientated magazine (...) We are jealous of our Belgian friends. Vreemd maar Vriend.*" In addition to the festivals in Brussels, *Vreemd maar Vriend* had started publishing a local newspaper and broadcasted a radio program in Antwerp.

Overall, the lifespan of this early Berber association was, especially when compared to the Dutch case, quite short. *Vreemd maar Vriend*'s members explained that the Moroccan community in Antwerp during the mid- and late nineties did not at all times agree with what the association printed or discussed on the radio, especially with regard to their emphasis on Berber culture and call for Berber culture and contributions to Moroccan history to be recognized. However, their failure in Antwerp was also explained in reference to Hassan II, who, until 1999, was still king. Not only were they pressured by consular employees to halt their activities, Moroccans in Antwerp were also afraid to speak up against his regime and oppression of Berber languages in Morocco. In short, both the association and the Moroccan community in Antwerp, Brussels and Mechelen felt surveyed by the Moroccan government. The 'Berber-Arab issue' remained a sensitive one, even after the 1994 king's Throne Day speech, when Hassan II promised a change in policy towards Berber culture and language.

The rising popularity of Berber identity and culture in Belgium from the late nineties onwards, within the historical framework of Moroccan migration, may henceforth in addition be explained by trends in Moroccan politics. Morocco has continuously sought to tighten relations between the state and its citizens abroad on both economic and cultural levels. The most logical reason would constitute the policy shift in Morocco, especially since Mohamed VI's rise to the throne towards citizens abroad, the *Marocains résidant à l'Etranger (MRE's)* (Belguendouz, 2006; 2009a & 2009b; Brand: 2008). Hassan II's *Amicales,* for instance, had by then been dissolved and consultative bodies were installed in order to assure participation of the *MRE's* in a more democratic way. The nineties were marked by a significant change with the creation of a Moroccan *Ministry for Moroccans residing Abroad*, quickly incorporated into the Ministry of Foreign Affairs in 1997. Nowadays, the *Fondation Hassan II pour les Marocains résidant à l'Etranger*, initiated in 1990, continues to take up this role as an informative and advisory body to which *MRE's* may appeal for economic, cultural and social affairs. An advisory board of MRE's, the *Conseil de la communauté marocaine à l'étranger (CCME)*, was founded in 2007 yet dissolved in 2012 in search of other institutions to guarantee bonds with the diaspora and promote participation.

Berber identity politics in Antwerp after 2000

Whereas members of the Berber Movement in the Netherlands have by now already started to reflect on the history of their movement, currently only one association in Flanders is active: the Antwerp based *Tilelli*, previously named *Umas,* signifying 'little brother' in Tarifit (Riffian Berber), but equally referring to *'Unie Multicultureel Antwerpen Stad'* ('Union Multicultural Antwerp City'). The members involved, however, were recent migrants, arriving in Flanders after 2000. But the earliest – albeit rather unsuccessful – initiatives in Flanders were undertaken by Moroccans who had migrated to Belgium at a younger age, having attended primary school in Morocco yet not having lived through youth and adolescence in Morocco. This particular migration pattern has impacted the development of associations in Flanders and explains the differences in their activities when, for instance, compared to the Netherlands. One of the founding members of *UMAS*, however, had been active in *Vreemd maar Vriend*. From 1995 onwards in Brussels associations *Jugurtha* and *Tiddukla n'Imazighen* were active. In Leuven, *Agraw Imazighen* co-organized activities of the *Rif Autonomy Group,* a grouping of Belgian and Dutch activist striving for more regional autonomy in Morocco, in 2011. *Tifawin* and *Yuba* are two younger associations active in Brussels. In Ghent, Tilelli organized a week-long festival in 1996, to which representatives from foreign associations were invited. No Berber activists active in Antwerp, Brussels and Leuven, nor in the Netherlands, however, knew the association had existed. Although the amount of local associations is thus far smaller in Flanders, a *Mouvement Amazigh Belgique* (Belgian Berber Movement) exists outside of a regular associative network similar to that of the Netherlands.

Ties between Flanders and the Netherlands are tight, also among those second-generation youth engaged in activism. Among the latter, those raised in the diaspora, language often poses problems. Whereas older activists who were born in Morocco maintain ties with France and are active in Brussels, younger activists (born in Morocco or in Belgium) focus on ties with the Netherlands because their mastery of French is insufficient. As a matter of fact, since those born in the diaspora often lack a thorough knowledge of the mother tongue, activities are not always fully conducted in *Tarifit*. As such, language acts as a divisive factor. Flemish Riffians often attended debates and festivals in the Netherlands because there are very little of those in Flanders itself.

The Arab European League joined the *Federatie Marokkaanse Verenigingen* (*FMV*) soon after its inception in 2000 and critiqued integration and anti-discrimination policies while boasting an Arab but more predominant Muslim identity, blending multiculturalism with pan-Arab nationalism. According to the president of *FMV*, the umbrella association had been wary of Arab and Berber initiatives, as they might divide the community of Moroccans in Flanders, who were already facing the threat of popular, discriminatory political parties in the late nineties and early two-thousands. Matters escalated in 2002, however, when *AEL* initiated civil patrols after police reports on monitoring of Moroccan youth had leaked, and the murder of a Moroccan by a Belgian caused riots after which *AEL* leader Dyab Abou Jahjah was arrested for inciting the violence. In early 2003 Dutch branches were set up, but *Amazigh* activists protested against these plans. *AEL* never attained similar popularity among Moroccan youth in the Netherlands. In Antwerp, however, the number of members among Moroccan youth grew.

A Flemish *Berber Movement,* initiated by local liberal politician Mohamed Talhaoui, was short-lived and never had a significant impact on Moroccan associative life in Antwerp. During my interviews in Antwerp, many *Amazigh* activists argued that Talhaoui had failed because he had created the movement solely on political and instrumental grounds, directed against Abou Jahjah, and not on an authentic attitude of *Amazighité*. *AEL* urged the Moroccan migrant population as the actor to bring about change in Antwerp and Flemish society, but all the while claimed 'Arab' domination over Berber culture, even though Abou Jahjah had stressed that from a pan-Arab ideal, 'non-Muslims' were to be tolerated (Jacobs, 2005: 105). In Antwerp, Arabism thus predominated Berberism.

However, the success of the *AEL* did not burry the Arab-Berber question altogether. In fact, some members questioned the predominance of Arabism over Berberism. This caused some Flemish Moroccans to refrain from further membership, though only very few of these considered founding an *Amazigh* association as an alternative. Rather, they would incorporate *Amazighité* in other ways: through social work or a broader framework of professional work with youth on a local level. Besides within *AEL*, during the nineties already, some youth centers had also debated the topic of *Amazigh* identity. The short-lived initiative 'SoRif' organized travels to Morocco for Moroccan youth attending centers of social work, in order to become more acquainted with their 'identity' and 'history' as Berber Moroccans. Some of these initiators had ended up in *AEL*. During the heydays of the *AEL* in Antwerp in 2002, the topic was subject to much debate. Some conformed to the overarching Arabism as the basis and structure of social organization, whereas others did not.

A clear *Amazigh* political answer to the *AEL* with regard to their Arabism, however, was never formulated. In Antwerp and Mechelen in particular, Berber identity was embedded in social work and thus took on a different shape than in the Netherlands, where it formed the basis of cultural associations. In Flanders, however, social workers of Moroccan origin in the late nineties and early two-thousands started to set up courses in Moroccan national history and paid particular attention to Riffian history and Berber identity, as well as focusing on the shared past of Moroccans and the Flemish, such as in the commemorative practice of the burial site of Chastre near Gembloux, where Moroccan soldiers, as part of the French army during the Second World War, were buried in Islamic fashion next to Christians (Karrouche, 2011). In Flanders, boundaries between cultural and social activism had thus become blurred.

Over the past years, cultural initiatives related to Berber culture and identity have been supported by local and national politics, such as the teaching of Berber on the level of higher education in Flanders, the founding of Moroccan-Flemish cultural center *Daarkom* in Brussels, which directed attention towards the Berber issue in Morocco. Cultural centers in Brussels (BOZAR), and Antwerp (Moussem) have increasingly incorporated Berber art and music in their programs. In Antwerp, Berber cultural festivals have now become a fixture in the city's cultural programming. Often, this has been due to the influence of individuals affiliated with the Berber Movement, without necessarily being involved with or being founders of a local Berber association, or intellectual elites of Berber origin. The accommodation of the Dutch *Berberbibliotheek* in

Moroccan Tirailleurs buried in the cemetery of Chastre (source: KADOC)

Flemish publishing has likewise popularized and mainstreamed Berber culture and languages.

Being Berber

In the Belgian-Berber diaspora, the Berber activist agenda and discourse varies according to the context and location of the member associations' actions, not only interpreted geographically in the strict sense of territoriality, but also in terms of discourses as mobile cultural practices (Clifford, 1992). The Berber elite that initiated Berber identity politics in the late sixties set up cultural and popular research associations both in Morocco and among the small Moroccan exile-communities, mostly in Paris. Nowadays, the movement has grown larger, more diverse. Moreover, it has lost its elitist character. The agenda of the Berber Movement is at once local, national, transnational and global. At times this renders the logic of the movement complex, even to such an extent that it may lead to the *"coexistence of multiple, incommensurable (yet not incompatible) logics of practice and knowledge operating in different spheres of social interaction"* (Silverstein, 2011: 68).

Today Morocco upholds its longstanding tradition with both internal and external migration, and it remains one of the leading emigration regions in the world. 'Moroccannes' is still mediated across national borders: politically, economically and culturally. Several institutions have done so in the past. During the past two decades in Flanders, the Moroccan Berber Movement has developed a cultural and political discourse with an emphasis on their difference from Arab-Islamic culture. Associations within this movement in host societies, established by highly educated first generation follow migrants, have faced a growing interest from second-generation youth. This opens up space for renewal: new ways of appropriating Berber representations of the past and rethinking current positions of Moroccan-Berbers, their transnational ties, cultural belongings and political engagements.

As culture makers Berber activists function altogether as the 'gatekeepers' (Hoffman – Gilson Miller, 2010: 10) to what is 'acceptably Amazigh'. Activists themselves in Belgium have acknowledged the disunity of the Movement and its inability to mobilize large masses with clear political demands, as for instance the *AEL* was able to do. Yet not the founders of these Berber associations are nowadays at the core of current developments within Berber activism in the diaspora; post-migrants are. They will inevitably impinge upon modes of identity-construction and collective, political action based on Berber identity.

More than forty years ago, in their seminal work 'Arabs and Berbers', Gellner and Micaud (1972) predicted that there was no 'Berber problem' in the Maghreb. The course of Moroccan history and migration history has proven them wrong. Developments as recent as the Arab Spring in Morocco in 2011 and the rise in interest among second- and third-generation youth in host societies, who attend Berber cultural festivals, point out that Berber culture can still be regarded as an identifier in multicultural societies, and that their Berber activism is still relevant. Whereas Berber activism in the eighties, nineties and early two-thousands was mostly a male affair, women and post-migrants are increasingly participating in Berber activism. Women have also started to establish their own associations and networks. This suggests that these women, often post-migrants, only partly identify with the men who founded the associations that got them acquainted with a thorough understanding of the relevance of Berber culture to Moroccan history in the first place. Nowadays, in young Berber women's lives in the Maghreb and the diaspora, Berber activism often intersects with feminism. In the diaspora-condition, Berber activists have viewed the Berbers as ethnic minorities living within Moroccan minorities in host societies.

On the other hand, Berber identity remains contested. What is needed, according to second-generation Moroccan migrant critics, is a uniting factor and not a divisive one. Given the focus of the Flemish integration debates on Muslim identity and 'radical Islam', stressing internal differences between Moroccan Belgians would only work in their collective disadvantage. This argument is precisely what held the development of Berber associations in Flanders back during the nineties. With which histories will post-migrants in the future identify, which collective histories will shape their identities, their cultural and political actions? Addressing such issues of plurality consists one of the main challenges not only policymakers are facing today, but Berber activists as well.

Notes

1   I use 'Berber' and 'Amazigh' ('free person') interchangeably for stylistic reasons. Many activists denounce the term 'Berber' because of its implicit negative bias.

2   The associations in Belgium that were researched between 2008 and 2012 were: Agraw Imazighen, Leuven; Jugurtha, Brussels; Tiddukla n'Imazighen, Brussels; Tifawin, Brussels; Tilelli/Thirelli (previously UMAS), Antwerp; Tilelli, Ghent; Vreemd maar Vriend, Antwerp; Yuba, Brussels.

Bibliography

Aouchar, A. (2005). *Colonisation et campagne berbère au Maroc*, Afrique Orient: Casablanca.

Belguendouz, A. (2006). *Le traitement institutionnel de la relation entre les Marocains rusidant àidant*. Le traitement insResearch Report CARIM-RR 2006-06, Florence: European University Institute.

Belguendouz, A. (2009a). *Le conseil de la communauté marocaine à l'étranger. Une nouvelle institution en débat*, Research Report CARIM-RR 2009-01, Florence: European University Institute.

Belguendouz, A. (2009b). *Le nouveau ministère chargé de la communauté marocaine résidant à l'étranger. Quelle stratégie?* Research Report CARIM-RR 2009-02, Florence: European University Institute.

Brand, L. (2008). *Citizens Abroad. Emigration and the State in the Middle East and North Africa*. Cambridge: Cambridge University Press.

Brouwer, L. (2006). Dutch Moroccan Websites. A Transnational Imaginary? *Journal of Ethnic and Migration Studies* 32, 1153-1168.

Burke E. III (2007). The Creation of the Moroccan Colonial Archive. 1880-1930. *History and Anthropology* 18 (2007), 1-9.

Clifford, J. (1992). Traveling cultures. In L. Grossberg, C. Nelson, P.A. Treichler, (eds.), *Cultural Studies*. New York: Routledge, 96-116.

Cottaar, A., Bouras, N., with Fatiha Laoukili (2009). *Marokkanen in Nederland. De pioniers vertellen*. Amsterdam: Meulenhoff.

Crul, M., Heering, L. (eds.) (2008). *The Position of the Turkish and Moroccan Generation in Amsterdam and Rotterdam. The TIES Study in the Netherlands*. Amsterdam: IMISCOE Research – Amsterdam University Press.

De Haas, H. (2007). Morocco's Migration Experience. A Transitional Perspective. *International Migration* 45, 39-70.

De Haas, H. (2009). International Migration and Regional Development in Morocco. A Review. *Journal of Ethnic and Migration Studies* 35, 1571-1593.

Entzinger, H., Dourleijn, E. (2008). *De lat steeds hoger. De leefwereld van jongeren in een multi-etnische stad*. Assen: Van Gorcum.

Feliu, L. (2006). Le Mouvement culturel amazigh (MCA) au Maroc. *L'année du Maghreb* I, 274-285.

Ferguson, H. (2009). *Self-Identity and Everyday Life*. London – New York: Routledge.

Gellner, E., Micaud, C. (eds.) (1972). *Arabs and Berbers. From Tribe to Nation in North Africa*. Lexington – Toronto – London: Lexington Books.

Glick Schiller, N., Fouron, G.E. (2001). *Georges Woke Up Laughing. Long-Distance Nationalism and the Search for Home*. Durham – London: Duke University Press.

Gross, J.E., McMurray D.A. (1993). Berber Origins and the Politics of Ethnicity in Colonial North African Discourse. *Political and Legal Anthropology Review* 16, 39-58.

Guerin, A. (2011). Racial Myth, Colonial Reform, and the Invention of Customary Law in Morocco 1912-1930. *The Journal of North African Studies* 16, 361-380.

Hammoudi, A. (1997). *Master and Disciple. The Cultural Foundations of Moroccan Authoritarianism*, Chicago – London: The University of Chicago Press.

Hart, D.M. (1997). The Berber Dahir of 1930 in Colonial Morocco. Then and Now (1930-1996). *The Journal of North African Studies* 2, 11-33.

Hoffman, K.E., Gilson Miller, S. (eds.) (2010). *Berbers and Others. Beyond Tribe and Nation in the Maghrib*. Bloomington – Indianapolis: Indiana University Press.

Jacobs, D. (2005). Arab European League (AEL). The Rapid Rise of a Radical Immigrant Movement. *Journal of Muslim Minority Affairs* 25, 99-117.

Karrouche, N. (2011). Naar het geval Gembloux. 'Heet' en 'koud' erfgoed van migratie en de omgang met 'interculturaliteit. *FARO. Tijdschrift voor cultureel erfgoed* 4/1, 23-27.

Kratochwil, G. (1999). Some Observations on the First Amazigh World Congress (August 27-30, 1997, Tarifa, Canary Islands). *Die Welt des Islams* 39, 149-158.

Maddy-Weitzman, B. (2007). Berber/Amazigh "Memory Work", in B. Maddy-Weitzman, D. Zisenwine (eds.), *The Maghreb in the New Century. Identity, Religion and Politics.* Gainseville: University Press of Florida, 95-126.

Maddy-Weitzman, B. (2011). *The Berber Identity Movement and the Challenge to North African States.* Austin: University of Texas Press.

Mamadouh, V. (2001). Constructing a Dutch Moroccan Identity through the World Wide Web. *The Arab World Geographer* 4, 258-274.

Martin-Alcoff, L. (2000). Who's Afraid of Identity Politics?. In Paula M. L. Moya, Michael R. Hames-Garcia (eds.), *Reclaiming Identity. Realist Theory and the Predicament of Postmodernism.* Berkeley – Los Angeles – London: University of California Press, 312-344.

Merolla, D. (2002). Digital Imagination and the 'Landscapes of Group Identities'. The Flourishing of Theatre, Video and 'Amazigh Net' in the Maghrib and Berber Diaspora. *The Journal of North African Studies* 7, 122-131.

Merolla, D. (2005). "Migrant Websites", Webart and Digital Imagination. In S. Ponzanes, D. Merolla (eds.), *Migrant Cartographies. New Cultural and Literary Spaces in Post-Colonial Europe.* Oxford: Lexington, 217-228.

Pouessel, S. (2010). *Les identités amazighes au Maroc.* Paris: Non Lieu, 2010.

Reniers, G. (1999). On the History and the Selectivity of Turkish and Moroccan Migration to Belgium. *International Migration* 37, 679-713.

Schrover, M., R. Penninx (2001). *Bastion of bindmiddel. De organisatie van migranten in historisch perspectief.* Amsterdam: Instituut voor Migratie- en Etnische Studies.

Silverstein, P. (2004). *Algeria in France. Transpolitics, Race and Nation.* Bloomington: Indiana University Press.

Silverstein, P. (2011). Masquerade politics: race, Islam and the scale of Amazigh activism in southeastern Morocco. *Nations and Nationalisms* 17, 65-84.

Van Amersfoort, H., van Heelsum, A. (2007). Moroccan Berber Immigrants in the Netherlands, Their Associations and Transnational Ties. A Quest for Identity and Recognition. *Immigrants & Minorities* 25, 234-262.

Van Heelsum, A. (2001). *Marokkaanse organisaties in Nederland. Een netwerkanalyse.* Amsterdam: Het Spinhuis.

Van Heelsum, A. (2003). Moroccan Berbers in Europe, the US and Africa and the Concept of Diaspora. In UCLA Centre for European and Eurasian Studies. Occasional Lecture Series, paper 1.

Vertovec Steven (2004). Migrant Transnationalism and Modes of Transformation. *International Migration Review* 38, 970-1001.

Vertovec, S. (2009). *Transnationalism*. London – New York: Routledge, 2009.

11. Fluctuating identifications among second-generation Moroccans in the Netherlands and Belgium: looking beyond personal experiences via social network analysis

Anna Berbers, Leen d'Haenens & Joyce Koeman

I have been born and bred here but with my parents I do have a certain label, that I come from Morocco and you keep that, it stays. My children will eventually have it, my partner, everyone will keep that label. But that does not mean I am not Dutch. [woman, 23, North-Holland]

The quote above shows the complexities and interrelatedness of the multiple ethnic identities of migrants and their offspring. Taking the second-generation Moroccan minorities[1] living in Belgium and the Netherlands as a case in point here, we look into the intertwined relationships between: (i) the manifestations and experiences of intra-group tensions within society at large (e.g., multicultural policies, media portrayal and social interactions), and (ii) Dutch or Belgian national-, Moroccan ethnic- and Muslim religious-identifications.[2] We present a mixed-method approach, combining personal network analysis with qualitative interviews, in an effort to provide a comprehensive account of minorities' life worlds (Cf. Bilencen, 2016). In this chapter, we discuss external-identification by others, as it is relevant for self-identification of minorities on the basis of nationality, ethnicity and religion (Van Heelsum, 2013), but we focus on the latter instead of the former.

Moroccan minorities are a relevant group to study for identification processes, as the majority population perceives the cultural distance to Moroccan minorities to be larger than to other minority groups. So, Moroccan minorities are perceived as the most 'different' by the majority population and consequently experience high levels of prejudice and stigmatization (Schalk-Soekar & Van de Vijver, 2008). However, while Moroccan minorities are perceived as most different, they actually show a stronger orientation towards the Dutch and Belgian society (e.g., identification with host nationality, language proficiency, contact with majority population) than for instance Turkish minorities (De Vroome, Verkuyten & Martinovic, 2014).

When discussing intra-group tensions in relation to Moroccan minorities, issues with regard to religious-identifications cannot be ignored. Most Moroccan minorities identify with Islamic religion and their identifications with Islam are often intertwined with their ethnic Moroccan identity, even more so for the second-generation than for the first (Van Heelsum, 2013). This can be difficult for establishing a positive sense of self for some Moroccan minorities, as many recent events have put migrants, Islam and Muslims in a negative daylight: the departure of numerous 'Syria fighters', the depiction of extremism among Muslim youth in the media, the terrorist attacks in Paris and Brussels, and so on. News media tend to frame such events in a way where Islam and/or minority groups pose a threat to 'fundamental European values' (Berbers, Joris, Boesman, d'Haenens, Koeman & Van Gorp, 2016; Wolska-Zogata, 2015), as well as European way of life in general. These representations and circumstances impact upon the daily experiences of Moroccan minorities living in Europe, as well as on the intergroup relationships between majority and minority groups.

The discussion in this chapter centers around identifications with both nationality, ethnicity and religion. These terms have acquired fuzzy boundaries, and especially the concept ethnicity requires clarification. We define ethnicity as feelings of belonging to a group of people, in which an intersubjective belief exists that one is different from other groups, based on characteristics like customs and language. The group shares a belief in a shared ancestry, as well as a common homeland. By presenting ourselves as a 'we'-group, the boundaries of what it means to belong to this group are socially constructed in interaction with out-groups, the 'they'-group. So, ethnicity foremost comprises the social organization that takes place, based on the cultural elements ethnic groups find most relevant themselves (Roosens, 1998). Hence, identification with Moroccan ethnicity refers to the extent to which Moroccan minorities feel that they belong to the ethnic group Moroccans. Our case study is limited to the second-generation migrants of Moroccan descent, i.e. whose parents have migrated to Belgium and the Netherlands as their host countries. The latter provide the basis for what we define here as identifications with nationality, i.e. the extent to which Moroccan minorities feel part of the Dutch/Belgian society, as indicated by the (double) nationalities in our participants' passports.

Ethnic-, national- and religious-identifications are important building blocks when constructing a social identity, which is dynamic and situational by nature, as people define themselves in relation to others (Tajfel & Turner, 1986). All human beings endeavor to achieve and maintain a positive self-image and construct social identities in relation to the various situations that make up the fabric of everyday life (Goffman, 1956). However, for people of Moroccan descent this has become problematic in a context where public discourses continuously link their religious identity (Islam) to terrorism (Berbers et al., 2016). And diminished feelings of acceptance in turn may reinforce their identification as a separate group, which is illustrated by the embedded use of the terms 'autochtony' and 'allochtony' that serve as a basis for belonging, and in which notions of 'primordiality' are at play by the formation of (fictive) ties and kinships that exclude individuals from certain rights. This stigmatizing process further sets Moroccan minorities apart as religious and ethnic outsiders (Slootman, 2014). Those who experience this are forced to renegotiate elements of their identity to maintain a positive self-image, for instance by downplaying or exaggerating certain elements, depending on the situation. Especially second-generation minorities show a certain situational flexibility in how they adapt and construct their social identities (Van Heelsum & Koomen, 2016).

In light of this, we aim to analyze the 'lived' experience of personal networks, with an emphasis on related identification processes, as well as the structure and composition of networks. Personal networks are essential drivers for an expansive range of behaviors, attitudes and phenomena, such as: the spread of obesity (Christakis & Fowler, 2007), mortality rates (Berkman & Syme, 1979), status attainment (Linn, 1999), minority groups' transnational practices and social identification processes (Bilecen, 2016; Lubbers, Molina & McCarty, 2007; Lubbers, Molina, Lerner, Ulrik, Ávila, & McCarty, 2010; Vacca, Solano, Lubbers, Molina & McCarty, 2016) and a plethora of other reasons (for an overview, see Hâncean, Molina & Lubbers, 2016). We will use the structure and composition of personal networks of minorities to provide a complementary view on commonly studies identification processes. Minority groups with a more dense and homogeneous network (in terms of ethnicity) and a smaller number of subgroups are more likely to self-identify ethnic-exclusively (e.g. Moroccan), whereas other types of networks may lead to ethnic-inclusive (e.g. Moroccan-Belgian) and generic identifications (Lubbers et al., 2007; Lubbers et al., 2010). This contribution aims to examine how personal networks and interactions of minorities with society at large shape their daily identity negotiations/ constructions. First, the main concepts and methods derived from social identity perspective and identity theory are introduced. Second, it is explained how these are applied to our study of second-generation Moroccan minorities living in the Netherlands and Belgium.[3] Third, the main identity negotiations/constructions discerned are presented. Finally, the limitations of our study as well as suggestions for future research are discussed.

Moving from Identity Theory towards the Social Identity Perspective in social network analysis

Within this chapter, we adopt a theoretical lens that joins perspectives from Identity Theory (IT) and the Social Identity Perspective (SIP), which both revolve around the dynamic construction of the self in relation to individual behavior and society, but each emphasizes a different aspect of the identification process. We argue that both perspectives should be utilized concurrently to gain complete understanding of the intricate identification processes under study. Hence, we set out with a description and comparison of both theories that will show their respective disciplinary origins, their subsequent focal points and complimentary views on identification processes.

SIP has disciplinary roots in psychology and provides a social psychological theory of intergroup relations, group processes and the social self. It is based on the notion that the social categories one feels to belong to (e.g., nationality, political affiliation, ethnicity), provide a definition of whom one is by means of the key characteristics of that category. In other words, individuals have a repertoire of distinctive category memberships or social identities that vary in importance for delineating the self-concept. Social identities both describe and prescribe group members' attributes, and evaluate social groups in relation to other relevant in- and out-groups. People endeavor to achieve and maintain a positive self-image and this self-image is sustained by identifying and constructing elements in which they evaluate their in-group as superior to the relevant out-groups (i.e. in-group bias). This positive identification allows people to boost their self-esteem (Tajfel & Turner, 1986). So, SIP focuses on cognitive processes through which people sharpen the boundaries between in- and out-groups.

IT[4] was established in the sociology domain as a micro theory about the self as product of social interaction and sets out to explain people's role related behavior. People come to know who they are by interacting with others and seeing themselves through the role they enact reflected in that social interaction. People claim a certain role identity through a process of labeling themselves as a member of a particular social category (Burke, 1980). The role identity becomes meaningful through reflexivity in social interaction, as others respond to the enacted role and these responses form the basis for developing a sense of self. When others confirm the enacted identity via social cues in interaction, this validates a person's status and can increase self-esteem. Alternatively, when others reject the enacted identity, this can cause psychological distress and diminished self-worth. So, people feel distressed when the reactions of others are different from what they would expect, based on the role they are performing (Hogg, Terry & White, 1995). People mostly change their behavior to be congruent with their internalized identity standards, but occasionally, they change their role identity to match their behavior (Burke, 1991). Role identities are organized hierarchically as some identities have more self-relevance than others with a higher probability that they will be used for action. Those identities positioned at the top of the hierarchy will be more likely to be enacted in a given situation, and thereby have implications for people's relationships and their perceptions and evaluations of others (Hogg et al., 1995). According to IT, which does not focus on cognitive processes but centers on social interaction, people's sense of self comes from the various roles they occupy in daily life (e.g., daughter, citizen). When people enact a certain role and this is not reflected in social interactions with others, this can cause psychological distress and low self-esteem (Hogg et al., 1995; Tajfel & Turner, 1986). In IT, social categories such as ethnicity or gender are viewed as master statuses (Stryker, 1987) and are not considered to directly evoke specific behavioral expectations, but to have an indirect impact on the constructed self through prioritizing certain role identities, as well as influencing their interactions with others (Hogg et al., 1995).

Following several scholars (Lubbers et al., 2007; Lubbers et al., 2010; MacFarland & Pals, 2005), we argue that SIP and IT are complementary theoretical lenses that, when combined, offer a more complete and nuanced picture of the subjective social world in which inter-ethnic relationships evolve. Both theories view the self as socially constructed and share the notion that people have a hierarchy of identities and the knowledge that the salience of these identities varies with different social environments. Whereas SIP focuses on the cognitive processes and structures (e.g. categorizations) that underlie identification processes (Hogg et al., 1995), IT focuses more on how the sense of self is reflectively constructed in social interactions. Additionally, the theories have a different interpretation of social environment: SIP views categories as social environments (e.g., ethnicity, gender), whereas IT refers to social networks (i.e., the structure of relationships between individuals; Lubbers et al., 2007). An integration of both theoretical stances allows a joint analysis of macro processes (SIP) and micro processes (IT) that drive social interactions and behaviors.

According to IT, there are several network properties that are related to behavior of actors within the networks. Conformity is expected to be greater in networks where actors are more densely connected in their relationships, as well as more homogeneous in background. Additionally, actors who have multiple cohesive subgroups in their personal networks have more unstable identities as they are confronted with diverse external-identifications (MacFarland & Pals, 2005). Several studies found that the ethnic or (trans)national-identifications and practices are associated with the types of networks in which individuals are embedded[5] (Bilencen, 2016; Lubbers et al., 2007; Lubbers et al., 2010; MacFarland & Pals, 2005; Vacca et al., 2016). For instance, Erasmus students who have high proportions of cross-national friendships are more likely to self-identify as Europeans. Additionally, friends from other countries with whom solidarity is strong are less likely to be considered as 'foreigners' by these Erasmus students (De Federico de la Rúa, 2013). Their personal networks were classified into network profiles on the basis of network structure (e.g., density and number of cohesive subgroups), as well as network composition (e.g., country of origin and percentage of family members), that were related to self-identifications of migrants. Personal networks in which network members, mostly family and people from the country of origin, formed one dense cluster were associated with ethnic exclusive self-identifications, whereas more heterogeneous personal networks tended to exhibit more plural definitions of belonging.

The relationship between personal networks, ethnic-identifications, social and economic integration has also been studied among migrant groups in Spain and Italy. The amount of majority members in personal networks of minorities was related to economic outcomes, with an average level of embeddedness most often leading to economic success. Low number of natives *was considered* as an indication of a lack of structural integration, while high numbers was viewed as a sign of insufficient social capital among other minority groups (Vacca et al., 2016). Additionally, personal networks were referred to as an explanatory factor for (trans)national-identifications of minority groups.

So, in our study we would expect that people of Moroccan background, who have a dense and homogeneous personal network in terms of ethnic and religious background, are more likely to identify themselves according to ethnicity or religion exclusively (e.g., Moroccan or Muslim). We expect that people of

Moroccan background who have loosely connected networks that consist of multiple subgroups with more heterogeneous actors (i.e. ethnically diverse) tend to identify in an ethnic-plural fashion (e.g. Moroccan-Belgian) or in generic terms (e.g. as a woman). Additionally, we expect those with loosely connected networks of heterogeneous subgroups to have more unstable identifications, as they meander through divergent social spaces, compared to those with a dense and homogeneous personal network. In the following, we describe how this manifests particularly among second-generation Moroccan minorities in the Low Countries.

Identification processes of second-generation Moroccan minorities

Identification processes related to ethnicity, nationality and religion operate differently for first- and second-generation minorities. Even if second-generation minority members feel perfectly at home in the country they were born in, societal discourse tends to highlight their ethnic minority background. For second-generation minorities, this can more easily lead to a *reactive identity*, whereby minorities are even more inclined to identify as a member of that particular ethnic or religious group. Where for the first-generation, a disidentification with Dutch/Belgian nationality can take place, this is less likely for the second-generation. The latter seem more confident in managing multiple identities and coping with negative societal discourse, discrimination and perceived group rejection (Van Heelsum, 2013). Recent research indicates that Moroccan minorities in the Netherlands, in contrast to Turkish minorities, do not have a lower identification with Dutch nationality compared to the majority group (De Vroome et al., 2014). In fact, most Moroccan minorities prefer a hyphenated identification (i.e. Moroccan-Dutch) above an ethnic exclusive-identification (e.g. Moroccan; Bochove, Burgers, Geurts, De Koster, & Van der Waal, 2015). The interrelatedness of ethnic, national and religious-identification (micro factors), alongside perceived group rejection and discrimination in the Netherlands and Belgium (macro factors) will take center stage in this study. Therefore, the policy context of both societies, with similarities and differences in integration policies and discourses will be sketched.

Immigration and integration polices

Over the past two decades more restrictive immigration/integration policies have been implemented in both the Netherlands and Belgium (Huddleston, Bilgili, Joki, & Vankova, 2015). To capture group-differentiated rights, the policy index of Indicators of Citizenship Rights for Immigrants (ICRI) is relevant. This index strongly represents religious rights and ranks countries based on their differential cultural rights (ranging from-1 to 1). Based on 23 indicators, five broad categories are distinguished: (i) absence of cultural assimilation requirements for access to rights; (ii) accommodation of religious practices outside public institutions; (iii) cultural rights and provisions in public institutions; (iii) political representation rights; and (iv) affirmative action policies. In 2008, overall ICRI scores were higher in the Netherlands (.42) than in Belgium (.15), and when the religious rights for Muslims are singled out, the discrepancy between the Netherlands (.79) and Belgium (.04) is even bigger (Koopmans, 2013). This indicates that immigrants in the Netherlands used to have more access to cultural rights, especially when it came to Muslim minorities. ICRI measurements have not taken place since 2008, however, more recent findings of other indexes show a decline in differential minority rights, especially in the Netherlands (Huddleston et al., 2015).

Research questions

Based on the literature described above, we pose the following research questions that contribute to a better understanding of the ethnic-identification processes among second-generation Moroccan migrants living in Belgium and the Netherlands:
- To what extent do participants identify with their ethnicity, nationality and/ or religion?
- Which strategies do participants adopt to construct a positive social identification?
- What are the differences between the Netherlands and Belgium?
- How are the composition and structure of social networks related to experienced identification processes?

Methodology

Approach

For this study, we adopted a mixed-method approach that combines qualitative and quantitative social network analysis in order to construct a typology of networks that encompasses the 'lived' experience of the network (Bilencen, 2016), with an emphasis on related identification processes and the structure and composition of networks. As we were interested in social identities higher in terms of hierarchy, we focused on the most important contacts in the network and asked participants for aliases of the most important people in their lives. We aimed to analyze up to 20 people, and asked for family, friends, acquaintances and colleagues, but not all participants were able to reach this number.[6] The computer-assisted approach was chosen so we could include more than two dimensions to visualize participants' networks, while generating a detailed picture of the personal network structures. Each participant was placed at the central point of the circle and the circle was divided in three sections, one for online contact, one for offline contact and one for contacts important for both online and offline communication.[7] All contacts mentioned were placed on concentric circles, representing the importance of the contact and the resources they represented. Interrelationships between reported contacts were also recorded, so the social structure could be analyzed. Information on the background of the participants was gathered (e.g., ethnic background, gender, age) to discern diversity within the network. Our approach here is inspired by the previously mentioned study that was conducted with various migrant groups in Spain and Italy, although we recorded a smaller number of actors (focusing on important contacts who they trust) to allow a more detailed discussion of identifications with the participants (Bilencen, 2016; Lubbers et al., 2007; Vacca et al., 2016).

Participants and procedure

Both in the Netherlands and Belgium, we approached second-generation Moroccan minorities aged 18 to 40, while aiming for diversity in terms of education, gender and age within our sample. We selected participants using theoretical sampling within the Grounded Theory framework, which led to more Belgian than Dutch participants. The participants were all born in their respective 'host countries' and at least one of their parents immigrated from Morocco. In total 41 interviews were conducted in April and May 2015, which were transcribed and analyzed in NVivo, software with a view to systematic, qualitative content analysis.

The participants (see Table 1) were interviewed by the principal investigator, as well as two student-assistants. Interviews took place in the informants' homes or at a location of their preference. On average an entire interview, including the mapping of the social network, lasted between one hour and a half to two hours. A discussion guide was developed as a part of a larger research project, focusing on the following topics: social and news media use, reception of media representations of Moroccan ethnicity and Islam, representation of Syria fighters, governmental policies, personal social networks and identification processes related to ethnicity, nationality and religion.[8] An in-depth analysis personal social networks and identification is discussed in this chapter.

Table 1   Age, gender and education of the participants

	Belgium (*n*=26)	The Netherlands (*n*=15)
Average age (years)	28,7	28,1
Gender (percentages)		
– Man	13	9
– Woman	13	6
Education		
– Primary education	1	1
– Secondary education	13	8
– Bachelor degree	9	4
– Master degree	3	2

Results

In this section, we describe the results for the four research questions that have guided this study: (i) the identification processes related to ethnicity, nationality and religion; (ii) the strategies employed by the participants to maintain a positive self-identification; (iii) the national context; and (iv) the relationship between composition and structure of social networks and identification processes. In this way we combine SIP, which can provide context to identification processes based on categories like ethnicity, with IT illustrating the importance of personal networks and social interactions.

Identification processes

We asked the participants to what extent they saw themselves as 'Moroccan' and/or 'Dutch/Belgian'. Some participants spontaneously mentioned that their religion was more important to them or that none of the categories were completely fitting or relevant. So, we broadened the identification question and asked specifically about religion, as well as other social categories that they felt were important for their sense of self. Participants identified with both their ethnicity and nationality, so we do acknowledge the complex intertwined relationships between national-, ethnic- and religious-identifications, but for clarity sake we choose to discuss them separately below.

Identification with Moroccan ethnicity was highly multiform and diverse among participants. Most of the participants in this study had a background in the Amazigh population, and identified with both Moroccan and Amazigh ethnic identity. There was a high variation in the presence of ethnic socio-cultural practices in their childhood homes (e.g., speaking Arabic and/or Amazigh languages, religious practices, culinary traditions, music) and this seemed to impact the salience of particular identity aspect. The participants who strongly identified with Moroccan and/or Amazigh ethnicity placed a higher value on ethnic socio-cultural practices, as well as visiting 'homeland' Morocco. The participants who identified less with their Moroccan or Amazigh background experienced pressure to conform to religious tradition in family context (e.g., fasting, wearing head-scarves), as well as disapproval regarding their acculturation to 'host' country practices:

> "Few dare to discuss it openly, but in the Moroccan community, ehm I am not seen as [first name participant], but as the 'Belgian'. For the real Moroccans, I have become too Belgian, especially with a Flemish partner." [man, 33, Flemish Brabant]

Among our participants, who were all born and raised in Belgium or the Netherlands, identification with the host country nationality was generally more pronounced than identification with Moroccan and/or Amazigh ethnicity. Some of the participants described feeling out of place when in Morocco, while feeling at home in the Netherlands or Belgium. Particularly the educational opportunities and citizen rights in the host country, compared to Morocco, were stressed as an asset to acquire a position in life. Many confirm that predominantly the Dutch and Belgian social norms and practices are leading in how they live their lives:

> "I have Moroccan background, but I think I inherited the Belgian norms and values. I'm born and raised there [Belgium] and I have learned much of what is important in terms of behavior here. I think I have inherited The Belgian code of conduct, being polite, and participating in society. So, I am Belgian in terms of nationality, but I have Moroccan roots so I can enjoy mint tea and Moroccan pancakes you know, but it does not play a huge role in my life." [women, 25, Utrecht]

The quote above illustrates how the participant associates her Belgian nationality more with the central values in her life, while Moroccan ethnicity is downplayed to culinary cultural traditions. This is reflected in her empathetic "I am Belgian". The participants that indicated that Islam was important to them viewed it as a guidepost to living a 'good' life and as a very positive force to society, regardless of the religiosity of the participants (i.e. the extent to which they practiced religious traditions such as fasting). Some participants explicitly related being Muslim to levels of religiosity, whereas other viewed it more as a philosophy than a strict guideline:

> "I have had a religious education (...) I am religious in the sense that I do believe in God and I get inspiration from the tradition of religion, but I'm not a practicing Muslim. I believe in the existence of a creative force and I believe in the good in Islam. There are many beautiful things I appreciate in Islam, but I also find these aspects in Christianity and even in other denominations. So, in that sense, when it comes to religion that spurs people to become a better version of himself, I have a great appreciation for religion." [man, 35, Flemish Brabant]

Maintaining a positive self-identification

All participants describe some difficulties related to being a minority group and having multiple sources of identification. In a way, they are caught in between two worlds and they are always the foreigner, whereby they are viewed as 'European' in Morocco and as Moroccan in Belgium or the Netherlands. The participants adopt several strategies to construct a positive identity and minimize psychological distress related to perceptions of external-identification incongruent with self-identification: (i) participants change their self-identification in response to incongruent external-identification; (ii) participants avoid situations that do not affirm their role enactment or self-identification; (iii) participants identify with a mixture of their nationality and ethnicity and describe themselves as both; (iv) participants identify mostly as Muslim but layer this identification with ethnicity and nationality; and (v) certain participants no longer identify with both ethnicity or nationality.

Some participants describe a reactive identification, with their ethnicity or religion, whereby external-identification leads to self-identification as mostly Moroccan or Muslim.

> "I used to be more Belgian than Moroccan. In my youth particularly and then at some point you clash with certain values and also people and then you think maybe they are right after all. So, I felt a little more Moroccan with the experiences I've had in my lifetime (...). Now, at this moment, I feel really Moroccan. But then I think why do I feel like that? (...) I would say I was born here, I am Belgian. But my surrounding likes to keep pushing. We are people so we like to put people in boxes and if you are put in the same box over and over again then yes, I am Moroccan and proud of it too. But I used to be proud to be Belgian, but if they begrudge you being Belgian then you have to change your thinking." [woman, 36, Antwerp]

This participant first describes a positive childhood self-identification, where she was proud to be Belgian and the Belgian identification was high in her identity hierarchy. However, this changed during the course of her life, due to experiences with 'othering' and perceived group rejection. It is striking how most participants who describe a reactive identity are very aware of and highly critical to media portrayals related to Moroccan ethnicity and Islamic religion, as well as associated governmental policies and politics. So, the experienced external identification as 'Moroccan' is shaped by media portrayal, governmental policy and political rhetoric, not just via interpersonal interactions in daily life.

Participants that describe a lessoned identification with their Moroccan or Amazigh ethnic identity, perceived disapproval and stigmatization in family context. They adopted behaviors perceived to belong to the majority group (e.g., secularism, interpersonal etiquette, romantic relationships with majority group members), and when they enacted this identity, they were confronted with disapproval and pressure to conform. In response, they avoided contact with their family and instead of changing their identification, they just engaged less in family gatherings and interacted less frequently with family members. Instead, they developed more relationships with friends, colleagues and acquaintances of non-Moroccan background, mostly Belgian or Dutch majority group members.

Participants who describe themselves as a mixture of both incorporate different aspects of both groups in their identification processes, which is reflected in the use of more inclusive pronouns (i.e., we and us) when discussing topics during the interview related to both Moroccan ethnicity and Dutch/Belgian nationality.

> "I am both. I am Dutch Moroccan. I know city hall better than the consulate. I live here, my house is on Dutch territory, my language is Dutch um so yeah, I've never known anything else. I live in the Dutch society (...) I see myself as from here, there in Morocco I am a foreigner, and here I am Dutch." [man, 28, Utrecht]

These participants, who identify with both Dutch/Belgian nationality and Moroccan ethnicity, tend to be relatively positive about their place in Dutch or Belgian society as an individual, stressing the civil and political rights, as well as educational and career opportunities. Nevertheless, most participants were relatively negative about the place of their ethnic/religious group in terms of societal hierarchy, and some described feelings of group rejection. These feelings stem from the perceived negative media portrayals on their ethnicity and religion, which participants considered a driving force in the polarization between majority and minority groups. It must be noted that the education level of participants seems a relevant marker here, as the more highly educated attributed feelings of group rejection more frequently to media representations, although they did not frequently describe personal experiences with discrimination. Instead, lower educated participants and women wearing a headscarf, regardless of their educational level, did describe personal encountered discrimination more often. Veiled women particularly hinted at discrimination during specific time periods when radicalization and terrorism were covered extensively in the media, like after Charlie Hebdo.

Participants who primarily self-identify as Muslim do not exclude identification with their Moroccan ethnicity or Belgian/Dutch nationality, but construct multiple layered identities:

"Above all, I feel I am Muslim. That is the most important to me. Secondly, I feel very Dutch. I'm really glad that I was born and raised in the Netherlands. I'm proud of it. I love to get back home when I return from vacation. There is nowhere else I'd rather live (...) I am also very proud I am of Moroccan origin (...) I see it as an enrichment. Two cultures that I have been given: great. In that sense, I see it more as a positive than a negative." [man, 34, Zeeland]

In contrast to participants who show reactive identifications, the participant above strikingly uses more inclusive pronouns (i.e., we and us) when discussing nationality, ethnicity and religion, but foremost his layered social identity is not constructed in response to (negative) external-identification.

Lastly, some participants reject the ethnic, national and religious labels, and instead describe themselves as 'just human' or as cosmopolitan in the sense that they support cosmopolitanism as an ideology; whereby all humans belong to the single community and based on shared morality. They argue that labels are predominantly used for exclusion of some groups and that these are no longer adequate as current identification processes transcend boundaries, like national boundaries:

"I'm not so keen on ethnic or nationalist labels, like Flemish or Belgian or Moroccan. I am just not keen on nationalism in general (...) It is the national dimension which I find just irrelevant. I'd say, look, I attach more importance to someone as a person than someone as a Belgian or a Moroccan. We are all people, right?" [man, 38, Genk]

National context

There were some differences between the Dutch and Belgian participants. The Belgian participants were less emphatic when they discussed identification to their nationality than the Dutch. This could be related to the sharp regional divisions in Belgium, a federal state where the northern Dutch-speaking region of Flanders, the southern French-speaking region of Wallonia, the small German-speaking region, and the bilingual capital region of Brussels are characterized by distinct political parties, institutions, discourses and regional policies.

"I think that Belgium is a harder identity issue than, say, the Netherlands or France because (...) even internally in Belgium is unclear, you have the Flemish identity and the Walloon identity and then there is even a small German community and how we are all still Belgians? I think that's a little more complicated than, than in neighboring countries."

So, the identification with the Belgian nationality is confounded by identification with feeling 'Flemish' or 'Walloon'. Most participants in Belgium live in the Flemish region, so many identify more strongly with their Flemish background. Some work or study in a Flemish institute or have a Flemish spouse, and therefore feel Flemish. Others rejected such regional distinctions as they felt the labels were related to group tensions and were used to exclude people.

Interestingly, all participants who describe a reactive identification were Belgian and were especially critical of the ban on headscarves that is currently implemented in many public schools, as well as in effect for civil servants:

"I don't care what politicians do, they are all corrupt. But what I do care about is the headscarf (...) That ban is irresponsible, I think personally. The most important thing is that the students get good grades, and you can get good grades with a headscarf and when they say, no more, then, the students will be too unmotivated to go to school (...) I know the press has a major role in how Islam is perceived, in their articles there is a sort of enemy and victim and certain roles and usually Islam is rather a threat and therefore an enemy (...) If it continues, you will see that they are going to integrate Muslims by making them cast their religion aside and then there will be a group that does not want to so they can no longer participate in society, you know?" [Man, 20, Brussels]

This participant views the headscarf ban as an exclusionary tactic, to deprive Muslims of education opportunities and blames the media portrayal of Islam, as well as 'corrupt' politicians for this development. In the Netherlands, where the ban is not in effect (except for judges, lawyers and police), participants seem less critical to headscarf issues. Also, Dutch participants did not feel restrained in expressing their religious identity and even expressed more understanding for this particular policy measure. Some compared it to the uniform they wear at work, others described situations where they themselves would not appreciate being confronted with civil servants wearing a religious symbol.

Identification processes and social networks

Previous research (Lubbers et al., 2007) indicated that a more dense and homogenous composition as well as a smaller number of subgroups in migrants' social networks can lead to more ethnic-exclusive identification (e.g. Moroccan). Migrants with networks encompassing more subgroups across divergent social contexts and therefore obtain a higher number of labels that are salient to them, consequently they more often identify as ethnic-inclusive (e.g. Moroccan-Dutch) or generic (e.g. man). We have analyzed the personal networks of our participants and discerned four distinct network types: (i) 'The densely connected family network', with a high proportion of family members in one densely connected group; (ii) 'The multiple subgroup network', with several cohesive subgroups that were not connected; (iii) 'The connected worlds network', with cohesive subgroups that were interconnected trough one or more central contacts; and (iv) 'The uniform network', where the participants only had a small number of contacts with high homogeneity of ethnicity and religion. All network types had some isolates (i.e. contact who do not have a relationship with others on the network) or duo's (i.e. two connected contacts who do not have relationships with others in the network). The density, size of the different network types are summarized in table 2, as well as the number of Belgian and Dutch participants with each type of network.

We will first discuss the network types before we explain the relationship with self-identification. 'The family network' type is very dense as most family members have a relationship with each other regardless of the participant. The networks are of medium size. This type of network is associated with participants who have a lower or medium educational attainment, and also applies to mothers. They do not have a lot of time to maintain close relationships outside of their family, so their networks do not contain many friends, but consists of mostly family and some neighbors. 'The multiple subgroups' and 'The two worlds connected' are very similar, as they both were large in number of people, more diverse in terms of ethnic and religious background, as well as the types of relationships (i.e., family, friends, colleagues, acquaintances). Both network types were more common among the more highly educated and also associated with being involved in associations (e.g., volunteer organizations, sports, advocacy groups).

As reported in previous paragraphs, most participants in our study displayed an ethnic-plural identification (i.e. Moroccan-Dutch), with those who viewed themselves exclusively as Moroccan or Muslim as notable exceptions. The participants who describe changing their self-identification as Belgian/Dutch to

Table 2 Average density, size of network types and number of Dutch/ Belgian participants (N=41)

Network type	Average density	Average size	Number of Belgian partici- pants (n=26)	Number of Dutch partici- pants (n=15)	Total	Primary Self- identi- fication
Family	0.36	11.5	6	8	14	Ethnic-plural
Multiple subgroups	0.21	18.2	8	5	13	Ethnic-plural, generic
Two worlds connected	0.27	17.9	9	2	11	Ethnic-plural, generic
Uniform	0.25	5.3	3	0	3	Ethnic/ religious-exclusive

Moroccan or Muslim in response to external-identification as Moroccan, they seem to have the same network type: they stand out for having smaller networks (between 4-8 contacts) of mostly family members and with homogeneous composition in terms of ethnicity and religion (i.e., Moroccan ethnicity and Muslim). We have dubbed this network type 'The uniform' network. These participants reported either very high or very low educational attainment and were frustrated with career opportunities as well as the position of their ethnic and/or religious groups in society.

The relationship between network composition and structure, and identification processes is not as straightforward as in previous studies described in the literature section (Lubbers, et al., 2007; Lubbers et al., 2010; De Federico de la Rúa, 2013). Most participants with a 'family', 'multiple subgroup' or 'two worlds connected' network show an ethnic-plural identification and either construct their identity along ethnic/national lines or layered their identification with religion as a primary identification. The participants who prefer not to use ethnic, national or religious labels self-identify more generically and have a 'multiple subgroup' or 'two worlds connected' network, indicating that switching between different social spheres with different hierarchies of identities can lead to a more unstable identification and to a critical stance towards any kind of labelling. The relationship between the composition of the network in terms of ethnicity and religion and identification processes was only found for those who had negative experiences with incongruent external-identification. The participants who reactively identified as solely Moroccan or Muslim showed high homogeneity of social network composition and one cohesive subgroup. Additionally, the participants who described lessoned identification with ethnicity and religion due to conformity pressure in family context identified more strongly with their Dutch or Belgian nationality and many of their voluntary contacts (i.e., friends, colleagues, acquaintances) were Dutch or Belgian majority members and non-religious or catholic.

Some participants have an ethnically homogeneous network (i.e., mostly people of Moroccan ethnicity and Muslims) but they do not show decreased identification as Dutch or Belgian. This might be related to the self-identification of the participants as Dutch or Belgian. Most of the friends and family of the participants with Moroccan ethnic background had Dutch or Belgian nationality and the participants typically describe them as being Dutch or Belgian, or emphasize that they are born in Belgium or the Netherlands. Moreover, the participants describe their friends and family as 'being' Dutch/Belgian, so a more homogeneous network does not necessarily lead to an ethnic-exclusive identification if the meaning of the national label (i.e., being Dutch or Belgian) is not restricted by ethnic background. Lastly, having a certain network type seemed to be more related to stages of life. Parents with limited responsibilities outside of the household are more likely to have a 'family' network, whereas working professions and students were more likely to have a 'multiple subgroup' or 'connected worlds' networks. This underlines the dynamics of identity construction and calls for research methods (e.g., panels, dynamic social network analyses) that can also capture the longitudinal and contextual factors that shape social interactions over time.

Discussion

Main findings
In this study, we analyzed personal networks, identification processes and strategies to maintain a positive self-image of second-generation minorities of Moroccan descent in the Netherlands and Belgium. The participants identified

with their ethnicity, nationality and religion in varying degrees, and constructed an inclusive identification by combining or layering the various labels that are commonly used or constructing a generic identification, to maintain a positive self-image. The exception referred to those who had negative experiences with ethnic, religious or national identification and felt their self-identification was not accepted by others. The participants who were not granted the label 'Dutch/ Belgian' reactively changed their self-identification to 'Moroccan' or 'Muslim'. The most relevant factor here appeared to be the perceived group rejection, as well as experiences of external-identification whereby the participants were excluded from the category 'Dutch' or 'Belgian' because of their ethnic and/or religious background. Women with headscarves were particularly affected, because they experienced more negative discrimination as they were easily identifiable as Muslim in their daily lives. These women also described feeling an increase in discrimination during times of high coverage on terrorist related events and some experienced difficulties with job opportunities because of the headscarf or had to remove it to partake in education. The participants who experienced lessoned identification to their ethnic and religious background and pressure to conform in family context, seemed to avoid those social situations in which their high identification with nationality (or socializing with majority Dutch and Belgians) was problematized.

These findings on negative experiences with ethnic, religious or national-identification show that IT and SIP both have a part to play in clarifying identification processes. SIP and specifically the in-group bias can explain how incongruent external-identification can sharpen boundaries between in- and out-groups, whereas IT can clarify how these boundaries affect social interactions. When the majority Dutch or Belgians do not affirm the self-identification as 'Dutch/Belgian', the participants experience psychological distress and change the hierarchy of identities. For those minorities, the 'Dutch/Belgian' identity moves down the ladder and becomes an out-group. The Dutch/Belgians majority is thereafter viewed in stereotypical ways and as inferior. Alternatively, the participants who experienced lessoned identification to their ethnic and religious background and pressure to conform in family context change the frequency of social contact in accordance with IT by interacting with others who have a similar identification to them.

The results also show that the association between network types and identification processes is less clear-cut for second-generation minorities, as a high homogeneity in networks was not necessarily associated with ethnic-exclusive identification. As the second-generation identifies relatively strongly with their nationality, the same relationship between network type (i.e., composition and structure) and identification (i.e., ethnic-plural, ethnic-exclusive or generic) was not found for all type of identifications. This could be related to the selection of participants, as we focused on second-generation minorities and the other studies on first-generation migrants. Yet, the classification of networks provides explanations to the divergent identification processes found in our study. However, looking at the participants 'lived' experience of identification in their personal network increased our understanding of how inter-group processes unfolded and how not have the self-identification affirmed can cause psychological distress and lead participants to change identifications or behavior (by avoiding the social settings in which this occurs).

Moroccan minorities are mostly oriented towards the host society, which is reflected in an identification with nationality as strong as that of the native majority population. However, the majority views Moroccan minorities as the most 'different' from 'them', compared to other ethnic groups (Schalk-Soekar & Van de Vijver, 2008) and this difference is experienced in external-identification, whereby the 'Moroccan minorities' are excluded of the category of being Dutch or Belgian. More highly educated minorities identify more strongly to their nationality, and have done everything they can to be considered 'integrated' in society, so the external-identification is probably more difficult for them than lower educated minorities. We would argue that this is related to their position on the bottom of the ethnic hierarchical ladder, in conjuncture with stronger national-identification. They are considered most different by the majority groups, more than Turkish minorities, but the Moroccan minorities identify more strongly with their Dutch/Belgian nationality (De Vroome et al., 2014), so personal experiences with discrimination, as well as negative stigmatization in media portrayal will impact them more strongly than other minority groups.

The results also show that outcomes of policy in relation to ethnic and religious difference as group rights can be a mixed bag. An example of this is allowing headscarves in education. On the one hand, being more accommodating in policy to acknowledge ethnic heritage and religious difference can decrease feelings of group rejection. On the other hand, there does appear to be some normative pressure in Moroccan communities in the Netherlands and Belgium on headscarf wearing. Policy should be mindful of trying to avoid such pressure. However, the participants who had to remove their headscarf because of policy, described feeling rejected by the majority group, and placed a strong emphasis on the importance of expressing one's religious identity. Putting pressure on them to take off their headscarf to ensure that others do not have to experience pressure to put it on does not seem like a satisfactory solution. The initiative of the Flemish catholic schools to give Muslim students more leeway in expressing their religious identity seems like a good step in the right direction (Maerevoet, 2016, May 4).

Limitations and suggestions for further research

We incorporated several data gathering methods, both qualitative and quantitative, and used a well-tested theoretical lens towards the sensitive topic of ethnic-identification. However, the study does have some limitations, particularly differences in the recruitment and selection of participants in both countries may have shaped our findings. In the Netherlands participants were recruited by a Dutch research company Labyrinth, with access to an extensive network of people of Moroccan descent and able to deliver a balanced sample based on education, gender and age. In Belgium participants were recruited via several associations (e.g., religious, student oriented, social); the higher educated and more active in associations seemed to be overrepresented. As these factors are usually also related to interest in political issues, awareness of migration policies and minority rights, we added additional participants to our Belgian subsample who were lower educated and not active in associations.

The study was explorative in nature and the findings are therefore tentative and need further testing. We would recommend a more large-scale study that combines IT and SIT, whereby a larger number of contacts would be registered per interview participant so that the social interactions could be investigated to a deeper and wider extent. We focused on the most important contacts; broadening this aspect might allow a more detailed and diversified study into the relationship between personal networks and identification processes. Additionally, we recommend a cross-cultural comparison with Turkish minorities, as they similarly identify strongly with their religion, but less strongly with their Dutch/Belgian nationality (De Vroome et al., 2014), which might yield interesting results.

This current project was conducted in a time when radicalization and terrorism were high on the political and media agenda, and the increased inter-group tensions allowed us to delve deeply into inter-group distinctions underlying identification processes. However, this timing can also lead to higher self-selection among participants, causing those who feel less secure in their self-identification to avoid participation in the study. Alternative methods should be used to reach this group, such as virtual ethnography on online forums. The online anonymity allows for analysis of identification processes and related inter-group viewpoints that would otherwise remain in the shadows (Berbers et al., 2017). The findings also indicate that policies in relation to minority integration and integration media discourses are relevant for identification processes. A such, a longitudinal study that encompasses both the Dutch and Belgian integration debate discourses seems a highly interesting avenue for further research.

Notes

1 Second-generation refers to people who were born in the host country, but one or two of their parents where foreign born.

2 Most Moroccan minorities have dual citizenship, so they have both Moroccan or Dutch/Belgian nationality. However, in this study, we focus on their identification with the host country nationality and the identification with Moroccan ethnicity.

3 The two main regions in Belgium have a notably different integration policy, both in terms of policy practices and vocabularies: while Wallonia (i.e. French-speaking Southern region of Belgium) applies French-style assimilationism, Flanders (i.e. Dutch-speaking Northern region of Belgium) follows Anglo-Saxon multiculturalism (De Raedt, 2004; Martiniello & Swyngedouw, 1999). The integration policy established in the Netherlands is comparable to the Anglo-Saxon multiculturalist model (De Wit & Koopmans, 2005). As the integration policy impacts on identification processes and diversity within social networks of minorities, we excluded Belgian participants from Wallonia.

4 Although IT was originally formulated by Stryker, it is now used more widely to refer to related theoretical work that recognizes the relationship between notions of self and wider society or social structure (Hogg et al., 1995).

5 Lars Leszczensky (2016) studied how the relationship between network composition among majority and minority groups and national identification emerged. He did not find evidence for a causal relationship, in the sense that the identification of minority groups is caused by the ethnic and/or national background of their friends. However, previous research demonstrated a relationship between identification and network composition, suggesting that a correlation between the two is more plausible than a unidirectional causal influence.

6 For a comprehensive account of difficulties with collecting personal network data, see Wellman (2007).

7 This distinction between online, offline and mixed contacts is used for a different study and will not be discussed here.

8 The topics discussed during the interview were partly about radicalization and depictions of 'Syria fighters' in news media, which could have impacted on the way the participants described their identification processes.

Bibliography

Berkman L.F., & Syme S.L., (1979). Social networks, host resistance, and mortality: a nine-year follow-up study of Alameda County residents. *American Journal of Epidemiology*, 109(2), 186-204.

Berbers, A., d'Haenens, L., & Koeman, J. (2015). Reception of media representations of Moroccan ethnicity and Islam in Belgium and the Netherlands: The case of the 'Syria fighters'. In S. Mertens & H. De Smaele (Eds.), *Representations of Islam in the media: a cross-cultural analysis*. Lanham, MD: Lexington Books.

Berbers, A., Joris, W., Boesman, J., d'Haenens, L., Joyce, K., & Van Gorp, B. (2016). Framing of the Syria Fighters in Flanders and the Netherlands: Victims or terrorists? *Ethnicities* 16(6), 798-818.

Berbers, A., d'Haenens, L., & Koeman, J. (2017). Worlds Apart? Exploring the News Framing of 'Syria Fighters' and Interactions and Identification Processes on Online Discussion Forums. In L. d'Haenens & M. Kayıkçı (eds.), *European Muslims and new media*. Leuven: Leuven University.

Bilencen, B., (2016). A personal network approach in mixed-methods design to investigate transnational social protection. *International Review of Social Research* 6(4), 233-244.

Bochove, M., Burgers, J., Geurts, A., De Koster, W., & Van der Waal, J. (2015). Questioning ethnic identity: Interviewer effects in research about immigrants' self-definition and feelings of belonging. *Journal of Cross-Cultural Psychology*, 1-15.

Burke, P. (1980). The self: Measurement requirements from an interactionist perspective. *Social Psychology Quarterly* 43, 18-29.

Burke, P. (1991). Identity processes and social stress. *American Sociological Review* 56, 836-849.

Christakis, N.A., Fowler, J.H., (2007). The spread of obesity in a large social network over 32 years. *The New England Journal of Medicine* 357, 370-379.

De Federico de la Rúa, A. (2013). *Networked identification with Europe: Friends and identities of the European students* (Unpublished doctoral dissertation), Université des Sciences et Technologies de Lille and Universidad Pública de Navarra.

De Raedt, T. (2004). Muslims in Belgium: A case study of Emerging identities. *Journal of Muslim Affairs* 24(1), 9-30.

De Vroome, T., Verkuyten, M., & Martinovic, B. (2014). Host national identification of immigrants in the Netherlands. *International Migration review* 48(1) 1, 1-27.

De Wit, T. D., & Koopmans, R. (2005). The integration of ethnic minorities into political culture: The Netherlands, Germany and Great Britain compared. *Acta Politica* 40, 50-73.

d'Haenens, L., Van Summeren, C., Saeys, F., & Koeman, J. (2004). *Integratie of identiteit: Mediamenu's van Turkse en Marokkaanse jongeren [Integration or identity: Media menus of Turkish and Moroccan youths]*. Amsterdam: Boom uitgevers.

Goffman, E. (1956). *The presentation of the self in everyday life.* Garden City, NY: Doubleday.

Hâncean, M., Molina, J., & Lubbers, M. (2016). Recent advancements, developments and application of personal network analysis. *International Review of Social Research* 6(4), 137-145.

Hogg, M., Terry, D., & White, K. (1995). A tale of two theories: A critical comparison of identity theory with social identity theory. *Social Psychology Quarterly* 58(4), 255-269.

Huddleston, T., Bilgili, O., Joki, A., & Vankova, Z. (2015). MIPEX: Migrant Integration (Policy Index). Retrieved 16 November, 2015, from: http://www.mipex.eu/play/

Lenszczensky, L. (2016). *Tell me who your friends are? Disentangling the interplay of young immigrants' host country identification and their friendships with natives* (unpublished doctoral dissertation). Graduate School of Economic and Social Sciences at the University of Mannheim.

Lin, N. (1999). Social networks and status attainment. *Annual Review of Sociology* 25, 467-487.

Lubbers, M., Molina, J., & McCarty, C. (2007). Personal networks and ethnic identification: The case of migrants in Spain. *International Sociology* 22(6) 721-741.

Lubbers, M., Molina, J., Lerner, J., Ulrik, B., Ávila, J., McCarty, C. (2010). Longitudinal analysis of personal networks: The case of Argentinian migrants in Spain. *Social Networks* 32, 91-104.

Koopmans, R. (2013). Multiculturalism and immigration: a contested field in Cross-National Comparison. *Annu. Rev. Sociol* 39, 147-169.

Maerevoet, E. (2016, May 4). Katholiek onderwijs creëert meer ruimte voor islam [Catholic education creates more space for Islam]. *De Redactie.be.* Retrieved from: http://deredactie. be/cm/vrtnieuws/binnenland/1.2647249#

Martiniello, M. & Swyngedouw, M. (eds) (1999). *Où va la Belgique? [Which direction will Belgium take?]*. Paris: L'Harmattan.

McFarland, D., and Pals, H. (2005) Motives and context of identity change: A case for network effects. *Social Psychology Quarterly* 68(4), 289-315.

Roosens, E. (1998). *Eigen grond eerst? Primordiale autochtonie. Dilemma van de multiculturele samenleving.* Leuven: Acco.

Schalk-Soekar, S. & Van de Vijver, F. (2008). The concept of multiculturalism: a study among Dutch majority members. *Journal of Applied Social Psychology* 38(8), 2152-2178.

Slootman, M. (2014). *Soulmates. Reinvention of ethnic identification among higher educated second-generation Moroccan and Turkish Dutch*. Amsterdam: University of Amsterdam.

Stryker, S. (1987). Identity theory: Developments and extensions. In T. Honess & In K. Yardley (Eds.), *Self and identity: Perspectives across the lifespan*. London: Routledge, 89-104.

Tajfel, H., & Turner, J. (1986) The social identity theory of inter-group behavior. In Stephen Worchel and William Austin, eds. *Psychology of intergroup relations*. Chicago IL: Nelson-Hall, 7-24.

Vacca, R., Solano, G., Lubbers, M., Molina, J. & McCarty, C. (2016). A personal network approach to the study of immigrant structural assimilation and transnationalism. *Social Networks*

Van Heelsum, A. (2013). Ethnic identity of Turks and Moroccans in Western Europe: position acquisition and position allocation. *IMISCOE conference*. 26-27 August 2013, Malmö, Sweden.

Van Heelsum, A., & Koomen, M. (2016). Ascription and identity. Differences between first-generation and second-generation Moroccans in the way ascription influences religious, national and ethnic group identification. *Journal of Ethnic and Migration Studies* 42(2), 277-291.

Wellman, B. (2007). Challenges in collecting personal network data: The nature of personal network analysis. *Field Methods* 19(2), 111-115.

Wolska-Zogata, I. (2015). The story of Chalir Hebdo: An analysis of European and American newspapers. *Mediterranean Journal of Social Sciences* 6(2), 353-362.

12. Migration and language use at school: an ethnographic close-up

Jürgen Jaspers

Introduction

Western schools are challenged by old and new migration waves, and Belgium is no exception to this trend. Although exact figures are unavailable, general estimations are that about 20% of pupils in Francophone Belgian schools speak another language than French at home, and that this can go up to 50% in Brussels' French-medium schools.[1] Official statistics in Dutch-speaking Belgium indicate that in Belgium's second city, Antwerp, some 44% of pupils in primary schools and 31% in secondary schools were registered in 2013-2014 as speaking another language than Dutch at home.[2] In Brussels' Dutch-medium schools, less than 10% of pupils going to kindergarten and primary schools were found to have two Dutch-speaking parents in 2014, and some 30% were registered as having no Dutch-speaking parents at all.[3] While this creates formidable pedagogical challenges in schools belonging to both of Belgium's linguistic communities, it also invites pronounced ideological concern in the Flemish Community, which as a political entity is itself the product of a movement that long contested, among other things, that Flemish pupils had to attend French-medium education in Belgium. Consequently, and in contrast with Francophone Belgium, the increasing number of pupils speaking other languages at home than Dutch in Flemish schools has not just become a difficult pedagogical hurdle to cross, but also an object of ideological problematisation. This makes Flemish schools a privileged site for observing the acute negotiation of linguistic diversity in monolingually organised Western schools.[4]

Testimony to this problematisation is that consecutive Flemish Education Ministers have each explicitly focused on language in their policy briefs, and in particular on pupils' acquisition of (Standard) Dutch. In 2007 Minister Vandenbroucke stated that "only by guiding each [pupil] to a correct and rich competence in the standard language will education be able to guarantee that social opportunities do not depend on [pupils'] origin but on the extent to which [their] talents have been strengthened and developed" (Vandenbroucke, 2007, p.6).[5] The Minister called on all schools to develop policies demonstrating their adherence to this concern and indicated that "[e]very teacher is a language teacher. Not just the teacher of Dutch. Also the kindergarten teacher. The PE teacher. The geography, accounting and carpentry teacher, up to the professor of constitutional law. The point is that teachers use correct language".[6] Vandenbroucke's emphasis on Standard Dutch was not just a matter of equal opportunities; it was also seen to be a practical solution to the problem of having too many languages than can reasonably be included at school. Vandenbroucke's successor staunchly supported this view. While recognising the value of other languages, he suggested a "rich knowledge of Standard Dutch [...] is *the* precondition for those wishing to learn, live and work in Flanders. Those who come from elsewhere and fail to learn Standard Dutch, remain in the privacy of their family or community and live – in Flanders – outside Flanders." (Smet, 2011: 3). Somewhat less pronounced on the issue of language, the current Education Minister nevertheless declares in her policy brief (2014-2019) that she "will follow up on recently introduced innovations regarding the knowledge of Dutch as instruction language" (Crevits, 2014: 28) and pointed out recently that "Dutch is and remains the language of instruction. It is the key to integration. I am hardcore in this: you need to learn and know the language. [...] We must not budge one inch from Dutch as instruction language."[7]

Flemish policy makers' devotion to Standard Dutch has subsequently inspired the formulation of strict Dutch-only policies in many schools across Flanders, and it has invited more attention to the difficulties that an academic register may pose in subjects like geography or maths. Such policies collide with pedagogical convictions, however, when teachers wishing to create a positive learning environment notice this is difficult to reconcile with punishing pupils' home language use (Harris & Lefstein, 2011; Jaspers, 2015b). Simply allowing these languages at school in its turn rubs against sensitivities about the fate of Dutch in a globalised world, and with concerns that pupils acquire a language of prestige. Schools are in this sense the barometers of wider-scale social and ideological tensions.

Dutch-only policies equally conflict with most linguists' emphasis on the pedagogical opportunities of pupils' primary languages. Local policy makers' interest in these opportunities has led to an experiment in the city of Ghent involving the use of home language in four primary schools from 2009 to 2012 (Ramaut et al., 2013). In particular this entailed that all pupils were allowed to use their home language at school in informal communication (e.g., during group work) and that pupils with Turkish-speaking backgrounds received extra tuition in their home language. The experiment was inspired by the growing scientific consensus that recognition of pupils' primary languages at school is pivotal for their well-being, and that these languages can scaffold the learning of new subject matter and, not least, the acquisition of the school language (Cummins, 2000; Ramaut et al., 2013). However, when the Ghent Education council member upon receiving the final project report in April 2014 suggested to the press that pupils not speaking Dutch at home would henceforth be allowed to use their home languages in city-run schools during informal communication, criticism came thick and fast from the then Flemish nationalist opposition who suggested that 'this choice in fact boils down to factual apartheid',[8] or that 'Flanders wholesales in scholars who are organising disadvantage on a scientific basis'.[9] PISA[10] results were called to mind to argue that pupils with migration backgrounds speaking Dutch at home outperform those with similar backgrounds but speaking other languages in the family. Such results reveal, opposition politicians argued, that rather than investing in home languages pupils should be exposed to Dutch to a maximum extent from as early an age as possible. Questions were also asked with respect to the 'impression that action must be taken against harsh repression [of other languages] in playgrounds' because 'that picture is wrong, the facts are different. Where does one get detention for an occasional chat in a different language?'[11]

Other linguists rose to the defense of their vilified colleagues and argued that even limited teaching in another language would be able to boost pupils' competence in Dutch; that recognising other languages would not cause harm to Dutch as instruction language; and that almost half a century of exposing pupils from non-Dutch speaking families to Dutch has not been able to prevent their consistently higher school failure rates than fellow pupils from Dutch-speaking homes (working class homes excepted). These arguments did not command much authority, however, characteristic of the dialogue of the deaf that advocates and opponents of multilingualism at school are developing around this issue.

Considering the political and professional backgrounds of the opposing parties, one would likely interpret this as a conflict between ideological reservations on the one hand and convictions based on objective facts on the other. Yet linguists were discreet about the fact that the Ghent experiment did not observably produce positive effects on pupils' learning outcomes (though no negative effects either) (Ramaut et al., 2013; Slembrouck et al. 2016). Neither are politicians alone with their reservations: many parents fear that multilingualism at school will negatively affect their children's Dutch; school directors occasionally find pupils' home languages a matter of cultural concern, but are far more worried about poor skills in Dutch and the expected effects on pupils' futures; and teachers suspect that allowing home language use will encourage pupils to form separate ethno-linguistic clans or invite secret communication in class. Even if language in public discourse has often come to replace (and so, hide) ethnic diversity as a more acceptable target of problematisation (Hill, 2000), it may be imprudent to brush these linguistic concerns aside as ill-informed or unfounded if the available knowledge of cause-and-effect relations is insufficiently convincing. More research would thus seem to be advisable.

Under the current Flemish political climate, however, now dominated by opponents of home language use at school, there are few signs that similar experiments will soon see the light of day. Language legislation in addition prohibits experimentation with methods that linguists find more promising, such as using pupils' home language as instruction language alongside Dutch. It therefore looks as though at least for a while, pending a shift in legislation or scientific breakthrough, schools will be facing ongoing challenges to reconcile a monolingual policy with a multilingual reality. This does not diminish their need for advice on how to take up this challenge effectively, however. If such advice is to be provided without the risk of seeing it dismissed out of hand as purely theoretical, we need to speak knowledgeably on how linguistic diversity and monolingual expectations are actually reconciled at Flemish schools today. In the coming pages I argue that ethnographic research offers a valuable contribution in this regard. On the basis of fieldwork involving pupils with a Moroccan background, I demonstrate that pupils and teachers were ambivalent about the language policy, imposing it on some occasions and bypassing it on others, and that these different responses to policy were not neatly divided over teachers and pupils. The friction between linguistic policy and reality thus compels all parties at school to find practical, ad-hoc solutions. Before I illustrate this I briefly situate this study into its research domain and provide more information on the types of data I have collected.

The ethnography of classroom interaction

The ethnographic study of classroom interaction is relatively recent. It stems from disciplines which in the 1960s and 70s picked up the baton of explaining why working-class and non-white children were disproportionately failing at school. Up till then – and sometimes up to the present day – it had been customary to blame this failure on these children's lack of intelligence, failing motivation, inferior genes or deprived home culture, but Anglo-Saxon sociolinguists and linguistic anthropologists looked for different explanations (Labov, 1972; McDermott, 1974). Partly based on new audiovisual recording techniques that permitted detailed observation of classroom interaction, scholars shifted the blame from pupils to specific communication patterns that produced pernicious misunderstandings in class. Pupils and teachers were demonstrated to have subtly differing communication habits (specific intonation patterns, storytelling templates, conversation-organisational procedures, ...) so that what working-class or non-white pupils considered polite or normal (e.g, interrupting others), teachers found inappropriate, resistant, or incomprehensible, with the expected negative consequences (Gumperz, 1982; Cazden et al., 1972). Experiments were set up to synchronise teachers' communication styles to those of their pupils. Later research showed however that even widely differing communication styles did not prevent school success, and that trust relationships, anticipated benefits of schooling, family histories and pupils' relative status vis-à-vis other pupils could be equally decisive (D'Amato, 1993).

Subsequent ethnographic research has been interested in examining the effects of handling linguistic variation in class on teacher-pupil relations, on pupils' positioning vis-à-vis discourses on regional, gender-, class- or ethnic identity, or on how linguistic resources are socially earmarked and impact on pupils' social statuses in and out of class (Jaspers, 2005; Rampton, 2006). Other scholars investigate how teachers implement language policies and which alternative routes they explore (Menken & García, 2010). Language use in class is also of interest to those examining how teachers switch between, or mix, languages for keeping pupils' attention or transmitting curriculum matter (Creese & Blackledge, 2010; Jaspers, 2014).

Ethnographic fieldwork is essential to these investigations since scholars work from the assumption that (1) pupils and teachers must be observed in their 'natural' habitat to understand what goes on in class; and that (2) explanations for behaviour must be found in a local social logic that is difficult to make explicit by those for whom it is self-evident (Erickson 1986; Snell et al. 2014). There is a preference therefore for long-term observation and recordings, allowing to distinguish what looks similar from the outside (e.g., a teacher asking a question to a pupil) as an invitation, reproach, request or directive depending on the setting, its participants, and the course of the interactional event. While scholars in this domain find questionnaires and interviews useful techniques, they usually treat them with caution: given that explicit accounts often provide idealisations of the ambivalent reality that people inhabit, they must be taken as a positioning in that reality rather than a transparent description of it.

The time required for observation is one of the main disadvantages of this approach. It typically leads to case studies of a singular school (or even a singular class). Panoramic accounts thus require questionnaires and targeted interview questions. The quantity and diversity of data in case studies also makes comparison between cases more challenging than with survey research that focuses on a limited set of specific variables. But the advantages are considerable. Ethnographic studies offer a wealth of information that only survives in diluted form in research that demands a limited presence at the scene. Long-term on-site experience also helps researchers to compare interview accounts with speakers' observable reality. Another asset is the flexibility of this type of research: ethnographic studies allow for a focus on data that were not taken account of at the research design stage but that turn out to be critical.

Context and data of this study

The data I report on here were collected at two secondary schools, one in Antwerp (Jaspers, 2005, 2011), the other in Brussels (Jaspers, 2014, 2015a). The Antwerp school (henceforth the 'City School') belongs to the city-subsidised net and offers technical and vocational education. Data collection involved 20 months of fieldwork in two electro-mechanics classes between May 1999 and April 2002, involving 35 pupils two-thirds of which were of Moroccan descent (the other third comprising three pupils with Turkish backgrounds and ten with a Belgian-Flemish one), all but one of them boys, with ages varying between 16 and 21. This amounted to daily fieldnotes, 35 hours of individual audio-recordings (with parallel recording during class), and 45 hours of interviews.

The Brussels school ('Sacred Soul') is a catholic, Dutch-medium school, also offering technical and vocational education. Distinctive of the school is that as a Dutch-medium school it hardly counts a handful of pupils speaking Dutch at home. Fieldwork lasted five months between September 2011 and May 2012 and concentrated on one class majoring in office skills with 17 pupils (seven girls, ten boys) between 13 and 16 years old. Eight of them spoke Turkish at home, six had a Moroccan background, two pupils a French-speaking Belgian one, and one pupil a mixed Dutch-Congolese background. The dataset consists of daily fieldnotes, 35 hours of individual audio-recording (and parallel classroom-recording) and 10 hours of interviews. The names of the schools are pseudonyms, as are all names used below.

Neither of these two case studies deliberately set out to focus on pupils with a Moroccan background. But such pupils were difficult to ignore in the City School due to their continuous linguistic experimentation and overall presence at the scene, reason why my research gradually started to focus on their language use. In Sacred Soul pupils with a Moroccan background did not so much stand out; I will discuss their language use together with that of their classmates.

How did pupils and their teachers at these two officially monolingual schools handle linguistic diversity? In brief, they tackled this issue by means of linguistic rules, humor, leniency and protest. I will address each of these in what follows, demonstrating that neither of these responses was the prerogative of pupils or teachers.

School rules

In both schools the rules and regulations were an important point of reference. The City School rules stipulated that "Standard Dutch is spoken at school", which was further elaborated for the two classes I observed:

Example 1
"Obviously we use the standard language (Standard Dutch) during class.
(...) We do not use any dialects and certainly no foreign languages that

are only comprehensible to a small group. Everyone must understand everyone else at all times" (Fieldnotes, September 2000).

In Sacred Soul pupils received a regulations booklet that reminded them and their parents of the school's Dutch-medium character. Various posters hung on walls that stated "I choose ... Dutch", or that advised in some more words:

Example 2
Sacred Soul is a catholic Dutch-medium school. The Dutch-language character of the school cannot be drawn into question. (...) You can be penalised if you do not speak Dutch. A small effort is thus enough to avoid any penalties (Fieldnotes, September 2011).

Different from what politicians above suggested, teachers did not hesitate to remind pupils of these rules, asking them time and again to 'speak Dutch', 'you have to speak Dutch', 'we agreed to speak Dutch'. Teachers in Sacred Soul punished home language use through giving notes in pupils' diaries that parents had to sign off. Those who collected a range of such notes could count on detention on Wednesday afternoon, or on a personalised contract that stipulated what was expected if pupils wished to avoid expulsion (see also Agirdag et al. 2014; Jalhay & Clycq 2014).

Also the quality of Dutch was given consideration. In Sacred Soul, where pupils struggled with a limited competence in Dutch, it was not uncommon to hear 'learn Dutch!', or, after an awkwardly formulated answer or question, 'and now in Dutch please?'. In the City School the standard quality of language was regularly in focus, with teachers insisting on the proper standard word rather than the dialectal alternative.

Soldiers of the system?

The above data suggest that teachers were behaving as loyal 'soldiers of the system' (Shohamy 2006: 78-79), in line with other analyses of Flemish teachers' very negative attitude towards pupils' home languages (Agirdag et al., 2014; Blommaert et al., 2006). A longer presence at the scene, however, reveals that teachers cannot simply be thrown into the same ideological pot. The following example already indicates that not all teachers were equally strict:

Example 3

"There are rules but rules are also there to be broken (...) I don't think you can always act repressively, that would be the wrong approach I think (...) You notice that some teachers who do act that way and who are constantly waving the rules around are not liked by [these pupils]. Which doesn't mean that you should ignore the rules to be liked by the class of course, but you do have to be somewhat flexible, and I think if they don't use that mother tongue to say things that don't belong in class, that [you shouldn't comment on it]. I do say sometimes 'no Chinese in class' or that kind of thing, but, I think you shouldn't be too strict" (English teacher, 45+, Interview, May 2000)

Others were not so strict either. One teacher said she would tolerate other languages in class 'as long as she didn't hear it', adding that she was slightly deaf in one ear. In Brussels older teachers said that while ten years ago pupils still risked being booked for detention until the end of the year for using their home language, the inspection had demanded a relaxation of the rules. Others formulated more substantial doubts, wondering whether they were not fighting an uphill battle on account of the large number of pupils who did not speak Dutch at home, and whether they were not undermining their authority by asking the impossible. Even those who were in favour of the language policy could have mixed feelings about it, like Mr S (30), a French teacher who as a French speaker had gone to a Dutch-medium school when he was younger:

Example 4

"I'm actually one of the strictest teachers when it comes to maintaining the school linguistic policy, in contrast to that whole table over there", he said, while pointing to a group of older teachers sitting nearby. "As a French speaker I know how difficult it is. But I'm really starting to ask myself questions about this policy, because it's hard to impose, and it creates negativity around Dutch" (Fieldnotes, September 2011)

Despite such intuitions many teachers wanted to be loyal to their colleagues and honour the commitments made. Many teachers also insisted on Dutch out of a sincere concern for their pupils' future opportunities. Such examples demonstrate that teachers' attitudes towards mono- or multilingualism could be much more diffuse and complex than the clear-cut negative stance that emanates from other, mostly quantitative, studies.

Leniency and humor

Also pupils' relation to the language policy could be called ambivalent. When asked what they thought of that policy, they often answered that it could have been worse. In Brussels pupils even said that 'teachers should be stricter', adding jokingly that in such case 'there would be less Turks and stuff, less Moroccans' (while they were of Turkish descent themselves). In Antwerp pupils said that 'rules are made to be broken', and when I asked Mourad (18) if he wasn't insulted that he was not allowed to speak Arabic he answered: 'but we hear this every day, as if we're going to feel insulted every day'. Others smirked that their teachers could not particularly be called devotees of the language policy themselves because of their dialectal language, with Adnan rhetorically asking: 'Have you ever heard Mr H talk Dutch?'

Various humorous reactions could be observed too. In Sacred Soul, Lionel (15) loudly liked to call other pupils to order for not speaking Dutch ("Hey! Dutch-medium school!"), something that teachers often found difficult to penalise given that it was indeed an official school rule. When I asked Bashir (19) at the City School what he thought of the rule that prohibited his use of Arabic, he said: "nothing, when I'm at school nothing, as long as I don't have my degree nothing [laughingly:] but when I've got my degree, death to all those teachers! [hilarity]". Some pupils mocked the secret communication that home language use supposedly involved:

> *Example 5*
> It's the Feast of the Sacrifice. Mourad gives a cookie jar to his French teacher. She thanks him with four kisses. Someone says *shukran* 'thank you'. To which another pupil responds mock-indignantly: "Hey, he said *shukran*!" Nordin then adds, equally ironic: "Oooh! They are all *shukran*!" (Fieldnotes, March 2000).

In light of these examples it was not surprising that home languages could be heard relatively often, in and out of the classroom. Yet this did not imply that once outside class, pupils resorted to using their home languages exclusively.

On the contrary, because Berber and Arabic are not mutually comprehensible, many pupils spoke Dutch with each other. In Antwerp pupils pointed out that they also used Dutch at home, mostly among siblings, often to the displeasure of their parents. Hence, the location was not all-determining for language choice. Neither did home language use necessarily mark off friendship groups, disturb classroom order or ensure secret communication. To be sure, all of this could be achieved by using Turkish or Arabic. But at both schools there also existed friendship groups with mixed language backgrounds, while home language use in class could also neutralise conflicts and even contribute to classroom order – which some teachers also recognised (Jaspers, 2005). Not to mention that secret communication and the construction of exclusive friendship groups also occurs at schools where multilingualism is less prominent.

Support from an unexpected quarter

In spite of their minimising of the language policy, pupils were at the same time imbued with it. So much was visible when pupils in Sacred Soul from other classes than the one I observed, said to me without a trace of irony that 'it's not good, is it, you're speaking French', when they heard me speak French with the pupils I observed. This adhesion also manifested itself in other ways. When I compared Faisal's (17) language use in Antwerp on formal, less formal and informal occasions it appeared that the higher the formality of the context, the more his language use displayed features of Standard Dutch. In their daily language use, then, pupils such as Faisal – he was not exceptional – seemed to take into account general expectations about polite, standard-like speech (Jaspers 2011).

There were also explicit expressions of support. Youssef (18) in Antwerp avowed that he understood teachers, 'since I only speak Arabic myself and most pupils in my class are uh Berbers, so when they start talking I also think they're on about me so I understand the feeling'. But rather than with pure comprehensibility the investment in the language policy more often seemed to be associated with what might be called social distinction. As Nordin (19) illustrates here:

Example 6
"But they're right when they say 'Dutch, Dutch', because some Moroccans or Turks *mouhiem* 'in any case' foreigners in general, you know, don't speak Dutch well. And that's a good tool for them, for

better Dutch yeah. [...] The more you speak Dutch, the better you learn it. You can hear it when I talk. [In Antwerp dialect:] I've always stuck to the rules." (Interview, May 2000).

Because it underlines his own fluency in Dutch, Nordin seems to find the existing language policy quite useful for less fluent pupils – although in suddenly switching to a distinctly dialectal voice he did not regularly use, his last comment ironically indicates that his love for linguistic rules needs to be taken with a pinch of salt.

Such examples illustrate that to some pupils the current language policy was not without its merits. After all, behind this policy lie a number of ideals about correct or competent language that create a symbolic hierarchy among those having to answer to these ideals. At both schools this implied that those who struggled to make themselves understood, spoke with a marked accent, or talked dialectally, were frequently ridiculed. "Dutch please!", pupils called out when one of their classmates had said something very disfluently. At the City School Turkish-speaking pupils were a favourite target, 'because they confuse *him* and *her*', Faisal said, at which point everybody started laughing. Even among pupils with Moroccan backgrounds it was not uncommon to find the ideals upon which the official language policy is based subsequently used to accentuate internal group dynamics. Thus, Nordin, a speaker of Arabic, at one point scornfully remarked that Berber-speaking classmates 'can't speak Arabic, neither can they speak Dutch, so they have to speak Berber!', in this way not so much underlining the objective facts as his higher position in the symbolic hierarchy on account of the fact that he speaks a 'real' language instead of a language variety that a range of Mediterranean countries are slow to recognise officially. Depending on the relation between speaker and listener such utterances could be interpreted as well-intentioned teasing or belittling comments. But the point is that they are based on a frame of reference that is whispered to these pupils' ears by the current language policy: within that frame disfluent Dutch is a formidable stigma, while 'real' languages (Standard Dutch, Arabic) prevail over what are seen as dialects. This produces scores of opportunities for those wishing to distinguish themselves from others within and across ethnic groups.

Such support for official policy could be interpreted as a sign of pupils' internalisation of the dominant perspective on language (Agirdag et al., 2014). But the above data demonstrate that such an internalisation is far from absolute or all-determining. Pupils differed in their investment in the language policy (with some being generally in favour while others were indifferent or opposed). Public displays of adherence to linguistic policy were moreover not to be taken at face value, and even those who were fluent in Dutch could be observed mocking linguistic expectations lucidly. Rather than the outcome of an internalised ideology, such behaviour is more usefully explained as an active and never entirely predictable negotiation of a discourse on language that may be temporarily circumvented, commented on, and manipulated, but that can never entirely be escaped. The fact that pupils could be observed fostering the negative attitudes towards other pupils' languages that are usually attributed to teachers, proves in addition that victims and offenders in this cannot be easily identified on the basis of their official status at school. In what follows I demonstrate that even playful negotiations of the language policy could not be attributed to pupils alone.

Home language use among teachers

Observe in the next example the teacher of French at Sacred Soul, who indicated above that he usually is one of the strictest when it comes to imposing the language policy, using Arabic during French class:

> *Example 7*
> *Participants and setting.* September 2011, French class. Mr S (30), Ilhame (15), Zaki (14). After his correction of their tests, Mr S emphasises impatiently that pupils write an 's' at the end of verbs in the second person singular of the simple present (e.g., *tu parles* 'you speak'). Mr S has told the class to do this a number of times already. I often participated in tests during French class. Arabic is in boldface.

French original	English translation
1 Mr S: 'TU' TOUJOURS AVEC UN S! [.]	'TU' ALWAYS WITH AN S! [.]
2 ?: ( )	( )
3 Mr S: la prochaine fois	next time
4 Ilhame:(non t'as dit) sur la table	(no you said) on the table
5 Mr S: | les él- [.] les élèves [.]	| the pu- [.] the pupils [.]
6 Zaki: c'est sur la table qu'on va danser	it's on the table we're going to dance
7 Mr S: non pas sur la table parce	no no not on the table because
8 qu'en effet les tables sont pas	in fact the tables are
9 solides [.] c'est la prochaine fois	not stable [.] it's the next time
10 [.] **wollah billeh**	[.] I swear I swear
11 Ilhame: [lacht]	[laughs]
12 Mr S: **wollah billeh** vous allez danser	I swear I swear you're going to
13 sur [.] vos chaises [..] et toi aussi	dance on [.] your chairs [..] and
14 Jürgen! Si je te reprends encore	you as well Jürgen! If I catch you
15 UNE fois à écrire 'tu' sans 's' à	ONE more time writing 'tu'
16 l'indicatif présent en plus [.]	without 's' in the present
17 la base!	indicative moreover [.] the basis!

After loudly proclaiming the rule (line 1), Mr S starts producing a threat in line 3 (made explicit by Zaki in line 6) that Ilhame deplores as less spectacular than promised (line 4) – viz. that pupils would have to dance on their table. Mr S first explains why the tables are not appropriate for what he has in mind (lines 7-9) before completing an adjusted threat in lines 9 and 12-13 ('you'll be dancing on your chairs'). Mr S switches to Arabic in line 10 (*wollah billah*, each word meaning 'I swear to God'), and he repeats this in line 12.

Mr S did not speak Arabic at home in contrast to about six of his pupils, nor had he learnt it in a foreign language course. This made his use of it marked, and by speaking it here in the frame of (re)formulating a mock-threat it looks as though he is trying to accentuate his language-pedagogical advice (writing 's' at the end of verb forms in the second person singular) in the hope that pupils will remember it better. Note that this was not the only occasion when Mr S switched to his pupils' home languages. He regularly asked pupils to teach him things in Arabic or Turkish and subsequently experimented with these languages, using Arabic *inshallah* 'if God wills', *smahli* 'sorry' or *salam aleikum* 'how are you' alongside

Turkish *merhaba* 'welcome' and various dirty words. While in the example above such use of home languages could be taken to support pedagogical aims, I argue elsewhere (Jaspers 2014, 2015a) that in other cases such experimentation created a certain playfulness that facilitated the transfer from one setting to another (e.g., from the relatively liberal regime of the playground to the stricter one of the classroom). Such playfulness could equally defuse emergent trouble, establish pupils' attention, and make life at school in general more humorous and thus palatable – something that many educational experts indicate is a major factor in pupils' well-being and motivation. At the same time however, this playfulness generally reproduced the symbolic hierarchy in which signs of urban heteroglossia are associated with activities, social personae, and topics that are orthogonal to what is considered crucial at school: a rational, curriculum-oriented, Dutch-only type of language use.

Discussion and conclusion

Space limits prevent further illustration, but the general picture that emerges from these two schools is more complex than a representation of teachers as absolute advocates of the language policy and pupils as their inevitable victims or opponents. Teachers *and* pupils appeared to develop ambivalent attitudes towards linguistic expectations, imposing them on some occasions and circumventing them on others. It was not uncommon to see pupils invest in language policy as way of distinguishing themselves from other, less fluent speakers. The humorous interactions above equally demonstrated that in the two contexts discussed, a fair number of pupils felt reasonably well at school, contradicting ideas that this is heavily dependent on the recognition of home languages. There are good grounds for arguing too that well-being is at risk among teachers seeking to be a loyal colleague and trying to construct a positive classroom climate with their pupils under the current circumstances.

I suggest this invites the following two conclusions. First, we can anticipate that the above pupils would have felt much less comfortable had their schools decided to increase the penalties for home language use. The ambivalence, humor and leniency in my data therefore have to be seen as strategies with which teachers and pupils are trying to keep a difficult situation still viable. Since Flemings themselves decided some 80 years ago not to tolerate similar difficulties any longer in the then largely French-speaking Belgian school system, and subsequently called for

Dutch-medium education, there is reason for asking why Flemish authorities today have reservations about recognising pupils' home languages as a matter of democratic principle. Such recognition could involve extracurricular language education, the introduction of (computer-based) multilingual content, or more ambitiously, a multilingual curriculum.

But, second, apart from the enormous political steps that need to be taken to achieve this, an ethnographic close-up of language use at school equally reveals that multilingual education will create new difficulties. We can expect pupils to explore to what extent a new linguistic framework can help them to distinguish themselves from other, less competent pupils. It will be challenging to cover all pupils' home languages in schools with a marked linguistic diversity. We can also expect that the recognition of home languages will imply the selection of a standard variety, at the expense of pupils' mixed or dialectal language use that so becomes available for negative earmarking.

In sum, introducing multilingualism at school will not change much about the fact that it remains a site of social tension and limited funding. Just as it will change little about the fact that schools, as they are organised today, by definition need to fail pupils if educational success is to keep its value. Multilingual instruction (in whatever form) would be a major step forward in the democratisation of education, but unless we wish to pin all our hopes on an institution that is required to produce failing pupils, we have to ask which other measures can be taken to provide for all citizens' emancipation. The history of Dutch speakers in Belgium has shown that this does not exclusively depend on the choice of instruction language.

Notes

1 Estimations provided by the Francophone Education Minister, reported in "Le français est peu maîtrisé par les élèves", *La Libre Belgique*, 26 October 2016, and by the French Community Conseil de l'Education et de la Formation in its *Migration et Education* report in February 2013.

2 Flemish Community statistics, provided to Parliament by the Minister of Education (Hilde Crevits) on 29 January 2015.

3 Flemish Community Commission year report 2014: http://www.vgc.be/sites/www.vgc.be/files/publicaties/2014vgcjaarverslag.pdf.

4 See, however, Hambye & Siroux (2008) for how pupils negotiate linguistic variation within French at two secondary French-medium schools in Belgium.

5 The policy brief is in Dutch. All translations henceforth are mine, unless otherwise indicated.

6 Suggested in a speech at the Symposium 'Standing tall in Babylon. Languages in Europe', 14 September 2007.

7 "We will not budge one inch from Dutch as instruction language", interview with Hilde Crevits and Raymonda Verdyck, *De Tijd*, 31 August 2016.

8 "Do we choose apartheid then?", Peter De Roover and Zuhal Demir, *De Standaard*, 11 April 2014

9 "No Dutch at school is organised disadvantage, disguised as progressiveness", Siegfried Bracke, *De Morgen*, 11 April 2014

10 Programme for International Student Assessment, an international comparative research into linguistic and mathemathic skills among 15-year-olds.

11 "Dutch does not belong to white authochthons", Zuhal Demir and Peter De Roover, *De Standaard*, 17 April 2014.

Bibliography

Agirdag, O., Jordens, K., Van Houtte, M. (2014). Speaking Turkish in Belgian primary schools. Teacher beliefs versus effective consequences. *Bilig* 70, 7-28.

Blommaert, J., Creve, L., Willaert, E. (2006). On being declared illiterate. Language-ideological disqualification in Dutch classes for immigrants in Belgium. *Language & Communication* 26(1), 34-54.

Cazden, C., John, V., Hymes, D., eds. (1972). *Functions of language in the classroom*. New York: Teachers College Press.

Creese, A.; Blackledge, A. (2010). Translanguaging in the bilingual classroom. *The Modern Language Journal* 94(1), 103-115.

Crevits, H. (2014). *Policy brief 2014-2019*. Brussels: Flemish Ministry of Education.

Cummins, J. (2000). *Language, power and pedagogy*. Clevedon: Multilingual Matters, 2000.

Erickson, F. (2016). Qualitative methods in research on teaching. In M. C. Wittrock (ed.). *Handbook of research on teaching*. New York: Macmillan Press, 119-161.

D'Amato, J. (1993). Resistance and compliance in minority classrooms. In: E. Jacob and C. Jordan, (eds). *Minority education*. Norwood NJ: Ablex, 181-207.

Gumperz, J. (1982). *Discourse strategies*. Cambridge: Cambridge University Press.

Hambye, P. & Siroux, J-L. (2008). Langage et 'culture de la rue' en milieu scolaire. *Sociologie et Sociétés* 40 (2), 217-237.

Harris, R., Lefstein, A. (2011). *Urban classroom culture*. London: King's College.

Hill, J.H. (2000). The racialising function of language panics. In R. Duenas Gonzales (ed.). *Language ideologies: critical perspectives on the Official English movement*. Urbana, IL: National Council of Teachers of English, 245-267.

Jalhay, S., Clycq, N. (2014). De percepties van leerkrachten en directeurs over diversiteit: is diversiteit gelijk aan taal?. In N. Clycq, C. Timmerman, P. Van Avermaet, J. Wets, and P. Hermans (eds). *Oprit 14. Naar een schooltraject zonder beperkingen*. Gent: Academia Press, 75-96.

Jaspers, J. (2005). *Tegenwerken, belachelijk doen. Talige sabotage van Marokkaanse jongens op een middelbare school*. Brussel: VUBPress.

Jaspers, J. (2011). Talking like a 'zero-lingual'. Ambiguous linguistic caricatures at an urban secondary school. *Journal of Pragmatics* 43(5), 1264-1278.

Jaspers, J. (2014). Stylisations as teacher practice. *Language in Society* 43, 373-391.

Jaspers, J. (2015a). Modelling linguistic diversity. The excluding impact of inclusive multilingualism. *Language Policy*, 14(2), 109-129.

Jaspers, J. (2015b). Tussen meervoudige vuren. De implementatie van eentalig taalbeleid in een context van taaldiversiteit. *Pedagogische Studiën*, 92(2), 344-359.

Labov, W (1972). *Language in the inner city*. Oxford: Blackwell.

McDermott, R. (1974). Achieving school failure: an anthropological approach to illiteracy and social stratification. In: G.D. Spindler (ed). *Education and cultural process*. New York: Holt, Rinehart & Winston, 82-118.

Menken, K., García, O., eds. (2010). *Negotiating language policies in schools*. New York-London: Routledge.

Ramaut, G. et al. (2013). *Evaluatieonderzoek van het project 'Thuistaal in onderwijs' (2009-2012): Eindrapport*. Gent & Leuven: Ghent University & KU Leuven.

Rampton, B. (2006). *Language in late modernity*. Cambridge: Cambridge University Press.

Shohamy, E. (2006) *Language policy*. New York & London: Routledge

Slembrouck, S., Van Gorp, K., Van Avermaet, P. (2016) Strategies of multilingualism in education for minority children. In P. Van Avermaet, S. Slembrouck, K. Van Gorp, S. Sierens, and K. Maryns, eds. *The Multilingual Edge of Education*. London: Palgrave (in press).

Snell, J., Shaw, S., Copland, F.(2015). *Linguistic ethnography. Interdisciplinary explorations*. Basingstoke: Palgrave Macmillan.

Smet, P. (2011). *Samen taalgrenzen verleggen*. Brussels: Flemish Ministry of Education.

Vandenbroucke, F. (2007). *De lat hoog voor talen in iedere school*. Brussels: Flemish Ministry of Education.

13. Same-sex sexualities and Belgian Moroccan communities

Wim Peumans

Introduction

It was my very first 'official' day of fieldwork, somewhere in October 2010, when I was introduced to the Syrian-Dutch writer and sociologist Omar Nahas by one of my interlocutors, Khalid. Omar, Khalid and I were both at the Brussels Rainbowhouse, together with dozens of others, to attend a lecture by the African American gay imam and convert to Islam, Daaiyee Abdullah. I shake Omar's hand and tell him I know his books. He gives me a faint smile. Omar seemed a bit annoyed with me, or at least he was acting quite distant and cold – very different from the other times I would meet him later during my fieldwork. I told him I read about him in the newspaper a few weeks earlier. Again, something between a faint smile and a grimace. I was later explained that Omar was feeling frustrated because the past weeks he had been giving interviews to Belgian newspapers about a newly set-up program in Antwerp which trained laymen –and women to become guides in their local mosques. Omar was coach and leader of the project. But instead of focusing on the program, which was to lead to mutual understanding between non-Muslim Belgians and Muslim Belgians in Antwerp, the article revolved around the reporter asking the newly trained guides 'what does Islam think of homosexuality?'

I told Omar about my PhD project on 'homosexuality and Islam'. "You know", Omar said, "if you do this kind of project, I think I have an angle for you, or rather three. First, what do Muslims in general think of same-sex desire? Second, why is society in general so obsessed with what Muslims think of homosexuality? Third, you have to look at the experiences of gay, lesbian and bisexual Muslims themselves."

While my PhD research[1] mostly focused on the third angle, the two other perspectives were of course always on the background during fieldwork.

It seems to be commonplace knowledge that the relationship between same-sex sexuality and Belgian Moroccan communities is a contentious and problematic one. Yet research which looks into this relationship is relatively scarce. When it comes to specific studies on Belgian LGBTs of Moroccan background themselves, it is virtually non-existent. Indeed, LGBT and Moroccan (and more broadly, Muslim) are considered an oxymoron.

The chapter will study the relationship between same-sex sexuality and Moroccan communities in Belgium from two interrelated perspectives. First, it will assess the attitudes of Moroccans towards same-sex sexuality and situate these attitudes in broader frameworks. Second, the relationship between LGBT issues and Moroccans (and more broadly, Muslims) stirs much public and sometimes political attention. I discuss a series of events around gay bashing that took place during my fieldwork. All events were heavily mediatized and caused public and political scrutiny as they revolved around same-sex sexuality, Islam, migration and often Belgian Moroccans.

In doing so the chapter provides a unique, complex and layered insight into the multiple intersections between race and ethnicity on the one hand and sexuality and gender in contemporary Belgian society. My project focused on same-sex sexualities, transnational migration and religion in Belgium, with specific attention towards lesbians, gays and bisexual of Muslim background (10 out of 28 participants had ancestral roots in Morocco). For this study I conducted ethnographic face-to-face and e-mailinterviews, did participant observation in the activities of the LGBT scene and I asked participants to maintain a diary.

The issue of gay bashing was the cause of heated debate in 2010 – 2012 and throughout my fieldwork I kept a binder with newspaper (From '*De Standaard*', '*Le Soir*', '*De Morgen*', '*De Tijd*' and '*Het Belang van Limburg*') and magazine clippings ('*ZiZo Magazine*', '*Brussel Deze Week*' and '*Inch/Labels*') on issues broadly related to same-sex sexualities and ethnic minorities. The chapter at hand seemed the perfect opportunity to do an in-depth analysis of the debates that happened at the time. I went back to the clippings and complemented them with online articles on the issue, whenever necessary ('*MO* Mondiaal magazine*',

'*ZiZo online*', '*Brusselnieuws*', '*De Standaard*', '*De Morgen*'). I did what is called an 'ethnographic content analysis'(Altheid, 1987): this particular type of content analysis is emergent, open-ended and an example of the partial and situated nature of ethnographic research. Ethnographic content analysis consists in looking for convergences and dissimilarities in themes, issues and frames in a set of collected media articles (Gormly, 2004). In total I analyzed 24 articles, both in print and online. Although I did not do an exhaustive analysis of everything that was published on the matter at the time, already the articles that were analyzed, provided me with sufficient insight to develop particular arguments and claims.

One of the strengths of an ethnographic approach to content analysis is that one does not see the researcher as exterior to the events discussed, but as talking from a particular location and positionality. Although as a researcher I acted more as an observer than a participant, whether in online or offline debates on these issues. When one Flemish socialist politician invited me to talk at a workshop on 'homosexuality and Islam' in the Flemish Parliament at the time when the issue of gay bashing was most salient I kindly declined. Firstly, as I had just started my PhD I did not feel ready to present any findings. This was decided in mutual accord with my PhD guidance committee in light of the highly sensitive nature of my research topic. Secondly, as I will explain later, I felt narrowing the subject down to 'homosexuality and Islam' was problematic as it set up a causal link between Islam and violence against queer people.

Belgians of Moroccan origin and same-sex desire: a contentious relationship?

Looking at the historic record, research on the attitudes of Moroccans towards (same-sex) sexuality or on same-sexual practices in guest worker communities is virtually non-existent, apart from incidental anecdotal evidence. This is a consequence of historiography being characterized by a persistent heteronormativity and heterosexism.

The history of the LGBT movement in Belgium mentions a few links between the guest worker movements and the struggles for LGBT rights. The Stonewall riots – commonly considered a watershed moment in the history of LGBT rights – led to the rise of the Gay Liberation movement, not only in the United States, but also in Europe. This new kind of activism stressed the importance of openness, pride, identity and confrontation. It was inspired by student, feminist,

Black Power and anti-war movements. In Belgium, LGBT activist groups such as *'Groep Rode Hond'* ('Group Red Dog', 1973), *'Rooie Vlinder'* ('Red Butterfly', 1976-1981) and *'Roze Aktiefront'* ('Pink Action Front', 1981-2001) were established along the lines of Gay Liberation. Inspired by Marxism and left-wing intellectual legacies, these groups sought alliances with other social groups, such as workers, women and ethnic minorities (Borghs, 2015). For example, in 1983, the *'Roze Aktie Front'* took part in a march for voting rights for guest workers and in 1986 for equal rights for youngster of second generation (Brys, 2015).

We have to look across the Dutch border, to the experiences of Moroccan first generation migrants in the Netherlands, to find anecdotal evidence of same-sex behavior amongst the guest worker communities in the 1960s and 1970s. David Bos for example interviewed a Dutch Moroccan man who came to the Netherlands in the golden sixties, a time of sexual revolution and liberation: 'In the sixties there were gays who came to visit the guest workers. And not just for intercourse. They also gave much money and helped us with documents, requests, and insurance. There was so much humanity amongst these people. And you know why? I only realize that now: because they were also a minority. Of course other motives played their part as well. They did not just come purely for the men. They were concerned about the wellbeing of guest workers' (Bos, 2010:271) (my translation).

Historian Andrew Shield analyzed personal ads in the periodicals of the Dutch COC (*'Centrum voor Ontspanning and Cultuur'*, considered the oldest LGBT rights movement in the world) between 1965 and 1976. Three percent of the ads was posted by men of color: they seeked friendship (*'vriendschap'*), a serious relationship (*'serieuze vriendschap/relatie'*) or they were interested in living together (*'samenwoning'*). Although Shield focused on personal ads, he mentions one COC issue with an interview featuring 'Abdou', a young man who fled Morocco at the end of the 1970s because of his sexuality (Shield, 2011; Shield, 2014).

Moving on to the present and back to Belgium we can find a number of studies, which have assessed the attitudes of Belgian Moroccans towards same-sex sexuality, yet they tend to confirm the clichés that are held commonplace.

In their book on Islam in the Netherlands and Belgium Shadid and van Koningsveld (2008) only mention that same-sex sexual acts are denounced in the same vein as adultery and sexual offence. Yet the authors do not draw on sociological data to make their case, but refer to the respective *suras* from the religious texts.

A sociological study by the University of Rabat on Belgian Moroccans made use of quantitative (surveys with 401 persons) and qualitative research methods (6 focusgroups and 50 individual interviews).

Whenever questions were asked about sexual freedom and same-sex sexuality, most people used the term 'immoral'. 53,44 percent of the surveyed persons stated same-sex sexuality poses one of the greatest dangers for morality (Saaf, et al., 2009:120). The authors found a correlation between the idea that same-sex sexuality is immoral and the degree of religiosity (Saaf, et al., 2009:121).

Six years later a new study on Belgian Moroccans found that the majority of respondents, 59,3 percent, disapproved of same-sex sexuality. One fifth of the participants thought same-sex sexuality was defendable in some circumstances. Respectively 8,9 percent of men and 10% of women of Moroccan background approves of same-sex sexuality in all circumstances, meaning the level of tolerance is only slightly higher amongst women compared to men (Torrekens & Adam, 2015).

The aforementioned studies do not provide us with much of a framework in which to situate such attitudes nor is much contextualization offered. While the numbers are clear, the reader is left asking why Moroccans feel the way they do about same-sex desire.

Such explanations are given in studies on the attitudes of Muslim minority youngsters towards same-sex sexuality. In a three-year panel study among late adolescents and young adults between 2008 and 2011, Hooghe and Meeusen (2012) found a correspondence between religious groups in terms of their displays of homophobia: 21,8 percent of Muslim youngsters of a variety of ethnic backgrounds avoid contact with LGBTs. Strong religious adherence is seen as the main explanation for the high prevalence of anti-gay sentiments. Another study, executed among pupils in 70 schools in Brussels, confirmed that young men and women of foreign origin – not just of Moroccan origin – hold more negative attitudes compared to Belgians. Contrary to the study by Hooghe & Meeusen, the authors suggest that 'youngsters of foreign origin seem to be less aware of societal normative pressure surrounding the expression of sexual prejudice compared to Belgians' (Teney & Subramanian, 2010:168). That is to say, amongst ethnic majority Belgians it is now socially acceptable and desirable to state one is tolerant towards or even acceptant of LGBTs. Yet ethnic minority youngsters grew up in backgrounds in which this is seldom the case: either same-sex desire is unspoken of or it is spoken of in negative terms. The degree to which one identifies with Belgian society and the perception of institutional discrimination are other factors, which contribute to the ethnic differences in sexual prejudice (Teney & Subramanian, 2010: 168).

The results of my own work offer complementary perspectives on the attitudes of men and women of Muslim background towards same-sex sexuality. My research found that instead of seeing LGBTs with a Muslim background as victims of the oppressing and totalizing forces of 'religion', 'culture', 'tradition' or 'honor and shame', it is better to understand their families' moral understandings of sexuality, gender and kinship within their particular life trajectory. Within a context of migration, relationships of power define which aspects of one's culture, religion and tradition become highlighted or downplayed as a way of marking one's boundaries versus the ethnic majority group (Espín, 1999). Norms, values, practices and discourses around sexuality and gender often play a crucial role in this ethnic and racial boundary-making process (Nagel, 2003). The persistence of the heterosexual family myth in society, together with the socio-economic background, education level, migration context and ethnic and religious belonging help explain why many Muslims in Belgium have negative attitudes and opinions on same-sex sexuality. Although there were familial and cultural differences in the role of religion in the everyday life of my interlocutors' families, religious morality often was very much part of the equation.

The importance of family, endogamous marriage and procreation was stressed and valued as a religious and cultural imperative. Matters of sexuality often raise the highest moral anxieties. Sexuality and morality in everyday life are deeply intertwined. Sexuality occupies the attention of many religions because it is a powerful way to organize and relate human beings, since sexuality and sex evoke strong emotions in people, touching on our most intimate assumptions, our routinized knowledge and moral dispositions (Peumans, 2015). Religions are preoccupied with defining the nature, purpose and boundaries of human sexuality, especially female sexuality. Through ideology, taboo and ritual, certain sexual acts, practices and desires are recognized as licit as opposed to illicit, good versus evil, natural vis-à-vis unnatural. In many of my interlocutors' families, out-of-wedlock sexual engagements are strictly forbidden and in hegemonic interpretations of the Qur'an and *hadith* sexual acts between persons of the same sex are considered *haram* (Peumans, 2015). Further, as I mentioned below, sexuality and gender are quintessential markers in ethnic boundary making processes: this process is gendered, as in a context of migration, women are often seen as the reproducers of the ancestral homeland's culture and religion (Espín, 1999; Yuval-Davis, 1996). Yet it should be noted that this process of 'ethnosexual frontiering' (Nagel, 2000) works both ways, that is to say: ethnic majority groups engage in such a politics of gender, sexuality and intimacy as well (Clycq, 2012).

'From gaybashing to mocrobashing'

In the following paragraph I wish to focus on a series of events that took place during my fieldwork, mainly through an analysis of online and print media articles. All these events revolve around same-sex sexualities, Islam, migration and often Belgians of Moroccan descent. They demonstrate how in public, media and political debates these issues are talked about and the contrasting ways in which these debates are framed. In 2011 – 2012 a number of incidents of gay bashing stirred much public, activist and political attention, beginning with the cases of two gay men being beaten up in June 2011 and a violent conflict in the gay café 'Le Fontainas' in November 2011, respectively happening near and in the gay neighborhood of Brussels. The absolute lowpoints were the murders of Ihsane Jarfi, a 32 year gay man of Belgian-Moroccan origin in May 2012, and Jacques Kotnik, a 61 year old gay man of Belgian origin in July 2012, both cases happened in the Francophone city of Liège.

In contrast to Liège, Brussels had been in the news before with incidents of physical and verbal aggression towards LGBTs, as the problem had been brought under attention by journalists nearly a decade earlier in 2004. A study (Poelman & Smit, 2007) on violence towards LGBTs in Brussels only confirmed these media reports, yet not much was being undertaken by police and politicians alike to come up with strategies to counter the violence.

The difference in 2011 – 2012 compared to 2004 was the availability of social media, which victims of violence could use to make their case public and heard. This makes it easier for these stories to be picked up by news media and to lead to intense debates and public indignation on social media themselves.

Seeing its salience in the media, the issue did come up in some of the interviews I did. For example, Meryem, who is in her thirties and identifies as lesbian, moved out of Brussels to a city in Wallonia, because she and her girlfriend were scolded when they walked hand in hand in public in the capital. Another participant, Brahim, grew up in Brussels, is in his thirties and identifies as gay. His parents are from Moroccan origin and migrated from Morocco to Belgium in the 1960s. Brahim was trying to make sense of why young men of Moroccan background engage in gay bashing, echoing the findings of studies mentioned above:

I think they feel frustrated. Frustrated because they experience racism every day, which is partly true. And then they see me, a gay man of Moroccan origin, someone who is in a weaker position than them. It allows them to vent their frustration. It [*gay bashing*] happened to me a few years ago actually. Three times as a matter of fact, two times by Moroccans ('*des Marocains*') and one time a black guy ('*un black*'). It was violent. They followed me to my home. They beat me up so hard I had to go to the hospital. But it only makes me stronger. I told myself: "OK, they might do this to me, but I will never feel sorry for being gay."

But also some persons who had migrated themselves to Belgium, from a variety of national and ethnic background would state they would walk hand-in-hand with their partner in only some parts of the city they lived in, out of fear of repercussions.

The prevalence of gay bashing laid bare the precarity of acceptance of same-sex sexualities and persons with same-sex desires or non-conforming gender behaviour. After the Netherlands, Belgium became the second country in the world to legalize marriage between persons of the same gender. Its state-laws allow adoption by same-sex couples and it has elaborate anti-discrimination laws. Yet changes in laws do not equal changes in the hearts and minds of all Belgians.

Politicians, both from left and right sides of the political spectrum, joined the discussion. The government was slow and, according to LGBT associations, too slow, to undertake initiatives to counter the violence. In the following I want to highlight some of the key moments in these debates as they were held in a variety of media platforms.

In an open letter titled 'Stop Gay Bashing' openly gay MP Jan Roegiers from SP.A (Flemish socialist party) urged politicians to undertake action to stop the violence against queer persons. Structural attention should be given to sexual identity and gender in education, especially in concentration schools ('*concentratiescholen*', referring to schools with a disproportionate amount of youngsters of ethnic minority background), as 'gay bashers are often youngsters of foreign origin ('*allochtone afkomst*')'(Roegiers 2012). The letter also asked 'imams and other spiritual leaders to play an important part' and 'for complaints to be effectively treated by police and gay violence to be prosecuted.' Politicians, radio presenters, media personalities, artists, writers and a few academics signed the letter. In an interview, titled 'from gaybashing to mocrobashing?', Jan

Roegiers countered the interviewer's critique of 'culturalizing' gay bashing in the aforementioned letter and other media interventions:

> I may have mentioned ethnic minority youth ('*allochtone jongeren*'), but we consciously did not speak of Muslim youngsters. Because what is a migrant ('*allochtoon*')? An American, Dutch person or French man is also a migrant, not just someone from Maghreb origin. (...) Apparently scientific reports contradict the experience of many LGBs ('*holebi's*'). It may be subjective, but in my experience gay-related violence is often related to guys with foreign roots (Serhane 2012).

In response to the above-mentioned letter 10 renowned persons with foreign roots wrote an open letter titled 'Stop Putting Labels on People'(Bahri, et al., 2012) warning readers about the pitfalls of the ongoing debates: "the demonization shifts from one group to another: 'the gay person' to 'the person of foreign origin' ('*allochtoon*')." In an accompanying letter, 'A kick under the ass of politicians', an openly gay journalist of Belgian-Tunesian origin expressed his anger over politicians who state everything was the fault of 'people of foreign origin' ('*allochtonen*'): "Those so-called people of foreign origin were born and raised here. They are part of your system, which is now showing cracks." (Bahri, 2012)

Another response in this particular debate was an open letter published by two Flemish Nationalist politicians, Piet de Bruyn (openly gay and white Belgian) and Zuhal Demir (of Turkish-Kurdish ancestral origin). The authors stated:

> a fundamental problem was young men of foreign origin. Their involvement was a common thread in the hundreds of reported cases of aggression towards LGBTs. In politically correct jargon the cause is their 'cultural background'. (...) As if a cultural background is ever a criterion to make behaviour acceptable or unacceptable. As if cultural background is a given which cannot be touched (De Bruyn & Demir, 2012).

Some of the solutions they offered were similar to the ones proposed by the socialist MP, although there were some differences. Instead of addressing 'spiritual leaders to take up their responsibility', the nationalists proposed 'structural consultations with the minority communities and clear engagements to respect the equality of LGBTs' and 'taking up homophobic violence as a point of interest in the action plan "Prevention of Violent Radicalization and Polarization". In doing so, both propositions implicitly refer to Muslim communities.

The extreme right party '*Vlaams Belang*', known for its racist and homophobic points of view, made several contradictory u-turns in order to capitalize on the issue and to make a case for its anti-Islamic agenda, although not nearly as successful as the homonationalist rhetoric of Dutch politicians Pim Fortuyn and Geert Wilders (Vlaams Belang 2012) (cfr. below). Their opinion pieces were not picked up by general newspapers or other media, but only published on their website. Running up to the gay pride in May 2012, an op-ed titled, 'Pride without Courage', appeared in '*Brussel Deze Week*', in which three Flemish nationalist politicians from Brussels complained the Pride organization did not make the theme of gay bashing central to this year's parade. They criticized using 'macho behaviour' as an excuse for anti-gay violence and instead explained, based on (non-cited) studies, that while socio-economic status and education level play a small part, religion does exert an influence. They concluded that 'Islam and Muslim culture have a place in our society if they show unconditional respect for essential values, such as freedom to look or live differently'(Van Caneghem, et al., 2012). The op-ed led to a response of Merhaba, the largest LGBT association for ethnic minority LGBTs. First they refuted the arguments, using the study by Teney and Subramanian (2010) I mentioned in the previous paragraph. Then they asked what courage is:

> Is it making certain groups in society responsible for homophobia while these groups themselves are confronted with structural forms of racism and discrimination? Is it a sign of courage to see homophobia as the problem of the 'Other', but in the meantime not do anything about the reception of gay bashing complaints in police offices?

To the dismay of the audience at a debate on 'same-sex sexuality and ethnic minorities', organized in Antwerp on June 8th 2012, the chair of the Federation of Moroccan Associations ('*Federatie Marokkaanse Verenigingen – FMV*'), Mohamed Chakkar, declared homosexuality is 'not an topic of concern for the Moroccan community, as we have other fish to fry'(Ankal, 2012; De Crom, 2012). According to his Dutch counterpart of the Cooperation of Dutch Moroccans ('*Samenwerkingsverband Marokkaanse Nederlanders – SMN*'), a dialogue should be engaged in, 'if you notice, based on facts and figures, that there is a taboo in your community. You should not look for arguments to not open up the theme for discussion' (De Crom, 2012). The persistent lack of a decisive overarching plan drawn up by politicians caused a lot of frustrations, especially since the Belgian prime minister between 2011 and 2014 was openly gay. The agreement of the new federal coalition between socialists, liberals and Christian democrats, which was formed in October 2011 after world record breaking negotiation talks of 541 days, contained a passage about its intention to tackle gay violence. Yet each mediatized incident of gay bashing led to more and more frustration amongst LGBT persons and organizations about the lack of political initiative. One answer was the formation of a new LGBT association named 'Outrage'. Outrage staged 'kiss-ins', whistle-concerts against homophobia and launched a bashing app, allowing victims of physical or verbal violence to submit their experience, including the location, time and a short description of the incidence. All these data were immediately made visible on a 'Bash-map'. Between January 2012 and mid-May 2013, there had been 469 reports of anti-gay violence, of which 249 took place in in Brussels. Merhaba launched a campaign to tackle multiple kinds of discrimination. The text on the poster, which was spread out, is translated as: 'You know where it starts, but you do not know where it ends. Discrimination, don't start with it.' On the poster a door is pictured containing stickers with various slogans: "No gays; brown skin not welcome; no women above forty, ...", 'Wel Jong Niet Hetero' ('Young but not Straight'), the Flemish umbrella group for youngster LGBT associations, made an undercover documentary, titled 'Hommes de la Rue' ('Men of the Street') in the tv-program 'Volt' in November 2012, in which two gay men walked hand in hand in public, showing the often hostile reactions of bystanders (often with visible foreign roots, judging from skin color or specific accents), which lead to even more indignation in media debates.

On a regional level political initiatives were already being taken: Pascal Smet, the socialist Flemish minister of Equal Opportunities and Education signed a charter in October 2012 making it obligatory for schools to discuss sexual orientation and gender. Amongst other things, the Brussels minister of Equal Opportunities Bruno de Lille (*Groen* – green party) launched the '*meld-it*' – campaign, pleading with victims of gay bashing to report to the police. He also cooperated with the Brussels police to organize workshops about the subject within the police corps.

When the Christian democrat and humanist (*CdH*) federal minister of Interior Affairs and Equal Opportunities, Joëlle Milquet introduced the new National Security plan in March 2012, this did not contain anything concerning the issue of gay bashing. Member of Parliament Jan Roegiers ominously warned: 'We should not wait until someone is killed before action is taken'(Junes, 2012).

A sign welcoming foreigners in Mechelen (source: KADOC)

Already in November 2011, Outrage wrote an open letter to the socialist mayor of Brussels, Freddy Thieleman, with the same warning: 'You made promises, but these remained unfulfilled. (...) We suspect someone has to die before you really take action. Take it from us we will not let it come this far'(Brussel Nieuws, 2011).

A few months later the Belgian LGBT communities were shocked by the murders of Ihsane Jarfi and Jacques Kotnik. Finally *çavaria*, the Flemish umbrella LGBT associations, received an invitation of the prime minister (Brambust, 2012). Still, it was not until January 31th 2013 when the different governments in Belgium released their 'Interfederal Action Plan against Homophobic and Transphobic Violence', nearly two years after the first incidents were reported in the media.

Following the launch of the plan, the president of the Federation of Moroccan Associations, Mohamed Chakkar, was interviewed in the politically centre-right Flemish daily newspaper 'De Standaard'. The first question was: "The action plan against homophobic violence does not pay attention to faith communities, a missed opportunity?" Mohamed Chakkar replied: "If this was explicitly mentioned, then it risked stigmatizing a whole part of the population. You cannot address leaders of faith of whichever religion on the behaviour of a few individuals. The people themselves are responsible for this" (Vanhecke, 2012). The journalist continued: "Is there a connection between violence against LGBTs and the Muslim community?" The president answered: "You find gay haters in every group. I do not want to justify these problems, but we need to put them in the right context. Violence against gays is a general societal issue, in which faith does not play a part"(Vanhecke, 2012).

Although all media outlets devoted attention to the issue of gay bashing, it is important to highlight the different ways the LGBT media published on the events, with particular attention to '*Zizo*' and '*Labels*' (later renamed '*Inch*'). Zizo was first published in 1993, merging out of the 'Gay and Lesbian Newspaper' ('*Homo- & Lesbiennekrant*') and the 'Faggot' ('*Janet*')(Borghs, 2015:210). It has a website for daily news affairs and a quarterly published printed version. It runs on a permanent and voluntary editorial staff and is housed in the offices of *çavaria*, the umbrella group for all Flemish LGBT associations. 'Labels/Inch' only appeared bimonthly between 2009 and 2014, was published in Brussels by a Dutch-speaking editorial staff with offices in the *Dansaertstraat/Rue Dansaert*, one of the trendiest neighborhoods of Brussels.

The way the issue of gay bashing was treated in both magazines was remarkably different. *ZiZo* for example published a special issue on violence in January 2012. This contained an article on 'gay bashing in numbers', only based on scientific studies; what to do if one is attacks or insulted; how to report violence; an overview of what initiatives were being taken by politicians and activists, with special attention to Merhaba and Outrage. Everything was reported in a balanced and neutral tone of writing.

Inch took a different and arguably much more sensationalist approach, yet they were the first ones to bring the issue to the attention of media and public early 2011, when the January/February issue cover said 'Hot in Brussels: hitting gays' ('*Hip in Brussel: homo's meppen*') and the accompanying article, 'growing gay hatred terrorizing Brussels' ('*Groeiende homohaat teistert Brussel*') with highlighted quotes such as "I am still not racist, but again it was a North African boy" and concluding with a quote by a 34-year old white advertiser who lives in the centre of Brussels: "They should all be deported from the country, those homophobic new Belgians. I should not have to adapt to their culture?"(Lemaire, 2011)

LGBT rights, moral panic and the ethnic/racial other

In January 2016 I took the last train from Antwerp to Tongeren on a late Sunday night. Upon arrival in Tongeren, my husband and I walked through the passenger's tunnel. As we were getting up the stairs to the exit, a guy came down and brushed past my shoulder in an aggressive manner. I ignored him and we went on and so did he, but while he was walking in the tunnel I heard him call out '*homo*' two or three times. I don't know whether he was referring to us or the other male person walking behind us, who could've been gay too. This was the second time – at least as I can recall – in the last decade I encountered homophobia in a public space. I was puzzled as what to make of this situation. I didn't feel insulted by someone calling me 'gay', I mean, that is stating the obvious. Surely, '*homo*' is only an insult to the man in question, not to me. I wear it as a badge of honor. I experienced a slight feeling of estrangement from my own surroundings: here in Tongeren, of all places? Reminiscing about my high school time there, it was not a complete surprise of course. To my own irritation the young man in question did have 'foreign roots' (Moroccan? Tunisian? Arab? I have no idea). This was probably what annoyed me most about the whole situation. I wish I had confronted him: "Listen, what is your problem? I mean, I'm writing this chapter about gay bashing and, and... " How ironic.

It made me reflect more on how in media and political discourse the violence against queer persons was linked to homophobia among ethnic and racial minority communities ('*allochtone gemeenschappen*') so the causes were sought in the cultural and religious realm. The explanations that were given or the links between ethnic minorities and gay bashing were often based on subjective judgment, as one politician phrased it: 'It may be subjective, but in my experience gay-related violence is often related to guys with foreign roots'. At the time of the events the only available research report on perpetrators of anti-gay violence was published in the Netherlands (Buijs, et al., 2009) and this was only mentioned a few times in these debates. Some politicians brought in statistics claiming the involvement of ethnic minorities was central in "hundreds of reported incidents", yet ethnic origin is not taken up in police reports.

At the height of the wave of gay bashing Sofie Peeters released the documentary '*Femme de la Rue*', about the verbal and sexual harassment of women in the streets of Brussels, often linked to men of foreign origin (Longman, 2013). Cologne witnessed hundreds of cases of assault on New Year's Eve 2015, events that have repercussions for Belgium as well. While some media outlets pointed out the perpetrators were asylum seekers, others were blamed for hushing their origin. In response to the events in Cologne, the Flemish Nationalist Belgian Federal Secretary of Asylum, Theo Francken, launched a plan to educate asylum seekers about Belgian values and norms, with special attention to the way women should be treated. As one feminist activist pointed out in an op-ed: 'Perhaps we should reserve the same indignation about rape and harassment when white men are the culprits'(Mangelschoots, 2016).

In other words, the case of gay bashing is not a singular one in the Belgian public debate and should be situated in broader societal debates. Over the past years there have been similar issues relating to sexuality, gender, Islam, migration and often Belgian Moroccans. This often caused a moral panic, which compresses 'social, political, media, and psychological fears and anxieties, whether real or culturally imagined (often a combination of both) and solidify the boundaries between victim and victimizer, safety and danger'(Herdt, 2009). One can witness a range of similar dynamics in the debates I discussed in this chapter. By putting all blame on a racial/ethnic Other's culture and ethnicity, public officials and politicians distance themselves from their own responsibilities in such matters: after all, as one journalist observed in an op-ed quoted above, these young men were born in Belgium, they are 'part of a system which is now showing cracks.' What is remarkable is how 'violence', 'Islam' (or more neutrally 'religion'), 'migrant', 'Moroccan' or 'foreign origin' are frequently used in the same sentence. As cultural theorist Sara Ahmed (2014) reminds us, the mere proximity of both words in a sentence in such a repeated manner makes their association 'essential', or as she puts it, these words become 'sticky'. One example is the question of a journalist to the president of the Federation of Moroccan Associations: 'Is there a connection between violence against LGBTs and the Muslim community?' In a similar vein, the categories of 'Muslim', 'migrant' and 'Moroccan' are often conflated, despite attempts by politicians to counter that 'they consciously did not speak of Muslim youngsters (…). An American, Dutch person or French man is also a migrant, not just someone from Maghreb origin.' In these debates we can delineate different degrees of what Jasbir Puar (2007) names 'homonationalism', a concept which investigates how in today's neo-liberal nation-states some queer subjects are included at the expense of others, namely ethnic minorities and migrants. The issue of gay bashing is used in variable degrees towards political gain.

It is precisely through its border politics that neo-liberal nation-states claim their sovereignty and determine who belongs to the national body and who does not. That is why asylum seekers need to learn about "Belgian values" and "how we treat women" upon arrival in Belgium. For both politicians on the left and right, sexual minority rights and gender equality have come to be seen as quintessential markers of what it means to be Belgian, modern, and European, even though they are only recent accomplishments in the scale of history and not achieved in an equal way in the whole European Union. Sexuality and nationalism have always been intertwined in the history of nation-states: the new sexual nationalism in Europe are, 'just like the old ones, not just about nationals and aliens; they are also about the distinction between "true" nationals and "others" that are suspect on account of their foreign origin – not citizenship'(Fassin & Salcedo, 2015:1119). The category of homosexuality has become racialized and tacitly equated with whiteness (which is one of the reasons why LGBT Muslims are considered an oxymoron): 'From the explicitly designated Other to a racially homogenous nation, it became an implicit racial foundation of a nation that may be no longer thought of as racial' (Dudink, 2011)

In these debates Moroccan and more broadly Arab men are represented in similar tropes. Much is being assumed about Arab masculinity, yet little is known. Academically speaking Arab masculinity remains a 'black box' to use Inhorn's (2012) term of phrase. Yet in representational terms they are considered excessively masculine, oversexed or hypersexual. In doing so, Arab men take up an ambiguous position: one the one hand they are a subject of fear, a threat to white women and gay men, but on the other hand, at least within gay men's circles, they are also a subject of desire and ethnosexual adventuring. Such fears and desires of the racial Other are deeply historically embedded and have colonial precursors (see Boone, 2014). In other words, the moral panics that ensues after events such as the ones discussed above is racialized and ethnicized. Intimate connections can be discerned between debates on multiculturalism and (hetero)sexism.

Conclusion

This chapter first provided the reader with an overview of existing studies on the relationship between Belgian Moroccan communities and same-sex sexualities. In the current literature that assessed the attitudes of Belgian Moroccans towards a variety of societal issues, same-sex desire was only a minor point of attention. Those studies which gauged specifically the attitudes towards homosexuality, focused on youngsters of a variety of ethnic minority backgrounds. When it comes to explaining why these youngsters hold more negative opinions, the arguments put forward by Teney & Subramanian (2010) were more convincing and in line with my own research.

Secondly, I looked at 'gay bashing', an issue that became very topical during my fieldwork, as is evidenced by the media frenzy and public outcry surrounding these events. A persistent thread in this discourse was the explicit and implicit causal links that were set up between gay bashing, Islam, migration and often Belgian Moroccans.

The subject of sexuality and especially same-sex sexuality is conspicuously absent in migration studies in general and in research on Moroccan communities in particular. If anything, I wished to demonstrate the necessity of research on these topics as public debate is often founded on half-truths and cultural stereotypes, with the concomitant risks to essentialize whole groups of society towards political gain.

Note

1 This research project was funded by the FWO Vlaanderen (Research Foundation Flanders), project number 1126711N (supervisors: Christiane Stallaert and Johan Leman). For this chapter I want to acknowledge the help of my father, who reads 5 newspapers and who, during fieldwork, helped me keep each newspaper or magazine article that was related to my research.

Bibliography

Ahmed, S. (2014). *The Cultural Politics of Emotion*. Edinburgh: Edinburgh University Press.

Altheid, D.L. (1987). Ethnographic content analysis. *Qualitative sociology* 10(1):65-77.

Ankal, H. (2012). *Holebi- en minderhedenorganisaties bespreken homoseksualiteit*. Brussel: MO*

Bahri, R. (2012). Trap onder kont van politici. *De Standaard*.

Bahri, R., et al. (2012). Stop met etiketten op te kleven. *De Standaard*.

Boone, J.A. (2014). *The Homoerotics of Orientalism*. New York: Columbia University Press.

Borghs, P. (2015). *Holebipioniers – een geschiedenis van de holebi- en transgenderbeweging in Vlaanderen*. Antwerpen: 't Verschil.

Bos, D. (2010).'Gewurgd door taboes'; veranderingen in de acceptatie van homoseksualiteit in de Marokkaanse gemeenschap in Nederland. In S.E. Keuzenkamp (ed.). *Steeds gewoner, nooit gewoon*. Den Haag: Sociaal en Cultureel Planbureau, 265-283.

Brambust, F. (2012). Çavaria opgelucht om uitnodiging Di Rupo. Gent: *Zizo Magazine*.

Brussel Nieuws (2011). Het zoveelste homofobe incident op rij. *Brusselnieuws.be*.

Brys, Y. (2015). *Holebi's aanwezig in de Sociale Strijd*. RAF – Info over 20 jaar Roze Aktiefront.

Buijs, L., Hekma, G., Duyvendak J.W. (2009). *'Als Ze Maar van Me Afblijven' – Een Onderzoek naar Antihomoseksueel Geweld in Amsterdam*. Universiteit van Amsterdam.

Clycq, N. (2012). 'My daughter is a free woman, so she can't marry a Muslim': The gendering of ethno-religious boundaries. *European Journal of Women's Studies* 19(2):157-171.

De Bruyn, P., Demir Z.(2012). Snelrecht voor Geweld tegen Homo's. *De Morgen*, 01.03.2012: 21.

De Crom, J. (2012). Homoseksualiteit is 'geen thema' voor Marokkaanse gemeenschap. *De Standaard*.

Dudink, S.P. (2011). Homosexuality, Race, and the Rhetoric of Nationalism. *History of the Present* 1(2), 259-264.

Espín, O.M. (1999). *Women Crossing Boundaries – A Psychology of Immigration and Transformations of Sexuality*. New York/London: Routledge.

Fassin, E., Salcedo, M. (2015). Becoming gay? Immigration Policies and the Truth of Sexual Identity. *Archives of Sexual Behavior* 44(5):1117-1125.

Gormly, E. (2004). Peering beneath the veil: an ethnographic content analysis of Islam as portrayed on the 700 Club following the September 11th attacks. *Journal of Media and Religion* 3(4):219-238.

Herdt, G. (2009). Introduction: Moral Panics, Sexual Rights, and Cultural Anger. In G. Herdt, (ed.). *Moral Panics, Sex Panics: Fear and the Fight over Sexual Rights*. New York: New York University Press, 1-46.

Hooghe, M., Meeusen C. (2012). Homophobia and the Transition to Adulthood: A Three Year Panel Study among Belgian Late Adolescents and Young Adults, 2008-2011. *Journal of Youth and Adolescence* 41(9), 1197-1207.

Inhorn, M.C. (2012). *The New Arab Man – Emergent Masculinities, Technologies, and Islam in the Middle East*. Princeton/ Oxford: Princeton University Press.

Junes, T. (2012). Minister Milquet belooft actie tegen homofoob en transfoob geweld. Brussel: *Zizo Magazine*.

Lemaire, E. (2011). Groeiende Homohaat Teistert Brussel. *Labels*, 28-35. Brussel.

Longman, C. (2013). 'Femme de la Rue': Sexism, Multiculturalism and Moral Panic. In *Exploring Sexual Hierarchies: Gayle Rubin's "Thinking Sex" Today*. Brussel: Université Libre de Bruxelles.

Mangelschoots, A. (2016). Eigen volk eerst, denk ik na Keulen. Brussel: *De Morgen*.

Nagel, J. (2000). Ethnicity and Sexuality. *Annual Review of Sociology* 26(1):107-133.

Nagel, J. (2003). *Race, Ethnicity, and Sexuality: Intimate Intersections, Forbidden Frontiers*. Oxford / New York: Oxford University Press.

Peumans, W. (2017). *Queer Muslims in Europe: Sexuality, Religion and Migration in Belgium*. London: IB Tauris.

Poelman, M., Smit, D. (2007). *Agressie tegen holebi's in Brussel Stad*. Brussels: EHSAL.

Puar, Jasbir K. (2007). *Terrorist Assemblages: Homonationalism in Queer Times*. New York: New York University Press.

Roegiers, J. (2012). Stop gaybashing.

Saaf, A., Bouchra Sidi Hida, and Ahmed Aghbal (2009). *Belgische Marokkanen – een Dubbele Identiteit in Ontwikkeling*. Brussels: Koning Boudewijnstichting.

Shadid, W.A.R., van Koningsveld P.S. (2008). *Islam in Nederland en België – Religieuze Institutionalisering in Twee Landen met Gemeenschappelijke Voorgeschiedenis*. Leuven: Peeters Publishers.

Shield, A. (2011). Moroccan Perceptions of Dutch (Homo)sexuality, 1964-1979. In *Sexual Nationalisms – Gender, Sexuality, and the Politics of Belonging in the New Europe*. University of Amsterdam.

Shield, A. (2014). 'Suriname – Seeking a Lonely, Lesbian Friend for Correspondence': Immigration and Homo-emancipation in the Netherlands, 1965-79. *History Workshop Journal* 78.

Teney, C. and S.V. Subramanian (2010). Attitudes Toward Homosexuals Among Youth in Multiethnic Brussels. *Cross-Cultural Research* 44(2):151-173.

Torrekens, C., and Adam I. (2015). *Marokkaanse en Turkse Belgen: een (zelf)portret van onze medeburgers*. Brussels: Koning Boudewijnstichting.

Van Caneghem, L., Godfroid O., De Visscher, J. (2012). N-VA over Pride en gaybashing: 'Geen fierheid zonder moed'. Brussel: *Brussel Deze Week*.

Vanhecke, N. (2012). 'Een Homo Sla je Gewoon Niet'. *De Standaard*, 01.02.2013.

Vlaams Belang (2012). *Die Arme Allochtonen Weer*. Brussel: Vlaams Belang.

Yuval-Davis, N. (1996). Women and the biological reproduction of "the nation". *Women's Studies International Forum* 19(1-2):17-24.

Part 5
Religion and devotion

14. Struggling with the Jinn: Moroccan healing practices and the placebo effect

Philip Hermans

The discipline of medical anthropology investigates from the holistic and cross-cultural perspective that is typical of anthropology the ways in which people in different cultures cope with sickness and try to preserve their health. It developed in the middle of the previous century and has become an important anthropological subdiscipline with a rich tradition and an interdisciplinary character. (Mc Elroy, 1996, Romanucci-Ross, Moerman & Tancredi 1997, Society for Medical Anthropology 1972-2016). Medical anthropology researches conceptions of sickness and health in different cultures, folk medicine, the universality and specificity of complaints and syndromes, the influence of socio-economic relations as well as gender and power relations on health seeking behaviour and access to health care, and the interaction between scientific medicine and folk medicine. The relevance of medical anthropology for our current society became clear when it became increasingly multicultural. In particular since the end of the sixties of the last century the Moroccan population has grown steadily and became one of the largest ethnic minorities in Belgium.

Many Moroccans and people of Moroccan descent who live in Belgium adhere to the belief that various illnesses as well as misfortune can be caused by supernatural agents and powers. Because of this, they often find themselves misunderstood by western therapists and seek help from traditional healers who use popular Islamic elements in their treatments. This article goes into the healing practices and rituals as they are still performed in Morocco and Europe and tries to explain the healers' relative successes as well as their patients' dependency on them.

Although these beliefs remain pertinent for Moroccans who live in Europe, they more than often have to rely on healers in Morocco for treatment. A few traditional healers are indeed active in Belgium but they are not seen as the most powerful and they miss the rich cultural context that is, as we shall see, still very much in existence in Morocco. So, although this article relates to fifty years of Moroccan migration in Belgium, practices and situations in Morocco appear to remain relevant and therefore received my focus in the first place.

In 1979 I got a job as a psychologist in a centre for mental healthcare in Brussels. I had studied psychology and anthropology, had developed an interest in Moroccan culture, and was learning Moroccan Arabic. The centre was set up as an answer to the growing number of immigrants, especially Moroccans and Turks, who needed psychological guidance and psychiatric care. It was one of the first in Belgium to opt for a transcultural approach which meant that clients could express themselves in their native language and that their cultural background was taken into consideration. Soon my colleagues and I became aware that many Moroccans lived through their illnesses in ways we were not used to. Not only were their complaints strange to us but they also held very different conceptions of the nature and cause of their disorders. Some patients told us about the healers they went to see in Morocco who seemed to understand them better. I wanted to figure out what really occurred during these traditional treatments. To that end I observed the practices of Moroccan faith healers in Belgium, the Netherlands and especially Morocco and interviewed them as well as their patients. Starting in 2002 I had the opportunity to focus on the religious shrine of Ben Yeffu in Morocco. It is situated in the countryside about 120 km south of the city of El Jadida and about 20 km inland from the Atlantic coast. People come to the shrine to call in the aid of two Islamic saints who lived in the fourteenth century A.D. Their living descendants continue to heal the sick and help the unfortunate. During four consecutive years I carried out ethnographic fieldwork for a month in the region of El Jadida, in particular the shrine of Ben Yeffu in collaboration with Mohammed Maarouf, a colleague of El Jadida University.

The shrine of Ben Yeffu (source: Philip Hermans)

The Jinn

Many Moroccans assume that illnesses can be caused by supernatural powers, especially spirit-like beings called jinn. This is probably the main reason why, notwithstanding the existence of a modern official healthcare system, traditional healing practices are still thriving in Morocco. Indeed all kinds of traditional healers are active here. Many operate from a personalistic understanding of the causes of illness. According to a personalistic aetiology illnesses are directly caused by another, often supernatural being that intends to harm deliberately. The sick person is therefore considered to be the victim of this being. In Morocco, jinn, a kind of spirits or demons, are perceived as playing the most important role in causing illness and misfortune. Other invoked personalistic causes are sorcery and the evil eye where it is human beings who bring about illness by supernatural means.

There might be some confusion concerning the English and Moroccan Arabic terminology. While in English jinn is the plural form of jinnee, in Moroccan Arabic *jinn* is the singular form and *jnun* the plural; a female jinnee is a *jinniya*.

The belief in jinn is very much alive in Morocco and like the belief in angels and the devil it is part of Islamic dogma. The Koran specifies that Allah created the jinn from smokeless fire. They are further mentioned in at least 15 of the 114 of its chapters. While orthodox Islam does not provide much detail about these spirits, Moroccan folklore does so all the more. The jinn are usually invisible and are not subject to the ordinary laws of nature. On the other hand, they are very similar to human beings. They are male or female and reproduce. They have been endowed with reason and especially emotion. Their social organization can be seen as a mirror image of the traditional Moroccan social order. For example they live in families, tribes and nations and have sultans who keep armies and hold court. They can be of Islamic, Jewish or Christian persuasion or pagan. Apparently they speak human languages. For their lodging and food they depend on what nature provides or what people produce. Jinn inhabit places of all sorts but prefer caves, sewers, rivers, lavatories and slaughterhouses. Sometimes they occupy the houses people are living in. They are particularly keen on blood and milk but loathe salt. Though normally invisible they can take on animal or human forms. Black dogs and cats, especially when caught sight of at night, are often thought to be jinn.

Some jinn have proper names and are known for their peculiarities. Most famous or infamous is the *jinniya* Aisha Qandisha. She may appear as a beautiful girl, seduces men and makes them her slaves. Such men are said to be married to her and will not be able to tie the knot or to make love to another woman.

Although jinn and people are thought to live in separate worlds, the demons take an important place in everyday Moroccan life and are called upon to explain unusual and uncanny phenomena. This has to be understood in the context of the traditional Moroccan worldview that is impregnated by supernatural phenomena receiving their meaning from popular Islam. A strange noise at night will easily be attributed to jinn, often jokingly, but one never knows for sure... Some people are known for the yarns they spin about jinn guarding treasures and about creepy encounters with these creatures. However, it is when people fall ill or are hit by misfortune that they will presume this may be the doings of a jinnee. Jinn are very capricious, unpredictable and revengeful. If a person inadvertently hurts a jinnee it will retaliate by making him ill or taking possession of him. The most common explanation is that jinn attack because people pour away hot water without enouncing the protective formula *b ismi llah* (in Allah's name) and then scold the demon. A jinnee may also attack or enslave someone because he is sexually attracted to him or her. Extraordinary circumstances make people more vulnerable, especially in situations of transition such as birth, circumcision and marriage. Emotional situations such as sadness, excitation and anxiety are also a case in point. People who do not comply with their religious duties should also fear the jinn. Finally women are more prone to become preyed upon by jinn as they are seen as weaker than men.

The most severe kind of affliction jinn cause is possession. In this case one or more jinn actually inhabit a person's body and take over his personality. Typical symptoms of possession are mental confusion, agitation and aggression as well as behaviour that would receive the label of psychotic, manic, hysteric, schizophrenic or melancholic in western psychiatry (Lim, Hoek & Blom, 2015). When a jinnee has only struck or touched a person the symptoms are different. Deafness, blindness, paralysis, pain and even death, especially when they occur suddenly are interpreted as such. However, all illnesses that are enduring will sooner than later be attributed to jinn. The same counts when modern medicine can bring no solution. Moreover when medical examinations cannot demonstrate an organic pathology it is often seen as proof of a jinnee's actions. Mental disorders for which modern psychiatry does not have an immediate solution and that are characterized by hallucinations, delusions and changes in personality are therefore easily credited to jinn. Vague complaints and life problems experienced as illness are also frequently understood in terms of such supernatural phenomena, as well as impotence, conjugal problems and bad luck in general.

Healers

The most important healer who works from a personalistic aetiology is the *fqih* (plural: *fuqaha*) or Islamic cleric. *Fuqaha* have had a traditional education that mainly consists of learning the Koran by heart. Many enter into an agreement with a local community to be appointed as imam in a mosque where they lead the believers into prayer and work as Koranic schoolteachers. Giving advice in matters of religion, reciting the Koran on special occasions and writing amulets belong to their standard activities. Not everyone can become an imam and therefore some self-assign themselves as healers. They receive their patients at home, in a shop or in a tent in the marketplace. They make their diagnosis by listening to their patients' complaints and by carrying out calculations on the letters of the patient's and his or her mother's first name as well as other esoteric means. As for treatment a *fqih* will usually start with reciting some verses from the Koran and imploring Allah and the saints. One of the important principles of prophetic medicine, a healthcare system based on the customs and sayings of the prophet, states that the Koran is the best of medicine (Ibn Qayyim Al Jawziyya, 1998: 47-48, 126-128, 132-141, 246-248). The Koran (17: 82) confirms 'That which We have revealed in the Koran is a balm and a blessing to true believers, though it adds nothing but ruin to evil-doers'. Suras useful in case of jinn afflicted illnesses are 'The Fatiha', 'The Jinn', 'Daybreak', 'Men' as well as 'The Throne Verse' from 'The Cow'.

While reciting the *fqih* will touch his client, hold or even slap him. All these procedures have the aim of expelling the jinnee. Koranic verses are said to scorch demons, break spells and neutralize the evil eye. Apart from Koranic verses also unintelligible, secret phrases are used.

A fqih writing an amulet (source: Philip Hermans)

Fuqaha also make use of written amulets (*hejab, sbub, harz, tslamin, tbarid*). These are bits of paper on which signs or words have been written. They are then inserted in a small plastic, leather or foil pouch which the client has to wear on his body. Water in which the ink of similar bits of paper has been dissolved is also used as a potion. The patient must drink it or rub it over his body for three or seven consecutive days usually at the time of evening prayer. Water over which

Koranic verses have been recited is used in the same way. Amulets can also be used as fumigation. Together with a handful of herbs they are thrown on a blazing charcoal brazier. The patient must stride over this to fumigate his body. Other specific techniques are practiced (see for instance Hermans, 1999) but the most impressive form of treatment is exorcism by which *fuqaha* try to expel one or more possessing jinn by engaging them in a kind of battle. Healers usually resort to this practice when they are presented with an unconscious, psychotic or aggressive patient. Exorcism is a well-known technique in Morocco. It usually starts with reciting verses from the Koran that provoke or scare the jinnee and trigger his manifestation. The healer then addresses the jinnee directly, interrogates him and forces him to leave. The jinnee answers through the mouth of the patient and complies or, as is more often the case, refuses to go. Some *fuqaha* can become very heavy-handed when jinn refuse to obey. They press their patients against the ground and hold them firmly. This goes along with a lot of yelling and scolding. In extreme cases patients get thoroughly beaten up. Other *fuqaha* believe they can obtain better results by staying kind and respectful towards the jinn.

Not all practicing healers are *fuqaha*. Fortune-tellers (*shuwwafa*) for instance are also active in the business, mainly women to whom the position of *fqih* is not open (Hermans, 2006). Fortune-tellers often claim to have been possessed by jinn, enabling them to gain access to their world and to receive their help. In vague terms they forecast the future and the fate of their clients and warn them of immanent dangers or predict important events in their lives. Especially 'the other' is pointed out as the cause of all misfortune. Fortune-tellers also uncover the causes of illness and misfortune which they mainly interpret in terms of jinn, the evil eye or sorcery. They may recommend or offer medicinal herbs, give reassurance, recite Koranic verses or other formulas and perform healing rituals themselves. They may also advise their clients to go on a pilgrimage, to sacrifice an animal or to take part in the rituals of a religious brotherhood.

Fuqaha and *shuwwafat* are not only active in the most traditional fringes of Moroccan society. Patients from all walks of society appear to consult them. Some of them practice through the telephone and the internet. They are also active in Belgian and Dutch cities with a large Moroccan population, such as Antwerp, Brussels, Rotterdam and Amsterdam. Generally they are not seen as potent as those who practice in Morocco. They also miss the importance of a supporting environment that is pregnant with meaning. Therefore many immigrants make use of their yearly holiday to visit healers and shrines in their country of origin.

Saints

Saints (*siyyed, wali, saleh, mrabit* or *marabout*) hold an important place in popular Moroccan Islam. They are not canonized by any religious authority but were recognized by the people as holy and as representatives of Allah on earth because of their remarkable religious lives. Many were historical figures but all kinds of myths and legends were made up around them that proved their exceptional standing. Saintly lineages played an important political role in Morocco's tribal past and important scions became local lords who were later venerated as saints. Descent from the prophet played an important role in becoming holy. Many saints are indeed *shurfa* which means they trace their filiation from the prophet via his daughter Fatima. This by itself is not enough and has to be paired with extraordinary actions and qualities such as exceptional power, piety, detachment or erudition. By performing miracles (*karama*) they showed they possessed Allah's blessing (*baraka*). Legends often relate that saints did not fear to summon the sultan because of his injustices. Tensions with the sultan were generally resolved with the saint withdrawing his curse and the sultan recognizing the saint's sharifian descent. Some saints founded religious brotherhoods such as the Hamadasha and the Aisawa that are also active in curing the afflicted. The Moroccan countryside is dotted with shrines and domes (*qubba*) that were built in the course of time to house the tomb of a saint. Every town has its patron *marabout* and many neighbourhoods have their own local saint. Inside these constructions a catafalque represents the saint's tomb. Some are small, some have not been maintained for many years while others have evolved into large complexes and institutions with multiple functions and receiving dozens of pilgrims on a daily base.

Pilgrims come to implore saints for all kinds of favours. They can call in their aid for every legitimate wish such as finding a spouse, having a child, succeeding in an exam, winning a lawsuit, breaking a spell, getting revenged for a perceived wrong but generally they come for a cure. Some saints are specialized in the healing of particular diseases, for instance jinn-caused illnesses.

The shrine of Ben Yeffu

A case in point is the shrine of Ben Yeffu on which I focused my later research. The name refers to Saint Sidi Abd l Aziz Ben Yeffu who, according to legend and semi-historical sources, founded the shrine and a fiefdom in the fourteenth century. Such a shrine is called a *zawiya* in Moroccan Arabic. The term denotes the quarters where the members of a religious brotherhood or the descendants of an Islamic saint meet and practice. It includes the mausolea and tombs of the saint and his descendants, a mosque, a Koranic school, meeting quarters, houses, shops and stalls. Legend lets Ben Yeffu descend from the prophet Mohammed via his daughter Fatima Zahra, Sultan Mulay Idriss, the founder of Morocco's first dynasty; and Mulay Abd s Slam Ben Mshish, one of Morocco's most important saints. The name Yeffu refers to the sound of the scorching breath he blew (*bukh*) to burn a monstrous jinnee. By this first miracle he established his sainthood.

Treating the eyes by blowing (bukh) (source: Philip Hermans)

Upon arrival pilgrims usually buy a few bundles of candles from one of the shops outside the shrine. They enter through the main gateway and cross two courtyards to arrive at the saints' cupola crowned mausolea (*qbab*, singular: *qubba*). Underway they pass the *mehkama*, literally the tribunal, where a selected number of the saint's descendants, called *hufdan* (singular: *hafid*) have taken place and who in turn run the shrine and act as healers. Only a few of them are trained *fuqaha*. The visitors offer candles and a few dirhams. Then they proceed

A hafid blessing and tapping with his kelkha (source: Philip Hermans)

to the mausolea. On entering they take off their shoes. Some kiss the doorposts. They then approach the tomb and kiss its four posts.

Pilgrims recite formulas as "Oh Lord Sultan! Oh Sidi Abd l Aziz! Oh Red Soil! I come to you but Allah is my destination. May my needs be fulfilled by your strength and the strength of Allah!' or `Oh Sidi Abd l Aziz! I call upon you to dry my tears. I come here with all my sorrow and complaints!" Some pilgrims ask Sidi Ali to curse someone: "Oh Sidi Ali! I have come directly to you but Allah is my aim. I accuse so-and-so before your court. He has wronged me and I wish his family to break up!"

People will light a candle and find a place against the wall or the tomb (*tabut*) to settle down for a while. Some will put their feet under the pall that is draped over the *tabut* or wipe their tears on it. Others lean against the *tabut* or press their painful limbs against it so that its *baraka* rubs off on them. Some people have brought orange blossom water *(ma zhar)* to sprinkle over the *tabut* and other visitors. Some put their hands under the *tabut* to gather dust that has collected there and rub the grime that is saturated with *baraka* over their faces. Meanwhile they express their wishes in whispers or in silence. Finally some people might stretch out on the floor and try to rest or dose away.

After their visit to the saints people return to the *mehkama*. A *hafid* will bless them. He takes the visitor's head in his hands and recites the appropriate Koranic verses. Then follows a short ritual exorcism *(sri'a)* by which he gently taps the pilgrim's body from top to toe with his *kelkha,* a light stick. Then he blows *(bukh)* on the face and in the ears. Meanwhile he murmurs a formula such as: "In the name of Allah, the Healer, the Curer. Oh Lord Sultan Ben Yeffu. Oh Red Soil. Oh Sid l Bdawi, judge of accusations. Oh owner of the white horse!' or `Oh rescuers! Oh preferred people of Allah! Here is your son! Allah heals and cures until you don't feel any pain!" The *hufdan* further recite from the Koran or from their own poetry. I often heard 'The Sword that rules the Jinn'. It starts with eulogising Allah and the prophet and goes on praising Sidi Abd l Aziz Ben Yeffu. He is compared to the beauty of the full moon and the break of day. He is the healer who helps everyone. With the will of Allah he heals all illnesses. He does not have to rely on herbs, powders, quicksilver, hot irons or cupping, the remedies of the time, but disposes of a treasure of secrets to cure the sick. He is a sultan who rules with wisdom. When his descendants blow, their breath turns into a scorching flame that burns the jinn. People appeal to him from overseas and offer him sheep and cattle to thank him. His brother, Sidi Ali, is compared to a hawk who chases jinn as if they were birds.

The mehkama (left) and the entrance to Sidi Ali's mausoleum (source: Philip Hermans)

Some men will ask to be tread upon *(afs)*. They will prostrate themselves in front of the *hafid* and remain lying at length on the ground, face down. The healer will put his right foot on their back and more or less gently start treading on the back, neck and back of the head as if giving a kind of massage by foot. After the blessing and treatment the visitor kisses the *hafid* on his forehead, hand or shoulder as a sign of respect. Then he slips him a few dirhams as payment.

The *hafid* continues with a supplication *(fatha)* for his patient, the other *hufdan* present joining in. The client will receive a few candles, some red soil or a written amulet, all said to contain the saint's *baraka*.

The shrine leases small rooms or rather cells where patients can stay for a few days to undergo the beneficial influence of being on-site and imbibing the saint's *baraka*. In a dream they might even receive a revelation or be exorcised.

This is how a regular benediction takes place. People who come for a particular problem or illness will inform a *hafid* and get more advice or a specific treatment.

Exorcism

An exorcism is such a specific form of treatment. While blessings and ordinary treatments proceed in a calm and easy manner, exorcisms are of an entirely

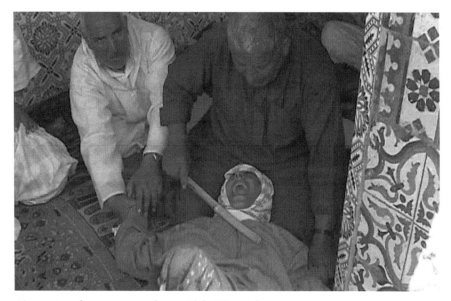

The exorcism of a young woman (source: Philip Hermans)

different order. They can be very animated, rowdy, even violent. Here follows the description of a ritual I experienced at Ben Yeffu during the *musem* (annual pilgrimage and fair) in August 2003.

A woman brings her subdued daughter to the *mehkama*. When the *hafid* takes the girl's head in both hands and starts to recite the Koran, she drops down and starts to yell. He grabs her hand and presses it to the ground. Another *hafid* joins in seizing her other hand. The girl shrieks and tries to pull herself loose but is pushed back to the ground. Meanwhile her mother holds on to her legs. As they all hold her under control the *hafid* continues to mumble. She goes on shrieking and shouting. A crowd of onlookers has gathered.

> Then the *hafid* orders: "Come, get out! Go away."
> The girl tries to wriggle herself free and keeps shouting.
> The *hafid*: "Off with you, get out! In Allah's name, get out, stop! What are you doing? Leave this woman and never come back."
> The *hafid* releases the hand he is holding to see if the girl will remain calm, but as this is not the case he grabs hold of her again and asks: "Are you a man or a woman? ..."
> The girl: "Ouch, oh, oh."
> The *hafid* grasps the other hand and holds the girl firmly to the ground.
> The *hafid:* "Are you a believer? Are you a Moslem, a Christian or a Jew? ..."
> The girl/jinnee: "Yes!"
> From now on the *hufdan* and onlookers presume and act as if it is the jinnee who answers through the girl's mouth. The unintelligible howling that follows apparently reinforces the onlookers' belief that it really is a jinnee who has taken over.
> The *hafid:* "Go away! Leave this woman. Hurry up! From where do you want to leave, from her hands, her mouth or her feet?"
> Jinnee: "Her hands!"
> The girl continues to shriek and moan.
> The *hafid* starts to beat her hands and breast with his *kelkha*.
> Jinnee: "Ouch."
> *The hafid:* "Leave! Hurry up! What are you playing at? Do you want us to make you suffer more?"
> Jinnee: "No! No!"

The *hafid:* "Then go! I will now take care of you. Put your hands down! Hurry up! Off you go! You are only making it more difficult for yourself."
Jinnee: "Don't make me suffer."
The *hafid:* "Then hurry up and leave."
The *hafid* hits her right arm and hand for a while.
Jinnee: "Ouch, ouch!"
The *hafid:* "Get out! If you return I promise you a terrible punishment."

The girl calms down. The *hafid* stops hitting her. He holds her head in both hands and starts reciting the Koran again. He then presses his thumbs on her eyes. The girl stays put. She winces in pain. The *hafid* starts to hit her hand again but now more gently than before. He softly massages her arm and upper chest. She is much calmer now. Lying on her back she seems to have fallen asleep. After a few minutes she wakes up, opens her eyes and looks bewildered. The *hafid* helps her up and encouragingly pats her on her back.

Roqiya

In contrast to popular Islam, orthodox Sunni Islam, that appeals more to the educated and sophisticated part of the population, accepts only koranic incantations (*roqiya*) and the use of hallowed water as healing methods. It rejects many aspects of traditional healing as described above such as the idea of the heredity of *baraka*, the power and status of *fuqaha* and the belief in saints as well as the obviously magical features of its techniques. These are all seen as *bid'ah* or heretical "innovation". The expansion of Salafism, as an ultraconservative and puritanical form of Sunni Islam, has given rise to a growing number of people practicing *roqiya* (Touag, 2013). In their eyes the healing power of the sacred word is hereby reinstated and in principle this method can be acquired by every devout Muslim without depending on inherited mystic powers.

The cure

First a visit to a healer and certainly a shrine is of a different order than a call on a doctor or a consultation at a hospital. There is an important devotional aspect. Of course patients expect a cure but at the same time they come to express their belief in and their dependency on the saints and the almighty, they come to submit to him and to lay their destiny in his hands. That being said it is not easy to establish if and how patients really get better at the hands of the *hufdan* at Ben Yeffu or of other traditional Moroccan healers. As an anthropologist in the field one can hardly organise medical check-ups. Though I did not witness a lot of striking recoveries during my years of research I did hear many accounts of patients who had benefited from traditional treatments. Above more healers at shrines such as that of Ben Yeffu continue to attract loads of patients. So, what can be the cause of their success?

Believers, healers as well as their patients, explain the traditional healing process in terms of the notion of *baraka*. This is a supernatural blessing, a miraculous force, an emanation of the divine into this world. It is this force that in one way or another vanquishes the jinn who are ultimately seen as the cause of all ails. Certain objects but also plants, animals and human beings possess *baraka* and are therefore able to generate prosperity. The Koran and its recitation hold plenty of *baraka*. Saints, as friends of God, par excellence possess *baraka*. Many thank their power to their descent from the prophet and have proven it by miracles they performed. Their descendants inherit their *baraka*. Where other healers also refer to their Koranic and esoteric expertise the *hufdan* at Ben Yeffu boast that their power to heal resides totally in their ancestor's *baraka* and works automatically, even involuntary. In one of their poems they praise Ben Yeffu as the doctor who cures all ails by Allah's will and without the help of other means or techniques.

Of course this explication can hardly be reconciled with the insights of modern bio-medical sciences. Anthropology and transcultural psychiatry have formulated a number of explications about the workings and successes of traditional healing. Many boil down to the idea that these treatments address in a symbolic way the social significances and tensions that are acted out or expressed in the behaviour and symptoms of the afflicted and by doing so reconcile them with their social environment and restore them to health. (Turner, 1968; Crapanzano, 1976; Kleinman, 1980; Dow, 1986; Devisch, 1993).

The placebo effect

The problem with these kinds of explanations is that they do not take into account enough the huge variation in complaints, symptoms, illnesses and other troubles that are presented. All these cannot be reduced to one sole social or cultural predicament. Above more the healers do not even try to pose a specific diagnosis or to make a psychological or social analysis. Every illness, whatever its nature, is ultimately perceived as caused by a jinnee who has to be cast out with the *baraka* of Ben Yeffu and by the grace of Allah. More or less every benediction, treatment or exorcism follows the same stereotypical pattern.

Therefore I have not tried to explain the *hufdan's* successes in terms of symbolic cultural transactions or psychoanalytical processes but actually in terms of the non-specific workings of the placebo effect. I will not use this notion as a *deus ex machina* that simply saves the plot without further explanation but I will try to analyse the basic sociological and psychological workings of this effect as they appear to operate at Ben Yeffu.

The placebo effect is the effect that a patient gets better because he believes he is receiving an effective drug or another form of therapy, even if this treatment contains no active ingredient or is inefficient. Apparently the significance of the treatment triggers psychological and even biological processes that lead to actually feeling and getting better (Torrey, 1986; Moerman, 2002; Evans, 2003; Singh & Ernst, 2008). The more a treatment is perceived as effective the stronger the placebo effect appears to be. Hence it is important the patient is convinced his treatment is extremely potent. It is even better if his healer believes this too. In this context symbols become important again at least on the condition that they support the conviction that a treatment is powerful.

The *hufdan* of Ben Yeffu appear to be masters in managing the placebo effect, which is in presenting themselves as majestic and powerful healers and in raising the hopes of their patients enormously (Hermans, 2015). To start with they share the worldview of their patients and operate in the context of popular Islam. This implies they have the power to exceed the laws of nature.

Moreover the Koran figures highly in their rituals. This is Allah's word. There is nothing more potent. The *hufdan* claim to be descendants in a long line of famous and powerful saints that goes back to the prophet Mohammed, the most important person that ever walked on the face of the earth. We already know they are endowed with a lot of *baraka*. Prayers and supplications to the saints and the Almighty are an integral part of their rituals. This way they fuse healing and religion, which enhances the perceived power of the cure.

But the *hufdan* also associate themselves with the symbols of secular power. Ben Yeffu is called a sultan, but, as the legend goes, a sultan who was much more powerful than the Black Sultan who reigned at the time and whom he defied and overpowered. He also showed himself more formidable than other saints in the neighbourhood. Above more he is a mighty judge, but rules not only over human beings but also over the jinn. Rituals of exorcism often take the form of a lawsuit with an interrogation and the conviction and eviction of the offending fiend. Exorcism rituals are very spectacular and emotional. The portrayed and perceived "reality" of these performances reaffirms the belief in the existence of these beings, the traditional worldview as well as the power of the *hufdan*.

In the past the *zawiya* received royal decrees (*dahir*) that allowed the descendants of the saint to exploit the land and that declared they had to be honoured and respected. Nowadays the Moroccan regime (*makhzen*) subsidises the sanctuary, undoubtedly to safeguard this aspect of the country's cultural heritage as well as for political reasons, but the healers and people see this as a recognition and approval of everything that occurs there. This of course increases the *hufdan's* prestige even more. The buildings of the hallowed sanctuary are imposing, certainly when they are compared to the humble dwellings of most of the pilgrims. Here everything is possible. Above more the surroundings of the *zawiya* are loaded with symbols that testify to Ben Yeffu's wondrous importance such as an imprint of the hoof of his white horse (*afsa*), a miraculous cairn (*kerkur*), a well (*bir*) containing healing water, a red hill (*'aqba hemra*) of which the soil is used to keep jinn at bay, a cavern (*khelwa*) where the jinn are imprisoned, and graveyards with numerous tombs of lesser saints.

The narratives, myths and rumours about Ben Yeffu and his successors also increase the prestige of the healers as well as the hope of their patients. During my visits nearly always someone was singing Ben Yeffu's praise and spinning yarns about miraculous cures spectacular exorcisms. Most impressive was the account about a Princess of the United Arab Emirates who obtained a miraculous cure for her incurable deemed paralysed son in 1985. By way of thanks she let a grand mosque be built next to the shrine and let the village of Ben Yeffu be electrified. Apparently she still provides the funds for maintaining the building and for paying the salaries of the imam and other personnel. All this has left a deep impression on the local population and pilgrims. They consider the miracle as a living proof that the saint and his descendants have not lost their power in any way.

Furthermore also the techniques of the *hufdan* are impressive. Their fast and categorical diagnoses correspond with their patient's worldview. Being blessed, touched and ritually beaten by one of these impressive robed and turbaned characters brings about intense emotions. The expectations of the patients are raised by mixing supplications and suggestions and by explicitly declaring that the treatment has been successful. Lastly, there is always a message of hope. The *hufdan* never predict a negative outcome nor will a patient hear that he has a ten percent chance to survive or that he must learn to live with his problem. Allah willing, Ben Yeffu and his descendants can always cure.

Of course an elaborate exorcism is not an agreeable experience for the patient but it remains a very dramatic and impressive event, even more so for the onlookers, whose belief in jinn is once more actualised. The genius and power of the exorcist as he evokes one or more jinn, the way he manages the dialogue and finally expels the fiend compels amazement and awe.

The sense of being able to master one's problems is also important in increasing a patient's expectations. The *hufdan* accomplish this by giving their patients assignments to deal with their problem, for instance by wearing a protecting amulet, preparing and drinking a concoction, by scattering some red soil in their house to keep the jinn at bay, sacrificing a chicken or a ram to the jinn, even organising a full blown nightly ceremony (*lila*) by a religious brotherhood involving ecstatic dancing, a sacrifice and a communal meal.

The placebo effect may be more important than we ever thought but after all its strength is limited. It goes without saying that the effect will be more obvious in the case of psychosomatic disorders, certain mental disorders and especially in situations where the burdens of poverty and a hard life are experienced as illness. The effect will also be greater on the subjective experience of an illness, which is influenced by culture, and less on basic biological dysfunction. For this reason a temporary improvement of the complaints is to be expected for these kinds of treatments. A traditional approach can mean an important support, but for many afflictions there is not much it can do. It cannot be that a section of the population must make do with therapies that only rely on the placebo effect while the advantages of scientific medicine remain reserved for the higher classes.

On the other hand, we may look down upon a form of therapy that is solely based on the placebo effect as well as on its practitioners and users. Let us not forget that many alternative therapies that are successful in our (post)modern societies such as homeopathy, acupuncture, chiropractic, and osteopathy as well as many forms of psychotherapy rely on this same principle (Torrey, 1986, Singh & Ernst, 2008).

Research at the shrine of Ben Yeffu gave rise to three monographs: Hermans (2007), Maarouf (2007) and Rhani (2014). They offer more insight than this short article could achieve in the practices and processes taking place at the shrine as well as further implications and interpretations of Moroccan faith healing.

Conclusion

Although traditional healing is probably becoming less important for people with a Moroccan background who live in Belgium, many still accept its beliefs and assumptions as true. It is in particular when they find no relief in the official health care system or when their symptoms suggest to them that their illness is of a supernatural order that some actively resort to traditional healers. Shrines even remotely resembling that of Ben Yeffu do of course not exist in Belgium but in all Belgian cities with a concentration of people from Moroccan origin some *fuqaha, shuwwafat* and even a few religious brotherhoods are active. Regrettably they miss the rich cultural context that prevails in Morocco and are not perceived as very potent so people will usually continue their quest for traditional therapies in Morocco itself.

However, it is important for Belgian therapists and healthcare workers to be aware of their patients' backgrounds in order to better understand their complaints and problems and to be able to engage with them and counsel them in more efficient ways. As the staffs of healthcare institutions become increasingly multiethnic this is happening already automatically. The ethnopsychiatric approach (Watrin, 2014) that is implemented in certain practices goes further. Here the patient is received and taken care of in a semi-public setting by a mixed group of specialised healthcare professionals and interpreters under the direction of a psychiatrist. Consultation is possible in the patient's own language and the patient's beliefs, feelings and experiences are taken seriously. Therapy consists in working with the patient's perceptions and combining them with the therapist's own theoretical perspectives.

Acknowledgements

Many thanks to my wife, Hilda Dorissen, for proofreading and commenting and to Nadia Fadil for her comments on a first version of this article.

Bibliography

Crapanzano, V. (1973). *The Hamadsha. A study in Moroccan ethnopsychiatry*. Berkeley: University of California Press.

Devisch, R. (1993). *Weaving the threads of life. The Khita gynecological healing cult among the Yaka*. Chicago: University of Chicago Press.

Dow, J. (1986). Universal aspects of symbolic healing: a theoretical synthesis. *American Anthropologist* 88, 56-69.

Evans, D. (2003). *Placebo. The belief effect*. London: Harper-Collins.

Hermans P. (2006). The success of Zohra, a female healer. Emancipation in a traditional Moroccan setting? *Kolor* 6(1) 71-80.

Hermans, P. (1999). Buzellum behandelen in El Jadida. In: M.C. Foblets & C. Pang (eds.), *Culture, ethnicity and migration. Liber Amicorum Prof. dr. E. Roosens*. Leuven: Acco, 29-42.

Hermans, P. (2015). Rituels de guérison et effet placebo: le cas de Ben Yeffou. In: B. Dupret, Z. Rhani, A. Boutaleb & J.-N. Ferrié (eds), *Le Maroc au present: d'une époque à l'autre, une société en mutation*. Casablanca: Fondation du Roi Abdul-Aziz Al Saoud / Rabat: Centre Jacques-Berque, 745-754.

Hermans, P. (2007). *De wereld van de djinn. Traditionele Marokkaanse geneeswijzen*. Amsterdam: Bulaaq.

Ibn Qayyim Al Jawziyya. *Medicine of the Prophet*. (Fourteenth century Arabic text translated by P. Johnstone, 1998. Cambridge: The Islamic Texts Society).

Lim, A., Hoek, H., & Blom, J. (2015). The attribution of psychotic symptoms to jinn in Islamic patients. *Transcultural psychiatry*, 52(1), 18-32.

Maarouf, M. (2007). *Jinn Eviction as a Discourse of Power. A Multidisciplinary Approach to Moroccan Magical Beliefs and Practices*. Leiden: Brill.

McElroy, A. (1996). Medical Anthropology. In: D. Levinson & M. Ember (eds), *Encyclopedia of Cultural Anthropology*. New York: Henry Holt and Company, 759-763.

Moerman, D. (2002). *Meaning, medicine and the 'placebo effect'*. Cambridge: Cambridge University Press.

Rhani, Z. (2014). *Le pouvoir de guérir. Mythe, mystique et politique au Maroc*. Amsterdam: Brill, 2014.

Romanucci-Ross, L., Moerman, D. & Tancredi, L. (1997). *The Anthropology of Medicine. From Culture to Method*. Westport: Bergin & Garvey.

Singh, S. & Ernst, E. (2008). *Trick or treatment? Alternative medicine on trial*. London: Transworld Publishers.

Society for Medical Anthropology, *Medical Anthropological Quarterly*, 1972-2016.

Torrey, E. (1986). *Witchdoctors and psychiatrists. The common roots of psychotherapy and its future*. New York: Harper & Row.

Touag, H. (2013). Guérir par l'islam: l'adoption du rite prophétique – roqya – par les salafistes en France et en Belgique. In B. Maréchal & F. El Asri, *Islam belge au pluriel*, Presses Universitaires de Louvain, 201-218.

Turner, V. (1968). *The drums of affliction. A study of religious processes among the Ndembu of Zambia*. Oxford: Clarendon.

Watrin, D. (2014). L'ethnopsychiatrie, une autre voie pour soigner les traumatismes des migrants. Retrieved 24 April 2016 from http://www.crvi.be/index.php/2014-03-03-15-37-14/revue-de-presse/4034-article-l-ethnopsychiatrie-une-autre-voie-pour-soigner-les-traumatismes-des-migrants

15. How do Moroccan Muslims in Belgium deal with death and dying?

Bert Broeckaert, Stef Van den Branden,
Goedele Baeke & Chaïma Ahaddour

Since the end of the Second World War, most European countries have gradually developed into postmodern multicultural and multireligious societies. In Belgium, as in the majority of European countries, within a few decades Islam has become the second largest religion (Barrett, et al., 2000). These evolutions constitute an important challenge to the ways in which our society deals with death and dying, as these are still deeply influenced by secular-Western ways of thinking and/or Christian approaches and thus tend to pay insufficient attention to the impact and the perspectives of other traditions (Halman & Draulans, 2004).

In the care for the elderly and more in particular in the end-of-life care this new cultural and religious diversity will become more and more tangible. At this moment, however, there is hardly any scientific research available on a national as well as an international level whose research data and informed policy proposals have enabled a well-founded policy in this field, a policy necessary to be able to guarantee people from minority groups decent and respectful end-of-life care.

At the same time recent studies indicate the ageing of the Belgian Muslim population: in 2008 13.381 elderly Moroccans (men and women aged 55+) were living in Belgium (Lodewijckx, 2010). This rapid evolution towards an increasing and socially significant group of elderly Muslim patients as such should not be problematic be it that the increase of elderly community members in need for adequate home care is not paralleled by the sociological evolutions within the communities. Whereas traditionally many Muslim families hold the ideal of taking care of sick and ageing family members within the extended family model, recent studies have observed that throughout the years a shift has occurred from an extended family model to a nuclear family model (Dami & Sheikh, 2000; Sokolovsky, 2009). This shift has resulted in an eroding of the traditional social safety net within Belgian Muslim communities and in an increase of the need for adequate organized support of elderly Muslims (Yerden, 2010). Yet, till today very little is known about the attitudes, beliefs and practices of Muslim communities in Belgium regarding healthcare, elderly care, death and dying.

Interdisciplinary research on end-of-life issues in contemporary multicultural and multireligious society has been one of the central research axes of the Interdisciplinary Centre for the Study of Religion and Worldview and the Research Unit Theological and Comparative Ethics (Faculty of Theology and Religious Studies, KU Leuven) since almost 15 years. Within the framework of this encompassing research programme, several lines of research have been developed. In this chapter we give the most important results of the research we have been doing on Moroccan Muslims in Belgium and end of life ethics since 2002 (Van den Branden, 2006; Van den Branden & Broeckaert, 2008, 2009, 2010, 2011a, 2011b, 2013; Baeke, 2012; Baeke, et al., 2011a, 2011b, 2011c, 2011d, 2012a, 2012b; Ahaddour, et, al., 2015). We will discuss the way elderly Muslims in Belgium deal with illness and health and more specifically with a number of delicate medical-ethical decisions that can or even have to be taken near the end of life.

Treatment decisions in advanced disease: a conceptual framework

Time and again we have pointed out that the ethical issues at the end of life are not just restricted to those of euthanasia. However, we have found that there is still much confusion about for example the difference or the boundary between pain control and euthanasia or between euthanasia and withholding life-sustaining treatment. Therefore, we developed, already in 2006, the following conceptual framework with regard to treatment decisions in advanced disease. It is endorsed by the Flemish Palliative Care Federation, that brings together all palliative care initiatives in Flanders, Belgium and i.a. spread through a brochure (6 editions, 30 000 copies distributed) and numerous lectures and workshops and as a result widely known and used in Belgium (Broeckaert & Federatie Palliatieve Zorg Vlaanderen, 2016). As in the Muslim literature too concepts like euthanasia are often used in many different ways, it is absolutely central, in order to enable a meaningful discussion, to start here too from a clear conceptual framework. The same is of course true for our own empirical work on the ethical attitudes of Muslims in Belgium. A meaningful exploration of views and attitudes regarding euthanasia and other treatment decisions at the end of life is only possible if we use terms and concepts in a univocal way. Therefore this paper too starts with a short presentation of our conceptual framework.

In our framework, we offer a typology of the different kinds of treatment decisions that can be taken in advanced stages of a life-threatening illness. In other words, it is about the different ways medicine can help and support patients with advanced disease. We do not do this because we are so keen on classifications, but because each kind of treatment decision brings about specific ethical issues which can easily be misunderstood when no clear boundaries and differences have been set. We distinguish three major categories of treatment decisions in advanced disease: (1) choices with regard to curative or life-sustaining treatment: is such a treatment initiated or withheld, continued or withdrawn?; (2) choices with regard to palliative treatment and symptom control, i.e. all treatments aimed at maximizing, in an active way, the incurably ill patient's quality of life and comfort; (3) choices with regard to euthanasia and assisted suicide, where lethal medication is purposefully administered.

In each category choices can and have to be made. A life-sustaining or curative treatment can be started or continued. But it can also be stopped or withheld and this for two reasons: because is no longer deemed effective or meaningful (non-treatment decision), or because the patient simply refuses the treatment (refusal of treatment). As far as our second category – pain and symptom control – is concerned we offer specific and strict definitions of pain control on the one hand and of palliative sedation on the other. A third category consists of voluntary euthanasia and assisted suicide –legalized in a few countries only– and of non-voluntary euthanasia – which is illegal everywhere. Our aim with this framework and these definitions is not to present an ethical evaluation, but just to clarify and separate the different concepts. From the fact that we mention and describe a certain act it cannot be deduced that that we approve of it or advocate it.

**TREATMENT DECISIONS IN ADVANCED DISEASE –
A CONCEPTUAL FRAMEWORK** (Broeckaert)

1. (FORGOING) CURATIVE AND/OR LIFE-SUSTAINING
   TREATMENT
- **Initiating or continuing a curative or life-sustaining treatment**
- **Non-treatment decision:** "withdrawing or withholding a curative or life-sustaining treatment, because in the given situation this treatment is deemed to be no longer meaningful or effective."
- **Refusal of treatment:** "withdrawing or withholding a curative or life-sustaining treatment, because the patient refuses this treatment."

2. PAIN AND SYMPTOM CONTROL
- **Pain control:** "the intentional administration of analgesics and/or other drugs in dosages and combinations required to adequately relieve pain."
- **Palliative sedation:** "the intentional administration of sedative drugs in dosages and combinations required to reduce the consciousness of a terminal patient as much as necessary to adequately relieve one or more refractory symptoms."

3. EUTHANASIA AND ASSISTED SUICIDE
- **Voluntary Euthanasia:** "the intentional administration of lethal drugs in order to painlessly terminate the life of a patient suffering from an incurable condition deemed unbearable by the patient, at this patient's request."
- **Assisted Suicide:** "intentionally assisting a person, at this person's request, to terminate his or her life."
- **Non-voluntary Euthanasia:** "the intentional administration of lethal drugs in order to painlessly terminate the life of a patient suffering from an incurable condition deemed unbearable, not at this patient's request."

Islamic end of life ethics

We cannot understand Muslim attitudes towards specific end of life issues if we do not put them in a much broader theological and ethical framework. In this framework the importance of Qur'an and Hadith cannot be overestimated. God appears in Qur'an as the almighty and all-knowing creator. Toward him submission (Islam) – not just a question of orthodoxy but foremost of orthopraxis – is the only appropriate attitude. At the Last Judgment God will decide the future of each and every man. In death and dying too this eschatological perspective is crucial. From his own analysis of the most important Hadith collections Van den Branden concludes that both illness and cure are attributed to Allah (Van den Branden, 2006). Confronted with unbearable suffering suicide is not an option; in these circumstances patience is the central virtue that holds out the prospect of paradise.

As a result of global migration Islam is confronted with a new reality in which large groups of Muslims are leading their lives in non-muslim countries. Globalization and the ever more important role of the internet have resulted in a globalized Islam and created what Olivier Roy has called a 'virtual ummah' (community) of which every Muslim all over the world is a member (Roy, 2002). An important characteristic of this new globalized Islam is that local traditions tend to disappear from the horizon. In an effort to find answers to the ethical questions of today and especially in a migrant situation Muslims tend to rely on and refer directly to Qur'an and Hadith, forgetting the mediation of local scholars, traditions and schools which used to be so important in traditional Islam.

In order to find out what within this contemporary Sunni 'virtual ummah' is thought about the big ethical questions at the end of life, we reviewed the rare available empirical literature (assessing real world attitudes and practices of Muslims in this area) and studied the views of influential international Muslim authors on these subjects (Rashid Gatrad, Abul Fadl Mohsin Ebrahim, Dadil Boubakeur,…). Special attention was given to the position of a number of influential Muslim organizations that have developed views on these issues (a.o. Islamic Organization of Medical Sciences, European Council for Fatwa Research, Islamic Medical Association of North America and Islamic Social Services Association). A lot of time was spent on a thorough analysis of so-called *e-fatwas*, more specifically decisions on medical-ethical issues around the end of life that can be found on a number of important Sunni websites (including for instance www.islamweb.net, www.islamonline.net, www.understanding-islam. com) – websites that are used in particular by young Muslims in the west to find 'the' Muslim view on specific issues: what do I have to do in this specific situation to be a good Muslim? (Van den Branden, 2006).

As far as the choices regarding curative and/or life-sustaining treatment are concerned, most organizations, authors and *e-fatwas* show only a very conditional and limited acceptance of non-treatment decisions and refusal of treatment. Such choices seem only acceptable when the patient is actually braindead or at least really dying. Artificial hydration and nutrition can never be withheld or withdrawn. Little is written on pain control and nothing on palliative sedation. As far as pain control is concerned, the dominant view is that pain control is acceptable, even in high doses, as long as the intention remains the alleviation of pain and not the shortening of the dying process. All forms of active termination of life (voluntary euthanasia, assisted suicide, non-voluntary euthanasia) are seen as radically forbidden by the organizations, authors and e-fatwas we reviewed. The reason for this blank rejection is clear: like suicide euthanasia denies that God is and should be in control; it is the opposite of a faithful submission to the divine will.

Real world Muslim end of life ethics – methodology

Is there any difference between these theoretical, normative ideals and 'official' positions on the one hand and the real world attitudes of ordinary believers on the other? To find out we did a series of empirical studies involving elderly Moroccan men and women in Belgium focusing on their religious beliefs and practices and on their attitudes and views regarding specific end of life issues.

Because of the delicate nature of the themes to be discussed (dying and death; religion) and the specific characteristics of the population (often illiterate; not speaking Dutch or French; difficult to access) we opted for a qualitative research method using Grounded Theory as our general framework. 35 Semi-structured interviews (till theoretical saturation) of each between one and one and a half hour were conducted with elderly (60+) Moroccan Muslim men and women from various districts in the city of Antwerp, Belgium (the Flemish city with the largest numbers of Muslims from Moroccan descent). Interviews were recorded, transcribed, coded and categorized using MAXqda.

We chose to interview *elderly* Muslims first because the Moroccan migrant population in Antwerp is ageing rapidly and because of their age they are the ones that are most likely to be personally confronted quite soon with the issues we are studying. Women and men were questioned about their religious views and practices; their attitude towards medicine, illness and suffering; their attitudes towards the active termination of life and finally their attitudes towards non-treatment decisions. Given the strong segregation of the sexes in this (age) group of Muslims and the sensitivity of the topics involved, women were interviewed by a female researcher and men by a male. Apart from these elderly men and women as a touchstone five specialists were interviewed: two well-known imams, two Moroccan physicians and one Moroccan nurse, all of them working in Antwerp and very familiar with the elderly Moroccan community our respondents belonged to. All results were compared to those of other empirical studies and the international normative Muslim literature.

Illness

For the elderly Moroccan men and women we interviewed illness is caused by God. But also cure is willed by him. They put their faith in physicians and medicine, though in the end only God decides whether one recovers or not. In any case man can and should fight illness. At the same time he must endure the illness faithfully and patiently; complaining is inappropriate.

"Allah gives illness but we have to do something against it. If we go to the doctor, we must do everything to be cured."

"Allah says 'you have to consult a doctor, and I will do the rest'."

"You must accept it. When you say 'Oh, I'm fed up with it', that's not good. Allah gives the pain, money or health, or... But you must accept. You must stay calm."

"We must be patient and say '*alhamdulillah*' (praise be to Allah). We must not complain."

For many illness is a test by God, a real exam that determines the fate that awaits a person after death. By illness and suffering a person is also purified from sin.

"If you accept your illness, you get another good mark. It's a test".

"Someone who behaved bad, someone who suffers a lot of pain, this means that his sins diminish. If Allah wants him to suffer, this means that he is a bit purified from sin. And if he dies, he will go to paradise".

"It's written in the hadith (words and deeds of prophet Muhammad) that people who are ill for a while pay the penalty, because they have done something wrong. But if they die, they go to paradise, they are purified".

These results are very similar to what we found in the international empirical and normative literature. Here too a theological framework plays an important role in shaping the way people are dealing with illness and suffering: especially in times of illness and suffering one has to submit, faithfully and respectfully, to the divine will.

Interestingly, one elderly Moroccan woman, though still a religious person, did *not* link illness and suffering to Allah. According to her suffering was not caused or willed by God. God only wants what is good for man; Suffering is just a very bad thing and nothing more or else. This very 'deviant' attitude could be linked to her personal confrontation with illness and death: she had lost her husband to cancer a few years before. On the other hand, she had no children, no family in Belgium, only a limited contact with other Muslims here and never attended mosque. This very specific situation too, very different from that of the other respondents, could explain the very different attitude she had towards illness and suffering. None of the male respondents had a similar attitude. Whether this is the result of gender differences remains to be seen.

Active termination of life

In order to learn more about the attitudes of our Moroccan respondents towards specific ethical issues at the end of life –including different forms of active termination of life– we presented them a number of concrete cases and asked for their reactions. How would they respond? And why? As an example we give here the cases that were introduced for the category of active termination of life:

Case 5: non-voluntary euthanasia
A patient is in a deep coma and is living already for many years without the aid of machines. Can a physician give him a lethal injection? Who can decide about this?

Case 6: voluntary euthanasia
A patient is terminally ill, has a life expectancy of only a few weeks and suffers unbearable physical pain that cannot be alleviated. Can the physician end the life of the patient in order to relieve him from his suffering?

Case 7: assisted suicide
A patient is terminally ill, has a life expectancy of only a few weeks and suffers unbearably psychologically or mentally. This suffering cannot be alleviated. Can the physician provide lethal medication to the patient so that he can end his life himself?

The arguments that both male and female respondents gave regarding euthanasia and assisted suicide are very different from the arguments centering around self-determination and quality of life that in a western context are very common. For our respondents active termination of is completely unacceptable.

"*La, haram, ha-ram, ha-ram* [No, Forbidden, Forbidden!, Forbidden!]."

"There is no discussion. There is no discussion, that [euthanasia] is totally *haram*. It is a sin, a sin really, a big sin. It is murder. That is a big sin really, there is no discussion."

"No, that is not allowed. Euthanasia forbidden in Islam. Forbidden. Euthanasia is murder in the Qur'an in the Islam. Euthanasia is equal to murder."

It is up to Allah and only him to decide the moment of death of each and every person. Whoever takes control of this himself, puts himself in the place of Allah and thus acts in an inconceivable and totally unacceptable way – this is nothing but pure blasphemy. Such a person does not show the patience that his expected from him and thus will not enter paradise. Patiently enduring suffering is the motto; decisions on life and death must be left in the hands of God. All forms of active termination of life (euthanasia, assisted suicide) are thus as forbidden as they are inconceivable.

"He [a person getting euthanasia] is not a Muslim, but a heretic. They have no patience. They must have patience and wait until death comes."

"He [a person getting assisted suicide] will go to the fire, because he committed suicide. Allah didn't, he didn't wait for Allah until he would die, he killed himself. Then he will go to the fire. Because he didn't have the patience to wait for his death."

"Someone who commits suicide, will not go to paradise. He does not earn *hassanat* (good marks)."

"It [active termination of life] is a sign that the person disagrees with what Allah has decreed regarding him, because everything what happens with people has already been written down ... So if that person says 'yes, an end to my life', that means that he does not belief in *qadar* [the will of God]. And believing in fate is one of the six pillars of *imaan*, of believing."

Strikingly one woman did show a certain openness regarding euthanasia. This openness could be linked to the suffering she had experienced in her personal life: her husband had died a few years earlier and had suffered a lot. It could indeed be the case that a very real confrontation with suffering and death changes the views and attitudes of people, though this is certainly not a necessity: another respondent, with a very similar experience, was indeed very negative about any form of active termination of life. What was clear however was the fact the respondent who in exceptional cases could accept euthanasia had an image of God that was different from that of the other women: suffering was for her certainly *not* caused or willed by God; she saw God as the protector of human being and could nog imagine that God wanted human beings to suffer. Whether the fact that none of the male respondents showed an openness regarding euthanasia can be ascribed to gender differences or whether it is mere coincidence cannot be concluded at present.

Life-sustaining treatment and pain control

The same theological framework that makes them reject euthanasia lies at the origin of the equally sharp rejection of the withholding or withdrawing of life-sustaining treatment by the vast majority of our respondents. Again they do not reason in terms of autonomy or quality of life. Instead they point to the divine command to take care of one's own body. Man should seek cure and take the treatment that is required. Not only illnesses, but also their remedies are given by God. For the rest it is a matter of trust and submission to God. God decides about life and death; he decides when will be the time of death. It is and remains *haram* to cross this divine plan, e.g. by withdrawing a life-sustaining treatment.

"Among Catholics or Belgian people, it happens, switching off machines or giving a lethal injection. For us, in Islam it is forbidden. It's *haram,* it is not allowed [...] In our religion, it does not happen. They are not allowed to switch off the machines. In our religion, life has to be ended by Allah, not by human being."

For a minority of the respondents refusing a treatment is acceptable, but only when certain conditions are met (including the fact that the patient already and unsuccessfully tried several treatments before). So here too we find important reservations. Refusing a treatment that would work is not an option.

"If they want to die, they turn away from God. That's my opinion, it is like not having faith in God, like taking the right in their own hands."

"Then she dies, Allah will tell her: 'why didn't you do what I... why didn't you have patience? I have given you an illness to be patient, to test your patience'."

Pain medication on the other hand does *not* pose a problem for our respondents, even when given in high doses and when one might think they could have a life-shortening effect. Again: treatment is given by God and can and must be taken. Important here is the belief that for our respondents it would not be the physician or the medication as such that would be causing death when giving these high and potentially life-shortening doses. According to them the possible life-shortening side effect will only be there if God wants it to be. Therefore it is him and no one else (nor the intrinsic effect of the drugs involved – which is denied) who would cause death when pain medication would shorten life.

"The doctor can do nothing actually because I believe in Allah. Even if the doctor says 'look, if you are going to take this [pain] medication, you will die tomorrow', I will take it, because my period of life is in the hands of Allah, not in the hands of the doctor."

"Even if the doctor says your days are limited [as a result of the heavy pain medication], you don't have to take this into account because as a believer you have to believe that nobody can know your lifespan except Allah."

Discussion

Religious motives play a central role in the answers of our respondents to the cases and ethical issues that were presented to them. Both male and female respondents refer very explicitly to general directions they find in Qur'an and Hadith. More importantly throughout the interviews they keep repeating that they want to be good Muslims and that precisely for this reason they are making this or that choice. Patience remains the central virtue. At all times people are requested to maintain a good relation with Allah and to be a good Muslim, not less so when one's health is failing and one is suffering. We hardly found any differences between the sexes regarding these basic views and attitudes (though there was one dissenting female voice as we mentioned earlier).

When we compare the results of our interviews of elderly Moroccan Muslims with what we learned about this group from the interviews with the imams, physicians and nurse, we find a perfect match. Not only regarding the specific attitudes towards specific treatment decisions at the end of life, but also regarding the religious vision and background that explains these attitudes: medical treatments are good and willed by God; a person can and should take them; putting oneself as a human in the place of God by taking control of one's own dying and death and thus determining oneself one's time of death is radically forbidden.

When we compare the attitudes of our Antwerp respondents with the answers we found in the international authors, the views of the international Muslim organizations and the most important e-fatwas, we find very striking similarities. Active termination of life in all its forms (voluntary euthanasia, assisted suicide, non-voluntary euthanasia) is radically forbidden. We find also a similar attitude towards the refusal of treatment – which for most respondents is only allowed if the treatment really doesn't work. As far as non-treatment decisions are concerned, we find some differences. Though if we look more closely the seemingly greater openness in the normative sources in reality amounts to the same dismissive attitude: withholding or withdrawing of artificial hydration or nutrition is never acceptable; only clearly ineffective treatments can be stopped or withheld.

We do however find an interesting difference between our respondents and the normative literature as far as pain control is concerned. For our respondents that see no problem in even very high doses of pain medication, God is in control of everything. There is no such thing as a certain autonomy of earthly realities (e.g. the intrinsic effects of certain chemical substances on the body). The normative sources on the other hand, most likely as result of a much greater familiarity with science, seem to take this intrinsic, automatic operation for granted ("when I give dose x, then, as a result of the intrinsic qualities of the medication given, in this patient the shortening of life is a possible or even likely consequence").

Striking is the big consensus we found between Moroccan Muslim elderly women on the one hand and the Turkish elderly women and Orthodox and Chassidic elderly women we interviewed in other studies on the other hand. All these groups of women are for the largest part very dismissive regarding all forms of active termination of life, including voluntary euthanasia, assisted suicide and non-voluntary euthanasia, and non-treatment decisions that have a life-shortening effect. The image of God of these respondents is very similar: God decides about everything, including illness and health; God judges man; God decides the moment of death. At the same time they experience God's nearness and live in a rather closed community with a strict social control. These factors are likely to explain the lack of variation in ethical positions regarding the topics discussed here. Though it should be noted that even in these very homogeneous groups still a few dissenting voices could be found. Maybe these find their origin in the personal confrontation with suffering and death, but this needs further investigation.

Of course we need to be careful with the results gathered so far. What can be said about these first generation Moroccan Muslims in Belgium cannot be generalized for elderly Moroccan Muslims in Morocco or in the rest of the world, let alone for elderly Muslim everywhere or Muslims everywhere. Elderly Moroccan Muslims in Belgium are far from a clear cross-section of the global elderly Muslim population. For this the group we studied is too specific and too homogeneous: unlike Muslim elderly in many other countries, these people share a very similar socio-economic and cultural background (coming from the same specific regions in Morocco), a similar socio-economic situation, very limited schooling, and a limited interaction with the Belgian and western context.

We are thus very well aware of the limitations of this research. This is not a large scale quantitative study that can test a carefully constructed hypothesis. And more important: very explicitly we have chosen to study the older generation of Moroccan migrants – a generation that is only in a very limited way influenced by the western context it is living in. A generation that is moreover illiterate, hardly educated, had and has a low socio-economic position and is confronted with important language barriers. But also a generation that brought its traditional understanding of Islam and its village religion to Belgium. It would be very interesting to compare the attitudes and ideas that they developed against this traditional background with those of younger Muslim generations that were raised in Belgium, much more exposed to western influences and are much more diverse as far as education and socio-economic position are concerned. And finally: we are of course still dealing with people that are in relatively good health. Not people suffering from an incurable disease of that are terminally ill. How people will respond and act and react when in real life they are confronted with the ethical challenges discusses here on a rather theoretical or hypothetical level is not certain. However, this group of elderly Muslims gives the impression, from their encompassing religious framework, to have deep convictions regarding the ethical choices to be made. The fact that the physicians and palliative nurse we interviewed in their concrete daily experience in the care for the ill and the dying finds the same views and frameworks, points in the same direction.

Future research

Only recently we finished a new series of interviews with both elderly and middle-aged Muslim women of Moroccan descent in Antwerp, Belgium. In this study we no longer focus exclusively on a number of medical and ethical issues at the end of life, but we chose resolutely for a broader perspective that goes from care for the elderly to the period after death. In future research we want to find out how the younger generations of Muslims in Belgium and Europe perceive illness, ageing and the subject of death and dying. In their case, it is no longer the traditional religiosity, which they have imported from their country of origin and have held onto in relative isolation since then, that determines their identity, beliefs and attitudes. They have been brought up in a western environment and have a strong connection with western society through language, education and work. And in that context – influenced by it but just as well reacting to it – they experience and develop their own (religious) identity in different ways and directions.

If we want to improve elderly care and palliative care, then it is of course important to conduct specific research on people, in this case Muslims, in formal elderly care and palliative care. Although, we have a lot of experience with palliative care research, we so far not wanted to conduct research on religious and ethical convictions among palliative patients with a Muslim background. Such research, barely offering immediate advantages for the patient in question, will only be done when we have acquired extensive general knowledge of Muslims and the end of life. We believe that research on these very vulnerable groups for whom time is very precious, is only justified once we have enough background knowledge at our disposal to minimalize the burden of the research for the patient and at the same time to ensure the maximum respect for possible sensitivities. We intend to conduct this research in the near future.

We sometimes receive the request from hospitals for concrete guidelines regarding best practice for dealing with patients belonging to religious or cultural minorities. Preferably, on one sheet of paper and as clearly, practically and univocally formulated as possible. We do, of course, not respond to these requests by providing this one-page document. Instead, in our answers and in the regular workshops and lectures we give on these topics, we try to show that our Belgian and European society has indeed changed radically in terms of religion and culture. Nowadays, our health care system is facing a diversity of attitudes, beliefs and practices that is not familiar to us and sometimes leads to new and unexpected choices and needs. It is of course important to see and understand the cultural and religious roots of some of these demands or refusals. On the other hand, it is equally important to clearly recognize the internal diversity in all religious and cultural groups. "The" Moroccan Muslim (or "the" Jew, "the" Buddhist, ...) does not exist. The only beliefs and attitudes relevant for the care given in the hospital or in the nursing home are those of the concrete patient who is looking you in the eye, not those of the group to which he or she according to your schemes belongs.

Bibliography

Ahaddour, C., Van den Branden, S. and Broeckaert, B. (2015). Institutional elderly care services and Moroccan and Turkish migrants in Belgium: a literature review. *Journal of Immigrant and Minority Health*.

Baeke, G. (2012). *Religion and Ethics at the End of Life. A Qualitative Empirical Study among Elderly Jewish and Muslim Women in Antwerp (Belgium).* Thesis (D Phil). Leuven.

Baeke, G., Wils, J-P. and Broeckaert, B. (2011). 'There is a time to be born and a time to die' (Ecclesiastes 3:2a). Jewish Perspectives on Euthanasia. *Journal of Religion and Health* 50(4), 778-795.

Baeke, G., Wils, J-P. and Broeckaert, B. (2011). 'We are (not) the master of our body'. Elderly Jewish Women's Attitudes towards Euthanasia and Assisted Suicide. *Ethnicity & Health,* 16(3), 259-278.

Baeke, G., Wils, J-P. and Broeckaert, B. (2011) American Jewish Approaches to Contemporary Ethical Issues in Medicine: The Case of Organ Retrieval from Brain-dead Donors. *Mortality* 16(4), 365-379.

Baeke, G., Wils, J-P. and Broeckaert, B. (2011). Orthodox Jewish Perspectives on Withholding and Withdrawing Life-Sustaining Treatment. *Nursing Ethics* 18(6), 835-846.

Baeke, G., Wils, J-P. and Broeckaert, B. (2012). 'It's in God's hands'. The Attitudes of Elderly Muslim Women in Antwerp (Belgium) toward Active Termination of Life. *AJOB Primary Research* 3(2), 1-12.

Baeke, G., Wils, J-P. and Broeckaert, B. (2012). 'Be patient and grateful'. Elderly Muslim Women's Responses to Illness and Suffering. *Journal of Pastoral Care and Counseling* 66(3/5), 1-9.

Barrett, D.B., Kurian, G.T. and Johnson, T.M. (2000). *World Christian Encyclopedia: A Comparative Survey of Churches and Religions AD 30-AD 2200*. New York: Oxford University Press.

Broeckaert, B. and Federatie Palliatieve Zorg Vlaanderen.(2013). *Medisch begeleid sterven. Een begrippenkader*. 6ᵈᵉ ed. Vilvoorde: FPZV. English Translation: *Treatment Decisions in Advanced Disease – A Conceptual Framework* (http://www.palliatief.be/accounts/143/attachments/Research/conceptual__framework_bb.pdf (accessed on April 20ᵗʰ 2016).

Dhami, S. and Sheikh, A. (2000). The Muslim Family: Predicament and Promise. *Culture and Medicine* 173, 352-356.

Halman, L. and Draulans, V. (2004). Religious Beliefs and Practices in Contemporary Europe. In W. Arts and L. Halman, (eds.). *European Values at the Turn of the Millennium*. Leiden – Boston: Brill, 283-316.

Lodewijckx, E. (2010). Demografische data over veroudering en allochtone ouderen in Vlaanderen en Antwerpen. *Tijdschrift voor welzijnswerk* 34(311), 5-19.

Roy, O. (2002). *L'islam mondialisé*. Parijs: Editions du Seuil.

Sokolovsky, J. (2009). Ethnic Elders and the Limits of Family Support in a Globalizing World. In Sokolovsky, J., ed.. *The cultural context of aging: worldwide perspectives*. Westport: Praeger Publishers, pp. 289-301.

Van den Branden, S. (2006). *Islamitische ethiek aan het levenseinde. Een theoretisch omkaderde inhoudsanalyse van Engelstalig soennitisch bronnenmateriaal en een kwalitatief empirisch onderzoek naar de houding van praktiserende Marokkaanse oudere mannen in Antwerpen*. Thesis (D Phil). Leuven.

Van den Branden, S. and Broeckaert, B. (2008). Medication and God at Interplay: End-of-Life Decision-Making in Practicing Male Moroccan Migrants Living in Antwerp, Flanders, Belgium. In John Brockopp and Thomas Eich, eds. *Muslim Medical Ethics. From Theory to Practice*. Columbia: University of South Carolina Press, 194-208.

Van den Branden, S. and Broeckaert, B. (2009). Globalisation and a Living Islamic Identity. English Sunni E-Fatwas on End-of-Life Decision Making. In Timmerman C., Leman J., Roos H. and Segaert B., eds. *In-Between Spaces*. Brussels – Bern – Berlin – Frankfurt am Main – New York – Oxford – Wien: P.I.E. Peter Lang, 203-218.

Van den Branden, S. and Broeckaert, B. (2010). Necessary Interventions. Muslim Views on Pain and Symptom Control in English Sunni e-Fatwas. *Ethical Perspectives* 17(4), 626-651.

Van den Branden, S. and Broeckaert, B. (2011). Living in the Hands of God. English Sunni E-Fatwas on (non)Voluntary Euthanasia and Assisted Suicide. *Medicine, Health Care and Philosophy* 14(1), 29-41.

Van den Branden, S. and Broeckaert, B. (2011). The Ongoing Charity of Organ Donation. Contemporary English Sunni Fatwas on Organ Donation and Blood Transfusion. *Bioethics* 25(3), 167-175.

Van den Branden, S. and Broeckaert, B. (2013). 'My Age is Predetermined by God'. Elderly Muslims and Pain Control. In: B. Broeckaert and S.Van den Branden, eds. *Perspectives on Islamic Culture. Essays in Honour of Emilio G. Platti*. Les cahiers du MIDEO 6. Louvain – Paris: Éditions Peeters, 249-264.

Yerden, I. (2010). Maatschappelijke implicaties van de veelkleurige vergrijzing. Over allochtone ouderen en informele en formele zorg. *Tijdschrift voor Welzijnswerk* 34(311), 20-34.

16. Islamic knowledge and pious becoming among Moroccan Muslims in the region of Brussels

Mieke Groeninck

Introduction to the field and methodology

Fifty years went by since the unilateral agreements between Morocco and Belgium, arriving nearly at the fourth generation of Moroccan immigrants since the 1960's. According to recent estimations, a number of 468.687 people with a Moroccan background reside on Belgian ground. 47% percent of them are living in the capital of Brussels, which in numbers results in around 218.870. Brussels contains in other words the largest number of inhabitants from Moroccan origin. They also make up the majority of the estimated 277.867 Muslims who reside in the capital (Hertogen, 2015).[1] It is nearly impossible to proclaim any generalizations about this faith group as a whole, considering its immense internal divergence. However, building upon historical evolutions within the Islamic tradition itself as well as within their former home countries, social researchers have nonetheless distinguished some apparently contradictory, and in itself far from homogenous, movements within the Belgian and broader European Muslim presence.

On the one hand, they perceive a tendency among Muslims to describe themselves as secular and whose religious adherence tends to be less outwardly performed, or at least less explicitly in the public sphere. On the other hand, there's a branch belonging to the Islamic 'revivalism', 'pietist', or 'reform' movement; it promotes an active return of Muslims towards Islam, also in the public sphere.[2] This dichotomy does not completely collide with other distinctions that are often made between so-called progressives and conservatives, or modernists and literalists, or whichever divisions based upon differences in epistemological methodology, juridical flexibility or practical rigor.

In any case, it remains difficult to classify people, let alone groups of people, under whatever label that exists; not in the least because of the personal evolutions and historical or discursive changes that occur, also in the short term. But for the sake of clarity and based upon emic distinctions made by my proper interlocutors, I would describe the places where I gathered the research material for this paper, as belonging to the pietist reform movement with a more conservative choice of methodology. These institutions' expressed desire contains a personal and communal reform through an increase of Islamic piety and in response to a variety of problems they perceive within their own, Brussels-based, community. The internal reform that should take place stands in a dialectical relation with the surrounding society, for example in their primary concern with the development of authentic individual identities on the one hand, and how these blend into public space on the other. But equally so in their choice of strategy to arrive at such a reform: it broadly reflects the modernist attachment to knowledge as the way to personal self-discipline, identity formation, and societal progress (Taylor, 1989; Giddens, 1991; Frisina, 2002).

Hence, since the late 1990's, the reform movement is becoming characterized by a proliferation of offers in Islamic education for lay adults (man and women) in the traditional religious sciences: Qur'anic recitation (*tajweed*), Qur'anic exegesis (*tafseer*), Islamic dogma ('*aqidah*), the biography of the prophet Mohammed (*al-sirah*), Islamic jurisprudence (*fiqh*) and Islamic ethics (*adâb*). The focus hereby lies on correct, authentic, purified and practical knowledge on the level of "informed citizens" – to use this Schutzian category (Schutz 1946: 465-66)[3] – which should enable adult students to perfect their Islamic practices, ethics and beliefs in a society that poses numerous challenges to this primordial aspect of their identity.

In the period between May 2013 and June 2015, I have been doing fieldwork at four different places from a Moroccan background in Brussels, where such an offer is provided for adults.[4] One of them was created in 1998; the others came into existence in the last five to ten years. I have been doing participant observation during a period between one semester and two years per class and per institute. I have also conducted numerous interviews and informal talks with male and female teachers and fellow students; before, during, after or completely outside of class. Three of the places where I've worked (of which two were primarily mosques and one primarily an educational institute) organized courses by and for women-only, the fourth (a mosque) gave mixed courses, but gender-separated. In one of the three women-only offers, a parallel male institute existed as well. In the other two cases no such structural offer for men-only existed, apart from traditional Friday-afternoon classes with the imam. Hence my fieldwork is gender-colored, in the sense that not only are the majority of my interlocutors female, but the female over-representation in courses that provide such practical 'day-to-day' knowledge is also obvious. Much can be said about this, but it will not be the primary focus here.

Nevertheless it should be noted that this large female presence is among others what differs these relatively new offers in comparison to older structures of Islamic knowledge transmission. Previously, structural courses in Islamic religion were mostly aimed at children or male authorities. Qur'anic courses for children under the age of twelve already existed since the creation of the very first mosques in Belgium in the early 1970's (Dassetto & Bastenier, 1984: 88-96; Kanmaz & El Battiui, 2004: 7; Van de Weteringen, 2013: 137). Shortly after the official recognition of Islam in 1974, arrangements were also made to provide more advanced courses in Islamic religion for the authorities needed in a diasporic context: teachers, chaplains and imams.[5] In first instance, their education was organized by the *Islamic and Cultural Center of Belgium*. But in the early 1990's, the latter's central role became more and more questioned (Leman & Renaerts, 1996; Kanmaz & El Battiui, 2004; Kanmaz & Zemni, 2008). Since 1998 the Erasmus Hogeschool provides an option Islam in their training of teachers, and later Groep T (2008-2009) in Leuven and the Thomas More Hogeschool (2015-2016) followed. To the contrary, no formal education of imams or chaplains exists up until now (Debeer, 2011), despite the fact that a number of academizing initiatives were taken both at universities[6] and in private, unofficially recognized institutes. The focus in this paper, however, lies not on the acquisition of such expert knowledge in preparation of professional careers, but on the kind of everyday practical knowledge that is perceived to be indispensable for a personal pious reform, and that attracts a larger number of women than men.

Embedded research question

Previous Belgian research about the role of Islamic knowledge acquisition has among others placed its focus on women's position within the Islamic community through knowledge. Els Vanderwaeren (2009a; 2009b; 2012) has emphasized how female Muslims' renewed interest in Islamic knowledge provides them with tools to perform a personal *ijtihad* (effort) in order to negotiate Islamic practices in a non-Islamic environment. Together with Iman Lechkar – who studied intra-Islamic conversion from Sunnism to Shiism and vice versa in a Belgian context (2012) – they both emphasize the influence of Islamic knowledge acquisition and personal affect in negotiating individual autonomy and working towards ethical self-formation. Nadia Fadil on the other hand, has studied how religious and secular subjectivities are both regulated through a liberal agency model, which is characterized by a specific search for personal authenticity in Muslims' relationship with Islamic knowledge and the Islamic tradition (2008; 2015). On a more general level, Felice Dassetto (1996; 2011) has written about the internal diversity in Islamic knowledge, authority and sects, or how the local and global collide in the Belgian Islamic community.

However, whereas this previous research into the role of Islamic knowledge acquisition mainly focused on processes of ethical self-formation and societal change, I would like to expand this focus towards the world *outside* the subject and society as well. Drawing on Talal Asad's argument that "the connection between religious theory [or knowledge] and practice is fundamentally a matter of intervention – of constructing religion in the world (not in the mind)" (Asad, 1993: 44), I expend this by arguing that this also implies a religious construction (though in the sense of 'unveiling') *of* the world. Therefore I connect the discursive/ethical turn in anthropology as exemplified in Asad's work, with the more recent ontological turn.[7] Rather than focusing only on the ethical self-formation of subjects, I underline the implications any epistemological investment has on ontological *as well as* ethical formation. This means that overall, my approach will be less immanent than those from authors in the ethical branch in the anthropology of Islam (see below), since the ontological turn provides the methodological opportunity to take into account *everything there is* for my interlocutors at a given time and place; human and non-human, visible and invisible (Pedersen, 2012).

I believe that for those who engage in an active and pious self-reform, this has ontological implications as well. In following courses, students are directly or indirectly confronted with moments of "strong evaluation" (Taylor, 1985: 3);[8] intense reflections on ontology, cosmology or metaphysics, concluding that what the world and everything in it *is* for believing subjects might not be what it is for others. Or in other words, the frequent acquisition or reminiscence of

Islamic knowledge is also aimed at a "*rappel d'appartenance à un ordre des choses*" (rappel of adherence to an order of things) (Ricoeur, 1977: 40). It's not that my interlocutors (most of whom are Muslims by birth) were completely unaware of the cosmological 'order of things' before they followed courses; nor that they generally pass from a non-religious 'common-sense perspective' towards a 'religious perspective', as if these two are existing next to and largely separated from each other (Geertz, 1973 [1966]). But in providing tools to enhance personal piety, one of the aims of these courses is to structurally *expand, concretize* and *prioritize* my interlocutors' understanding (discursively and on the level of the heart; see below) of how and what the Universe is to which they 'adhere', and also *how* they should act ethically upon it at more and more moments and towards more and more (material and immaterial, human and non-human) objects of the Divine Creation. Besides a focus on disciplinary bodily praxis with the aim of ethical self-formation, I thus argue that the process of becoming pious is equally occupied with ontological sensibilization and humans' correspondingly '*apt*' (Asad, 1986: 15) responsibilities, desires, priorities,...

In asking how knowledge acquisition is related to pious becoming in everyday life, my focus is threefold: it deals with epistemology, the formation of an ethical self, but in relation to an ontological awareness and corresponding relational responsibilities. I will start by trying to unravel the kind of knowledge that is being transferred, which will also put a different light on the Cartesian understanding of knowledge. Consequently and closely related to previous research in discursive and ethical anthropology, I will elaborate on the relationship between knowledge, praxis, and not only ethical, but also ontological formation.[9] Finally, with this in mind, I will return to the conceptual understanding of piety to see how all this fits together in the everyday process of becoming pious.

The acquisition of correct practices and beliefs

"Even though we're supposed to know most of what is treated here, it's always a reminder. Especially for those things you don't practice daily. It helps us in our attempt to adore Allah correctly." This was the reaction given to me by one of my female fellow students at the beginning of our first joint course on *fiqh* (Islamic jurisprudence) in an Islamic institute that organized courses for women-only. The syllabus that we received at our inscription, dealt with the *kitaab al-tahârah* (book of purification) and the *kitaab al-salât* (book of prayer). Although as this woman explained, much of its content is already known, our teacher, whom I will call Nour,[10] emphasized in her introduction why frequent repetition of the jurisprudential rules concerning purification and prayer is important: "Islam is a religion of facilities. It's not only a matter of spirituality between us and Allah, but it is also important in our normal everyday life. We are Muslims 24/7: on the street, in our conduct, ... We are disciplined, for example in public transportation, while being in traffic, ... Non-Muslims don't understand that it is not only something private. It's a way of life, even in very intimate matters like going to the toilet; everything is regulated (*tout est inscrit*). (...) The rules make your aware (*te prennent conscience*) of the act you do for Allah. Previously, you may have done some things out of *fitrah*.[11] But at a certain moment you become conscience about a specific rule or hadith; from that moment on you may add *niyyah* [intention] to your act after which it becomes an act of adoration. Everything that is prohibited is known. For everything else the rule is that if there's no text, it is permitted. This is not only in matters of cult, but equally so in daily life and in the intimate sphere. (...) We don't have prescribed rules for everything. The only thing that always has to be present is good conduct. That has to become instinctively. (...) Lack of good conduct is often due to a lack of knowledge. We have to practice what we learn here, but everyone at his own pace. We don't have the right to judge others. The most important thing is *that* we are on the right track; the results are in the hands of Allah."

In her explanation, Nour touched upon what appear to be three different sorts of knowledge that are being transmitted in most of the Islamic courses for a lay public of Islamic students: what we could call bodily, intellectual, and spiritual knowledge. However, I prefer to combine this trichotomy with a division that is often made within Islamic sciences itself, namely a combination of external (exoteric) aspects of knowledge, mostly situated on the level of what we would call 'body and mind'; and internal or spiritual dimensions of knowledge situated in the heart (*qalb*) and related to esoteric insights (Bakar, 2012 [1998]: 166).[12] The heart has a special place in Islamic spirituality and epistemology as well. It is not only seen as the place where our spirit resides, but also as a source of knowledge. The heart is where the direct connection to God is situated, and which may be the source of internal meaning and insights through intuition and devotional feelings (Bakar, 2012 [1991]: 49-50). In other words, whereas empiricism only focuses on what we experience with the senses, in Islam internal experiences may also be a trustworthy, sometimes even *the* most trustworthy, source of knowledge (Bakar, 2012 [1998]: 194). The Cartesian dichotomy between outer objectified knowledge and inner mental comprehension based on a correct representation of knowledge (Taylor, 1989: 144), is contradicted by the fact that also inner experience provides on certain conditions an autonomous source of insight and knowledge.

Both external and internal modes of knowing may come in different stages and grades of intensity. Exoteric knowledge has its experts among the *'ulama,* while only Sufi mystical *shoyoukh* have access to true esoteric knowledge on the condition of having obtained a certain degree of internal or spiritual development (see Nasr, 1987). For the "not-(yet-)experts" among my own interlocutors, the internal/spiritual and the external/bodily dimension go hand in hand; the bodily acts help in establishing an internal disposition through the evocation of inner senses and a profound feeling of spiritual connection to God, which in turn may lead to additional insights and a stronger commitment to bodily acts (see also Nasr, 1987: xvii-xviii). In other words, although by way of analysis I will start by elaborating on the exoteric aspects of knowledge, in practice there's a continuous connection between both dimensions.

Among the exoteric aspects of Islamic knowledge are understood the correct practices and beliefs Muslim subjects should try to embody (Lambek, 1993: 6). This contains first of all a revivification of practical knowledge regarding the *'ibadât,* or the personal acts of faith and ritual worship based on the *shari'ah* (Wadud, 2006: 95). The above mentioned course about the *kitaab al-tahârah* (book of purification) and the *kitaab al-salât* (book of prayer) provide clear *shari'ah*-based rules on what kind of water should be used to purify oneself before prayer; in what cases one's state of purification is annulled and when not; how one should correct mistakes while in prayer; which prayers can be combined, etc.

Most of my fellow students see these courses as a kind of reminder to practice their daily rituals correctly, or to adjust small mistakes they've inherited from others over the years. But during these courses they also learn more about ways to negotiate practices and use certain facilities that Islam provides in enabling them to perform these practices correctly, while being in a non-Islamic and secular environment. An often heard example is the possibility (or the legitimacy) of combining certain prayers if one's daytime job doesn't provide an opportunity to do otherwise.

Besides correct practices during ritual acts, the emphasis also clearly lies on scripture-based ethical behavior outside of rituals, which my interlocutors often describe as *comportement* (conduct), but which in the literature is called *al-mu'amalat* (rules concerning conduct in social contracts and relations),[13] *akhlâq* ('ethics' regarding the self, family, society, animal world, physical environment and the Creator),[14] or *âdâb* (the good manners adopted by Islam derived from its teachings and instructions).[15] As Nour said, they are "Muslims 24/7", which should reflect itself in good conduct inspired on, deduced from, analogous with, or not contradictory to the Islamic scriptures (the Qur'an and the Hadiths). Through effortful repetition (*jihad al-nafs*)[16] it should eventually become more and more interiorized (or "become instinctively", as Nour described it) by the subject.

Whether it is through courses on the biography of the Prophet (*al-sirah*), courses on 'Islamic ethics', or through exegesis of Qur'anic verses (*tafseer*): in each of them the emphasis lies on the exemplary behavior of the Prophet and his companions, which provide sometimes clear-cut guidelines and at other times more abstract inspiration for contemporary conduct. This may include ethical behavior vis-à-vis family members, children, husbands, other community members, and non-Muslims (often exemplified in 'neighbors'). But it also concerns ethical behavior towards the invisible world: angels, *shaytan* (the devil), *djinn*, and most importantly, God. Personal sincerity (*ikhlas*) in one's desire to "please" God (*plaire à Dieu*) – which is indispensable for the believing subject – reflects itself in *akhlâq* towards the Universe in general, that in Islamic cosmological ontology means both the visible and invisible world (Al-Attas, 1995: 1).[17]

However, as my interlocutors say, "humans can only adore Allah rightfully, if they get to know Him correctly." And that is what the courses on the Islamic creed and dogma (*'aqidah*) are for. At the beginning of those courses, the teachers explain that concerning the fundamental matters of faith (*iman* (Ar.), *la foi* (Fr.)), there exists no divergence among Muslims. The *shahada* (or "testimony" of faith)[18] is ultimately what is most important and "what comes closest to a central creed in Islam" (Denny, 1994 [1985]: 107). It underlines the fundamental idea of *tawheed* (Oneness of God), and it ideally implies a strong belief in the other elements of faith and obedience to the five pillars of Islam.[19]

The teachers continue by saying that every Muslim, besides uttering the *shahada* and performing his religious duties (the five pillars of Islam and the other acts of '*ibada*), should also have a strong belief in the six 'pillars' or 'doctrines' of faith (*iman*): belief in the Oneness of God (and His names and attributes), belief in angels, belief in the prophets, belief in the Scriptures, belief in the Final Judgment and belief in the Divine Decree and Predestination (Denny, 1994 [1985]: 107-12). In her own course on '*aqidah*, Noor commented on this list saying that all the people in class would surely feel they have a strong belief in these six pillars of *iman* (faith). "But," she said, "you'll be surprised when we go deeper into each one of them what it actually means to embody this belief in your daily life affairs. You'll see there are moments in life at which your behavior seems to implicate that you're not always entirely convinced. Because when you would be truly convinced of the presence of angels, for example, your attitude would change."

Hence, the emphasis in the courses doesn't lie on the theological divergence within Islam, but rather on how a strong belief in the six pillars of *iman* can be maintained (by reading Qur'an, by attending frequent rappels, by witnessing the beauty of Nature, by self-reflexively meditating about events in daily life, ...); and which kind of agency such firm beliefs should exercise in the creation of certain virtues towards God and the Universe in general: *taqwa* (God-consciousness), *tawakkul* (trust in God), *ikhlas* (sincerity), and *akhlaq* (good behavior vis-à-vis fellow creatures). Through personal stories and questions, the practical 'applicability' of '*aqidah* thus becomes concretized. Or in other words, attention is paid to how correct beliefs can become embodied in daily life situations, and how people should act according to the agentive influence this creed has on the subject.

Rappel of adherence to an order of things

Through continuous repetition from the part of the subject, as well as through frequent discursive rappels from the part of the teachers, the embodiment of correct practices and beliefs may become less effortful, but part of a 'disciplinized ethical subject'. Scholars within the anthropology of Islam have often described this process in terms of ethical self-cultivation through bodily practices. Authors such as Talal Asad (1987), Saba Mahmood (2005), Charles Hirschkind (2006) and Jeannette Jouili (2015) perceive the ethical self-discipline of Muslim practitioners in a Foucauldian way as a "modality of power" (Mahmood 2005: 28; Jouili 2015: 15), that "permits individuals ... a certain number of operations on their own bodies and souls, thought, conduct, and way of being" (Foucault

1997: 225, quoted in Mahmood 2005:28 & Jouili 2015: 15). Adult courses in Islam, then, are perceived as self-disciplinizing ways to acquire Islamic virtues through repeated praxis (in the Aristotelian sense), in order to "regulate, inform and construct religious subjects" (Asad: 1987: 159). More recently Webb Keane extended this argument to explicitly include the element of 'belief' as well: "With the possible exception of divine revelation unmediated by any prior practices, institutions, or discourses, belief ontogenetically follows on practice. (...) Even the most spiritualized or scriptural religions teach doctrines through concrete activities" (Keane, 2008: 117).

However, this doesn't mean that there's a clear dichotomy between orthodoxy and orthopraxy within Islam, where orthopraxy per definition precedes 'right ideas or faith' (Wadud, 2006: 92). As Talal Asad has argued, "correct practice always has to conform to a correct model conveyed in authoritative formulas in Islamic traditions," which relates itself to the founding texts of the Qur'an and the Hadith (1986: 14-15).[20] Practical knowledge about the orthopractic and cognitive 'skills' concerning *'ibadat, al-mu'amalat, akhlaq/adab* and *'aqidah* is only meaningful if placed against the background of a cosmological description of the world; or in other words, within the frame of a "grand-scale ontological system" based upon the Revelation (Al-Attas, 1995: 4; Bakar 2012 [1991]: 21).[21] A subject cannot attempt to be sincere according to Islamic norms during *'ibadat* if one does not have at least a vague idea about the function of prayer for human beings as it is emphasized in the Scriptures. Nor can one act according to the islamically inspired *akhlâq* (vis-à-vis oneself and everything there is in this world) if one doesn't *recognize* or *read* the situation, relation or creation as an opportunity to do so.

Therefore, I believe that an investment in Islamic knowledge functions as a "rappel of adherence to an order of things" (Ricoeur, 1977: 40). Though the intensity depends on the ability of the teacher to "touch the students' hearts", as well as on the students' preparedness to be touched by it, it revitalizes and reconfirms not only my respondents' Islamically inspired ontological understanding, but especially also how they should embody their own responsibility therein: through ethical behavior, self-disciplinary efforts, bodily obedience, or pious dispositions. It thus implies specific duties, conduct and practices, always *in relation to* visible and invisible, human and non-human others, *because of* one's own and their place in the ontological scheme. In the words of Al-Attas:

"Knowledge is both the arrival of meaning in the soul as well as the soul's arrival at meaning. (...) Meaning is arrived at when the proper place of anything in a system is clarified to the understanding. The notion of 'proper place' already implies the existence of '*relation*' obtaining between things which altogether describe a *system*, and it is such relation or *network of relations* that determines our recognition of the thing's proper place within the system. By 'place' is meant here that which occurs not only in the spatio-temporal order of existence, but also in the imaginable, intelligible, and transcendental orders of existence." (Al-Attas, 1995: 14. My emphasis).

If considered in this regard, the pursuit of knowledge is a religious activity which in itself may testify for or against you on the Day of Judgment. It is not enough to gather knowledge in what is perceived to be a 'Western consumptionist way'. Islamic knowledge in particular has to become embodied, believed, practiced, *enliven* (Lambek, 1993: 6). The real effort doesn't lie in gathering knowledge, but in making it an inherent part of a 'reformed self' that realizes its true place in the world with and among the visible and invisible, human and non-human o/Other(s), *and* that acts ethically upon their true recognition in a Divinely created Universe.

Piety outside of the courses

In other words, any evolution on the epistemological path towards piety equally holds an influence on the level of a subjects' ontological understanding, and a clear emphasis on one's ethical responsibilities in the ontological frame. It should affect his/hers ethical behavior vis-à-vis the Universe, while it may also help reading the Universe's behavior towards them. Because besides keeping in mind their proper responsibilities in order to behave intentionally and ethically within their ontological and metaphysical frame, behind the Universe's behavior also lies a Divine intention which they sometimes are able to recognize and 'read', while they may fail to understand it or tend to forget it at other times.[22]

Because humans are by nature 'forgetful beings',[23] the large majority of believing subjects need frequent 'reminders' which come in different forms and practices, and which allow them to make the effort of 'returning' (*retourner vers*) or 'getting closer to' God (*se rapprocher d'Allah*) on a regular basis. The practice of *salât* (daily prayer) is traditionally seen as one of those moments during which the subject finds itself alone before God – an opportunity to return to the Ultimate Priority.[24] During courses students learn ways to improve the regulated performance of this *'ibada*, externally (exoterically) as well as internally. External rules may concern the prescriptions of purity, vestimentary rules, correct posture, or rules in case of mistakes during prayer. Internal efforts concern the attempt to focus solely on God during prayer (*khushu'*), or to perform the prayer consciously with the right and sincere intention (*niyyah*). If thus done 'felicitously' (Austin, 1962), the act of adoration may succeed in such a way that it touches the believer spiritually (on the level of the heart (*qalb*)), by which it at the same time functions as a reminder to what is truly important.

But also outside the prescribed daily rituals various practices may actively provide 'rappels', if performed felicitously by the subject (i.e. with the attempt of adding a sincere intention and a clear focus). The examples given by my respondents are practices of *dhikr* (verbally and repeatedly remembering God and the Prophet), reading Qur'an, performing *dua's* (supplications), going to *jalsahs* (prayer or Qur'anic circles), listening to sermons, performing good deeds, or attending Islamic courses. In the words of one of my respondents, such practices "provide rappels to boost one's *iman* (faith)". Islamic courses hold a specific position because, as already mentioned, in ideal circumstances such courses contain both exoteric *and* esoteric elements; they may speak to body, heart and mind at the same time. To paraphrase the Islamic scholar al-Ghazali (d. 1111), where there are thoughts of doubt (*waqa'i*), the acquisition of religious knowledge may provide certainty and appeasement of the heart (Amin Faris, 1962: 29).

However, the need for rappels, for consciously returning to God, for remembering Him in order for people to act in adoration of Him, is ongoing. Piety isn't an achieved state of being, but rather a continuous effort of a relational, ontologically inspired choice of action.[25] Among my respondents, one of the most frequently cited 'tools' of consciously placing one's efforts in the process of pious becoming, is the concept of *niyyah:* "acting out of a sincere intention to please God". Any act that is conform or not contradictory to the rules of Islam and is performed out of a sincere intention to please God, can be transformed from a mere spatiotemporal bounded act into an act of adoration with extensions until the Day of Judgment (and even beyond).[26] Therefore, Nour mentioned that a realization of "the rules make you aware (*te prennent conscience*) of the act you do for Allah. (...) At a certain moment you become conscience about a specific rule or hadith; from that moment on you may add *niyyah* to your act after which it becomes an act of adoration." In other words, from the moment any act (within the daily life sphere, for example) becomes 'encoded' within the system of scriptural references, its ontological status changes and it has the potentiality of becoming an act of adoration. "To place your *niyyah*" before, or at the beginning of any such act, is an agentive, internal performance (for example, through the use of 'inner speech') that may help to keep this pious relationship with Allah in order.[27] I use the word 'performance', because it is a conscious act that is per definition established within a relationship to the Divine, Who is present as a 'witness' at all times.

Nour explicitly extends the sphere of *din* beyond 'what was written', when she says that: "Everything that is prohibited is known. For everything else the rule is that if there's no text, it is permitted. This is not only in matters of cult, but equally so in daily life and in the intimate sphere." To say it otherwise, the whole of life can become a form of adoration for Allah, whether very explicitly and externally manifested, or implicitly and internally felt. The only condition is its conscious and knowledgeable relation – in any form – to Divinely prescribed rules, and the presence of a religious disposition that results in a kind of sincerity towards God. Placing your *niyyah* is a relational act from the subject towards the Divine; whereas devotional feelings of *taqwa* (God-consciousness) or *tawakkul* (trust in God) are the result of such an awareness of the Divine relation to His Creation. Piety, then, consists in the repeated act of remembering and acting ethically upon this remembrance, which bares within itself also an ontological consciousness (whether very explicit, or rather vague) on one's place and position in the world as a creation of God among other creations.

Conclusion

In order to understand the process of pious becoming through religious knowledge acquisition, I started by elaborating on the kind of knowledge that is being transferred. I have focused not only on the practical/exoteric and internal/dispositional knowledge transmission, but also on how it offers a "*rappel d'appartenance à un ordre des choses*". Therefore, I perceive piety as a continuous becoming that is above all *relational*; not only based on the mere presence of others, but upon the awareness of one's and others' place in the Universe in relation to the Ultimate Other. I believe that for my own respondents, any effort in piety is not limited to the self, but also includes such an ontological awareness of what 'I' actually am, what the world is, what others in it are, and which opportunities (or responsibilities) of adoration any event, relation or creation therefore may offer. In other words, I argue that for my interlocutors, Islamic knowledge acquisition not only has the possibility to change the body, mind and heart of the subject. It changes the world for them as well.

Notes

1 These data stem from 2015 (www.npdata.com Last visit 2/02/2016).

2 Literature on this movement in Europe, see for example: Amiraux (2001), Amir-Moazami & Salvatore (2003), Bowen (2011), Césari (1994), Dassetto (1996), Fadil (2008), Jouili (2015).

3 Schutz (1946) made a distinction in knowledge distribution between experts (whose knowledge is restricted to a limited field but therein it is clear and distinct); man on the street (working knowledge of many fields which are not necessarily coherent with one another); and well-informed citizens (who aim at being well informed, so he can form reasonably founded opinions in fields which as he knows are at least mediately of concern to him). See also Lambek 1993: 68-70.

4 During this period, I also did fieldwork in two other institutes; but since their aim was more to provide a descriptive academic background of various religious sciences rather than providing practical knowledge that should lead to personal reform, I focus less on them in this paper. Nonetheless, a number of elements I will analyse count for them as well.

5 In 1975, the Minister of Justice wrote a circular that foresaw in the official organisation of courses in Islamic religion from the moment parents asked for it (both in public as in private, mostly Catholic, schools). In 1978 a Royal Decree obliged the organisation of Islamic education and the appointance of Islamic teachers by the formal representative of Islam; a role which in those days was taken up by the *Islamic and Cultural Center of Belgium* (Kanmaz and El Battiui 2004: 13; Kanmaz and Zemni 2008: 3-4).

6 The university offers are: the 'Master of World Religions – Option Islamic Theology and Religious Studies' at KU Leuven (started in September 2014) and the '*Formation continue sur l'Islam*' (since 2006) at the Université Catholique de Louvain-la-Neuve.

7 More on the ontological turn in anthropology, see: Viveiros De Castro 1998, 2004, 2013 [2002]; Henare, Holbraad & Wastell 2007; Scott 2007; Carrithers, Candea, Sykes, Holbraad & Venkatesan 2010; Alberti, Fowles, Holbraad, Marshall & Witmore 2011; Scott 2013.

8   "A background of distinctions between things which are recognized as of categoric or unconditioned or higher importance or worth, and things which lack this or are of lesser value" (Taylor 1985: 3).

9   "Ontological formation" as in, quite literally, the formation of an understanding of being and consequential responsibilities (not of being itself, in the structuralist way).

10 This is an alias. Out of privacy concerns, no names of individuals, mosques or institutes where I've worked will be given.

11 Which may be understood here as "natural predisposition".

12 The famous Islamic scholar Abu Hamid ibn Muhammad al-Ghazali (d. 1111) equally so makes this distinction in his *Ihya' 'ulum al-Din* (Revival of the religious sciences) which deals with what he calls "practical religion" (as opposed to science of revelation or esoteric knowledge): "The sicence of practical religion is divided into outward science, by which is meant that of the functions of the senses, and inward science, by which is meant that of the functions of the heart." (Amin Faris 1962: xv).

13 More on the role and meaning of *al-mu'amalat*, see: Bowen 2012: 43; Deeb 2006: 171; Wadud 2006: 36.

14 Based on definition from Al-Qardawi 1981: 106-9, quoted in Halstead 2007: 285.

15 Based on definition from Al-Kaysi 2003: 13, quoted in Halstead 2007: 285.

16 *Jihad al-nafs* or "the struggle against the lower self" [implying its passions, drifts, character, etc.] (Jouili 2015: 37).

17 "Islam does not concede to the dichotomy of the sacred and the profane; the worldview of Islam encompasses both *al-dunya* and *al-akhirah*, in which the *dunya*-aspect *must* be related in a profound and inseparable way to the *akhirah*-aspect." (Al-Attas 1995: 1)

18 *Laa illaha illa Allah. Muhammad rasul Allah.* ("There is no god but God. Muhammad is the messenger of God.)

19 Which are besides uttering the *shahada*: *salat* (prayer), *zakat* (religious tax), *Ramadan* (yearly fast), and the *hajj* (pilgrimmage).

20 It is important to note here that for Asad, any understanding of 'correct models' is subject to historically situated debates and orthodoxical power relations. Since I believe ontology, or literally the 'talk about being as such', is an inherent part of the Islamic tradition, this too is not homogeneous, although attempts for homogenization are made by orthodoxy (Asad 1986: 15-16).

21 "It is therefore the Islamic revelation which defines the whole domain of study to which the Islamic sciences should be directed. The Muslim mind which accepts such a view of the cosmos has, prior to that, already accepted revelation as the highest source of knowledge." (Bakar 2012 [1991: 21).

22 "The world is, as it were, an immense book in which those who have eyes to see and ears to hear can recognize God's signs and thus be guided by their contemplation to the Creator Himself. Sensual and spiritual levels meet through and in the signs, and by understanding and interpreting them one may be able to understand the Divine wisdom and power." (Schimmel 1994: xii)

23 The forgetfullness of humans is often referred to in the Qur'an as well. For example: "And remember thy Lord when thou forgettest" (Q. S.18: 24)

24 More on the practice of *salât*, see Bowen (2012); Henkel (2005).

25 I understand Muslims' 'religious consciousness' to center around the unity of God (Bakar 2012 [1991]: 1).

26 Therefore Annemarie Schimmel perceived "niyyah" as the borderline between the "profance" and the "ritual state" (1994: 102). However, I would prefer to describe it in terms of the explicit presence of a relational religious consciousness upon which one chooses to act.

27 John Hick calls this the move from "self-centeredness to Reality-centeredness" (Hick 1989: 14). However, I would like to emphasize that this isn't a completed linear move from one state to the next, but rather gets repeated during moment of "returning to" God.

Bibliography

Abdur-Rahman, I.D. (1987). Sunnism. In S. Hossein Nasr (Ed.), *Islamic Spirituality: Foundations*, New York: Crossroads, 147-159.

Al-Attas, S.M.N. (1995). *Prolegomena to the Metaphysics of Islam. An exposition of the fundamental elements of the worldview of Islam*. Kuala Lumpur: International Institute of Islamic Thought and Civilization (ISTAC).

Alberti, B., Fowles, S., Holbraad, M., Marshall, Y., Witmore, C. (2011). "World otherwise": Archeology, anthropology, and ontological difference. *Current Anthropology*, 52(6), 896-912.

Amin Faris, N. (1962). *The book of knowledge. Being a translation with notes of the Kitab al-'ilm of Al-Ghazzali's Ihya' 'ulum al-din*. New Delhi: Islamic Book Service.

Amiraux, V. (2001). *Acteurs de l'islam entre Allemagne et Turquie*. Paris: L'Harmattan.

Amir-Moazami, S. & Salvatore, A. (2003). Gender, generation, and the reform of tradition: From Muslim majority societies to Western Europe. In S. Allievi & J.S. Nielsen (eds), *Muslim networks and transnational communities in and across Europe*. Leiden: Brill, 52-77.

Asad, T. (1986). *The idea of an anthropology of Islam*. Occasional Papers. Washington, D.C.: Center for Contemporary Arab Studies.

Asad, T. (1987). On ritual and discipline in medieval Christian monasticism. *Economy and Society* 16(2), 159-203.

Bakar, O. (2012 [1991]). *The history and philosophy of Islamic Science.* Cambridge: Islamic Texts Society.

Bakar, O. (2012 [1998]). *Classification of knowledge in Islam.* Kuala Lumpur: Institute for Policy Research.

Bowen, J. (2011). *Can Islam be French? Pluralism and pragmatism in a secularist state.* Princeton, Oxford: Princeton University Press.

Bowen, J. (2012). *A New Anthropology of Islam.* Cambridge: Cambridge University Press.

Carrithers, M., Candea, M., Sykes, K., Holbraad, M. & Venkatesan, S. (2010). Ontology is just another word for culture: motion tabled at the 2008 meeting of the group for debates in anthropological theory, University of Manchester. *Critique of Anthropology* 30(20), 152-200.

Cesari, J. (1994). *Être musulman en France. Associations, militants et mosquées.* Paris, Aix-en-Provence: Kharthala, IREMAM.

Dassetto, F. (1996). *La construction de l'islam européen. Approche socio-anthropologique.* Paris: L'Harmattan.

Dassetto, F. (2011). *L'Iris et le croissant. Bruxelles et l'Islam au défi de la co-inclusion.* Louvain-La-Neuve: Presses Universitaires de Louvain.

Dassetto, F. & Bastenier, A. (1984). *L'Islam transplanté. Vie et organisation des minorités musulmanes en Belgique.* Antwerpen: EPO/EVO.

Deeb, L. (2005). *An enchanted modern. Gender and public piety in Shi'I Lebanon.* Princeton, Oxford: Princeton University Press.

Denny, F. M. (1994 [1985]). *An introduction to Islam.* New York: Macmillan Publishing Company.

Fadil, N. (2008). *Submitting to God, submitting to the Self: secular and religious trajectories of second generation Maghrebi in Belgium.* Unpublished Doctoral Dissertation. Catholic University of Leuven.

Fadil, N. (2015). Recalling the 'Islam of the parents' liberal and secular Muslims redefining the contours of religious authenticity. *Identities: Global studies in culture and power* 24(1), 82-91. DOI: 10.1080/1070289X.2015.1091318. Last visit 1/04/2016.

Fakhry, M. (1970). *A history of Islamic philosophy.* New York, London: Columbia University Press.

Frisina, W.G. (2002). *The unity of knowledge and action: Toward a nonrepresentational theory of knowledge.* SUNY Series in Philosophy. New York: State University of New York Press.

Geertz, C. (1973 [1966]). Religion as a cultural system. In C. Geertz, *The interpretation of cultures: selected essays.* New York: Fontana Press, 87-125.

Giddens, A. (1991). *Modernity and Self-Identity. Self and society in the Late Modern Age.* Stanford: Stanford University Press.

Hallowell, A.I. (1960). *Ojibwa ontology, behavior, and world view.* New York: Columbia University Press.

Henare, A., Holbraad, M. & Wastell, S. (Eds.) (2007). *Thinking through things. Theorising artefacts ethnographically.* London, New York: Routledge.

Henkel, H. (2005). Between belief and unbelief lies the performance of Salat: Meaning and efficacy of a Muslim ritual. *The Journal of the Royal Anthropological Institute* 11(3), 487-507.

Hertogen, J., Non-Profit Data, www.npdata.com Last visit 2/02/2016.

Hick, J. (1989). *An interpretation of religion. Human responses to the transcendent.* London: Macmillan.

Hirschkind, C. (2006). *The ethical soundscape. Cassette sermons and Islamic counterpublics.* New York: Columbia University Press.

Jouili, J.S. (2015). *Pious practices and secular constraints. Women in the Islamic revival in Europe.* Stanford: Stanford University Press.

Kanmaz, M. & El Battiui, M. (2004). *Moskeeën, imams en islamleerkrachten in België. Stand van zaken en uitdagingen.* Brussels: Koning Boudewijnstichting.

Keane, W. (2008a). On the materiality of religion. *Material Religion,* 4(2), 230-231.

Lambek, M. (1993). *Knowledge and practice in Mayotte. Local discourses of Islam, sorcery, and spirit possession.* Toronto: University of Toronto Press.

Lechkar, I. (2012). *Striving and stumbling in the name of Allah. Neo-Sunnis and neo-Shi'ites in a Belgian context.* Unpublished Doctoral Dissertation. Catholic University of Leuven.

Mahmood, S. (2005). *Politics of piety. The Islamic revival and the feminist subject.* Princeton: University of Princeton Press.

Moosa, E. (2005). *Ghazali and the poetics of imagination.* Chapel Hill and London: The University of North Carolina Press.

Nasr, S.H. (Ed.) (1987). *Islamic Spirituality: Foundations.* New York: Crossroads, 147-159.

Nasr, S.H. (2006). *Islamic philosophy from its origin to the present. Philosophy in the land of Prophecy.* New York: State University of New York Press.

Pedersen, M.A. (2012). Common nonsense: A review of certain recent reviews of the ontological turn. *Anthropology of this Century,* 5, http://aotcpress.com/articles/common_ nonsense/ Last visit 19/02/2016.

Ricoeur, P. (1977). Herméneutique de l'idée de révélation. In P. Ricoeur, E. Levinas, E. Haulotte, E. Cornélis & C. Geffré, *La Révélation.* Brussels: Facultés universitaires Saint-Louis.

Schimmel, A. (1994). *Deciphering the signs of God: A phenomenological approach to Islam.* Albany: State University of New York Press.

Schutz, A. (1946). The well-informed citizen: An essay on the social distribution of knowledge. *Social Research* 13(4), 463-478.

Scott, M.W. (2007). *The severed snake. Matrilineages, making place, and a Melanesian Christianity in Southeast Solomon Islands.* Durham: Carolina Academic Press.

Scott, M.W. (2013). The anthropology of ontology (religious science?). *Journal of the Royal Anthropological Institute* 19(4), 859-872.

Taylor, C. (1985). *Human agency and language. Philosophical Papers Volume 1.* Cambridge: Cambridge University Press.

Taylor, C. (1989). *Sources of the self: The making of modern identity.* Cambridge: Cambridge University Press.

Vanderwaeren, E. (2009a). A religious and feminine counter-discourse in Flanders revealed. In C. Timmerman, J. Leman, H. Roos & B. Segaert (Eds.), *In-between spaces. Christian and Muslim minorities in transition in Europe and the Middle East.* Brussels etc.: P.I.E. Peter Lang, 113-130.

Vanderwaeren, E. (2009b). 'Moslima's aan de horizon'. Islamitische interpretatie als hefbomen bij de emancipatie van Moslima's. *Ethiek en Maatschappij* 7(4), 95-111.

Vanderwaeren, E. (2012). Muslimahs impact on and acquisition of Islamic religious authority in Flanders. In M. Bano & H. Kalmbach (Eds.), *Women, leadership and mosques: Changes in contemporary Islamic authority.* Leiden: Brill, 301-322.

Van de Wetering, S. & Karagül, A. (2013). 'Zoek kennis van de wieg tot het graf'. Islamitisch godsdienstonderwijs. Antwerpen, Apeldoorn: Garant.

Viveiros De Castro, E. (1998). Cosmological deixis and Amerindian perspectivism. *The Journal of the Royal Anthropological Institute* 4(3), 469-488.

Viveiros De Castro, E. (2013 [2002]). The relative native. *HAU: Journal of Ethnographic Theory* 3(3), 469-471.

Viveiros De Castro, E. (2004). Exchanging perspectives. The transformation of objects into subjects. *Common Knowledge* 10(4), 463-484.

Wadud, A. (2006). *Inside the gender jihad: Women's reform in Islam.* Oxford: OneWorld Publications.

17. The power of affective encounters and events: why Moroccan Belgian Sunnis become Shia

Iman Lechkar

Situating Moroccan Belgian Shia

While academic research on Moroccan Belgians mainly explores Sunni and secular variations of Islam/Muslims (Fadil et al, 2015), there is a significant but rather unknown community of 8000 to 10,000 Moroccan Belgian Shia (Lechkar, 2012, 2017). Already In the 1970s, Morocco saw its national religious organization in Belgium (Widadiya) being challenged by the Saudi Islamic Cultural Center (ICC) which was inaugurated in 1975. However, it's only in 1986, when Khomeini banners were very visible at a demonstration in Brussels, condemning the US Bombing of Tripoli and Benghazi, that it became clear that another Islamic power, Iran, is also expanding its sphere of influence in Brussels (Dassetto, 2011; Fadil et al, 2015).

Academic research on the 'Shia revival' has identified four important developments in Shia revival (Dabashi, 2011; Louër, 2008; Lechkar, 2017; Mabon, 2013; Maréchal, & Zemni, 2013; Nasr, 2006): (a) The Iranian revolution in 1979, (b) the growth of political and military power of Hezbollah, leading to the withdrawal of Israel from South Lebanon and the (c) the transition of political power from Sunnis to Shias in Iraq after the American invasion in 2003 and (d) the Arab uprisings from 2011 onwards, intensifying the Sunni-Shia tensions in the Middle East and other parts of the world.

As Dassetto rightly states in his books, while the 1980s are viewed as the beginning of the affirmation of Muslim religious identity in Belgium, the germs were already present in 1970s but were difficult to interpret (Dassetto, 2011). My own research also shows that the origin of Belgian Moroccan Shiism coincides with Khomeini's presence in exile in Neauphle-le-Chateau, France in 1978 and therefore I designate this phase as the first of six important Shiitization waves observed among Belgian Moroccan Shi'ites (Lechkar 2017, 2012). The first wave is characterized by a small group of Moroccan Belgians who went to pray the Friday prayer in France behind Khomeini. The second wave is situated during the first years of the television coverings of the Iranian Revolution and the establishment of the Iranian Embassy and Iranian cultural organizations in Brussels. The third important phase was the presence of the Iraqi dawa movement in Brussels. The fourth wave was triggered after the Iraq-Iran war, the extensive coverage of one of longest conflict of the twentieth century and the decision of Brussels imam Ouadrassi to pray for a Shia war victim and confided to his congregation that he had discovered the Shia message. The fifth period coincides with Hezbollah's political stance against Israel in 2000 and 2006 and the rise of Shia Satellite channels such as Al Manar covering Shia politics. The final but very important wave is the impact of Moroccan Belgian Shiites on other Moroccan Belgians.

While Belgium has recently witnessed an increase of Shia Lebanese, Afghan and Iraqi migration, it remains unclear how the relationship is between Moroccan Belgian Shi'ites and these relatively new Shia immigrants.

In the following part I will show how the impact of the abovementioned events and encounters could be understood. Brian Massumi rightly connects "the ability to affect and be affected" to "the dynamic unity of an event" and argues that any discussion on religious or interpretational change or other transitions should depart from an "affectation that is happening in-between" (Massumi, 2015, p. 9). Before we illustrate which events and encounters prove to be conducive for the Shiitization of Moroccan Belgian Sunnis, we will first address the notion of conversion.

Revisiting conversion

Sunni Moroccan Belgians who become Shia Muslims don't speak of conversion but rather of guidance (*hudaa*), the opening of the eyes (*istibsaar*), becoming Shi'ites (*attashayyu'*), or partisans of the 'family of the prophet' (*ahl al bayt*). Sunni Moroccan Belgians underscore the importance of a conviction that has always been present in their lives but became marginalized because of circumstances.

They therefore relate the discovery of the Shia message to guidance and *istibsaar*. Although these notions are used as emic categories to talk about themselves, Moroccan Belgian Shi'ites are aware the they are viewed or spoken about as 'converts' or in certain circles, among certain orthodox Sunni groups, as deviant.[1] This part will only draw on the etic notion of 'conversion' to revisit certain assumptions that are questioned by the data I gathered and to explain my non-usage of the term.[2]

As stated earlier, Sunni Moroccan-Belgians becoming Shi'ites don't consider themselves converts. They regard themselves as Muslims that are engaged with the primary sources of Islam. *Attashayyu'* (shiitization) is a revisionist articulation based on the engagement with the foundational Islamic texts, i.e. the Qur'an and hadith. This connects completely with Asad's definition of Islam as a discursive tradition, marked by discussion and contestation and based on the primary Islamic sources i.e. the Qur'an and Hadith (Asad, 1986).

Instead of seeing Shiitization as a schism with their previous beliefs, it is more correct to view it as a revision located within a discursive tradition constituted by discussion and contestation within the Islamic tradition. If we understand Islam as a tradition, then translating *attashayyu'* as conversion would be inadequate. Fatima and many others explain it to me in the following way:

> "*Tashaya'na* [we have become Shia]. We are followers of the *ahl al bayt*, family of the prophet, his daughter Fatima, her husband Ali and their two children, Hassan and Huseyn. So whether I am a convert, I don't think so, that would imply that I am not a Muslim anymore. Instead of conversion, I prefer *istibsaar*, because I believe that I just developed new insights on the basis of the same sources as other Muslims. Instead of just accepting what our parents said, I searched for my own information. (Fatima, 25, University student, Brussels, Shia)".

Shia Moroccan Belgians return to the death of the prophet, the succession disputes, the period of the compilation of the hadith and demonstrate that: "reflection upon the past is a constitutive condition for understanding and reformulating the present and the future" (Asad, 1986). I argue, in the line of Talal Asad, that the engagement of Moroccan Belgian Shiites with what it means to be a proper Muslim, their reinterpretation of the Sunni sources for example, is part of the ongoing debates that characterize Islam as a tradition. The process of reinterpretation and the repudiation of the dominant Sunni version is a hermeneutic exercise through which the subjectivity and self-understanding of a tradition's adherents are constituted (Mahmood, 2005).

In *"Comments on conversion"*, Talal Asad calls attention to Karl Morisson's formulation that: "It is a confusion of categories to use the word conversion as though it were an instrument of critical analysis, equally appropriate to any culture or religion" (Asad, 1996). My doctoral research shows that the conventional conversion paradigm (Lofland & Stark, 1965) draws on four problematic assumptions: (a) false consciousness, (b) radical change, (c) delineated conversion process, (d) rational choice (Lechkar, 2012).With the arrival of the alternative approach to conversion, these assumptions were enfeebled by some important researchers on conversion (Rambo, 1993, 1999; Coleman, 2003; Gooren, 2005, 2006). Lewis Rambo's indication of conversion as an open-ended process, Simon Coleman's focus on continuous conversion and Henri Gooren's elaboration of conversion careers countered Lofland and Stark's fixed stage model. However, the alternative approach does not explore sufficiently the power of encounters in producing particular affects.

In this paper I will put to the fore the notion of affect in order to fully understand the process of becoming Shia in a Belgian context. Conventionally distinctions were made between an 'intellectual' versus an 'affectional' conversion or 'rational' versus 'relational' conversion, separating the intellectual, and thus rational, from the affectional and relational (Lofland & Skonovd, 1981; Allievi, 1998). While conversion based on reason is understood as an authentic practice, conversion based on emotion is viewed as influenced, coerced, anachronistic and less authentic. In the following part, I will undo this dualism by introducing the notion of affect and the power of an encounter.

Abdullah's affective encounters and events

I employ 'affect' in order to indicate the inseparability of emotion and reason, and emphasize that reason and emotion are mutually constitutive and present in affect (Rosaldo, 1984; Massumi, 1987, 2015). Affect "arises in the midst of in-between-ness: in the capacities to act and be acted upon" and "is found in those intensities that pass body to body (human, non-human, part body or otherwise)" (Gregg & Seigworth, 2010:1).

In this part I will draw on the life story of Abdullah to show that the Shiitization of Moroccan Belgian Sunnis is informed by a series of encounters and events that affect their understanding and stance and sensibility towards belonging or not belonging to a particular religious tradition; i.e. Sunni or Shia tradition.[3] All of the interlocutors I spoke with were affected in some way or another by a Shia person they encountered or Shia event that they witnessed. The intensities and forces produced in those encounters and events brought about different feelings, thoughts and actions among Moroccan Belgians.

By drawing on Abdullah's account, I will try to show how these in between spaces look like, which intensities are produced that eventually led to the Shiitization of most of my respondents. When I met Abdullah in 2009, he was 55 years old and was married with 5 children, all of them raised as a second generation Moroccan Belgian Shiites. As a barber, he lived in the commune of Anderlecht, Brussels. When I asked him about his religious trajectory he takes me back to Tangier, Morocco in 1960s when most schools in big Moroccan cities were associated with a Christian education by catholic nuns and his father opposing this development and therefore sending his son to his grandmother in the countryside to study Quran.[4] After a decade of Quran school, the 17 year old Abdullah went back to his family in the city of tangier where he started a shop-based training of becoming a barber. It is because of his father's visits at the lunch moments of the main barber, when he took off his turban, and functioned as a barber model, letting his son experiment with his hair, that Abdullah mastered the craft of barbering.

When his father died in 1966, Abdullah liberated himself from what he calls the two "prison" experiences that he associated with his father's aspirations for him; i.e. the mosque and the barbershop. He bought a new car, started going out, went on adventure excursions with friends and broadened his limited and hierarchical frames received and lived during the countryside Quran training and barber experience in Tangier.

In the 1970s he encountered the Benseddik brothers, a renowned religious family in Tangier whose ancestral *zawiya* (religious school) is still much known among North Moroccans. Ali was particularly affected by one brother, Sheikh Sidi Mohamed Zemzemi Benseddik. He described him a brave man who was not scared from government reprisals and who tackled issues of poverty, inequality, colonialism and foreign interference.

During his adherence to Sheikh Zemzemi, his interest in Islam and its contemporary relevance also grew by the cassettes of the prominent Azhar University graduate, Egyptian scholar Abdel-Hamid Kishk, whose political and social sermons echoed not only in the streets in taxis of Cairo but also in many cities of the Arab world.[5]

In 1978 Abdullah moved to Brussels to join his newly wedded wife, who was the daughter of one of the first migrant workers who arrived in Belgium a decade earlier to work in the mining industry. 1978, Abdullah recalls, was also the year that Khomeini had to leave Iraq and went to exile in Neauphle-le Chateau, Paris. Abdullah describes this event in the following way:

> "The image of Khomeini will never disappear. Here I was in a foreign country, in a foreign family and I see this person on television who is so familiar. I saw all these characteristics that made me think of my youth, the countryside where and the imams (fuqiaan) with whom I studied. I saw my grandfather, my own father with his turban (razza), all in this one person who had fled Iran, Iraq and sought refuge in Paris."

Abdullah was clearly affected in a positive way by Khomeini because of the identification with many elements he embodied: exile, migration, identification with the countryside, Quran studies, his youth, father and grandfather. However, his positive affectation conflicted with the reaction of his father in law who designated Shia as false and not recognizing Prophet Mohamed.[6] He remembers the event very vividly:

> "while I was so impressed by this simple, authentic, deep-spiritual and knowledgeable man, my father in law kept on saying that they are Persians (Furs) and not Arabs; that they were impure and false, having their own belief and saying angel Gabriel erred in delivering the divine message to prophet Mohammed while it was meant for Ali, the cousin of Mohammed."

Abdullah puts his hand on his heart and says that it really hurt when he heard his father in law saying such things. While he was positively affected by the personality of Khomeini, he was very much interpellated by the utterings of his father in law and could not understand how a man and his entourage, who looked like Muslims, were not considered Muslims.

> "Light shines over them, they are so courageous but why do they doubt the prophet? I felt tormented."

Abdullah's affect of contentment, of identification is very important because it forms the basis of his power to search for and to craft his own religious identity. For many years, a decade to be precise, a feeling of unrest, affliction was part of his life, Abdullah confides to me. The Iraq-Iran war, one bloodiest and longest armed conflict of the twentieth century, affected him daily and pushed him to engage even more with the troubling ideas he had.[7]

> "I was always talking to my friend about the war, the Sunni-Shia divide, and one day he said to me there is celebration of the revolution at the Iranian Embassy. He suggested that we should go and finally meet Shia for the first time and experience from close by what Shiism is about. I was very anxious. For more than five years I was affected (t'atharrt) by world politics, troubled by my own Islamic identity and now I could finally make acquaintance with people about whom so many things circulated."

Abdullah uses the Arabic verb *athara*, meaning affected, to explain what the Iraq-Iran war did to him. He went to a Shia celebration for the first time and listened to the Sheikh reciting from the Quran and delivering an empowering political and Islamic preach. He prayed with Shia for the first time and describes the food as 'delicious' food. The positive titillation he felt when he first saw Khomeini on the TV screen returned completely. He was very anxious and curious but encountered no fundamental differences between the two tendencies. Moreover, he was relieved and again positively affected when he heard a special invocation in the middle of the prayer and saw everyone praying with their arms along their bodies:

> "We prayed (*sadlan*) with our arms along our bodies. I remember that from the time I was in Morocco. We prayed the same way and it was Sheikh Zemzemi who introduced *Salat al kapt*, whereby we started putting our arms on each other while praying. You know, he was a saint in Tangier, but when he did that, he was practically excommunicated (*kaffrouh*). Also the *dua al kunout*, the invocation in the middle of the prayer, was something that existed among Moroccans during morning prayers. The Shia however do it at each prayer."

Abdullah noticed authenticity in the Shia practices he witnessed that evening.[8] Praying with his hand along the body, the invocation during the prayer were Islamic practices that he related to the Islam lived and practiced when he was a child but which he remember were altered in Morocco during the 80s and 90s under Saudi globalizing influences.

Abdullah also noticed many books and Qurans and recalled all the utterances by his father in law and other people regarding a different Koran, a different belief, deviant practices. Since Shia books were not yet very available in Brussels, he asked an employee whether he could take home a Quran.

> "I went outside and couldn't wait to arrive home to read the whole Quran. I first read particular verses of which several Sunni sources had said Shia had changed them. But when I went to surah 94- *al inshirah*, I read the same surah that I also memorized at the age of five."[9]

Abdullah's agency, power to act increased again after the participation at the celebratory event. Abdullah was very happy to discover that Shiites do not have a different Quran since the chapter he read was the same as the one he knows by heart. Furthermore, he started to really question those who accuse the Shia of being deviant, impure, unislamic and each time he approached a Sunni religious authority, the same message was given: i.e. Shiism is a deviant form of Islam.

> "I remember exactly what the last Sunni imam I spoke to said when I asked him what differentiates Shia from Sunna. The imam, as so many others, didn't have any knowledge about Shia Islam. He only said that they have gone astray (*dalleen*), they are far from the religion (*b'adeen min deen*) and that they are closer to disbelief (*kufr*) than to Islam. I went outside and was really disappointed."

Abdullah is disappointed in the imam that fails to give detailed info about the specificity of Shia Islam and reduced the Shia community to a community gone astray. His father in law, the many Sunni imams and their stereotypes about Shiites do no longer agree with Abdullah's own knowledge and experience of Shia Islam. Abdullah remained questioning and searching until one day he realized that the Lebanese doctor he always went to was also Shia:

"I had a terrible stomach ache and went to see Doctor Abu Halima, a Lebanese doctor, also in Anderlecht whom I had known for many years and besides being my doctor, he was also my translator because my French was certainly not so good when I first arrived here. When I took a seat I noticed a book on his desk: 'Why are we Shia'. I was surprised and asked him whether he was Shia. I also asked him whether I could read that book. Jokingly, he said 'are you sure it will have any benefit for you?' 'Yes', I answered affirmatively, went home, even forgot about the stomach ache and dissected the book."

Abdullah felt outraged and offended because he thought of himself as someone with a lot of religious background but what he had read, he had never read or heard before. It was about the history of Islam but it was another history. That moment he realized that history has different faces, different versions and he had, up until then, only accessed one.

A couple of months later, he found out that he was not alone in discovering a new interpretation. His friend told him about Imam Ouadrassi who for many years has a particular Shia sensibility:[10]

"Hamdullilah, I cannot describe what I felt when I spoke to Oudrassi and when he told me to come and join his congregation because he assembles Muslims who see themselves as Muslims and respect both Sunnis and Shia because they are both the true followers of the Prophet."

Abdullah joined Arrahman mosque whose imam completely fit with his own sensibility as he was also a Moroccan migrant to Belgium, brought up in a Sunni household but having also discovered and respecting Shia doctrine. Abdullah launched himself in the study of Shia history, tradition and through a final event, he felt profound peace (*rtaht dbassah*):

"In 1989 al-Tijani al Samawi published his book 'Then I was guided' (*thouma htadayt*), Tijani refers to the Sufi order he belonged to and as a Tunesian Sunni he also adhered to the teachings of imam Malik ibn Anas. His book told not only the story of his life, but also of my life. For almost 35 years, I was in mosques and never did I hear about the story of injustice upon the prophet's family, Ali, Fatima and his children, Hassan and Hussein, while Allah says that the whole truth should be shown."

The publication of this book was a milestone in the religious and interpretational quest in which Abdullah was engaged. The book is an account of Muhamed Al Tijani al Samawi, pertaining to the Tijani sufi order, which is very known sufi order in the whole of North Aftica. Al Tijani accounts how, since he was a child, he was a very practicing and engaged Muslim but as an adult he undertook a trip to the Middle East that was life changing. On a ship he encountered an Iraqi Shia lecturer who affected him, triggered his interest in Shia Islam and made him feel disturbed about how and which Islamic knowledge is transmitted.

Abdullah's own experience and knowledge of Sunni Islam, the troubling reactions towards Shi'ites and the other (unknown) face of Shia Islam were all elements that are explored in the narrative of Muhamed Al Tijani. This led Abdullah completely identifying with the Muhamed Al Tijani's own road to Shia Islam.

By focusing on affective encounters and events and the impact they have, I do not want to downplay the intellectual, rational and/or autonomous dispositions of my informants. What I want to argue for, rather, along with Kenneth Gergen who inscribes himself in the same philosophical tradition, is that any will, reasoning or judgment is situated in a relational web.

In *Relational Being, Beyond Self and Community*, Gergen formulates a critique of the conventional emphasis on the individual mind and develops a framework based on the primordial importance of relational processes. "I am linked therefore I am" is Gergen's response to the Cartesian maxim: "I think, therefore I am." Gergen proposes: "an account of the human action that can replace the presumption of bounded selves with a vision of relationship." Gergen doesn't just encourage us to focus on relationships between two autonomous agents, but rather refers to: "a process of coordination that precedes the very concept of the self." (Gergen, 2009, p. 15)

Gergen goes on to argue that: "virtually all intelligible action is born, sustained and/or extinguished within the ongoing process of relationship." It is inconceivable to exist without relationships and therefore he sees human action as "co-constitutive". Gergen argues that:

"There is no isolated self or fully private experience. We exist in a world of co-constitution. We are always, already emerging from relationship; we cannot step out of relationship. Even in our most private moments, we are never alone."

(Gergen, 2009) I see echoes of this sentiment in the work of Bakhtin where he writes:

> "To be, means to be for the other, and through him, for oneself. Man has no internal sovereign territory, he is always on the boundary; looking within himself, he looks in the eyes of the other; I cannot become myself without the other, I must find myself in the other, finding the other in me in mutual reflection and perception." (Bakhtin, 1981, pp. 311-312)

Concluding remarks

Moroccan Belgian Sunni Muslims who became Shia have all been affected by a particular encounter or event. While one respondent tells me about the impact of meeting Khomeini, another respondent puts to the fore the intriguing conversion with the Iraqi missionary in Brussels hearing for the first time what shia Islam is about or one of the commemoration of the Iranian revolution at the Iranian Embassy. Another respondent can't stop talking about the courageous political stance of Hezbollah and its resistance to Israeli occupation and its affect on his understanding Shia ideology. Many of the first Belgian Moroccan Shiites speak of the 'open' but practicing and spiritual attitude of another Belgian Moroccan Shiite that triggered their curiosity and sense of sense of belonging.

While being affected has normatively been understood as the counterpart of reason, I argue that being affected does not exist somewhere outside of the rational and the rational not outside the being affected. I employ 'affect' in order to transcend the emotion/reason duality, and to emphasize that reason and emotion are mutually present in affect.

I contend that dialogical practices are fundamental for the revision of interpretations, identifications, conduct and decision-making of my interlocutors and therefore I pay particular attention to the importance of the other in the constitution of the self.

Personal identities, I argue, are constructed relationally. This relationality is understood as a dialogical construction of identity. We should go beyond the prevalence of the autonomous individual because these hegemonic understandings of the self-reduce all relationality to non-authentic selves.

For a layered account of how the Moroccan Belgian community evolved after 50 years of migration, one has to elaborate on the different encounters and events that that community is affectively linked with. The Islamic revolution in Iran has proved to be an important event among Moroccan Belgians. In the case of Moroccan Belgian Shiites, affect is very much embedded in events that are historic, brave, revolutionary and political and encounters with people who are open, modest, spiritual and practicing. These encounters and events produced an affect of contentment, which forms the basis of the Sunni-Shia religious or interpretational change.

Notes

1 This article is based on the ethnographic research I conducted for my doctoral dissertation between 2007 and 2010. After the 2013 arson in the Shia Rida center in the commune of Anderlecht, Brussels, I returned to the field and noticed that the Sunni Shia rivalry was intensified and that certain Salafi groups and Islamic State viewed Shiites as 'heretics' and 'apostates'.

2 Instead of using the ethic notion of conversion, I will describe the change of Sunni Belgian Moroccan to Shia Islam in more emic terms such as "Shiitization", "becoming Shi'ites" or members of the *ahl al bayt*.

3 Abdullah is a pseudonym and a couple of other minor changes have been included in order not to reveal the respondent's identity.

4 For a profound elaboration on education in Morocco see (Ennaji 2005).

5 For a fascinating ethnography on the impact of cassettes on the development of religious sensibilities see Charles Hirschkind (2009).

6 for more information on Shia belief and teaching, see Nasr et al (1988).

7 For a detailed account on the Iran-Iraq war, see Hiro (1991).

8 See Lechkar (2012) for an account on modalities of authentification among Moroccan Belgian Shiites

9 Immediately after this quote Abdullah does refer to a different reading: *Hafs* replacing that of *Warsh*, but this distinction does not refer to a Sunni-Shia difference but to two known methods of recitation named after the leaders of two schools. *Warsh* method was often used in North Africa while *Hafs* is more dominant in the Middle East. See, an interesting chapter on this topic: Michael, M. J Fischer& Mehdi Abedi (1990)

10 For an interesting article on sensibilities and the reproduction/ contestation of a particular order, see (Fadil, 2009) For a specific article on Sunni sensibilities and the headscarf, see Lechkar, I. (2009) and a specific article on Shia sensibilities and Ashoura, see (Lechkar, 2017)

Bibliography

Allievi, S. (1998). *Les convertis à l'Islam. Les nouveaux musulmans d'Europe*, Paris: L'Harmattan, pp 97-138.

Asad, T. (1986). The Idea of an Anthropology of Islam. *Occasional Papers Series Centre For Contemporary Arab Studies*, Washington: Georgetown University.

Asad, T. (1996). Comments on Conversion. In P. van der Veer. (ed.) *Conversion to Modernities: The Globalization of Christianity*. New York: Routledge, p 266.

Bakhtin, M.M. (1981). *The Dialogic Imagination*, Austin: University of Texas Press.

Coleman, S. (2003). Continuous Conversion? The Rhetoric, Practice and Rhetorical Practice of Charismatic Protestant Conversion. In A. Buckser and S. Glazier. (eds) *The Anthropology of Religious Conversion*, Oxford: Rowman and Littlefield Publishers.

Dabashi, H. (2011). *Shi'ism. A Religion of Protest*, Cambridge: The Belknap Press of Harvard University.

Dassetto, F. (2011). *L'iris et le croissant, Bruxelles et L'Islam au defis de la co-inclusion* (Louvain: UCL Presses.

Ennaji, M. (2005*). Multilingualism, Cultural Identity, and Education in Morocco*. New York: Springer

Fadil, N. (2009). Managing affects and sensibilities: The case of not-handshaking and not-fasting. *Social Anthropology* 17(4) 439-454, 441.

Fadil, N., El Asri, F. & Bracke, S. (2015). Islam in Belgium. Mapping an emerging interdisciplinary field of study. In *The Oxford Handbook of European Islam*, ed. J. Cesari, Oxford: Oxford University Press.

Fischer, J. M.M. & Abedi, M. (1990). Qur'anic Dialogics: Islamic Poetics and Politics for Muslims and for Us. In Tulio Maranhao (ed.), *The Interpretation of Dialogue*. Chicago: The University of Chicago Press.

Gergen, K. (2009). *Relational Being: Beyond Self and Community*. Oxford: Oxford University Press.

Gooren, H. (2005). Towards a New Model of Conversion Careers: The Impact of Personality Factors. *Exchange*, 34 (2): 149-166.

Gooren, H. (2007). Reassessing Conventional Approaches to Conversion: Toward a New Synthesis. *Journal for the Scientific Study of Religion*, 46(3): 337-353.

Gooren, H. (2006). The religious Marker Model and Conversion: Towards a New Approach. *Exchange* 35(1): 39-60.

Gregg, M. & Seigworth, G.J. (2010). An Inventory of Shimmers. In Gregg, M. & Seigworth, G.J. (eds.) *The Affect Theory Reader*. Durham: Duke University Press.

Hiro, D. (1991). *The Longest War: The Iran-Iraq Military Conflict*. New York: Routledge.

Hirschkind, C. (2009). *The Ethical Soundscape: Cassette Sermons and Islamic Counterpublics*. New York: Columbia University Press.

Lechkar, I. (2009). De Keuze voor de Hoofddoek. *Karakter: Tijdschrift van de wetenschap* (Leuven: Academische stichting Leuven).

Lechkar, I. (2012). *Striving and Stumbling in the name of Allah: Neo-Sunnis and Neo-Shi'ites in a Belgian context*. Unpublished doctoral dissertation, Leuven: KU Leuven.

Lechkar, I (2012). Quelles sont les modalités d'authentification parmi les chiites belgo-marocains? In *Islam Belge*, eds. B.Maréchal & F. El Asri. Louvain La Neuve: Presses Universitaires de Louvain.

Lechkar, I. (2017). Extinguishing fire in Brussels: Moroccan Belgian Shiites in the aftermath of the Syrian civil war, *Journal of Muslims in Europe* (forthcoming).

Lofland, J. and Stark, R. (1965). Becoming a World-Saver: a theory of conversion to a deviant perspective. *American Sociological Review* 30 (6): 862-875.

Lofland, J. (1977). Becoming a world-saver revisited. *American Behavioral Scientist* 20(6): 805-18.

Lofland, J. & Skonovd, N. (1981). Conversion motifs. *Journal for the Scientific Study of Religion* 20(4): 373-385, 375.

Louër, L. (2008). *Transnational Shia Politics: Religious and Political Networks in the Gulf.* London: Columbia University Press.

Mabon, S.(2013). *Saudi Arabia and Iran: Soft Power Rivalry in the Middle East*. London: I.B.Tauris.

Mahmood, S. (2005). *Politics of Piety. The Reform of the Feminist Subject*. New Jersey: Princeton University Press.

Maréchal, B. & Zemni, Z. (2013). *The Dynamics of Sunni-Shia Relationships: Doctrine, Transnationalism, Intellectuals and the Media*. London: Hurst & Company.

Massumi, B. (1987). Foreword. In Deleuze, G. and Guattari, F. (1987). *A Thousand Plateaus: Capitalism and Schizophrenia*. Minnesota: University of Minnesota, xvii.

Massumi, B. (2015). *Politics of affect*, Cambridge: Polity Press.

Nasr, V. (2006). *The Shi'a Revival: How Conflicts within Islam will Shape the Future*. New York: W.W Norton & Company.

Nasr, H., Dabashi, H., & Nasr, V. (1988). *Shi'ism: Doctrines, Thought, and Spirituality*. Albany: State University of New York Press.

Rambo, L.R. (1993). *Understanding Religious Conversion*. New Haven: Yale University Press.

Rambo, L.R. (1999). Theories of Conversion: Understanding and Interpreting Religious Change, *Social Compass*, 46(3): 259-71.

Rosaldo, M. (1984). Toward an anthropology of self and feeling. In R. Shweder and R. Levine. (eds.), *Culture Theory: Essays on Mind, Self and Emotion*. Cambridge: Cambridge University Press

About the authors

Christiane Timmerman is a full professor at the University of Antwerp and is as Research Professor (ZAPBOF) academic director of the Centre for Migration and Intercultural Studies (CeMIS – University of Antwerp) that focuses on multidisciplinary research on migration, integration and ethnic minorities. In her function as director of CeMIS, she has built extensive experience coordinating large scale research projects on international migration and integration.

Nadia Fadil is Associate Professor at the Interculturalism, Migration and Minorities Research Centre (IMMRC) at the University of Leuven. Her primary research interest pertains to the presence of Islam as a lived and embodied reality in Europe. More broadly, her theoretical interest extends to questions of subjectivity and power, ethical selfhood, postcoloniality, race and secularism.

Karim Ettourki is a consultant at KADOC, Documentation and Research Centre for Religion, Culture and Society (University of Leuven) and staff member of Archiefbank Vlaanderen. From 2008 till 2013 he was member of the KADOC research department. Since 2013 he operates as a consultant for the heritage of ethnic-cultural minorities in Flanders and participates in different projects concerning migration and cultural diversity.

Sam De Schutter is a PhD candidate in History at Leiden University. He has studied History and Anthropology, and his previous research has focused on issues of migration in postcolonial contexts, especially between Congo and Belgium. Currently he is preparing a study on the history of disability within the context of international development. His research is part of an ERC funded project on 'Rethinking Disability'.

Idesbald Goddeeris is Professor of History at the University of Leuven, where he teaches (post)colonial and migration history. His research largely focuses on the history of migration, the Cold War, and the dealing with foreign cultures. He is also a senior member of the Leuven Centre for Global Governance Studies, where he coordinates the Leuven India Focus.

Albert Martens is emeritus professor Labor Sociology, Industrial Relations and Urban Sociology at the University of Leuven (Belgium). He has published in the fields of labor markets, social inequalities and discrimination, migration policy and urban social movements.

Emilien Dupont is a PhD student working at the Department of Sociology at Ghent University. She is affiliated to the research group Hedera. Her research focuses on the partner choices of ethnic minorities in Belgium, with a focus on Turkish and Moroccan migrants. She also examines divorce and remarriage patterns within these groups.

Bart Van de Putte is a professor at the Department of Sociology at Ghent University and is affiliated to the research group Hedera (Health and Demographic Research). He teaches specialized courses in social demography, besides introductory courses in sociology and courses in general sociology. His research focuses at topics in social demography, social stratification and historical sociology.

John Lievens is associate professor and chair of the Department of Sociology at Ghent University, where he teaches several courses in statistics and demography. He is affiliated to the research group CuDOS. His research focusses on culture and art participation, perception of culture, lifestyles, methodology in the social sciences, sexual behavior, and partner choice in ethnic minorities. Since 2001 he has been involved in the coordination of several Centres for policy relevant research on culture.

Frank Caestecker is a Doctor in history. He read history at Ghent University, and after his undergraduate studies he worked at the Universities of Brussels, Warsaw, Osnabrück and Madison (Wisconsin-USA). He is affiliated to the Department of Economics of the University of Ghent where he teaches public management of migration.

Jonas Wood is Postdoctoral Researcher and Visiting Professor at the Centre for Longitudinal and Life course Studies (CLLS) at the University of Antwerp, Belgium. His work focusses on socio-economic and migrant-native differentials in family formation and work-family combination, but also on context-contingencies such as the effects of economic cycles and social policy.

Layla Van den Berg is PhD Student and Teaching Assistant at the Centre of Longitudinal and Life Course Studies (CLLS) at the University of Antwerp, Belgium. Her work focusses on family formation and dissolution among migrant populations and in particular on the role of socio-economic status and household characteristics.

Karel Neels is Associate Professor of Demography and Statistics at the Centre for Longitudinal and Life course Studies (CLLS) at the University of Antwerp, Belgium. His work focuses on education, labor market trajectories and family formation of majority and migrant populations in Belgium and Europe.

Noel Clycq holds a MA in Communication Sciences, an advanced master in Anthropology and a PhD in Social Sciences. He is a visiting professor at the University of Antwerp and holds the chair in 'European Values: Discourses and Prospects' at the History Department. He is also senior researcher at the Centre for Migration and Intercultural Studies. He teaches four courses and studies issues related to migration, diversity, education, family and identity.

François Levrau holds a MA in Clinical Psychology, a MA in Moral Philosophy and a PhD in Social Science. Currently he is a doctoral-assistant at the Centre Pieter Gillis of the University of Antwerp. His research considers political philosophical issues related to the multicultural society. He also teaches a course on Religion and Diversity.

Nicolas Van Puymbroeck obtained the degree of doctor in Sociology at the University of Antwerp. His dissertation 'From Civil Society Innovation to State Control. Immigrant Citizenship and Configurations of Governance in Antwerp, Liège, Ghent and Rotterdam' discusses the historical development of migrant integration policies and immigrant non-profit organizations. He is also the author of 'Migratie en de Metropool' and published widely on immigrant politicization.

Rilke Mahieu is a research fellow at CeMIS (University of Antwerp) since 2009. Currently, she coordinates the evaluation study of the project "CURANT – Cohousing and case management for unaccompanied young adult refugees in Antwerp" (2016-2019). Besides, she works on a doctoral dissertation entitled "Fostering the ties with home: Moroccan diaspora policies for the post-migrant generations". Previously, she has conducted research on the gender/migration nexus and the school trajectories of youth with a migratory background.

Norah Karrouche specializes in historical culture and memory in Morocco, Algeria and among North African communities in Europe, with emphasis on the history and representation of Berber (material) culture, literature and arts (19th and 20th century). She received her PhD from Erasmus University Rotterdam (Erasmus School of History, Culture and Communication) in 2013 and is currently a lecturer in global history and anthropology at Vrije Universiteit Amsterdam, and a post-doctoral researcher in digital humanities at Erasmus Universiteit Rotterdam.

Anna Berbers is a lecturer Communication Science at the University of Amsterdam. Her academic interests revolve around identification processes of ethnic and religious minorities, (social) media use, news media portrayal and diversity in corporate communication. She conducted her doctoral research at the KU Leuven, where she investigated the media portrayal of Moroccan minorities, social media use, identification processes and social networks in a mixed-method project.

Leen d'Haenens is Professor in the Institute for Media Studies at the University of Leuven, Belgium, where she teaches media policy, analysis of media texts, and media and diversity. Her research interests include media policy, media and ethnic-cultural minorities, media and youth, media governance and accountability mechanisms. Together with other members of the Euromedia Research Group, she co-edited and co-authored The Media in Europe Today (Intellect 2011).

Joyce Koeman is Assistant Professor in the Institute for Media Studies at the University of Leuven with a research interest in the media uses and representations of ethnic minorities as well as the impact of emerging ethnic and Islamic marketing practices.

Jürgen Jaspers is a sociolinguist and associate professor of Dutch linguistics at the Université Libre de Bruxelles (ULB), Belgium. He publishes widely on classroom interaction, urban multilingualism and linguistic standardisation. His recent work has appeared in Language in Society, Language Policy, Science Communication, Journal of Germanic Linguistics, Applied Linguistics Review, Annual Review of Anthropology, and International Journal of the Sociology of Language, as well as in the Routledge Handbook of Discourse Analysis, the Oxford Handbook of Language and Society, and the Oxford Handbook of Language Policy and Planning.

Wim Peumans is an associated researcher at the African Centre for Migration and Society (University of the Witwatersrand, Johannesburg), where he was a postdoctoral fellow in 2016. As a Research Foundation Flanders fellow he obtained his PhD in Anthropology at IMMRC – University of Leuven. He has been a Visiting Trainee Fellow at the University of Kent – Canterbury. Peumans' award-winning Master's thesis was published as a book (Acco, 2011) and his latest book is titled 'Queer Muslims in Europe: Sexuality, Religion and Migration in Belgium' (IB Tauris, autumn 2017).

Philip Hermans studied psychology and social anthropology and earned a PhD in anthropology at the University of Leuven. He has worked as a school psychologist, intercultural therapist and as a researcher and professor. He has been a lecturer in intercultural pedagogy at the University of Groningen. Since 2006 he serves as a guest professor at the University of Leuven. His research interests include educational and psychological anthropology, healing, and Moroccan culture.

Bert Broeckaert is professor and member of the Research Unit of Theological and Comparative Ethics, Faculty of Theology and Religious Studies, University of Leuven) and a specialist in comparative ethics and end of life ethics. Since 2001 his research and that of his research group focuses on the way world religions deal with death and dying and more particularly on the way these influence treatment decisions near the end of life.

Stef Van den Branden studied Religious Studies, Theology and World Religions at the Faculty of Theology and Religious Studies, University of Leuven. In 2006 he defended his PhD in Religious Studies, entitled "Islamitische ethiek aan het levenseinde. Een theoretisch omkaderde inhoudsanalyse van Engelstalig soennitisch bronnenmateriaal en een kwalitatief empirisch onderzoek naar de houding van praktiserende Marokkaanse oudere mannen in Antwerpen" (promoter: Prof.dr. Bert Broeckaert).

Goedele Baeke studied Religious Studies and Theology at the Faculty of Theology and Religious Studies, University of Leuven. In 2012 she defended her PhD in Religious Studies (KU Leuven / Nijmegen University), entitled "Religion and Ethics at the End of Life. A Qualitative Empirical Study among Elderly Jewish and Muslim Women in Antwerp (Belgium)" (promoter: Prof.dr. Bert Broeckaert).

Chaïma Ahaddour studied Arabic and Islamology at the Faculty of Arts, University of Leuven. She is currently finishing a PhD Project (Faculty of Theology and Religious Studies, University of Leuven) on Moroccan women in Antwerp, Belgium and their views and attitudes regarding death and dying (promoter: Prof.dr. Bert Broeckaert).

Mieke Groeninck holds a PhD in Social and Cultural Anthropology from University of Leuven. Her research centers on issues related to Islamic religious knowledge transmission for adults in informal institutions like mosques and Islamic centers from a Moroccan background. She has conducted over two years of fieldwork in Brussels, during which she attended courses in six places. Her current research delves deeper into different types of traditional and academized forms of religious authority and knowledge construction.

Iman Lechkar is professor Islam and Gender, Fatima Mernissi Chair holder at the Vrije Universiteit Brussels and a research fellow at IMMRC – University of Leuven. Her doctoral dissertation (2012) researched conversion and religious practices in a Belgian context. Her teaching and research engage with Islam and gender, questions of violence, multiculturalism, secularism, conversion, religious practice, religious identities/authorities, ethnicity, citizenship, subjectivity, agency and the significance of media in self-fashioning processes.